D1748272

The Strassmanns

The Strassmanns

*Science, Politics, and Migration in
Turbulent Times, 1793–1993*

W. Paul Strassmann

Berghahn Books
NEW YORK · OXFORD

Published by
Berghahn Books

www.berghahnbooks.com

German edition
© 2006 Campus Verlag GmbH, Frankfurt am Main
Originally published as
W. Paul Strassmann: *Die Strassmanns. Schicksale einer deutsch-jüdischen Familie über zwei Jahrhunderte*

English-language edition
© 2008 W. Paul Strassmann

All rights reserved.
Except for the quotation of short passages
for the purposes of criticism and review, no part of this book
may be reproduced in any form or by any means, electronic or
mechanical, including photocopying, recording, or any information
storage and retrieval system now known or to be invented,
without written permission of the publisher.

Library of Congress Cataloging-in-Publication Data

Strassmann, W. Paul (Wolfgang Paul), 1926–
    The Strassmans : science, politics, and migration in turbulent times, 1793–1993 /
by W. Paul Strassmann ; translated by Evelyn Zegenhagen.
    p. cm.
Includes bibliographical references and index.
ISBN 978-1-84545-416-6 (hardcover : alk. paper)
    1. Strassmann family. 2. Jews—Germany—Biography. 3. Jewish physicians—Germany—Biography. 4. Jewish soldiers—Germany—Biography. 5. Jews, German—United States—Biography. 6. Germany—Ethnic relations. I. Title.

DS134.42.S77S77 2007
929'.20973—dc22

2007025077

British Library Cataloguing in Publication Data

A catalogue record for this book is available
from the British Library.

Printed in the United States on acid-free paper

For Betty, with Love

Contents

Preface *by Jutta Lange-Quassowski* — viii
Acknowledgments — xiii
Introduction: A Family en Route — 1

1. A Father against Orthodoxy: Heiman in Rawicz — 13
2. From the Revolution of 1848 to Reforms in Berlin after 1863: Wolfgang and Ferdinand — 21
3. Medical Achievements and Disappointments: Paul and His Siblings — 35
4. Golden Years of the Women's Clinic and of Forensic Medicine: 1909–1933 — 46
5. Soldiers — 64
6. Stage and Sky: Antonie I — 74
7. A Zenith in Heidelberg with a Bitter End: Gisela and Max — 92
8. Stalked by Nazis in the Schumannstrasse: 1933–1936 — 108
9. Inseparable despite Emigration: Erwin and Ilse — 124
10. Transatlantic Tensions in New York: Antonie II — 135
11. Old Trees, Transplanted: Paul and Hedwig in Dahlem — 151
12. Beginning Again in Minnesota: Erwin and Family — 166
13. On to Houston, Texas: City of the Future — 176
14. Destination Auschwitz: Reinhold 1944 — 189
15. Leading a Liberal Resistance Group: Ernst Karl Otto — 202

Epilogue: Looking Back — 213
Notes — 231
Appendices: Family Trees — 242
Bibliography — 247
Index — 254

Preface

Here we are presented with two hundred years of a kaleidoscopic story. First comes the swirling ascent of a family of migrants into the academic and social elites of Germany. Then we see the wreckage of their vocations and finally their hard-earned achievements in a new society, America.

This book, with its prompt translation and publication for German readers, is part of the bridge building that has characterized the Strassmann family. Although forced to give up life in Germany, they renewed contacts soon after World War II. As early as the 1960s, therefore, two Strassmanns, Erwin and Georg, were awarded the Federal Order of Merit by a new democratic president of Germany.

German readers still face the question, how can we picture what happened in the Nazi period? The crimes and their extent cannot be fathomed despite all our efforts. Nor can the consequences. The people who were murdered could not live their lives. They could not make their contributions to the development of society. The loss suffered by us Germans cannot be measured—its magnitude remains abstract. But we can approach the question by dwelling on the fates of individuals. Personal stories can make us conscious of the loss that our community has suffered because of National Socialist policies. A family story can fascinate, can let us identify with persons, can arouse sympathy or affection toward an individual or an entire family. The fate of one family can make us sad. Its loss becomes painful.

For twenty-five years I have directed the Ernst Strassmann Foundation within the Friedrich Ebert Foundation and have focused on the theme "Aufarbeitung der Vergangenheit" (Working with the Past, or Coming to Terms with Our History). When I married Bernd-Peter Lange in 1971 and thereby joined the family of Hermann and Margarete Lange, Ernst Strassmann had been dead for more than a decade, leaving no descendants. The reminiscences of my parents-in-law, however, inspired me with such deep admiration and respect that I wished I had known him.

Ernst led the resistance group that both my parents-in-law joined and that met at their house whenever Ernst was in Hamburg. Ernst's widow asked us later to organize and lead the Ernst Strassmann Foundation after her death. Together we felt a need to strengthen the federal democracy by letting the repressed past become known through research. Our goal has been to call forth a valid democratic German identity through open acknowledgment of the past as part of the culture.

We had worked for more than five years when a researcher, Horst Sassin, approached us about the resistance group that Ernst had led. Only then did my parents-in-law and I learn how large and extensive the group was to which they had belonged. As a security measure, the group had functioned from 1934 to 1945 according to the principle that "individuals need to know as little as possible." After the war, one did not talk much about resistance. After all, we had not succeeded, so why waste words about it? Apart from military conspiracies, resistance activities were hushed up as late as the 1980s in the Federal Republic, as were the crimes, although for opposite reasons. Resistance and exile were both taken as a form of treason in the atmosphere of postwar restoration.

Thorough research showed us much that seemed new about our honored and beloved Ernst Strassmann. In 1993 appeared Sassin's book, *Liberals in the Resistance: The Robinsohn-Strassmann Group, 1934–1942*.[1] It began a scientific reformulation of the history of the resistance because so far no liberal or left-liberal resistance group had been identified.

Ten years later, as always happens, history once again caught up with the present. Before explaining, I will cite some recent examples. In the years 2003, 2004, and 2005, a number of cities and communities organized memorial services. Sixty years earlier, these cities had experienced devastating bomb attacks that resulted in immense and ghastly suffering by the population. In the parliament of Dresden in January and February of 2005, the National Democratic Party and unreformed neo-Nazis carried historical distortion to a hysterical extreme that was condemned worldwide. Far right-wing parties, which have never come to terms with National Socialist crimes, now accuse the rest of the world of crimes against Germany. This shows that the past does not simply go away. Nevertheless, as early as the 1980s, even less extreme conservative circles began to admonish others to forget the past.

A few years ago, the Ernst Strassmann Foundation received a letter from W. Paul Strassmann in the United States. "Dear Sirs," the letter began, "I am a distant cousin of Ernst Strassmann and am writing a book about the fate of our family." He wrote a few sentences about important people portrayed in chapters in the present book, enough to make us very curious. Then he added, "Most of us emigrated. I was eleven years old." Horst Sassin's book had led him to contact us. Now he asked, "Do you have a report about the activities of the Strassmann Foundation? Apparently, you have a portrait of Ernst Strassmann. I would be very grateful for a picture and for other photos, which I could use in a chapter about Ernst Strassmann." Soon Professor Strassmann visited us, together with his wife and a granddaughter, and we were impressed by these people and all the information about the family that gradually reached us.

The two-century history of this family is moving. I devoured every chapter as it arrived here, neglecting other work. This dynasty of physicians fostered the health of human beings in many ways. They advanced surgical techniques, health care policies, the condition of hospitals, scientific research, instruction, and popular awareness of all these fields. In this family one finds noble persons who were respected and loved by their fellows.

How grateful the reader must be to know that many in the family survived because they made an early decision to give up their German livelihoods to avoid the impending disaster. They were fortunate to know Americans—quite famous ones—who were ready to swear out affidavits promising economic support, should that be needed. Many others had no such luck. The author himself does not brag or complain. He brings the reader close to the persons described, which may account for the pain one feels about the disgrace inflicted on them by others in our midst. Anyone concerned with the development of Germany will be sad, thinking of the emptiness that the loss of such personalities has meant for our society.

Yet all the more is it a joy that W. Paul Strassmann had access to so many private letters and diaries. After years of additional research, he presents us with a valuable family story based on historical facts and scientific sources, with episodes dating from 1800. Since the author is a member of the family and knows lore told by his relatives, every single story brims with life. The reader should be aware that many persons who appeared in the original manuscript had to be cut to stay within the constraints of a publishable book.

The author himself is exceedingly modest. He and his current family remain almost fully in the background, with the focus on his great-great-grandparents, great-grandparents, grandparents, and parents. With them he illustrates major accomplishments in assimilation, successes in spite of rejections, total ruination, and new efforts after emigration. The book's tone is not mournful but matter-of-fact, while the writing is suspenseful. The reader is keen to know what will happen next. The author stresses major issues, above all, professional accomplishments and successes, while social affairs, clubs, hobbies, and the like are mainly left out. Despite some appropriate pride in the vision and capacity of his ancestors, the author is by no means uncritical. He writes with substantial perspective and without any sentimentality.

The theme "Coming to Terms with Our History" has many aspects. In the course of its twenty-five years, the Ernst Strassmann Foundation has used different approaches. One goal is to keep victims from being forgotten. But victims are not only people who lost their lives or were tortured. Everyone who fled into exile to survive deserves recognition.

When the Ernst Strassmann Foundation began its work in 1981, public discussion in the Federal Republic was dominated by a so-called historians' dispute. Not just certain historians but many others wanted to move on and forget the burdensome past once and for all. Local groups who researched the hushed-up past were scolded and reprimanded as spoilers. Politicians especially wanted no part in sorting out complicity in past crimes.

Forty years after the end of World War II, when Federal President Richard von Weiszäcker said in his great speech that for Germans also May 8, 1945, was a day of liberation, indignant protests blazed forth in periodicals. But ten years later, when President Herzog declared January 27 (the anniversary of the liberation of Auschwitz) to be a memorial day for the Holocaust that had been perpetrated by Germans, no outbursts followed. A public reappraisal had begun.

Another decade after that, in January 2005, Chancellor Gerhard Schröder said that "the memory of war and genocide … has become part of our national identity," and President Horst Köhler assured the Knesset in Israel that responsibility for the Shoah was part of our German identity. President Köhler's award of the Distinguished Service Cross (2004–2005) for the Ernst Strassmann Foundation's efforts in "Working with the Past" expresses the changed attitude of many Germans. A "specific German identity" recognizing responsibility for the Nazi past had still been generally rejected in 1988. At that time, I wrote an essay, "The Contribution of Memorial Sites toward Forming a Democratic Identity," in which I called for associating such recognition with democratic traditions as occasionally revealed by the resistance.[2] The response was antagonistic.

For us, "Working with the Past" was not research for its own sake but a step toward making a culture of memory part of a new German identity. Nowadays, it is not only political leaders who caution us, as did the president of the Bundestag, Wolfgang Thierse, on the occasion of the sixtieth anniversary of the liberation of Auschwitz: "It is not just a matter of the correct or erroneous attribution of past guilt, but the growing responsibility for the present and the future in the light of this shameful memory." On the local level as well, recognizing victims, perpetrators, and occasional humanitarians who actively questioned these events at the time has become part of countless memorial occasions. They are often accompanied by school projects that inspire works of art expressing students' reactions to questions that include, for example, how can something as repulsive as forced labor exist in a civilized world? Such examples are no longer unusual, as Ari

Primor, Israel's ambassador to Germany from 1993 to 1999, has attested. In a memorial lecture to the legislature of North Rhine-Westphalia, he spoke of crimes "without precedent" committed in the name of Germany. He regretted that their recall in Germany had been long delayed, but he noted that now German acknowledgment of these crimes "is also without precedent."

The Ernst Strassmann Foundation has supported publication of other correspondence recovered from persecuted and murdered compatriots, such as the Glücksmanns of Düsseldorf.[3] In the Strassmann book, another aspect of memory is at hand: exile. Here we see how members of a family who migrated from the Posen or Poznan region of Poland in the nineteenth century rapidly became leading citizens in the German capital by virtue of their diligence, ambition, intelligence, and social commitment. We see how family members were then disenfranchised, degraded, driven out, and in some cases murdered if they did not flee the Nazi rule in time.

It is fascinating to read how Heiman in the province of Posen at the beginning of the nineteenth century lived a traditional Judaic life but, in contrast with his fellow Jews, educated his children to be open, farsighted, and oriented toward the future. It is exciting to experience the Revolution of 1848 from the perspective of the student rebel, Wolfgang Strassmann, joining him in the midst of the action. We meet not only famous personalities but tragic ones. The story of the "black sheep" of the family raises the question, did his life have to proceed that way or did the constellation of siblings and his parents' consequent response push him out? It hurts to read about the idealistic German patriotism of highly talented Hellmuth, who sacrificed his young life in World War I. His father, Paul Ferdinand, who found much consolation in German literature and music, was so rooted in his faith in a good Germany that up to his death in 1938, despite all the anti-Semitic racial abuses, he kept believing that soon everything would turn out well again. After emigrating to America, Ilse Strassmann wrote, "We shall always keep a piece of our German homeland here within our four walls with our books and our furniture." Antonie Strassmann, loaded with energy, surprises us with her quick decisions. Who cannot admire her courage or be struck by her uncompromising spirit? The bold resistance fighter, Ernst Strassmann comes to life in the book and continues to help through our foundation. But not all survived, and the author does not pass over this in silence.

The merits of this volume are many. First, the story is interesting because it shows the changing setting for two hundred years of assimilating Jewish life. Second, the book is filled with suspense and excitement about fascinating people. The reader's curiosity is far from exhausted by what is said about colorful personalities who achieved much—in one case, becoming an Honorary Citizen of Berlin—and who are even now mentioned on the Internet. They were members of the leading elite of Germany in cultural, intellectual, scientific, and political fields spanning generations. The challenge to come to terms with the past and the bridge-building spirit are additional reasons for reading the book.

But something else makes this book valuable and worth reading. In the last ten years, much effort has been given to recovering an extinguished, broken, lost, and displaced history. In Berlin, the former Women's Clinic and Hospital of Paul was placed under historical protection in 2003 as the Strassmann-Haus. The Forensic Institute of the combined Humboldt and Free Universities has been renamed after Fritz Strassmann, together with a medal created in 2004, dedicated to the centennial celebration of the founding of the German Association for Legal Medicine, of which Fritz Strassmann was the first chairman. Today, colleagues who knew the discriminated professors Strassmann as little as I knew Ernst Strassmann have seen to it that their graves are cleaned and honored. Scientific articles about Paul as well as about Fritz are being written, and lectures are being given. And that after 100 years! This means that their achievements remain models worthy of recognition. Antonie Strassmann, at least as an aviator—one of her three dream-like professions—is already well represented in exhibits and books and is being rediscovered.

I highly recommend this well-written glimpse into a fascinating family history!

Jutta Lange-Quassowski
Koblenz, Germany

Acknowledgments

Help from experts, friends, and relatives was crucial to the writing of this book about medicine, politics, and persecution. After two years in the US Navy decades ago, I began keeping notes on reminiscences by my parents, grandmothers, aunts, uncles, and cousins, both near and far, without any definite idea of ever publishing. Curiosity moved me. Had the Doctors Mayo really helped us to emigrate? Were there heavily burdened Nazis on my mother's side of the family? Did grandfather Strassmann sympathize with their ideology? Did he commit suicide? When were the first Strassmanns baptized? Were Strassmanns military heroes in any war? Were any of them concentration camp victims? What was Polish Rawicz like? If great-uncle Wolfgang was a famous revolutionary and Lord Mayor of Berlin, why is he not mentioned in history books? Was Antonie's celebrity as an actress and a flier justified? And why did the Gestapo try to kidnap her in New York?

For decades, my eventual profession of economist kept me too busy teaching and traveling to do more than ask and listen. To preserve bits of the past for our daughters, nephews, nieces, and grandchildren, I translated some of great-grandfather Heinrich's memoirs of emigration from Rawicz and uncle Max Gutzwiller's account of life in the Strassmann household in Berlin in the 1920s. In the 1970s, I asked my mother to transcribe ten long volumes of grandfather Paul Ferdinand's 1936–1938 diary into legible German, and she taught herself to type.

In 1994, I completed my last overseas projects dealing with housing policy in the Philippines and South Africa, and in that same year more cartons of letters, albums, memoirs, and documents came to me in Michigan from Houston, Texas. My mother had died, and my sisters had no time to sort out these materials. What would become of it all if I did not sift through it and put the salient events into perspective? I looked on our German past as a flawed treasure that would reward its exploration if faced honestly. Some relatives who had emigrated to Australia or England had changed their names and tried to expunge their German past, both Jewish and Gentile, but that had never appealed to me.

I began with the letters and accounts of my father's older brother, Hellmuth, who was killed in the Battle of the Somme in 1916 at age twenty-two. It was the shortest possible assignment, a sad but manageable task, and it encouraged me to proceed with others—first my parents, Erwin and Ilse, and then my aunts, Gisela Gutzwiller of Heidelberg and "Tony" (Antonie). After that came the stories of the emigrants from Rawicz, followed by the most central figure of the entire clan, my grandfather Paul Ferdinand. His long life began in pre-imperial Berlin among the Rawicz immigrants and ended with his being shunned by Nazis and left by those of us who were emigrating to the Americas, Australia, England, and Switzerland. Finally, I organized material about Strassmanns more distant from us—Fritz, Walter, Georg, Reinhold, Fred, Elisabeth, Annemarie, and Ernst—some famous, others not. Some died in concentration camps, others hid in villages, and one organized a resistance movement.

Since medicine and politics dominated these lives, I needed professional advice to sort out various technical problems and achievements. In the 1990s, I was fortunate to encounter three medical historians in Berlin: Dr. Matthias David of the Universitätsklinikum, Rudolf Virchow of the Freie Universität Berlin, Dr. Andreas Ebert of the Universitätsklinikum Steglitz of the Freie Universität Berlin, and Dr. Manfred Stürzbecher, who had earned doctoral degrees in both medicine and history and may be considered the dean of German medical historians. All of them clarified my understanding of medical issues and of the internal and external politics of the profession.

For help with the history of Jews in Prussia—migration, assimilation, and conflicts—I am particularly indebted to Professor Reinhard Rürup, then Professor für Neuere Geschichte Emeritus of the Technische Universität and Direktor of the Stiftung Topographie des Terrors. When I needed help with the origins of my great-great-grandfather, Joseph Bender Levy, with the work of Wolfgang leading the Berlin City Council around 1870, or with the hidden SS affiliation of a Bremen cousin after 1930, I depended on the archival skills of Frau Dagmar Giesecke, now of the Stadtarchiv und Landesgeschichtliche Bibliothek Bielefeld. My oldest Berlin friends, Hans and Eva Reis, supported me with affectionate hospitality and legal expertise and had the wonderful idea of visiting Rawicz.

Antonie left hundreds of clippings and letters about her life as an actress, a flier, and a business executive, but gaps existed nevertheless. I am thus grateful to the Staatstheater Stuttgart for sending archival information about Antonie's roles in 1921 and 1922 in *Götz von Berlichingen, Jungfrau von Orleans, Penthesilea,* and *Faust I* and *II*. The theatre was then called the Würtembergisches Landestheater in Stuttgart. Dr. Gertrud Pfister, Professor of Sport History at universities in Berlin and Copenhagen, sent me other valuable items, including stories from Brazilian newspapers on Antonie's flight in South America in 1932. In 2004, Frau Barbara Waibel, archivist and librarian at the Zeppelin Museum Friedrichshafen, organized an exhibit on women in aviation. She featured Antonie among others and found significant photographs, letters, documents, and a recorded 1932 lecture that she shared with me.

Correspondence with Dr. Horst Sassin first informed me about the resistance plots of Ernst Strassmann, and he eventually put me in touch with Dr. Jutta Lange-Quassowski, Director of the Ernst-Strassmann-Stiftung, who provided me with a comprehensive set of documents about Ernst's life and achievements and a great variety of expert suggestions for organizing and publishing the entire manuscript. Her unstinting support has been unique and very much appreciated. Another source of documents and photographs was Gisela Strassmann of Berlin, a great-great-granddaughter of Chune Strassmann of Rawicz, via Ephraim, Arnold, and Reinhard, and hence a niece of Ernst. I thank her.

A niece and a grandson of Fritz Strassmann, the main promoter of legal medicine a century ago, live in the United States: Annemarie Springer of Bloomington, Indiana, and Fred Strassmann of Belmont, Massachusetts. The two have generously made anecdotes, letters, diaries, and photographs available to me, their distant third cousin. Exchanging visits with them after all these years has been a joy. The same applies to most of my first, second, and third cousins in Europe, only two or three of whom refused to cooperate at all.

Generous with time and ingenious suggestions at the United States Holocaust Memorial Museum were Benton Arnowitz, Director of Publications, and Dieter Kuntz, co-editor of the 2004 volume, *Deadly Medicine: Creating the Master Race,* and associate organizer of the 2005 exhibit by that name.

Friends in Michigan and Texas were kind enough to read this or that chapter, to reminisce, and to make zestful comments. Also helpful were Ms. Lisa Moellering, Curator of

Acknowledgments

Collections of the Holocaust Museum Houston, Ms. Mary Schiflett, Vice President of the Texas Medical Center, and Ms. Elizabeth Borst White, Curator of the Center's John P. McGovern Historical Collections. On numerous occasions, the wizardry of Lana Davis kept three successive computers and their user-unfriendly software from sabotaging the entire project.

Difficulties with many a nuance were solved by Ms. Evelyn Zegenhagen, my ingenious translator, who luckily chanced into the project with an initial curiosity about Antonie and then dedicated herself to the whole enterprise. In both English and German the entire work flows better because of astute and subtle improvements suggested by Tanja Hommen of the Campus publishers of Frankfurt. I also thank Ms. Shawn Kendrick of Berghahn Books for vigilant refinement of the latest version. Meanwhile, Dr. Marion Berghahn proved time and again that even hurried e-mails could be scholarly and witty.

I gratefully acknowledge the financial support that Dr. Lange-Quassowski has mobilized for publication and distribution through German medical institutions, especially those in Berlin, where so many Strassmann doctors plied their trade. I treasure their endorsement of the 2006 German edition, *Die Strassmanns: Schicksale einer deutsch-jüdischen Familie über zwei Jahrhunderte.*

My wife Elizabeth (Betty) and our daughters, Joan, Diana, and Beverly, were the most energetic yet patient support group, reading version after version, improving proportions and length, and providing psychological and philosophical insights, all the while scrutinizing my style word by word. I cannot thank them tenderly enough.

Introduction: A Family en Route

A Memory

When I saw the New York World Trade Center aflame and collapsing on television that September morning in 2001, I remembered a childhood event. From an attic window of our Berlin apartment building, I had seen the German parliament, the Reichstag, in flames, its glass dome incandescent and its windows orange, smoke swirling into the night sky. It was February 27, 1933. Our nanny, thin-lipped Fräulein Emmy, whom we hated, brought us to the attic for the view, just under the roof, telling us it was important. I was six years old and in first grade, and my sister Renate was eight. Emmy carried sleeping Angelika, aged two. Our parents were skiing in the Silesian mountains, the Riesengebirge, so Fräulein Emmy wrote them a postcard about the fire, adding that our head colds were better. We hated her because of her obsession with dirty hands, but taking us into the scary attic was an adventure. It smelled of sawdust and moldy leather up there, many strange things.

The Reichstag fire allowed the Nazis to ban one political party after another until Adolf Hitler had power to rule Germany by decree. The building was left as a sooty ruin across the Spree River from us, beyond the elevated train tracks only a quarter mile from our apartment. We passed the ruin daily, walking home from Kritzinger's School on Klopstock Strasse, two miles away, and passing the neighboring Königsplatz playground with its swings and sandboxes. Sometimes we played around the base of Bismarck's statue in front of the Reichstag. Bismarck had a repulsive walrus mustache like my grandfather, Paul Ferdinand Strassmann, who owned and operated a clinic-hospital for women around the corner from us on the Luisenstrasse. If you walked a half mile south along the Luisenstrasse, you came to Berlin's most grandiose boulevard, Unter den Linden, and its monumental symbol, the six-columned Brandenburg Gate, topped by a green four-horse victory chariot. Our street's name changed to Wilhelmstrasse there, and in the next blocks you found the palatial residences of the German president, the chancellor, and various ministries. We lived close to the middle of things.

Everyone talked about who had started the Reichstag fire, usually saying it was Communist pigs, but when my parents returned from vacation, they said it was Nazi pigs. That was confusing because the Nazis in their brown uniforms with diagonal belts were the new government and the Reichstag was a government building, so why would they burn it? The new government had a novel symbol, the swastika. A school friend tried to show me how to draw it, the way we learned letters in class. It was not obvious but challenging, like imitating a Chinese character. When I had it figured out and drew it on the paths near the Königsplatz sandbox, Fräulein Emmy and my parents were not proud of my accomplishment.

Adolf Hitler was the head of the new government, together with old Field Marshall Paul von Hindenburg, who had a walrus mustache like Bismarck and my grandfather. Hitler wore a swastika on a red armband and, like all my male relatives, an Iron Cross military medal. His mustache was too small to get soggy with soup—you could say that for him. I remember seeing him four times. Twice he was standing and saluting in an open Mercedes with little swastika flags on the fenders and with black-uniformed SS men lined up spread-legged along the curved route toward the Kroll Opera House on the Königsplatz. The Nazi parliament now met there, and it was on our way to school. Another time he appeared on the small balcony of the Wilhelmstrasse Chancellory. And once I heard him give a speech on the steps of the art museum at a plaza, the Lustgarten, at the far end of Unter den Linden. The speech was amplified by loudspeakers on lampposts, but I could not understand his hoarsely shouted German at all. What was he saying? Maybe it was Austrian. How could a man unable to speak our language lead our country? Was he a foreigner?

Other foreigners, usually Americans, were introduced to me at my grandfather's clinic around the corner, where my father, Erwin Strassmann, was the new chief of staff. The foreigners talked to children as if they were grownups, addressing us as *Sie*, not *Du*, and they had no idea which things were masculine, feminine, or neuter (*der*, *die*, or *das*). I usually felt embarrassed and never answered their questions with more than one syllable, thus spreading embarrassment to my parents and grandfather. Before I was eleven years old, I had read German versions of *Tom Sawyer*, *Huckleberry Finn*, *Uncle Tom's Cabin*, *The Last of the Mohicans*, and the *Ted Scott* aviation series, and I soon believed that I knew more about their country than they knew about ours. I knew about skyscrapers, Indians, the Mississippi, the Civil War, Hollywood, Shirley Temple—everything. My grandfather subscribed to *Time* magazine and the *National Geographic*, and I spent hours looking over the pictures. His passion was lecturing me about history: Greeks and Romans, Italian princes and painters, Frederick the Great, and, above all, the five Strassmann brothers, who had migrated to Berlin from somewhere and had become incredibly famous and important. However, I did not believe one could take them seriously, with their long beards and odd collars. And besides, they were now all dead, so I would never meet any of them.

In addition, they were Jews. I had no clear idea what that meant. I knew about Adam and Eve, David and Goliath, Joseph and his brothers, Moses leaving Egypt through the Red Sea, and Mary and another Joseph fleeing back there with infant Jesus. With all that wandering, it was not amazing that some would have come to Germany—just surprising that I should be their descendant. My grandfather sounded quite proud of that and explained that moving about was all part of seeking a "Promised Land." After wandering through the Sinai Desert for years and finally approaching Canaan, the first Promised Land, Moses had sent two scouts ahead to learn if the land was really that good. I do not recall the words my grandfather used in telling the story, but here is the relevant text from the Bible, Numbers 13, verses 17, 20, and 23: "And Moses sent them to spy out the land of Canaan, and said unto them, Get you up this way southward, and go up into the mountain.… And be ye of good courage, and bring of the fruit of the land. Now the time was the time of the first ripe grapes.… And they came unto the brook of Eshcol, and cut down from thence a branch with one cluster of grapes, and they bare it between two upon a staff; and they brought of the pomegranates, and of the figs."

These scouts and their grapes were on the Strassmann coat of arms, which my grandfather had engraved on rings of lapis lazuli and seals of onyx. The great dining room of Schumannstrasse 18, their apartment in front of the clinic, had a stained glass window with these grape carriers. The idea originally came from my grandfather's great-grandfather, Schmuhl Molower, who had adopted the name Strassmann around 1793. He was a prosperous trader in Rawicz, Poland, and he had the scouts and their grape cluster sculptured in a relief above the front door of his house. To him, Poland was a promised land, one that had welcomed Jews fleeing from wars and pogroms in Germany after 1600. Napoleon's blockade and Russian tariffs put an end to Schmuhl's thriving business, however, and his two sons, Heiman and Chune, were poor. Among Schmuhl's grandsons were the five brothers who sought a better promised land in Prussian Berlin around 1840. Their sister, Bertha, married a court official in nearby Lissa and cared for the parents in their old age.

Medicine in History

Throughout history, medical practitioners have used their specialized experience and their apparent magic to gain social power. Healing skills gave physicians and shamans direct access to elite persons, and this access could be used to promote all sorts of projects. Their aura could also lead popular opinion in new directions. But their attempts to assert power at times involved them in persecution as either villains or victims. As Geoffrey Cocks has put it, "The growing power and prestige of doctors ... tended dangerously to convince many of them—and much of the public—of their expertise in a wide range of social, political, and philosophical matters."[1]

These generalities can be illustrated by the role of Jewish physicians in Germany from the eighteenth through the twentieth centuries, seen partly through the experience of several generations of Strassmanns. During the Middle Ages, a superior knowledge of healing was the best way for a Jew to interact with the predominantly Christian community. A medical career was more respectable than commerce. It was not rabbinical and yet was in line with Judaic values and traditions. Jewish medical students continued to study at Italian and Dutch universities (especially Padua and Leiden), but as the Enlightenment spread, a few German universities began to admit Jews on the condition of conversion. By the 1720s, here and there (e.g., Frankfurt/Oder and Heidelberg) conversion rules were waived. The first medical doctor title for a Jew was awarded at Frankfurt in 1721, and the second at Halle in 1724.[2]

Around 1750, Berlin had only two practicing Jewish physicians. During his decades-long reign (1740–1786), King Frederick the Great did little to further the rights and welfare of any Jews, especially physicians. In his opinion, physicians were typically engaged in "fruitless speculations while ignoring the moral implications of their science." To Voltaire he wrote on April 28, 1759: "I have as little faith in doctors of medicine as I do in theology, but I will not carry it to the point of doubting the curative effect that a proper diet can have. I never would have survived the ghastly fatigues that I suffered if I had not resorted to a diet that strikes all who come by as military."[3]

Medical studies were seen as the best path for Jews to join the German intellectual mainstream. They could not own land, could not be soldiers or government officials, and could not join or compete with any trades dominated by guilds. Even Moses Mendelssohn (1729–1786), the leading philosopher of cultural assimilation, had to face these constraints with regard to the prospects of his own son, Joseph: "He has no inclination for medicine, and as a Jew he must become a physician, a merchant, or a beggar."[4] It helped that universities were entered more easily than gymnasia (academic high schools) and that medicine was least preferred by Christians. Only 10 percent of German Christian students were in medicine, compared with over 50 percent of young Jews, with well over two hundred graduating by 1800. By 1798, eight Jewish physicians were practicing in Berlin, and three more joined them within four years.[5] In all Germany, Jews made up some 2 percent of physicians around 1800.[6]

The Napoleonic era widened educational opportunities in both annexed lands and in the allied German principalities of the Confederation of the Rhine. Prussia followed with reforms in a matching bid for popularity. By the mid-1820s, four to six Jews, half of whom were the sons of physicians, graduated annually from the new University of Berlin. One physician, Dr. N. J. Friedländer, became the first unbaptized adjunct professor (*Privatdozent*).[7] In the nineteenth century, Jews composed a third of medical students in Berlin and Breslau, although they were barely 5 percent of all Prussian university students. Their entry to medical schools was unrestricted.[8]

Post-revolutionary Change

The Revolution of 1848 brought another transition. The military aristocracy attributed the event to Jews, especially to Jewish students, and hence physicians in training. Without doubt, medical students were on the barricades to an extent out of proportion to their share in the population, but both shares were minute.[9] One Jew, Wolfgang Strassmann (brother of my great-grandfather), a student leader, was banned from the city for proclaiming a republic in a revolution that merely sought a constitutional monarchy. Years later he returned to lead the elected Berlin City Council for twenty-three years (1863–1885), including a dozen as chairman, the highest elected office ever held by a Jew in Germany. His story is told in the second chapter. Together with four brothers, Wolfgang had migrated to Berlin from Rawicz near the Polish-Silesian border.

The conservative opposition saw in Wolfgang the principal inspiration for a new phobia—anti-Semitism.[10] Many measures that Strassmann and his 1848 medical comrades, including Rudolf Virchow and Paul Langerhans, promoted on the council, such as a safe water supply, a sewer system, building codes, food inspection, public hospitals, and a variety of services, had health aspects. Their medical credentials helped the doctors to overwhelm any opposition. These were the years of political medicine (*politisches Arzttum*), when leading physicians saw themselves as the "natural attorneys for the poor." Without even mentioning wars and expanding industries, Virchow insisted that "inevitably and closely, practical medicine depends on the political process."[11] Poor relief, he asserted, should not be a matter of charity but one of the "equal right of all to a healthful existence.... [A]dmission to a hospital must be possible for anybody who stands in need of it, no matter if he has money or not, if he is Jewish or a heathen."[12]

The Hohenzollerns and Bismarck could have ruled Berlin more aggressively in the late 1800s, but they were satisfied with consolidated power over national affairs, especially the imperial budget and the military. They did not view Jewish and liberal management of urban problems as a threat. Jews and the anti-military Progressive Party (Fortschrittspartei) elected majorities to the City Council because of a voting system that practically disenfranchised the poor. Those who paid the top third in direct taxes could indirectly elect one-third of representatives, giving each rich voter (males only) at least a hundred times more power than any member of the masses of poor who earned few seats with their meager taxes. A one-man-one-vote system would have given Socialists urban power with three-quarters of the seats, but the Hohenzollerns and other elites preferred middle-class Jews to that outcome. Nevertheless, Bismarck made one unsuccessful attempt to remove Wolfgang Strassmann from the council.

Meanwhile, in the medical profession, especially in the universities, unquestioning adherence to ancient traditions was being displaced by a new code of skepticism and empirical science. Universities had previously taught medicine by lectures, with neither laboratories nor clinical treatment of patients forming part of the curriculum. The right of professors and students to observe hospital patients as part of medical instruction had to be fought for in mid-century, since municipal operators of hospitals saw their involvement as an inconvenience.[13] With experiments, one could learn how the body actually functioned and how it responded to medicines, while anesthetics and antiseptics allowed massive progress in surgery. The share of Jews among German physicians rose from one in fifty to one in six, and in Berlin about half of all doctors were Jews. At the same time, nearly half of all Jewish doctors practiced in Berlin.[14] Still discriminated against in the more traditional fields, many Jews turned toward new specialties, such as ophthalmology, dermatology, psychiatry, urology, gynecology, and even obstetrics. Here midwives were still the most common practitioners. In 1904, Fritz Strassmann took the lead in expanding legal medicine as a field and in organizing a corresponding national association with its own journal. In 2004, its centenary was celebrated by naming the legal medicine facility at the Humboldt University of Berlin the Fritz Strassmann Institut. Wolfgang's brother Ferdinand was in charge of Berlin's health for three decades (1889–1919) as medical magistrate, receiving no pay for years but instead an honorary citizenship.

Opportunities to be innovators also took Jews to developing spas, such as Bad Nauheim in Hessen, that specialized in heart ailments. Foreign aristocrats, industrialists, and celebrities—the Romanovs, Habsburgs, Roosevelts, and Hearsts—came to Bad Nauheim to be treated by Isidor or Franz Groedel, August or Theodor Schott, or Sally Schoenewald, all Jews, not by just any Nauheim doctor.[15] In general, Jews were twice as likely to be specialists as others and hence were more advanced in most fields.

Nevertheless, even if they had converted religiously, Jews were given university chairs more slowly than others, although the share grew. At the University of Berlin, 44 of 113 adjunct medical teachers were Jewish in 1908, but no Jew was among the 19 highest-level Ordinarius professors. The first unconverted Jew to attain the rank of Ordinarius professor of gynecology in Germany was Wilhelm Freund at Strassburg in 1878.[16] That was nineteen years after Moritz Stern became the first German-Jewish Ordinarius in any field (Göttingen, mathematics, 1859).[17]

Equally important as university chairs were appointments as director of a public hospital. Otto Spielberg was an early director of the University Women's Clinic at Breslau. He had converted and expected other Jews seeking tenure to do the same. But in 1906, Paul Strassmann, although converted, was rejected as director of the women's division of a large, new Berlin medical complex, the Virchow Klinik, named after Rudolf Virchow, despite an outstanding record with innovations in his own small hospital-clinic. So Paul borrowed a fortune and built his own teaching and research hospital in art nouveau style almost across the street from the largest public hospital complex, the Charité. Among his patients were the artist Käthe Kollwitz, Ellen von Siemens-Helmholz, and Princess Hermine von Schönaich-Carolath, second wife of the Kaiser. In 1923, finally as professor, he was elected to the Senate of the University of Berlin. His principal clinic building survived both world wars, was taken by the Nazis, was restored after German reunification, and in 2003 was historically designated, with a plaque and ceremony, as the Strassmann Haus (Strassmann House).

The Lost World War and Transformed Illusions

Losing the 1914–1918 war and being forced to submit to the punitive Treaty of Versailles was traumatic for most Germans, who had come to think of themselves as second to none in world science, industry, culture, and benevolence. With the final crumbling of feudal institutions, however, citizens of Jewish descent, many thoroughly assimilated and intermarried, seemed to have reached their goal of full emancipation. The last barriers to their free participation in politics, business, science, and the arts seemed to vanish at the onset of the Weimar Republic. But others saw cosmopolitan Jews as the untrustworthy elements that had led to national defeat and disgrace. Jewish artists, actors, and writers who scorned military pretensions and social inequities were seen as degenerate and shameful. When the economy collapsed in 1930 and hardship spread, paranoid fantasies about Jews helped bring Adolf Hitler to power.

Many Jews had been conspicuous in promoting German political reforms, and some—like the radical Rosa Luxemburg, at one end of the spectrum, and Walther Rathenau, industrialist and foreign minister, at the other—were assassinated. Fritz Strassmann performed the autopsies and identified their deaths as murders. Right-wing fanatics found these murders justified and welcomed the Nazi era as a time for vengeance. During that era, one of Fritz's sons, Georg, had to emigrate, while the other, Reinhold, was killed at Auschwitz.

While discrimination against Jews was ameliorated during the Weimar period (1919–1932), the medical profession as a whole did poorly even beyond the effects of hyperinflation and worldwide depression. The profession was more easily entered than others and hence was crowded and competitive. In addition, it was pressed by the public health insurance companies that Bismarck had brought into being in 1883. Physicians looked on these companies "with their single-minded concern for cheap, mass treatment ... as the enemy of good medical practice."[18] In their view, the companies treated "panel doctors" like employees, which the physicians hated and fought with two lobbying associations, the Verband der Ärzte Deutschlands and the Deutsche Ärztevereinsbund. In 1869, to forestall regulation, German physicians had collectively and legally classified themselves as a trade rather than a profession, a strategy that backfired by enhancing unfettered competition from an additional 30 percent of practitioners, or fourteen thousand lay healers (*Kurpfuschers*), often quacks without any medical training. As a result, by 1932 many young doctors were unemployed, with the lowest 10 percent earning too little—less than three thousand marks (or $5,700 at 2000 rates) annually—to get married.[19]

The Nazi Takeover

Despite these pressures, fewer than 7 percent of German physicians had joined the Nazi Party before Hitler took power in 1933. By the end of 1937, however, nearly half of all doctors (and by 1945, 44.8 percent) had come aboard because they liked how things were going—protection of their privileges, weakened control by insurance bureaucrats, and less Jewish competition due to emigration or decertification.[20] A larger share of doctors had now joined the Nazi Party than had signed up from any other German occupational group: two-thirds had party or some other Nazi affiliation. The joiners were doctors less than forty years old to an extent that offset relative hesitation among older physicians. The middle-aged and old were actually underrepresented in the Nazi elite. Joiners preferred the SS to the SA storm troopers because it matched their elitist aspirations combined with simple opportunism or even resignation. Leaders of the actual Nazi medical bureaucracy, such as Gerhard Wagner, head of the Nazi Physicians' League (NS Ärztebund), and his successor, Leonardo Conti, however, were "fanatical believers ... not opportunists in the conventional sense." They were typically suspicious of modern hospitals and academic "school medicine," identifying instead with the *Kurpfuschers* as folkish holistic alternatives, as authentic Aryan National Socialists. Their corporate dictates could never be opposed or even discussed by practicing physicians or professors, but the leaders complained throughout the Nazi years that universities were neglecting their exciting new field, *Rassenkunde*, a racial "science" mixing medicine with anthropological and sociopolitical elements.[21]

After 1933, non-Jewish physicians had the task of turning these eugenic and anti-Semitic racial theories into action programs. Hans Auler, one of Hitler's favorite physicians, shared the Führer's view that cancer cells were like Jews and Communist conspirators in the national organism. Auler made educational movies on the topic, and Hitler liked to spend time with him. Nazi eugenics maintained that non-Aryans were a biological menace to Germany and that the nation could be cured only by weeding out Jews and Gypsies, not by their religious conversion or education. Another Hitler favorite was Fritz Lenz, a geneticist who had not been anti-Semitic in the early 1920s. Now he wrote that "Jews do not transform themselves into Germans by writing books on Goethe."[22] What was needed was physical excision of these corrosive elements, if not by expulsion then by lethal extermination.[23] Established non-Jewish scholars in psychiatry, genetics, and anthropology, such as Heine Fischer, director of the Kaiser Wilhelm Institute for Anthropology of Berlin (1927–1942), legitimized Nazi fantasies with elaborate measurements and reoriented medical ethics from individual care to seeking the hereditary health of the larger community.[24] With enthusiasm they participated in research to calibrate the nature of Jewish subhuman inferiority and to measure how much "mongrelization" was tolerable. Scientific papers by Jews could no longer be published after a decree of October 4, 1933, because their aim was said to be the destruction of the host culture or simply the goal of making money, mere business, unlike the creative approach and dutiful aims of German science.

A single Jewish grandparent could condemn two million inhabitants as pariahs, and, in the calculation of political tacticians, that could alarm too large a segment of the national population. When the initial specification in 1933 of one Jewish grandparent as being fatal was raised to three in 1935, however, the outlaw population was held below one million. At the same time, the "Hindenburg exemptions" for World War I veterans and for close relatives of the war dead could now be dropped as "unscientific." But if Gerhard Wagner, the physicians' Führer, had had his way, even those who were one-eighth Jewish, those with a single Semitic great-grandparent, "would have suffered the entire impact of the [Nuremberg] provisions." In some German cities, half- and quarter-Jewish doctors had to be reinstated, and in 1937, hundreds of them were still practicing.[25]

Cruelties

An astonishing number of German physicians and university laboratory managers were flattered by the new power and privilege to "purify the race" by discarding the alien and unfit. They worked out ways of identifying and sterilizing the congenitally deformed and the mentally deficient, leading to the forced sterilization of some four hundred thousand persons by 1945.[26] From sterilization it was a small step toward euthanasia for children who were born with defects and hence were "unworthy of life." In the process, why not carry out a few experiments? Carl Schneider, director of the Heidelberg Clinic for Psychiatry and Neurology, together with Konrad Zucker, professor of psychiatry, began a children's euthanasia program with research in 1938. Full-scale extermination of children expanded at thirty clinics, with over five thousand children being killed from 1940 to 1945 as a result of this program.

In October 1939, Hitler put his personal physician, Karl Brandt, in charge of Aktion T4, a new program of "mercy deaths for incurably ill adults" to be carried out at six German and Austrian gassing centers. After killing seventy thousand people and causing unrest, including protests by outraged judges and clerics, the project was nominally ended in August 1941. Because of such anti-Hippocratic measures, a handful of outstanding physicians who had previously been sympathetic to Nazism, including Ferdinand Sauerbruch, Karsten Jasperson, and Werner Kirchert, or who were Catholic, such as Franz Büchner, became alienated from the regime. They were the exception. The murders went on surreptitiously by means of starvation and overdoses, eliminating an estimated additional one hundred thirty thousand Germans and Austrians.[27]

The doctors in charge of Aktion T4 were then ordered to apply their technology to the Holocaust killing centers in Poland; ultimately, the gas chambers using hydrogen cyanide or Zyklon-B. They also continued with inhuman research of various types, including fatal experiments involving biological and chemical injections, bone transplants, and extreme pressures or temperatures. After the war, seven of the most sadistic physicians were condemned to death at the Nuremberg trials in 1947, nine were jailed, while others, Josef Mengele among them, fled to South America. Most were "denazified" on the testimony of fellow citizens within a few postwar years.[28]

The number of doctors guilty of crimes against humanity in laboratories and killing centers has been estimated at between three hundred fifty and four hundred, less than 1 percent of the fifty-nine thousand German physicians of 1939.[29] Most German doctors might not have approved of the violation of human rights involved in all those experiments.[30] The damage to Central Europe, however, was not only the monstrous actions of these criminals, but also the distorting effect of surveillance, fear, and intensive racial indoctrination on an entire profession. The ethical relation between patient and healer had been corrupted. As Michael Kater has summarized: "[A] conventional medical culture [was] infiltrated from one side by a science alienated from humanity and from another by charlatanry." The deluded and fearful majority of doctors worked very hard in Hitler's war but inevitably grew callous toward atrocities and "failed in the end to keep quacks in abeyance."[31]

Movable Expertise

Estimates are that over a quarter of German-Jewish physicians, that is, more than two thousand, were killed in the Holocaust, unable to flee despite a shortage of doctors throughout the world. Five percent committed suicide. Some two-thirds of German and Austrian physicians classified as Jewish by religion or descent did find new promised lands—Palestine, Britain, Australia, Brazil, Turkey, and especially the United States—although still less than five thousand in this case.[32] Migrating was hard, but unlike their compatriots in law, commerce, and industry, doctors had a movable skill that could find work anywhere. By 1939, only 285 Jewish physicians (0.3 percent of 1933) still practiced in Germany, no longer as doctors but as decertified *Krankenbehändler* (sickness treaters). They were allowed to treat only Jews and could not drive cars or work in spas.[33]

Two-thirds of emigrating doctors were under forty-five years old. In the United States, medical colleagues welcomed them generously in 1933 but grew nervous about competition within five years. Despite a physician shortage in small towns and counties, the newcomers were criticized in medical journals and meetings as incompetent quacks with socialist inclinations who should not get a license without being completely retested, and then after waiting five years for US citizenship. Only New York and Massachusetts did not make US citizenship a prerequisite for a medical license.[34]

Personal contacts dating back decades eased the entry of a few doctors. The Strassmanns, for example, had the benefit of a long association with Will and Charles Mayo of the celebrated Minnesota clinic. The Mayo brothers had studied Paul Ferdinand's operative innovations in Berlin and knew of Erwin's prize-winning discovery about the process of ovulation. In 1935, they invited Erwin to join their staff in Rochester as a base for looking around for a permanent American residence. In 1938, Erwin's choice was Houston, Texas, where he played a part in organizing the Texas Medical Center, now one of the world's largest. When half of American physicians were drafted for service in World War II, those who remained behind were busy and prosperous at last. Erwin's cousin, Georg Strassmann, had meanwhile emigrated in 1938 and became the leading pathologist at the Metropolitan State Hospital at Waltham, Massachusetts.

An Overview

Of the fifteen chapters of this book that follow, five cover 1800 to 1920, and ten go on from there. A Rawicz chapter follows this introduction and begins with Heiman's radical decision to send his children to German-speaking Prussian schools, instead of the traditional Hebrew cheder, so that they could qualify for university admission in Breslau or Berlin. Soon the rest of Posen was legally pressured to follow this pioneering example. Then comes a chapter that describes Wolfgang's rise in the City Council.

Two chapters tell about Paul and his brother, Ernst (1868–1923), a charming but compulsive gambler, who failed at his studies and tried to cover his casino losses by fraud. He was disinherited and sent with a one-way ticket to Puntarenas, Chile. Years later he came back a rich man who lost it all again, gambling.

Central to this book are the careers of Fritz Strassmann, the pioneering forensic pathologist, and of Paul Ferdinand Strassmann, who established a ninety-bed clinic-hospital in the Schumannstrasse. Fifteen thousand babies were born there (two busy storks lived in the courtyard), twenty-six thousand gynecological patients were treated, and four thousand physicians were trained over the course of twenty-seven years. The clinic was sought out by doctors from around the world seeking advanced insight and training. But in 1933, two of the most trusted staff physicians denounced the Strassmanns as Jews and sought to take over the facility. Declared unfit in 1935, Paul, Erwin, and Georg were dismissed from university faculties, while Fritz had already retired. Erwin, Georg, and their families emigrated to America, and Paul was forced to sell his clinic-hospital.

As celebrated as any political physician was Antonie Strassmann (1901–1952), Paul's youngest daughter, who at age sixteen left school for the stage and within a decade had triumphant reviews for twenty-eight roles, including Maria Stuart, Iphigenie, Penthesilea, Saint Joan, Portia, Salome, and Lady Macbeth, on Berlin and Stuttgart stages. By 1930, her interest had shifted to acrobatic flying. She crossed the Atlantic in one plane and soloed along the entire coast of Brazil in another. After she emigrated to the United States, the Gestapo unsuccessfully tried to abduct her in New York to take her back to Germany as a counterspy. In 2004, her exploits were celebrated at an exhibit entitled "Frau und Flug" in Friedrichshafen, Bavaria.

Antonie's sister Gisela married a Swiss attorney and diplomat, Max Gutzwiller, later a Heidelberg professor, who battled against the notion that law was now whatever suited the inner soul of German folk as determined by Nazis. He was forced out of the university partly for being "clanned up with Jews."

Two chapters near the end are about a few Strassmanns who stayed in Germany as World War II started. Their stories stand for those of thousands of others during these times. Elisabeth and her daughter Annemarie hid in villages, and Reinhold was murdered at Auschwitz. Ernst Karl Otto, however, led a resistance group until he was caught by the Gestapo. Although employed as a judge and thought to be a loyal Aryan, Ernst set up a secret opposition movement that planned to re-establish the rule of law and democratic procedures after conspiring Wehrmacht officers had carried out a revolt. These officers failed in several attempts. Ernst was caught in 1942, but he hoodwinked his Gestapo interrogators and survived. The Strassmann Foundation established in his honor has supported anti-authoritarian research and progressive art.

The book concludes with an epilogue about emigrants who revisited Germany after the war. They felt alienation tinged with nostalgia and a striving to reconcile weighed down by bitterness. Annemarie has told me that she never again felt comfortable in Germany, but that hearing the language, especially the Berlin dialect, makes her feel connected in some crazy way. Hearing about his brother's last months before being murdered at Auschwitz made Georg, the pathologist, physically too ill to continue an itinerary in Berlin. After decades, his adopted son, Fred, learned that his natural parents had been part of a boldly heroic family of military aristocrats involved in anti-Hitler assassination plots.

Beyond medicine and politics, the Strassmanns were an assimilating Jewish family, successful in many ways but ultimately scourged by fellow citizens who saw them only in terms of anti-Semitism. In the early nineteenth century, the Strassmanns had sought to extricate themselves from provincial turmoil, dogmatism, and poverty in Posen through education and migration to Berlin. A new world, industrializing and expanding, opened up for them there. They enthusiastically joined the movement and advanced both science and civil institutions. The next generation, born around 1870, was even more ambitious than their parents had been. Always ready for another advance and seeing themselves as German patriots, they were hit by the catastrophe of World War I and its aftermath. In old age, this generation was at a loss about dealing with military defeat and rejection by neighbors who had become unhinged by Nazism. Their children, born after 1890, are the last generation wholly covered in this book. More sophisticated than their parents in many ways, they still wanted to excel. Their education was interrupted by the 1914–1918 calamity, and they found a world less welcoming than that of their parents and grandparents. As Nazi chauvinists came to power and turned bestial, emigrating overseas gave this generation of the 1890s its particular challenge.

The Strassmanns were not just political physicians but also parents who tried to direct their children in the context of changing fads and dangers. With six connected generations from 1793 to 1993, one can see evolving perspectives, ambitions, and illusions about careers, social status, national identity, and philosophy.

This book illustrates the interaction of medicine, politics, persecution, and migration in Germany primarily during 1845–1945 but also for about half a century before and after these years. My sources consist in part of letters, diaries, and Strassmann memoirs from some sixteen cartons that have come my way. As an academic economic historian,[35] however, I have tried to do more than report one family's association with both medical and political change in the context of assimilation. I have consulted German experts and archives, as well as hundreds of scholarly publications. Much of relevance has been published within the last dozen years, as the citations show, and that has helped.

At the book's end comes an account of my own first return to Berlin in 1952 and my 1993 visit to Rawicz, once again Polish. This introduction concludes with our 1936–1937 emigration from my point of view.

Emigration

Typically, first our father, Erwin, sailed alone. After he boarded the *SS Manhattan* in Hamburg on March 11, 1936, my grandfather wrote in his diary: "His decision was free, and I could neither promote nor oppose it.... As a combat officer, physician, and young professor, he has been hardworking and flawless. Nothing matters anymore. He is no longer regarded as a German physician.... As 'fully Jewish' he is bound by ever tighter restraints." When the rest of our small family followed seventeen months later in August 1937, Grandfather wrote: "Adieu! Adieu! Go find happiness, feel free and be respected!"

It was hard for me to understand what those long-dead bearded Jews had to do with my father's job of treating patients and delivering babies. In my class at the French gymnasium were four "fully Jewish" boys, and being "half-Jewish" myself, I pondered if any of us were really different from the others. Rosenthal was short, had long eyelashes, and was very shy, always sitting near the windows. Grünfeld had curly red hair and was sassy in an amusing way. Heavy-set Boris was the son of the Bulgarian ambassador and as ordinary as everyone else. The fourth was an enviably blond athlete, but I don't remember his name. On Saturday mornings, those four were not allowed in school to take part in art and gymnastics or to hear about General Franco's heroism in battling godless Bolsheviks in Spain. None of the four Jews seemed religious, so I assumed they were playing at home.

The best thing about emigrating for me was the hope of avoiding the next German war. Both of my parents had a brother killed in World War I—Hellmuth Strassmann and Ulrich Wens. Twenty-seven Strassmann relatives had fought in that war, and nine did not return. Since my sisters had only me as a brother, I already saw myself as a corpse hanging on barbed wire in a gray-green uniform somewhere in France or along the Polish Corridor. My mother would then wear my Iron Cross as a brooch, decorated with tiny gold oak leaves, as both my grandmothers had worn those of their sons. Hellmuth's and Ulrich's photos as boys and with Iron Crosses were everywhere. I would rather be around in person. There was this Polish pink strip on the map separating Pomerania from blue East Prussia, and Alsace was in French purple yet outlined in maroon on the far side of the Rhine. We had arithmetic lessons about how much territory was lost in 1918 and how Germans were outnumbered in that war. Nevertheless, I did not want to get hit by real shrapnel or be blinded by poison gas to revise the map, an imaginary thing. I can tell you that. Better to cross the gray Atlantic. In Berlin we already had air raid drills, and the attic from which we had seen the Reichstag fire had to be cleared of flammable junk. French bombers might come at any moment after the Olympic Games of 1936.

That is how I saw things long ago. The first chapter shows how it all began two hundred years ago in Rawicz.

Chapter 1

A Father against Orthodoxy: Heiman in Rawicz

Heiman was the first Strassmann to defy rigid traditions. Born on May 8, 1797, he was the son of a wealthy trader of Rawicz, a western Polish town that was temporarily the Prussian Rawitsch and that would change nationality five more times over the years. Rawicz was a clean town neatly laid out among rye and potato fields stretching flat toward a forest along the eastern horizon. In the west, a range of hills carried ninety-nine windmills, with a hundredth, according to legend, invariably burning down. Poland was the granary of Europe in the eighteenth century, and exports flourished, as did the Rawicz wool trade, which had four hundred looms active in good times. Rawicz snuff was prized by connoisseurs.

Count Adam Obracht Przyna Przyjemsky had founded Rawicz in 1638 as a profitable textile-weaving town on his ancestral estate. The Thirty Years' War (1618–1648) was in progress, and hundreds of people had already fled Austrian, Swedish, and French armies fighting in nearby Germany and had settled on his estate. But a formal arrangement would attract still more workers and taxpayers. Count Przyjemsky did not care about the refugees' religious beliefs, and within a year or two he had both a Protestant and a Catholic church built in the new town.

Jewish merchants arrived somewhat later in Rawicz, were expelled in 1648 at the time of the Chmielnicki massacres, returned, were expelled again in 1674, came back, and were finally allowed to stay. In 1698, an organized Jewish community existed, and by 1719 the twelve Jewish families in Rawicz as a group received an official letter of rights and privileges that also specified their taxes. The first rabbi, Menachem Mendel Gradenwitz, was appointed in 1755, but no synagogue was built until 1783. By then, nearly two hundred Jewish families lived in Rawicz.[1] To them and the German settlers, Polish was a foreign language. In the next century, Jews composed one-fifth of the Rawicz population of some nine thousand, making it the third largest town in the province of Poznan. Altogether, forty-three thousand Jews lived in the province, about 6 percent of the Poznan population.[2]

A month before Heiman was born, a paternalistic Prussian regulation of April 1797 allowed all Jews who earned an "honest" living and had regular last names to become *Schutzjuden*, protected Jews with privileges. The wealthy trader, Reb Schmuhl Molower, however, delayed changing his name until he was stopped on the street (*Strasse* in German) by a police officer and was told harshly, "Reb Schmuhl! Choose a German name!" "Well," said Schmuhl, "I'm on the street, so call me Strassmann."

Until Napoleon's invasion and blockades, Schmuhl made a fortune transporting goods by way of Kalisch to a White Russian entrepôt at Mohilew—hence his provisional last name, Molower. Schmuhl, his sons Heiman and Chune, and the rest of the family (names now lost) lived in a house at Judengasse 166 that had a large courtyard with stables and coach houses. The second floor of the house, with its large windows, was elegant and called a *belle étage*. Below on each side of the front door were shops, and above the door was the great sculptured relief showing two scouts of Moses returning from Canaan with a colossal bunch of grapes hanging from a pole across their shoulders.

These grapes and their carriers, which have remained the Strassmann family emblem, symbolized for Schmuhl and his descendants the promise of travel and migration to new lands. But Schmuhl's promised land was disappointing since his trade and net worth never recovered from Napoleon's anti-British continental blockade of 1806, nor from the high Russian tariff of 1820. After Schmuhl's death, by 1825 the family was poor.

Son Chune Strassmann took up farming at the nearby village of Borek, talking, dressing, and working like a Polish peasant. That was unusual for a Jew, but not unheard of. Once a week Chune came to Rawitsch to sell produce in the market and to bring cheese and eggs to brother Heiman. As described by his grandson, Heinrich, my great-grandfather, whose memoirs are the main source for this account:

> [Heiman] was a tall, strong man, a little irritable and violent, indulgent toward his children, but strict to the point of cruelty about dishonesty and bad report cards. Father had a sharp intelligence and an excellent memory and was learned in Judaism, even the Kabala, and apocryphal scriptures. He was a friend of the good *bon mot*, a double-edged sword, and especially popular among our Christian fellow citizens. Although those of our faith rightly did not take him as entirely Orthodox, they nevertheless sought his advice in learned and mundane matters. Our father was a proud man who saw value only in education … being rich was to him almost synonymous with ignorance.[3]

Against all local Jewish tradition, in 1821 Heiman named his oldest son Wolfgang, after two Germans whom he considered the greatest of recent times, Mozart and Goethe, who was still living. Heinrich went on:

> To be sure, our father never really knew the joys of a livelihood. An attempt to earn his bread as lottery collector ended with a loss. His later posts were honorific.… His own requirements were exceedingly modest; a glass of beer and Rawitsch snuff were his only luxury.… His "knowledge" of medicine and meteorology gained him a certain recognition, but especially his political views were respected in bourgeois circles. He was a democrat and more than somewhat proud that in 1847 his fellow citizens elected him their *Wahlmann* [one who could vote for their actual representative in Prussia's indirect balloting system] for the United Prussian Assembly.[4]

What was eccentric, ahead of his time, about Heiman was his enthusiasm for modern reforms, not his lack of regular employment. Sophia Kemlein has summarized life in Posen around 1800 as follows:

> The daily life of Posen Jews was determined by fulfilling the Law as set forth in the Torah and the Talmud; their identity was exclusively religious. Yet being a rabbi was not seen as a profession.… Books in languages other than Hebrew were not read.… Occupying oneself with matters other than one's own religion was not deemed as worthwhile.… With men

absent in learning centers or synagogues, women took over businesses, if they could afford it.... Contacts with non-Jews [involved] no efforts to bridge the abyss caused by differences in religion, legal status, language, culture, or life style.[5]

The Family Income

Part of the Strassmann family income came from the rental of the two shops in front of the house. A widow on one side sold dried fruit, pickles, and other groceries, while Schaje Zotenberg sold scrap iron on the other side. Schaje was called "ganef" or rascal because his wares were of dubious origin. The Strassmann boys, among others, sold him any metalware that was loose and some that was not. Schaje went through the motions of weighing things scrupulously but never paid more than three pfennigs. Neither he nor the widow paid the rent on time. Chune was supposed to receive half of the rent payments, and disputes about that led to bad relations—hatred, almost—between the two brothers. Heinrich noted: "Besides, our proud, educated, and respected father did not find it agreeable to have a peasant brother, as even we children noticed."[6]

Most of the income was earned by Heiman's wife, Judith (1795–1875), whom he had married when she was twenty-three and he was only twenty-one, an unusual age disparity for those times. Wolfgang was born a year later. Judith and her three sisters were blond and said to be great beauties. All four supported their families by selling textiles while their husbands indulged in learned but unremunerated pursuits. Their maiden name was Guhrauer, presumably because the family had emigrated to Rawicz and Leszno (Lissa) from Guhrau in Silesia around 1640. Generations earlier, they had lived in the Rhineland. By the nineteenth century, the Guhrauers claimed to have sired a hundred rabbis, an assertion that was not as certain as their wealth. The family owned the largest store in Rawicz, selling linen, ribbons, gloves, and other luxury goods.

Four times a year, Judith traveled thirty-five miles by coach (a trip that lasted all day) to the great fairs of Breslau and with borrowed funds bought cotton cloth to be retailed personally in Rawitsch. Clients usually sent for her, but if they were old customers, she might visit them on her own. Heinrich recalled: "With her soft, gentle manner, she knew how to nudge a sale toward a close."[7] During the 1840s, however, her business declined, as crops failed and depression spread throughout Europe. Judith had trouble repaying her debts and getting credit and therefore shifted her source of supply to odd-lot shops in Lissa. She sold her last stock to provide a dowry for her only daughter, Bertha, in 1852. "I still recall my intense fright at seeing the empty storeroom," wrote Heinrich decades later. "Mother now decided to go from house to house, selling goods from the larger stores of Rawitsch itself. Earnings under a middleman were much smaller but enough to see us through scantily."[8]

The Strassmanns lived in two rooms behind the sculpture of grapes from the Promised Land. The larger room had the parents' bed and the kitchen stove, and the smaller room had one bed for three children, while others slept on the floor. Although Heiman had no definite job, tasks like nursing sick children were Judith's responsibility: "If we ever returned home ill or with a bleeding head, it had to be a secret from Father. He would add a spanking to a light injury, especially if clothes were torn; but at the sight of a bleeding wound, our tall, strong father usually fainted, thus adding a second patient for our poor mother. And yet in the community Father was admired as something of a healer, knowledgeable about headaches, toothaches, and other ailments, and even acquainted with some Latin terminology."[9]

The Strassmanns were too poor to afford cookies and candy, yet when the circus came to town, their children shared everyone's joy at seeing camels, apes, bears, acrobatic riders, and tightrope walkers. Mother Judith made further sacrifices, or parental friends arranged their admission. But the town's most popular recreation was cost-free: "The pride of Rawitsch was the Promenade set on the remains of demolished fortifications that had encircled the town.... Raised high, well-graded, and landscaped with trees and occasional flower beds, the Promenade allowed vistas of the town from all sides. Almost everyone circled the Promenade daily, and on Sundays and holidays it was a 'Corso' for showing off a fashionable wardrobe and important family members who had returned from abroad."[10]

West of Rawitsch below the hills with the windmills, water collected every autumn (no one knew why), and that made for the best skating in winter. "On Sundays and holidays, old and young, all classes, even army officers romped and capered on the ice." Among the crowd were the daughters of Herr Müller, the prison director. This large, powerful man with military bearing had a gloomy face and a piercing stare. People said that, unlike his guards, he dared to walk among the prisoners unarmed and alone because he could tame them with his stare, the way cobras hypnotize rabbits. Heinrich recalled how everyone avoided Müller timidly and that even local dignitaries "felt uncomfortable on the occasions that he joined them for beers at their pub, the Ächten Seidel. The man's isolation would have been complete if his daughters had not been so beautiful that all young men were infatuated with them."[11]

A Pivotal Decision

Despite poverty and tradition, Heiman resolved to have his children educated in Christian rather than Hebrew schools. The Hebrew cheder school of Rawitsch taught the alphabet and spelling but no grammar or arithmetic before going on to the Pentateuch and the Talmud. The teachers had little training, and the curriculum was unsystematic and lacked standards. According to Heinrich: "Spankings were common in the cheder, since the teachers were usually in a bad mood because they lived in poverty and were rarely paid in cash.... In the winter we students had to bring a candle every week and a piece of firewood daily, but we froze because it warmed only the teacher and his family after school was over." No instruction at all was given to Jewish girls in Rawitsch.

> So our wise and courageous father made a decision that, given his own upbringing, was positively astounding and that shaped the character and intellect of his children in a conclusive and fortunate way: he sent brother Wolfgang (born 1821) and sister Bertha (born 1824) to Christian elementary schools.
>
> If you consider that Father ... had concentrated on Hebrew studies in the usual manner and was considered an authority as a preacher, kosher butcher, and circumciser ... and that his decision put his standing and income in the community at risk, then I say that his step must be seen as heroic. It was not only a break with tradition but, from the viewpoint of Rawitsch Jews, a break with religion altogether. Nothing like it had ever happened in Rawitsch.
>
> After growing up, I often spoke to our blessed father about his unprecedented step and heard the following. As an intelligent and prudent person who read the political news and who discussed religion, science, and public affairs in a friendly manner with Christian fellow citizens in the pub (itself unprecedented for a Jew), he easily concluded that the one-sided instruction of Jewish children qualified them for only two occupations: scholar or trader.... Father wanted something better for his children and saw that suitable schooling was the only way.[12]

The Protestant and the Catholic elementary schools of Rawitsch refused to admit little Wolfgang and Bertha because no precedent existed for doing so. But a third elementary school was attached to the local teachers college, and its director, Herr Hippauf, although believed to be hostile to Jews, admitted Wolfgang unconditionally in 1827. For Bertha, a place was found in the village school of Scyrakawo, an hour's walk away.

Compulsory education, stressing German grammar and arithmetic, was later mandated by the Prussians, but rabbis and Orthodox community elders opposed this intrusion into their ancient routine. Enforcement would mean paying for buildings and for teachers whom they could not control. Eventually, Jewish elementary schools had to teach secular disciplines, and in communities without such schools, parents had to arrange for private tutors or send their children to Christian schools. Teachers had to pass government examinations and were compelled to teach in German, rather than Yiddish or Hebrew, even in religious courses. All books naturally had to be in German. Most cheder teachers failed their examinations, and in any case, religion could not be more than a quarter of the curriculum. Jewish families often could not muster the resources for new schools and teachers, so many children eventually had to be sent to Christian schools, or they were kept home illegally. As late as 1833, in the district of Posen (the southern half of the province) 26.3 percent of Jewish children (mostly girls) had no schooling, and among the rest, 14.3 percent attended Christian schools.[13] Thus, Heiman's enthusiasm was a harbinger about a new direction that at first offended other Jews.

Heinrich reported: "Brother and sister studied industriously, and since both were exceptionally talented and had outstanding memories, they were soon the best pupils.... Neither brother nor sister suffered from anti-Semitic outbursts; on the contrary, they were admired by their fellow pupils as surprising white ravens and were favored by their teachers because of their industry and good behavior."[14]

Samuel Strassmann (born 1826) followed Wolfgang to the Hippauf school. Both studied Latin on the side and did well enough to be admitted to the gymnasium in Lissa, a town twenty miles north of Rawitsch. Wolfgang went in 1835 and Samuel in 1840. The gymnasium in Lissa was one of three in the province and had 370 students in 1830. Of these, half were Polish, 44 percent were German, and only twenty (5 percent) were Jewish. By the end of the next decade, a third of the students were Jewish.[15]

Bernhard Strassmann (born 1831) was sickly and attended a new and better Hebrew elementary school for both boys and girls that had replaced the cheder. The ambitious Rector Kohn brought in well-trained young teachers and, except for Latin, kept his school on a par with the other public schools. Bernhard, however, showed mechanical aptitude in making his own toys, so Heiman resolved that he should become a master mason.

> One does have to acknowledge the energetic and radical ways of our father. He persuaded a Christian master mason to accept brother Bernhard as an apprentice. Imagine the amazement and horror of our fellow believers seeing a Jewish lad in a mason's apron carrying lime and bricks on a shaky scaffold up to the roof and handling a trowel or hammer. Never before had they seen anything like that. At first the Gentile journeymen would haze and tease Bernhard, but he had pluck and was cooperative and, above all, good-natured. His instructor was sensible and unprejudiced. In three summers Bernhard became a journeyman himself and also finished his building studies during three corresponding winters in Breslau.[16]

Bernhard then joined his older brothers, Wolfgang and Samuel, in Berlin, where they were already finishing their medical studies. He enrolled in the Building Academy of Berlin, worked on construction sites, and eventually became a master mason.

Heinrich, the fifth child, was considered too delicate to attend school, so Heiman himself taught the youth at home for five years and then enrolled him in the new Hebrew school directed by Kohn. The precocious twelve-year-old had to sit with beginners half his age. He was destined for the gymnasium at Lissa like the oldest two, so extra lessons in geometry, Greek, and Latin were needed. These subjects Heinrich learned from the Protestant minister, Schück, of the penitentiary, a man who charged nothing for his time and even provided coffee and sandwiches. Heinrich recalled: "With the daily visits I gradually lost my childish horror at the ghastly institution and learned to ignore the screams of prisoners being whipped while I capered in the garden with Müller's daughters. In April 1849, at fourteen years old, I entered the Lissa gymnasium."[17]

Rawitsch in Revolt

After Heiman's older sons moved to Berlin, Rawitsch experienced the same pressures as the rest of Europe. In Prussian towns the Revolution of 1848 came and went. The downfall of King Louis Philippe in Paris and Prince Metternich in Vienna within a month had persuaded King Friedrich Wilhelm IV in Berlin to agree to a constitution with civil liberties (which he later revoked). Crop failures and bankruptcies throughout Europe in the late 1840s had made people receptive to deposing princes, and the Prussian king lost his nerve for half a year.

Hearing all this, almost everyone in Rawitsch joined a democratic club, and with enthusiasm Heiman became one of the leaders. After all, with no occupation, he had the time for military drill and nightly meetings at the beer hall. As Heinrich recalled:

> Imagine what a tremendous impression words never heard before made on us: fatherland, freedom, equality, emancipation of Jews, national assembly, the right of all citizens to bear arms, etc. Even greater was our impression of the club president, who read out his program on three successive evenings. The good fellow, a surveyor named Heinemann, was most radical and proposed a comprehensive reorganization of the state to promote the happiness of the people and the renown of our beloved hometown, Rawitsch. All were firmly convinced that only this man could save the state, and we could already picture him at the pinnacle of authority.[18]

Except for a squad at the penitentiary, the Prussian military garrison was withdrawn from Rawitsch and deployed in more strategic places. After all, Poles were also in rebellion and saw Russians, Prussians, and Jews alike as alien intruders. After the failed harvests of 1846, Polish peasants, perhaps incited by the nobility, had rioted against Jewish traders in a number of towns, and the Prussians had to restore order. So Jews now looked to Germans for protection, as well as for economic and political advancement, especially if the movement for constitutional democratic reforms succeeded. Joining a rebellion against the czar in Russian Poland did not interest the Posen Jews, and the Poles accused them of ingratitude for all the rights and benefits they had enjoyed over the centuries. Jews joined clubs for the protection of German interests in Posen, and in Lissa, wearing nationalist black-red-gold cockades, they assailed Poles to remove their red-white ones.[19]

With muskets that had been left behind and with broomsticks, the people of Rawitsch organized a "citizens' guard" and held amateurish military exercises.

> One day Father himself came home with a heavy, black "cow's hoof," as the infantry musket of those days was called because of its plump, black stock. Imagine with what joy we

three younger boys looked on this promising new toy. As soon as our parents went out, we took the musket out of the corner, right-shouldered and presented arms, just as we had often seen it done. Commands thundered through our house, and the heavy weapon banged the floor.

For Mother, these were times of continual fear. During her daily rounds she feared her return to possibly burned or mutilated children. While her somewhat hot-headed husband stood guard, she was afraid the Poles would attack the town. Indeed, the Polish insurrection suffered its final defeat fifty miles away at Xions.... Some nights Mother was startled by the drunk mason, Heinze, who expressed his love of freedom by running up and down dark streets, shouting "Garibaldi!" Most patrols led to extended inspections of various taverns.

Eventually, the revolutionary movement faded away, the stormy waves were calmed, and the secretly resentful partisans of the king rose back to the top. The citizens' guard was dissolved; the democratic club was closed; and Rawitsch resumed its former aspect of a very quiet provincial town. Sadly, we took our musket to the town hall—but our good mother breathed more easily. Father went to bed at a suitable bourgeois hour, and we boys lost our toy.[20]

One Letter That Survived

Heiman was eighty-four when he died in Berlin on November 17, 1881. He had lived independently with Judith in Lissa, Posen, until she died in 1875, and they had celebrated their fiftieth wedding anniversary in 1868. As a widower, Heiman moved to the nearby house of his daughter Bertha and her husband Louis Meyer, a court official. Judith was buried in the Jewish cemetery of Lissa, where Guhrauers had been buried for nearly two hundred years. All five sons came to the funeral, and Heinrich later wrote: "Our mother had no enemy, and as we carried her to the grave, her coffin was followed by old and young, Christians and Jews, Poles and Germans. She died as she had lived, without struggle or pain, calmly and peacefully, laying her industrious hands with a blessing on our heads and muttering Hebrew prayers."[21]

In 1878, father Heiman, aged eighty-one, wrote to Heinrich in Berlin that it was Judith of whom he still thought daily and whom he missed every moment. What he longed for now in the evening of his life was a final reunion with his sons and grandchildren in Berlin, perhaps in the spring of 1879. The wish was fulfilled, and Heiman moved a final time. I found his letter of November 28, 1878, a few years ago while sorting through family papers. It is the only direct memento to survive that remarkable man of Rawicz, who determined that his five sons and daughter must defy tradition and move into a larger world. I shall copy the letter as completely as I can decipher it both in German and English.

Lissa 28/11/1878
Geliebter Sohn, Tochter, und Kinderleben,
    Über euere so überaus sehr grossen Anhänglichkeit zu euerem alten Papa, welche mir die Bertha aus euerem Brief an ihr, vorgelesen hatte, bin ich ... sehr gerührt worden. [Fünf schwer zu entziffernde Zeilen, zwei Sätze, folgen. Sie erwähnen, "unser grosser Lehrer M."]
    Macht euch meines gar keinen Kummer. Noch bin ich Gottlob nur physisch schwach. Die Ursache ist nur dies wahre und einzige. Indem euere Gottselige Mutter mich mit die geringste nur anstrengende Arbeit verschont hatte, dem zufolge ich ausser Stande bin, ihrer nur einen Augenblick zu vergessen.

Ihr werdet euch nun zu richten wissen, dass selbst die delikatesten Angelegenheiten unserer Familie, mir nicht verborgen bleiben. Für meinen Lebensabend sehnt sich mein Herz euch auch einmal unberufen zusammen zu sehen, in Berlin. Es drängt mich mein Inneres an Euch etwas zu sagen, und weiss nicht was. Da aber im Winter gar keine Rede davon sein kann, will und muss ich es der Zukunft und auch der Zeit überlassen, und hoffe dass Er, der Weltlenker, mir die Gnade schenken werde, mich noch bis zur gewünschten Zeit leben zu lassen. Bleibt mir nur recht gesund und lebt froh. Das ist der Wunsch eueres Euch sehr liebenden

Vater Heiman Strassmann

[Translation]
Lissa, November 28, 1878
Dear Son, Daughter, and Children,

Your very great devotion to your old papa, which Bertha read to me out of your letter to her, has touched me very much. [Five indecipherable lines, two sentences, follow, mentioning 'our great teacher M.']

Do not worry about me. Thank God, I am still only physically weak. That is explained by only one true cause, that your blessed mother spared me the least and strenuous tasks, so that I cannot forget her even for a moment.

You will now see to it that even the most delicate concerns of our family will not be kept from me. For the evening of my life, my heart longs to see all of you together in Berlin without some formal cause. I have a pressing urge to tell you something but don't know what. Since we cannot consider it during the winter, I have to leave it to time and the future and hope that He, Who Steers the World, will graciously allow me to live until that desired time. Stay healthy and live in good cheer. That is the wish of your always very loving

Father Heiman Strassmann

Heinrich later recalled that his father had never been severely ill in his life. He had been a strong man (taller even than brother Ferdinand), a man with an excellent memory and a hefty temper. A month before he died on November 17, 1881, arterial sclerosis had caused his ankles to swell, rendering walking difficult. But otherwise, "Father had nothing wrong with him, looked well-preserved for his age [eighty-four], and had ample gray hair and many teeth. He died while I read the newspaper to him, without struggle or pain." He was buried at Weissensee, Berlin, in the family burial site. On the large granite plaque, his name is spelled "Heimann Strassmann" in German Gothic letters with "born in Rawicz, 8 May 1797, died 17 November 1881" below. Above are twelve lines in weathered Hebrew script that I cannot decipher.

Chapter 2

From the Revolution of 1848 to Reforms in Berlin after 1863: Wolfgang and Ferdinand

During the Revolution of 1848 in Berlin, Wolfgang and Samuel Strassmann were both student leaders in the college of medicine. In a *Medicinische (sic) Club*, students tried to reform the system of instruction and examination in a way that threatened the university's elite establishment. Wolfgang and Samuel also sought constitutional liberties and favored a republic in place of the Hohenzollern monarchy. A group of young physicians, who had formed the Society for Scientific Medicine (Gesellschaft für Wissenschaftliche Medicin) in 1844, shared their views and endorsed revolution. In medicine they demanded the rejection of all hypotheses and rules not based on scientific observations. Thus, they opposed unempirical, unprovable theories that diseases were due to "imbalances" among four basic bodily fluids—blood, phlegm, yellow bile, and black bile.[1] Because of their political activities, men such as Rudolf Virchow (1821–1902), a pioneer in cellular anatomy, were under surveillance and eventually left the city. Wolfgang (1821–1885), who was Virchow's age, twenty-six, was even banned from the city after spending six weeks in prison. Samuel was spared because he was the tutor of young Count Lucchesini, whose father was a marshal to the king's brother, Prince Karl. Eventually, Wolfgang became the chairman of the City Council and posthumously had a street named after himself. The chapter concludes with brother Ferdinand, the youngest, who was named an Honorary Citizen of Berlin after thirty years of directing public health and sanitation.

Wolfgang in 1848 was remembered by Heinrich as being handsome (*bildschön*) with wavy blond hair, a pale complexion, a high forehead, and a Greek nose. Typically, he wore a black velvet jacket and a nationalist black-red-gold sash. He had a "refreshing, engaging nature, idealistic ardor, a poetic gift, and a good-natured sense of humor."[2] He had begun his university studies with philosophy in Breslau but had switched to medicine in Berlin around 1845. When the revolution broke out, he was in his last semester of medical studies. Because of jail and exile, his revolutionary activities led to a six-year delay in his final examinations.

Social grievances, unemployment, and economic misery in Berlin as elsewhere in Europe were the underlying causes of the Revolution of 1848. The potato and grain harvests of 1846 were down by a quarter, and prices had risen by over 50 percent. On April 21, 1847, demonstrations broke out in Berlin markets and led to the storming of bakeries and restaurants, the smashing of windows in palaces, military intervention, and three hundred arrests. King Friedrich Wilhelm IV convened a novel United Prussian Assembly (Preussischer Landtag)to draft a constitution, but he dismissed it two months later, saying that he would "never agree to having a piece of paper crowd in between this country and the Lord God in Heaven."[3] Meetings at beer gardens, populist marches, and petitions resumed. People called for a constitution with freedom of speech, press, and assembly, and for independent judges, habeas corpus, trial by jury, the right to bear arms, and equal rights regardless of property or religion. Demands grew ferocious after the successful revolution in Paris in February 1848, and in early March some demonstrators were attacked by cavalry, slashing with swords, wounding many, and killing some.

As tensions rose and the news of Metternich's dismissal in Vienna arrived, the king apprehensively thought that concessions had to be made. Royal proclamations were issued to ease censorship and to support constitutions for all German states. Feeling victorious, a crowd of over ten thousand gathered on Saturday, March 18, at the Schlossplatz square just south of the royal palace to cheer the king, who appeared on a balcony. The boisterous crowds made military officers nervous, and they made a display of marching in troops. Their presence changed the crowd's jubilation into fear of betrayal. Officers ordered all squares near the palace to be cleared at once. Two shots were fired, perhaps unintentionally. People fled and erected barricades in all the streets leading toward the palace. Within an hour civilians shot at soldiers, and the battle was on. According to the historian Hajo Holborn, "the number of active fighters was probably not greater than a few thousand because of the scarcity of arms.... The largest group of insurgents were members of the craft guilds, but there were a good number of merchants and students on their side.... It was a general uprising without any general plan."[4]

Wolfgang Strassmann led a group of students at the great barricade of the Königstrasse just east of the Schlossplatz, facing the Kurfürsten Bridge. When that barricade was overrun by troops, Wolfgang and eight comrades fled into the house of Major Meno Burg on the corner of the Poststrasse, a block inward from the river. Meno Burg (1789–1853) was the first Jew to become an officer in the Prussian army, and as a protégé of Prince August, he had been promoted to the rank of major in 1847. Never baptized, Burg believed "in the essential goodness of man, and a visionary hope that the gentile world could be taught to abjure anti-Semitism by contact with responsible and honorable Jews."[5] On that day in March 1848, Major Burg, an artillery officer, was not at home. Prussian soldiers pursued Wolfgang and his friends into Burg's house. As Heinrich recorded: "Wolfgang managed to reach the top floor, where a servant girl was probably moved by the sight of this powder-blackened handsome young man. She saved him from death by hiding him in her own bed. 'Only Major Burg lives here,' she bravely told the soldiers rushing in, and they hurried back downstairs. Wolfgang often told me that it was the worst hour of his life, lying quietly under the blankets hearing musket shots and the dying screams of his comrades, fearing any minute a deadly bullet for himself."[6]

Accounts of the Königstrasse battle have varied with the observers' political preference. Prince Hohenlohe-Ingelfingen's version was that "a lively resistance was offered in the narrow Königstrasse. Here barricades stood one behind another at every intersection. Each barricade was first pounded with artillery, then stormed, and the adjoining houses taken in turn.... The resistance of the rebels was not in the least heroic.... In hand to hand fighting they were mostly cowards." Carl Frenzel, however, reported that "regarding [the soldiers'] exhaustion, anger, and brutality, where they had forced their way into houses, all accounts agreed."[7]

Sunday morning, after fourteen hours of fighting, two hundred forty civilians were dead, as were twenty soldiers and police. The government was winning, but the king had lost his nerve. He issued a conciliatory proclamation: "My dear Berliners.... My troops, your brothers and compatriots, have used their weapons only when they were compelled to do so by the many shots fired at them, as in the Königstrasse. The victorious advance was a necessary sequel.... Clear away the barricades ... and I give you my word that the troops shall be immediately withdrawn." The barricades were not cleared away, but the king withdrew the army from Berlin anyway and agreed to wear the black-red-gold sash of the revolution and to pay homage bareheaded to the slain civilians. Their bodies, wounds showing, were brought to the inner courtyard of the palace in a macabre procession. On Tuesday morning, the king and queen moved past the cadavers with feigned reverence. On Wednesday, a long funeral cortège was led by Alexander von Humboldt.

Among the two hundred forty bodies were the eight found in Major Burg's house. A rumor spread that they had been enticed there only to become victims of military rage. Their friends and relatives sought revenge on the occupants and wanted to demolish the building. Wolfgang, however, contradicted them and said that Major Burg and the other occupants were innocent. He made a poster to that effect and set up an armed guard of students for the occupants' protection.

A Victory Squandered

With the army out of the city, the revolutionaries now formed a civil guard and placed the palace under its protection. The king sent his notoriously autocratic brother Prince Wilhelm (later the first Hohenzollern Kaiser) to London and tried to adjust to becoming a constitutional monarch. He enjoyed the warmth with which his subjects received his concessions. The United Prussian Assembly was reconvened and drafted a constitution that left substantial prerogatives to the king.

Wolfgang was dissatisfied with that trend. "With all the enthusiasm of his idealistic nature, he plunged into further revolutionary activities and played a big role in clubs and meetings, giving speeches and drafting documents. He carried arms and stood guard.... One fine day from the balcony of Kranzler's Konditorei, he told a jubilant assembled crowd, 'The Hohenzollerns are no longer worthy of the throne of Prussia! I declare a republic!'"[8] That same day, Wolfgang was arrested and jailed for six weeks. When released, he was banned from the city.

A conflict about the duchies of Schleswig-Holstein was under way since a new king of Denmark sought to integrate the area fully into his realm on the basis of a dynastic claim. Although mainly German-speaking, Schleswig-Holstein had been loosely affiliated with the Danish royal house for nearly four hundred years. Wolfgang had no hesitation about joining German troops in three campaigns against Denmark to "liberate" the duchies. In those times, German nationalist fervor was seen as democratic because it confronted the class-biased systems of feudalism and dynastic absolutism. Prussia sent an army to cater to the nationalist vogue, but in July 1850 it agreed to peace terms favorable to the Danes. The Schleswig-Holstein army, which included Wolfgang, fought on for a few more weeks until it was defeated at Idstedt on July 24–25. As a result of that battle, Wolfgang, now a lieutenant, was decorated for "special personal courage."

In the meantime the Prussian revolution ended with the Assembly's final attempt to change the constitution. It sought to establish that the king no longer reigned through "God's Grace" and to modify his sole control over the army. That was too much for Friedrich Wilhelm, and on November 10, 1848, he ordered General Friedrich von Wrangel to return to Berlin with thirteen thousand troops. Wrangel thus marched back, announcing that "the troops are good, their swords are sharp, and bullets are in their rifles. But not against you, Berliners! No, they protect your true freedom, as granted by the king, and they preserve the law."[9]

Sources of Income

Wolfgang remained in the Holstein area, practicing medicine among the poor without a license, and did not return to Berlin until 1854. He was then allowed to complete his medical studies and to take his examinations on the strict condition that he should leave the city every night and sleep in Potsdam. In 1855, Wolfgang finally took his Prussian state medical examination and passed with the grade of "very good." The wars had given him much experience in surgery, but he was also outstanding in anatomy and laboratory work. This skill paid off with bits of extra income. Some fellow students who were assigned analyses of tissues smuggled these "in night and fog" to Mittelstrasse 20, where the brothers lived, to retrieve them with the solution the following night. The price for this service was seventeen marks, a *Friedrich d'or*, more than brother Bernhard, the mason, was paid in a week. Wolfgang still had his "indestructible optimism" and "high enthusiasm" for medicine, according to brother Heinrich, but although he could practice in the rest of Prussia, his revolutionary past barred him from being a doctor in Berlin.

The principal income of the brothers in the mid-1850s came from editing medical publications. A Guhrauer cousin had married Eduard Aber (1810–1899), who in 1840 had bought the Hirschwald bookstore on Unter den Linden, an enterprise founded in 1816 by yet another Guhrauer cousin. This bookstore published a series called *Graevelsche Notizen für praktische Aertzte über die neuesten Beobachtungen in der Medizin mit besonderer Berücksichtigung der Krankheitsbehandlung* (Graevel's Notes for Practical Physicians about the Latest Medical Findings with Special Stress on Healing), called "GNfPA" for short. F. Graevel had started the series in 1848 under the auspices of A. Hirschwald, but now the books appeared under Samuel Strassmann's name for an honorarium of five hundred talers annually (fifteen hundred marks).

Since he had a superb writing style, Wolfgang was thoroughly involved in this work, reviewing books of the past year in all medical specialties and writing introductory surveys of each field. Samuel had the tedious task of going through professional articles. Soon after his arrival, Heinrich helped with classifying publications and making bibliographies. The GNfPA was a well-organized digest of medical progress and sold well, even abroad, especially in Russia.

Work for Julius Sittenfeld, the renowned publisher of medical books, brought the Strassmanns into renewed contact with Rudolf Virchow, who was editing a journal, *Archiv für Pathologische Anatomie und Phisiologie*, and writing a six-volume handbook. A student of the former rector, Johannes Müller, Virchow had become professor of pathological anatomy at the University of Berlin in 1856. Like Wolfgang and Samuel, he had been a republican in 1848 but had fled to Würzburg with the approval of the king of Bavaria. After his years of exile in Würzburg, Müller had called him back. Virchow made important contributions to several branches of medicine and anthropology but is best known for founding cellular pathology and for his progressive politics. He became a founder of the Progressive Party in 1861, served on the City Council for an uninterrupted forty-two years, and was a member of the Prussian legislature and the Reichstag (1880–1893), where he steadfastly opposed Bismarck.

The Daily Routine

After breakfast, Samuel held his brief office hours and left for the hospital. Wolfgang began work on GNfPA, and Heinrich went to the university four blocks away. After a shared noon meal, the three medical brothers resumed their editorial work together. In the late afternoon, Wolfgang and Heinrich took long walks through the Tiergarten and talked about medicine, the Revolution of 1848, the Holstein campaigns, and literature (*Faust* and Shakespeare's royal histories were favorites).

After supper, all four usually went to Restaurant Hasteli on Unter den Linden a block away, where Wolfgang and Samuel played billiards, while Bernhard (nicknamed "Shorty") and Heinrich shared a single mug of beer, smoked, and read newspapers. On Sundays, the two older brothers were often invited for dinner at Eduard Aber's house, while Shorty took Heinrich on walks through the city to explain the architecture of prominent buildings. For fifteen pfennigs they shared a hot chocolate in a small café in the Luisenstrasse and then crossed to the Tiergarten to hear a military band at a beer garden. His weekly pay of fifteen marks made Shorty "a Croesus" for these treats.

At this time a cholera epidemic broke out, and Wolfgang volunteered as a physician for an eastern district near the Schlesischer Bahnhof, where they had all arrived in trains from Posen. This service made Wolfgang a Berlin citizen, although the police never revoked the ban on his presence. Wolfgang now rented rooms in the eastern Breslauer Strasse and moved there with Shorty. Heinrich reported: "Apart from his official tasks, Wolfgang had an extended private practice, at first only among the poor. Later his practice became almost universal in that district since he was competent, energetic, and never insisted on payment.... Above all, his reputation depended on his skill as a surgeon and an obstetrician. Night and day he was tirelessly on the job and became a widely known and beloved personality. He raised this poor and neglected district by founding a community club and organizing the Stralauer Bank [a cooperative]."[10]

These initiatives followed Wolfgang's association with Herrmann Schulze-Delitzsch (1808–1883), another 1848 revolutionary and co-founder of the Progressive Party and an elected member of the Prussian Assembly and later the Reichstag. Schulze-Delitzsch believed that a truly democratic constitution could come only from the masses of artisans and workers if they were economically well off, especially through self-help. He therefore started a nationwide movement for cooperatives in finance and purchasing, but he opposed any state support on their behalf, other than recognizing their legality. What was needed were a free economy, national unity, and universal and equal suffrage.[11]

In 1862, when he was forty-one, Wolfgang married Louise Cohen from Hanover. She was described by Heinrich as "no longer very young [being twenty-seven!] but well-educated and energetic, an excellent spouse and housekeeper, and at the same time undemanding and happily adaptable to our intimate circle.... We were impressed with the determined way that she could make her views decisive in anything controversial." In a sober and practical way, she toned down the "rough but hazy idealism" of the brothers, including that of Wolfgang, still "our oldest [and] most beloved."[12] They lived at Holzmarktstrasse 53, near the Jannowitz Bridge and railway station.

The Conciliatory Progressive and Anti-Semitism

In 1863, Wolfgang was elected by his district to the Berlin City Council in accordance with Prussian procedures, making him a *Stadtverordneter*. Twelve years later he became the chairman of that council, the *Stadtverordnetenvorsteher,* and he was re-elected annually to that post until he died eleven years later in 1885, aged sixty-four. In Prussia, with its semi-feudal constitution, no elected office had more power, and few elected officials were attacked as rabidly as Wolfgang Strassmann by conservative monarchists, specifically by the imperial court chaplain, Adolph Stoecker, and his right-wing movement. In its obituary on December 8, 1885, the conservative newspaper, *Deutsches Tageblatt,* wrote: "Everyone familiar with Dr. Strassmann's service to the city knows how to respect that. We acknowledge it frankly but cannot forget that it was mostly Dr. Strassmann, with his attacks on ecclesiastical councils and the Christian church in general, who set anti-Semitism in motion. His opponents fully recognize his efforts in promoting the welfare of the poor, both as chairman of the City Council and for nearly a decade as delegate to the Prussian Assembly. But his attacks explain why a large part of the citizenry opposed him so sharply." How did all this come about?

Until a year before the Revolution of 1848, meetings of the City Council were closed to the public, and at any time the minister of the interior could call for new elections. The chief of police, who was not under the council's jurisdiction, could initiate and carry out policies without its approval. "A kind of guerilla warfare was carried on between the Prussian government and the city of Berlin … under Bismarck and later under the Kaiser."[13] Throughout these years, the *Polizei-Präsident* of Berlin, appointed by Bismarck, kept an active file on Wolfgang.

Members of the City Council, like those of the Prussian Assembly, were not elected directly by universal secret franchise. According to the constitution decreed by the king in 1850, voters chose electors who then made the final choice, yet even this process involved a major inequality. Under this system, three classes existed: a class of the rich, who paid one-third of the taxes and chose one-third of the electors; a bigger middle class, who paid another third of the taxes and chose a second third of electors; and finally a very large class of poor taxpayers, who also chose a third of electors. Those men who were too poor to pay taxes, or too poor to own a dwelling, and all women were disenfranchised. Boundaries between the three classes of voters varied according to the income levels and tax payments of each district. According to a principal historian of the period, "application of these rules varied from district to district and any clear-cut [brief] explanation of the workings of the electoral system is impossible."[14] As a further safeguard against radicalism, half of the members of the City Council had to own real estate in Berlin. Making up about 4 percent of the city's population, Jews were wealthy enough to pay more than one-third of the taxes. Thus, they easily secured one-third of the effective votes under the three-class system and had ample representation on the City Council. This was not a result intended by the framers of the reactionary constitution.

Since Jews were disproportionately prosperous and mainly favored the Progressive Party, the system kept that party in power. While Progressives had less power in the countryside, and therefore in the Prussian parliament, they were unusually strong in the municipal councils, and "all the liberals cherished their leadership in the administration of the modern German cities."[15] Herzfeld has written that under the Progressives, "already in the 1880s Berlin had the reputation of being one of the best administered large modern cities."[16]

The City Council

Berlin withdrew from the province of Brandenburg in 1881 to reduce Prussian Junker interference in its affairs, but royal permission was still needed for setting up monuments, choosing street names, and some building plans. Numerous urban improvement projects were launched during the twenty-three years that Wolfgang Strassmann was on the City Council (1863–1885), especially during the last eleven years when he was the chairman. His predecessor as chairman of the council during 1863–1874 was Heinrich Kochhann (1805–1890), a baker and revolutionary of 1848 who stressed educational reform.

Another revolutionary council member was Rudolf Virchow, easily the most energetic promoter of new plans. Like Wolfgang, he was born in 1821, but he finished his medical studies eleven years earlier in 1843 and became radical and republican after battling a typhus epidemic among destitute weavers in Silesia. When he returned from exile in 1856, he became a principal opponent of Bismarck in the Prussian Assembly, in the Reichstag, and on the Berlin City Council. When he questioned Bismarck's veracity in the Prussian Assembly in 1863, the chancellor demanded a duel with pistols that the minister of defense, Count Albrecht von Roon, forestalled. Virchow now sought to establish complete and unrestricted democracy in place of the old authoritarian state, bigoted churches, inadequate schools, and an all-powerful police.

He worked with Wolfgang to achieve systematic garbage collection, meat inspection, new hospitals, and hygienic housing regulations and to compel indoor piped water, parks, and medical supervision of students' health in the schools. The English waterworks at Stralau were bought by the city in 1873, and new works were set up at Tegel and the Müggelsee. Landlords protested against the cost of installing water and sewer pipes in their buildings. A notable project of this time was the system of sewers and sewerage treatment that was begun in 1869. The waste water was channeled to fields around the city for aeration. It was Wolfgang and Virchow's favorite project, cost over seventy million marks, and was built mainly by the unemployed and homeless. Many government administrators and taxpayers thought it was inordinately extravagant, but better water and good waste disposal were the only way to prevent ever greater epidemics.

Virchow's passionate belief was that "[e]pidemics come from poverty, hunger, filth, and unsanitary living conditions." Hence, radical politics and better health were inseparable.[17] "I don't want to mention cholera, smallpox, and worse epidemics brought to us by expanding business or wars. I only want to remind you how inevitably and closely practical medicine depends on the political process.... [We] know how dangerous it is simply to ignore scientific principles or to treat them superficially in judging social conditions."[18]

City Council Meetings

City Council meetings were normally opened by Strassmann in the late afternoon without any ceremony. The council met under pseudo-Renaissance chandeliers in the exquisitely paneled and carpeted chambers of the new City Hall, which was designed by Herrmann Friedrich Waesemann in red-brick Tuscan style and inaugurated in 1870. Apart from the delegates, the mayor and the administering magistrates were usually in attendance, sitting at a separate *Magistratstisch*. The chairman began by simply declaring the meeting in session and reporting new business that had arrived in the form of letters and documents. After that came suggestions for new appointments that the session would have to approve, followed by elections to various committees, especially in the January sessions opening the year. In 1875, Strassmann's first year as chairman, the agenda included converting a private school to public use, the reconstruction of canals, a variety of building plans, organizing a weekly market, the construction of a curb and a latrine near a bridge, the purchase of a variety of sites for public use, and a number of procedural issues.[19] Wolfgang was so busy with it all that he gave up his medical practice that year.

In January 1877, Chairman Strassmann welcomed new and old delegates to the City Council. He read a letter from Crown Prince Friedrich, who hoped that "the true cause of economic decline would be diagnosed so that hard work would once more make trade and industry blossom and flourish in the Fatherland." Strassmann called for three cheers for his majesty, the king and emperor, as well as for the crown prince, and the dynasty: "Hoch!—Hoch!—Hoch!" He had acquired much tact since proclaiming a republic on Unter den Linden in 1848.

Strassmann continued the meeting by summarizing the council's activities in the previous year, 1876. There had been seventy-nine sessions during which 2,257 measures had been considered. Of these, 239 were still pending, especially questions of appointments and accounts. With thanks, he then resigned his position, as was the custom at the beginning of each year. The oldest delegate, Dr. Tappert, expressed the council's gratitude, and Strassmann received a standing ovation for his services. Strassmann was then re-elected by a vote of 89 to 2, plus one abstention.[20]

In 1878, Wolfgang Strassmann was again elected with a nearly unanimous vote of 77 to 1, plus three abstentions. He accepted again, saying that "with the best of intentions, it is not always possible to decide correctly at once, to stay clear of misunderstandings and error. But, gentlemen, with your care and friendly good will from all sides, you will improve where I fail because of those misunderstandings and errors."[21] This ritual would be repeated every January seven more times, until 1885, the year that Wolfgang died in office.

Achievements

Among major projects of these years, parks and public bathing facilities were established throughout the city to improve health conditions among the poor. The old city walls, except for the Brandenburg Gate, were demolished in 1868. The first city hospital was built at Friedrichshain in 1874, encompassing eight buildings and six hundred beds. Patients with cholera, syphilis, typhus, and smallpox, however, were not admitted for fear of contagion. In 1875, the city took over the care of streets and bridges, including the cleaning and repair of pavements. The city assumed responsibility for the prevailing gas lights and in 1882 began a shift to electric street lighting. As early as 1879, the world's first electric streetcars replaced horse-drawn cars. Five new railway stations were added to the four built before 1860, and a *Ringbahn* connecting them all in a great circle was completed by 1877. The inspection of meat and the organization of a central slaughterhouse (including fifty-three buildings) were established at Lichtenberg in 1881. Meatpackers objected to the accompanying severe controls against trichinosis. A central market hall for farm products was set up at the Alexanderplatz in 1884. However, nearly a quarter of the city's budget was spent on education, and between 1861 and 1881, the number of grammar schools (*Gemeindeschulen*) more than quintupled. The demand for education had increased that much because in 1870 the City Council had eliminated tuition. Nevertheless, the need to work and earn a living kept many children out of school.

All these urban achievements of the Progressives were viewed with mixed feelings by conservatives because they were the works of the foes of Bismarck and the Hohenzollerns, enemies who thus gained credibility in their quest to modify the monarchy with a constitution, perhaps even a bill establishing human rights and the separation of church and state. Since such constitutional advances were actually popular, and since the urban improvements themselves could not be criticized, reactionary critics had to look for other targets with mass appeal. They focused on the displacement of handicraft workers by factories and on the unsettling of ancient values through widespread commercialization. Both trends went easily with insinuations against Jews under the novel label of "anti-Semitism." A suitable personal target for these insinuations was the chairman of the Berlin City Council, Wolfgang Strassmann, the first Jew in that position.[22]

In the single remaining photograph of middle-aged Wolfgang, he looks out forcefully as if he were about to speak. He has a high forehead, shiny white hair combed back in a bush, and a square, clean-shaven jaw. A newspaper described him as "virile and loyal, solid and thoughtful, [a man who] knew how to stimulate and preserve the harmonious cooperation of all units of the city's administration with his humane and conciliatory spirit. His insights, his sense of justice, his impartiality assured the success of his administration."[23]

During 1871–1877, the paper merchant and printer, Leopold Ullstein (1826–1899), a dear friend of the brothers Strassmann, was also on the City Council. In his memoirs, Fritz Strassmann recalled that because the brothers' families socialized so much with one another, "other close friendships could hardly develop ... with the exception of some who were undoubtedly intelligent, like the founder of the Ullstein Publishing House, Leopold Ullstein."[24] On the City Council, Ullstein shared Virchow and Strassmann's concern for better sanitation, whether in the form of improved sewerage systems, public toilets, or cleaner markets and slaughtering facilities. He attributed his electoral defeat in 1876 not to anti-Semitism but to his support of otherwise free markets and to his advanced age (fifty-one). He refused to be reinstated through various possible stratagems after 1876 and instead expanded his business interests from paper and printing for others to his own periodicals, merging several acquisitions in 1878 into the *Berliner Zeitung*, a leading voice critical of Bismarck and his policies.[25]

Apart from his position on the City Council, Wolfgang was also elected to the Prussian Assembly, was founder and director of the Cooperative Bank of Stralau (Genossenschaftsbank des Stralauer Stadtviertels), was founder and chairman of the Berlin Union against Impoverishment (Berliner Verein gegen Verarmung), and was chairman of the German Union for Caring for the Poor and for Charity (Deutscher Verein für Armenpflege und Wohltätigkeit), all unpaid positions. He saw these activities and the policies of the Progressive Party not only as meritorious in themselves but also as a way of steering the poor away from revolutionary socialism. Yet conservatives were not impressed since these movements were all secular, not Christian conservative, and in the mid-1870s they began attacking Wolfgang with anti-Jewish slurs.

Attacks

The word "anti-Semitic" was first conspicuous in the pamphlets of a polemicist, Wilhelm Marr, and in the reply to his diatribes in a Jewish periodical, the *Allgemeine Zeitung des Judenthums*, dated September 2, 1879. The journalist Marr had coined the word in 1873, partly to stress that Jewish capitalism and political liberalism—not the Jewish faith—were the real danger. Marr had warned against electing Jews, and the periodical had responded that the absence of five or six talented Jewish delegates would hurt the general public more than it would the small Jewish community. A year later, the distinguished historian, Theodor Mommsen, wrote that all this incitement against Jews (*Judenhetze*) inflamed public opinion like a contagious disease.[26] Other prominent writers and historians, such as Otto Glogau and Heinrich von Treitschke, followed Marr's lead.

Given his close association with the Jewish financier, Gerson Bleichröder, Chancellor Bismarck had learned to favor wealthy conservative Jews, yet he despised liberals of the new Progressive Party, including Ludwig Bamberger and Eduard Lasker, both Jewish, as well as Eugen Richter and the former revolutionary, Rudolf Virchow. Indeed, to remove Virchow from the Berlin City Council, Bismarck even supported the candidacy of the blatantly anti-Semitic imperial court chaplain, Adolf Stoecker, writing to his own son, "Stoecker's election is highly desirable: first, as the nonelection of [Virchow] and, second, because he is an extraordinary, pugnacious, useful comrade-in-arms." Nevertheless, Bismarck did not openly champion Stoecker because it could be taken as an endorsement of anti-Semitism that would push more Jews into the Progressive Party. Stoecker lost but continued his political career without Bismarck's support.[27]

A petition against the "Jewish menace," calling for legal restrictions on Jews, was circulated, and 250,000 people signed.[28] Among other demands, the petition stated that Jews should never teach German children nor hold significant public offices. Despite his famous good nature and equanimity, Wolfgang Strassmann spoke up against this campaign and was then defeated for re-election in his district. But a vacancy arose in another district, and Wolfgang was elected there. On January 6, 1881, he was again chosen as chairman of the City Council by a vote of 97 to 16.[29]

Stoecker had been elected to the Reichstag on an anti-Jewish platform, and at a mass meeting at a brewery, the Bockbrauerei, he took the floor:

> They say we are inciting ... but I ask this gathering, who in Berlin has incited? [audience: "The Jews!"] ... I know that the liberal press, the Jews, and their fellow travelers denounce us as Jew-baiters, me above all. But it makes me happy ["Bravo, bravo"] that here in Berlin I have begun to stop Jewish overbearing [continuous thunderous applause]....
>
> Gentlemen, a word from Dr. Strassmann has set the pebble rolling; this word will keep on rolling as a great boulder, and will, I hope, pulverize Herr Strassmann and his entire City Council chairmanship (*Stadtverordnetenvorsteheramt*) [lively bravos]. The anti-Jewish movement will not let up.... No, it will roll around the earth.... Gentlemen, wherever Jewish overbearing becomes insupportable, people will rise up to throw off the yoke ["Quite right!"].
>
> We are challenging the Jews to a fight to total victory ["Bravo!"], and we will not rest until here in Berlin they have been thrown off their high pedestals, down into the dust where they belong [spirited applause].... Gentlemen, with joyous hearts we want to be a city of Hohenzollerns, and we want to keep Berlin from turning—as it now looks—into a city of Jews![30]

Virchow commented on this development with extraordinary foresight: "Although nowadays scientific attitudes are secure and victorious, we may still overlook the strong mystical stirrings that individual adventurers can generate in the public. Science seems at a loss in dealing with the puzzle of anti-Semitism, whose aims no one can understand in this age of equality before the law.... The human spirit is too inclined to forsake the troublesome path of orderly thought and to sink into delusions.... One should not mistake a dark unknown for some new truth and make it a point of departure for fantastic conclusions."[31]

The City Council continued to be hostile to the court chaplain and officially refused to acknowledge any Hohenzollern baptism, wedding, or funeral because Stoecker might officiate. That policy of ignoring *familiäre Ereignisse* of the court actually began in 1863 as a response to Bismarck's curtailing of the freedom of the press. But even with criticism muzzled, in the 1871 elections for the new Reichstag, only twenty-one Berliners voted for Bismarck. The liberal crown prince, Friedrich, ignored these disputes, attended a benefit concert for Silesian flood victims at the new Oranienburger Street synagogue, and declared anti-Semitism to be "a disgrace of the century" with deplorable participation by some in educated circles. Stoecker wrote to his wife that the Prince's comments had made

Jews and Progressives "very insolent." But Friedrich's mother, Empress Augusta, said that her son's remarks made her happy as proof of her own good influence. She added that she was not inclined to become excited about any Jewish issue.[32]

The claim of Stoecker and his associates that Wolfgang had attacked the church and was an open foe of all Christian dogma was false. The chairman of the City Council simply withheld support for whatever smacked of medieval superstition and intolerance. Wolfgang was thus against the exclusion of Jews from public office and public school teaching. But even his moderate opposition to Christian exclusive dominance was "Jewish intolerance" to the group around Stoecker. The canceling of City Council sessions because of Yom Kippur and other Jewish holidays especially enraged them. Stoecker supporters feared that progressive liberalism was a first step toward republican socialism and atheism. Conservative schemes gathered strength, however, and Stoecker gained control of the "inner mission" of the Protestant church in 1877 and founded a Christian Social Workers Party in 1878. In 1881 he declared that "social revolution has to be overcome by healthy social reforms, built on a Christian foundation. I want a culture that is Germanic and Christian. That is why I am fighting against Jewish supremacy."[33]

The main social revolution that Wolfgang favored, like Virchow and other Progressives, was the separation of church and state. Such separation, however, went against the doctrine of the "Christian state" under an anointed king, a doctrine that Friedrich Wilhelm IV had fervently believed in decades earlier and that Stoecker still promoted. This ideology did not allow Jews to teach or to give orders as officials or judges to Christian subjects. Ironically, the doctrine was most formally expressed by Friedrich Julius Stahl (1802–1861), a converted Jew and the principal founder of the Prussian Conservative Party. Stoecker's Christian Social Workers Party was a last German effort to base anti-Semitism partly on religion.

A Sudden End

After a three-day illness, Wolfgang died on Sunday, December 6, 1885, aged sixty-four. At that time, he still lived in the poor eastern section at the Wallnertheaterstrasse near the Jannowitz Bridge. The City Council met two days later, and the oldest member, Dr. Schultz, delivered the eulogy, while all members and visitors stood. Schultz stressed Wolfgang's policies for preventing poverty through creating employment opportunities, rather than relieving it through welfare. Thousands of families had benefited. Schultz concluded: "Gentlemen, all of you know what he meant to us as chairman, a man of high scientific and ethical standards, and you also know … how political currents impinged on his sphere of action.… Since 1848 I have had the honor of seeing City Council chairmen come and go … but I never met anyone who functioned as objectively as Strassmann.… Take care in replacing him that you do not hammer a nail into the coffin of our self-government. A false move could wreak a heavy revenge on us."

Another delegate, Dr. Horwitz, took the floor and called for a letter to the widow, Louise, because her "tender, loyal friendship had given [Strassmann] the strength and endurance for his almost superhuman activity." In that letter, members of the City Council stated: "As we contemplate the painful gap that his death leaves, we think … of the way he combined resolute commitment with mildness and with fairness for any opposing view, the way his impartiality overcame his passion for truth itself in emotionally tense moments.… He used his best strength, not for transitory things, but for enduring innovations."[34]

The obituary in the *Deutsche Illustrierte Zeitung* dwelled on Wolfgang's humble beginning without saying it was Jewish. Was that considered too unimportant or too controversial?

One of Berlin's best men has passed on, one who gave everything in the service of self-government for the capital, one who could claim credit for many of the great achievements of the past twelve years, which inspire the pride of Berliners and the admiration of visitors. As a member of the City Council for twenty-three years and chairman for eleven, he devoted his strength, knowledge, and ability to the steady development of our urban community with restless fervor and selfless sacrifice....

He rose from the poorest of circumstances through a bitter struggle for survival with almost no outside support, and yet even in his youth he dedicated himself to the highest goals of mankind.... No disappointment, no deprivation upset him. In a few years of practicing medicine among the poorest people and advancing science, he saved enough money for his own livelihood and for the education of his brothers, who, one after another, achieved positions of respect.[35]

The *Vossische Zeitung* on December 8, 1885, recalled: "Court Chaplain Stoecker and his comrades tried to entangle him in the anti-Semitic conflict, but Strassmann knew how to avoid this temptation to step into the gutter. In time, conservatives who had participated in that nevertheless had to cooperate with his leadership and farsighted vision for Berlin."

A secular funeral, planned by the lord mayor and paid for by the city, was held at City Hall and described at length in the press. A thousand dignitaries were invited, and the imperial family, as well as ministers Bismarck and Moltke, were informed but did not attend. A choir from the Nicolai Church sang in the auditorium, which was filled with Berliners of all classes. The Empress and the Crown Prince sent condolences, and government offices were closed so that officials could attend. Since the death of the operatic composer Giacomo Meyerbeer (1791–1864), no official funeral for a Jew had received such honors in Berlin. A eulogy was spoken by Rudolf Virchow, who said: "Neither he nor the City Council were spared vicious attacks. He himself was attacked because of his religion, and the council had to face a severe crisis under his leadership as never before."

The long funeral procession began at City Hall and included almost all members of the city's administration, members of the Prussian Assembly and the Reichstag, leading merchants and other citizens, and finally the adjutant of the imperial crown prince. Flags flew at half-mast. Wolfgang was buried at the Schönhauser Allee Jewish Cemetery under a high, fluted column of shiny black granite on a simple pedestal. Today, the gold-lettered inscription reads simply, "Dr. med. Wolfgang Strassmann, *Stadtverordnetenvorsteher*," and gives the dates and places of his birth and death. Below is similar information for his wife, Louise (née Cohen, 1835–1889).

One newspaper published an anonymous poem in his honor:[36]

Strassmann
Your enemies' hatred pursued you since
You gave your life to citizens' welfare,
And without pause they poured
Venom on you and your brave efforts:
Unblemished you left this world on clean paths,
Followed to the grave by the people's blessing.

At City Hall (the "Rotes Rathaus"), a memorial plaque and a marble bust of Wolfgang were set up right away, and in the 1890s his portrait was added to eleven others along the grand stairway. The Nazis took it away and probably burned it, thus sparing it from Allied bombing. Now his brother Ferdinand's portrait hangs in a corridor together with other Honorary Citizens

Wolfgang and Louise had two children, Wolf and Henrietta ("Henni"), who were in their twenties when their parents died in 1885 and 1889. Wolf became a mathematics teacher, never married, and died of tuberculosis at age thirty-five. Henni was a well-known painter and writer, a stout woman, beloved in the family, who married Karl Lehmann, a law professor at the University of Rostock on the Baltic coast. Their son, another Karl Lehmann, was born in 1894 and became an archeology professor. After the Nazis took power, he lived in Italy for two years without a paying job but found a professorship at the Institute of Fine Arts at New York University in 1935. Wolfgang would have been proud of this grandson but saddened by Henni's suicide in Nazi Berlin in 1937.

Ferdinand, Honorary Citizen

I close this chapter with a few words about Wolfgang's youngest brother, Ferdinand (1838–1931), who promoted further urban health reforms and who learned much about political tact from his older brother. As late as 1905, the mayor of Berlin, Georg Reicke, declared that "the city is not obligated to provide hospital care for every inhabitant who expresses that wish or whose doctor does." With the support of the City Council, Ferdinand countered such harshness for thirty years, and in 1915 he was named the fifty-third Honorary Citizen as a reward.

Like his brothers, Ferdinand (nicknamed "Nante") left Rawitsch in 1851 for the gymnasium in Lissa, where for five years he shared poverty and even a bed with brother Heinrich. In 1858, he followed the others to Berlin to study medicine, but the older brothers thought that three Strassmann physicians were already enough for the town, and they urged Nante to join the paper business of Joseph Bender Levy, Samuel's father-in-law (and later Heinrich's). They believed that such work would make Nante rich and independent. He tried it for six months but was so unhappy that the brothers let him study medicine after all and join university events. Throughout his life, Nante, like Heinrich, treasured his acceptance by the "Westfalen" student fraternity and participation in its social life, but he was too poor to join formally. In 1863, he was certified as a physician and was soon engaged in fighting a cholera epidemic. During the French war of 1870, he became the directing physician of an improvised military hospital.

Ferdinand followed Wolfgang into city politics in 1884, beginning with school reform and becoming an unpaid medical magistrate in 1889. As the only medically trained member of the government, he became indispensable and was too busy to continue his own private practice, although he remained unpaid until 1911. The inherited fortune of his wife, Margarethe (Gretchen, née Rosenthal, 1846–1919), allowed him to continue in public service. Under Ferdinand's direction, the city built hospitals, recuperative centers, and mental health facilities; enforced disinfection measures; and promoted better sanitation everywhere.

At the ceremony for his honorary citizenship in 1915, Ferdinand's thanks stressed that to him this meant an expression of friendship and good will from rich and poor, old and young, liberal and conservative, and especially Christian and Jew. For Berlin he would now work all the harder. His "only wish was that the harmony and understanding that have fostered the work so far would continue to prevail, a blessing for the community."[37]

Gerhard Masur (a historian and Heinrich's grandson by way of his daughter Frieda) has described Ferdinand as "a man of great modesty in appearance and assertions, even in his evaluation of his own capacities. Yet he was a man of unshakable equanimity whom nothing could disturb."[38] My mother remembered him as a sweet old man, who addressed her with the endearing diminutive, "Ilschen." Although he was nearly ninety years old, he stood up from his wheelchair and told my father, using another diminutive, "Erwinchen, how nice of you to introduce me to your wife. I am so happy to know you."

The Strassmann Street

Some people said that the Strassmann Street (Strassmannstrasse) was so named to honor Ferdinand as much as Wolfgang. During 1938–1946, it was renamed Ermelerstrasse. I first saw it as once more the Strassmannstrasse in Friedrichshain on a sunny June afternoon in 1989 when Communists ruled there. It was pleasant, with young trees and an outdoor café—a residential street five blocks long between a slaughterhouse and a cemetery. Later, in 1998, I saw it flourishing under capitalism with some twenty new stores, pubs, and restaurants, including a Strassmann Bistrot. Its strapping owner, Reinhard Klamm, was astounded to meet an authentic Strassmann descendant, but that did not help his beef-broiling enterprise to survive a change in taste. The pride of the street was still an old five-story library built in Amsterdam style, with a high gable patterned in white and red bricks like those of City Hall. In a *Rathaus* corridor, I later saw the portrait of Ferdinand displayed among all other Honorary Citizens.

Photograph of 1913 shows eight physicians of three Strassmann generations. Pictures on the wall from the left are Wolfgang (1821–1885), Heinrich (1834–1905), and Samuel (1826–1879). Seated are Ferdinand, left, aged 75, and on the right, Fritz, aged 55. Standing from the left are Erwin, aged 18, Paul, aged 47, and Georg, aged 23.

Paul Ferdinand and Hedwig Strassmann in front of the Reichstag (Parliament) around 1930 with Moki, Mieke, and Hexe.

The library in a street named after Wolfgang Strassmann (1821–1885).

The Frauenklinik of Paul Strassmann, Berlin, 1926.

The City Hall of Rawicz.

Scouts of Moses bringing a giant cluster of grapes from the Promised Land. This event was celebrated with a sculptured relief on Schmuhl Molower's, later Heiman Strassmann's, house in Rawicz and became the Strassmann symbol.

The church of Rawicz, built in 1639.

The Woderynskis of Rawicz help Hans and Eva Maria Reis in their search for Strassmann roots.

The four older Strassmann brothers in Berlin around 1857.
Master mason Bernhard (left rear), and three physicians,
from the left, Samuel, Heinrich, and Wolfgang.

Four Strassmann physicians in the Bismarck era. Top left: Samuel in 1875, aged 49, and, on the right, Wolfgang in 1880, aged 59. Below: Ferdinand in 1885, aged 47, and, on the right, Heinrich aged 37 in 1871.

Ferdinand Strassmann's portrait as Honorary Citizen still hangs in Berlin's Red City Hall.

Heinrich, aged 30, as an officer and physician with the 6th Infantry Division in the Danish war of 1864.

On March 18, 1848, Wolfgang Strassmann fought on the barricades of the Königstrasse opposite the royal palace in Berlin. Later, he served on the City Council.

The anti-Semitic court chaplain, Adolf Stoecker, fought Strassmann's plans to modernize Berlin.

Rudolf Virchow, the distinguished physician, scientist, and politician, fervently supported the reforms of Wolfgang Strassmann, his revolutionary comrade from 1848.

Heinrich Strassmann's family around 1891. From the left: Ernst, aged 23, Frieda, aged 22, Louise, aged 47, Paul, aged 25, Heinrich, aged 57, and Helene, aged 19.

Louise Levy (1844–1915) around 1885. In 1865, she married Heinrich Strassmann.

The Strassmann family tomb at Weissensee, Berlin. In the foreground is the author with his grandchildren, Daniel and Anna Mueller, 1998.

Chapter 3

Medical Achievements and Disappointments: Paul and His Siblings

The five Strassmann brothers from Rawitsch married rich Jewish women around 1860 and had thirteen children—six sons and seven daughters—whom they brought up in a secular way, stressing Goethe more than Moses. Not all were talented, and they confronted more challenges than necessary. Medical historians still write about Paul Ferdinand and Fritz Strassmann, and two Berlin buildings were historically dedicated to them in 2003 and 2004. Paul Ferdinand was the oldest child of Heinrich Strassmann and Louise Levy, and Fritz was the oldest of Samuel Strassmann and Flora Levy. The two women were sisters, daughters of Therese and Joseph Bender Levy, a wealthy paper maker from Birnbaum in Posen.

Paul and Fritz are the two Strassmanns around whom one can best frame a story of frustrated migration from one promised land to another, a theme of this book. Their fathers and their grandfather, Heiman, had come from Rawitsch to Berlin, and after them, two generations left for the United States, Australia, England, Switzerland, and Latin America. Born and buried in Berlin, Paul Ferdinand and Fritz lived at a time when they could picture the migrating experience of both the two earlier and the two later generations. When their grandfather Heiman died, Fritz was twenty-three and Paul fifteen, old enough to have caught the flavor of the old man's reminiscence of Jewish life in Rawicz. Their fathers and uncles told them about their medical careers in revolutionary Berlin, and indeed it was Paul who encouraged his father, Heinrich, to write those memoirs. As Paul himself approached the age of seventy, his remaining three children (Hellmuth was killed in France in 1916) had already emigrated to Switzerland and the United States. His wife's brother, sister-in-law, and their children had gone to Australia and changed their name from Rosenberg to Rodgers. He followed the way these closest relatives adjusted to new surroundings and how his eight grandchildren melted into new national identities. Paul Ferdinand did not live to see one of his own sisters emigrate to South America or to learn that the other sister died while at the Theresienstadt concentration camp. Fritz saw one son, with his wife and child, emigrate to America, but did not live to find out that the other son was killed at Auschwitz.

So here I tell first about Paul's ascent, his education, his marriage to Hedwig Rosenberg, and his professional development until the great disappointment of 1906. Then comes the founding of his private clinic-hospital and its flourishing in the Schumannstrasse, its good years, despite the lost war, depression and turmoil, until 1933. How Paul coped with the Nazis stalking his clinic during 1933–1936 and his two years of retirement are told later. Paul died of pancreatitis during a visit to his daughter Gisela in Switzerland, on August 15, 1938. After World War II, his grave at Wannsee was designated as honorary, and memorial tributes for him have been organized from time to time. Paul Strassmann was a man of great energy, superb organization, and fine achievements, celebrated (when it was safe) by patients and colleagues alike. I describe the similar career of Fritz in the following chapter.

Student Years

Born on October 23, 1866, Paul completed his early schooling during the 1870s while the family lived on the Oranienburger Strasse, one of Berlin's most elegant streets in the late nineteenth century, one especially favored by Jews. A massive, orientally domed synagogue, designed by the celebrated architect, Eduard Knoblauch, was built there in 1859–1866. About six blocks toward the east, between the Linienstrasse and the Münzenstrasse, was the *Scheunenviertel* (barn quarter) district, where poor immigrants created a kind of Eastern European *shtetl*. To the south, Joseph Bender Levy and Therese had their mansion and warehouse at the Fischerbrücke on the small Spree island where Berlin began and where the imperial palace stood. All his life Paul remembered playing under a horse chestnut tree leaning over the Spree River. Whenever he passed it, he mentioned it in his diary. The gnarled old tree survived there to be painted by Philip Franck in 1909 and Otto Nagel in 1942 and to be photographed by me and my own grandchildren a few years ago.

Heinrich coached and supervised Paul and his younger brother Ernst closely, observing on the next-to-last page of the draft of his memoirs:

> The duties of father and physician now fulfilled my life, especially the former duty. Teaching my boys took up almost all my time. Until their ninth year of school [*Ober-III*, in the early 1880s], I devoted myself completely to the education of my two sons, Paul and Ernst, even at the expense of my medical activities. Whether or not that was practical is not for me to say, but I happened to have something of the schoolmaster in me, and from my own schooldays I retained the firm conviction that the higher school years should not be wasted.
>
> I concede frankly that ambition also led me, but not just personal ambition, rather, the conviction of all five brothers to make special efforts on behalf of our name and to admonish our children to do likewise.

At the Friedrichsgymansium, Paul took his written Abitur examination early at age seventeen. He placed first in his class and passed with such distinction that the oral part was waived. Forty-one years later, for the Friedrichsgymnasium's seventy-fifth anniversary on October 5, 1925, Paul composed a poem of eighteen humorous and affectionate five-line stanzas. He mentions both teachers and classmates, as well as subjects taught, *Faust*, the *Iliad*, the *Odyssey*, Horace, Schiller, Humboldt, music, physics, and physical education. I will translate only one verse:

> Modern languages with loving care,
> Superior grammar came from there.
> Yet in Paris and in London

— When we tried to be heard —
No one understood a word.

Paul went on to study medicine, and within five years, at age twenty-three, he was a licensed physician, ready to specialize in gynecology and obstetrics, as his father had wanted to in vain two decades earlier. In April 1884, he entered the Friedrich-Wilhelm University of Berlin and joined a mainly Gentile dueling fraternity, Arminia. One year later, he transferred to Heidelberg where he obtained his first degree, the Physikum, on February 27, 1886. He had time to sing in a choir and to while away spring afternoons wandering the countryside with friends, lying on hillside meadows, playing the flute. He fought four major duels with sabers against competing fraternities in 1884 and 1885, notching these events into the pewter cover of his decorated beer stein. In one duel he received a wound that became infected in a way that he believed affected his health for the rest of his life. In later years he played a major part in a national fund-raising campaign to equip Heidelberg University with a large new pipe organ.

Paul resumed studies in Berlin in 1886 and passed his preliminary examination, *tentamen medicum et rigorosum*, in February 1888. Meanwhile, he was an assistant in the surgical clinic of the Charité university hospital under Geheimrat Ernst von Bergmann, known for introducing steam as a sterilizer for surgical instruments. He also spent three months assisting Professor Robert Olshausen (1835–1915) at the University Women's Clinic. Back in Heidelberg for another year, Paul passed his state examination in medicine on March 15, 1889. Ten days later, he successfully defended his dissertation, *The Study of Multiple Pregnancies*, in Berlin and officially received the title of "Doctor" on April 25, 1889. For that ritual, one had to recruit three friends as "opponents," and Paul chose his brother Ernst, his best friend, Siegmund Ginsberg, and Arthur Levin, who was already a physician. In his 119-page dissertation, Paul analyzed the records of 476 women who had delivered twins and of 12 who gave birth to triplets. Twenty of the mothers had died in childbirth, primarily of infections, but Paul concluded that multiple births were, nevertheless, no more hazardous than others and should rarely be artificially accelerated.

Two Years in Giessen

Later in 1889, Strassmann moved to Giessen in Hessen to be an assistant to Professor D. N. Löhlein at the Grand Ducal University Women's Clinic for two years. Löhlein was pleased with Paul's work and wrote a strong recommendation when the young man moved back to the Charité's Women's Polyclinic in Berlin: "With unfailing cheerful enthusiasm and devotion from his first to his last day, he fulfilled duties that were often disturbing, given the high percentage of difficult cases.... Either operating himself or assisting others, he distinguished himself through assurance and dexterity" (*Zeugnis* signed by Löhlein on October 1, 1891).

Paul was the impresario of theatrical and musical performances in the clinic's casino and was clever on the piano. After two collegial years, Paul found it "not easy to leave a circle of friends, as well as the institution that I had helped to inaugurate, and also the small town of Giessen with its university, so small and yet so impressive!" (July 3, 1892). Especially hard in 1891 was leaving Hedwig Rosenberg, to whom he had become engaged on February 23, 1891. She was a local beauty, aged twenty-two, and Paul was then only twenty-four. Hedwig was the daughter of a second-generation jurist, Dr. Anton Rosenberg, and of Julie Homberger, whose father, Heinrich, had inherited a cotton and linen textile mill in Giessen.

Reminiscing about those times, Hedwig wrote: "No girl could have enjoyed a happier and more stimulating youth than mine in those peaceful times in a small university town." In the ballroom of the Giessen Klub, the daughters of professors, bankers, lawyers, and doctors danced with students, young professionals, and the military elite. All her life, Hedwig remembered how often she had waltzed with Ernst Ludwig, the crown prince of the Grand Duchy of Hessen Darmstadt and a student. Writing her memoirs in 1941–1942, she catalogued the names of everyone she considered distinguished in those years and mentioned several ladies who had hoped she might someday be their daughter-in-law. But Paul Strassmann from Berlin had won her heart. In 1937, forty-six years to the day after their engagement, Paul wrote in his diary: "The bond between us has held and become ever stronger. We easily became fond of one another, but I am convinced that the decision to marry was based on a mutual evaluation of character, common values, and ideals for life. This feeling has been confirmed by our life together, building our home, educating the children, religious, moral, and civic views, as well as by intellectual activities and sport."

Marriage and Conversion

Paul and Hedwig married in April 1893 after Paul had returned from a study tour of England in 1891–1892 and had found a choice position in Berlin. After his two years in Giessen, accepting a position in another small town right away would have inconveniently delayed his availability for a major move. The conventional study tour to Britain and Ireland was therefore not just professionally valuable but a way of keeping his options open. The strategy worked. Two months after arriving in London in November 1891, Paul had an offer to be the principal assistant of Professor Adolf Gusserow (1836–1906), who had organized and directed the Second University Women's Clinic in Berlin at the Charité. Gusserow was a native of Berlin, the son of a physician, and a friend of Paul's father, Heinrich. Gusserow considered thorough training in obstetrics of greater importance for popular welfare than gynecology, and this priority included the training of midwives. During 1882–1892, Gusserow was three times the chairman of the Berlin Society for Obstetrics and Gynecology (Berliner Gesellschaft für Geburtshilfe und Gynäkologie) and the editor of the journal, *Archiv für Gynäkologie*. Above all, Gusserow valued practical skill over theoretical sophistication.

Paul and Hedwig honeymooned in Italy in April 1893, and exactly nine months later, on January 21, 1894, Hellmuth was born. Paul always thought of him as "our child of sunny Lugano." Erwin followed in July 1895, Gisela in October 1896, and Antonie in April 1901. Max Gutzwiller observed later: "From the beginning, [Hedwig] served her children and tactfully shared their inner and outer problems, gaining their love and devotion through an exemplary renunciation of a life of her own. Her countless letters add up to a colorful chronicle of the family and illustrate her principle of never giving unsolicited advice or sermons."[1]

In 1895, on Easter vacation in Hessen, Paul and Hedwig had themselves baptized by Pastor Füllmann of Grünberg, a village about twenty kilometers east of Giessen. The ceremony took place at five in the afternoon on April 23, 1895, and included Hellmuth, aged fifteen months. Hedwig was already six months pregnant with Erwin. Until I came across a stamped copy of the baptismal certificate in February 1999, I never knew the place or the date. The Strassmann and Rosenberg families had both been secular for decades, but official conversion meant that henceforth the church-designated share of taxes would go to the Evangelical Lutheran Church, not to Jewish congregations. Paul and Hedwig were among some thirty thousand German Jews who were baptized during the nineteenth century, about 5–6 percent of the Jewish population, which was around 530,000 in 1875.[2] Quite a few of these conversions were no doubt insincere and opportunistic, but not, I believe, that of my grandparents. They did not refer to their baptism as a watershed or a momentous transformation. Rather, to them it seemed like a natural and pious step along the assimilation journey from Rawicz and Ortenberg to life among the prevailing bourgeoisie. They attended church regularly and deplored the fate of outspoken pastors like Martin Niemoeller in Nazi times. My grandmother's letters are full of invocations of God's will and thanks for His blessings. I have never found a hint of cynicism in Paul and Hedwig's makeup, and I believe that they took Christianity more seriously than did the vast majority of Germans. In a memoir, their daughter Gisela's husband, Max Gutzwiller, wrote: "Hedwig Strassmann, born Rosenberg, also had a cheerful, active, yet thoroughly sensible nature that was rooted in a deep Lutheran faith." She seemed to have acquired that faith during her Giessen childhood and probably took the initiative in her and Paul's joint conversion.

In 1897, Hedwig gave her "beloved Paul" the Bible as translated by Martin Luther and chose two verses from Deuteronomy as a dedication:

Thou shalt remember the Lord thy God: for it is He that giveth thee power. (8/18)
Thou shalt rejoice before the Lord thy God in all that thou puttest thine hands unto. (12/18)

This copy of the Bible is now in my possession and looks well used, a repository of clippings, photographs, and notes. Conspicuous are references to son Hellmuth killed in France during World War I, as well as photographs of him in the trenches and of soldiers in spiked helmets carrying his coffin. A verse from Revelations (14:13) is designated for their own tomb in Berlin: "Blessed are the dead which die in the Lord from henceforth: Yea, saith the Spirit, that they may rest from their labors; and their works shall follow them."

Ernst Exiled

In 1904, problems with brother Ernst (1868–1923) turned into a crisis. He had never been a good student, as Heinrich recorded in his memoirs: "Despite the same help, supervision, and encouragement, I could not achieve [any good] result with my second son, Ernst. At nineteen he barely scraped past his Abitur examination (*recht und schlecht*). He studied medicine like Paul, but after sixteen semesters at several German universities, he never made it to an examination." Since Heinrich's training had worked brilliantly with the oldest, Paul Ferdinand, it was all the more disappointing that Ernst was a failure in medicine. Ernst liked languages, literature, and history, which were seen as useless by his mother Louise, and considered insufficient by his father, although he had himself excelled in these very spheres. Louise's brothers, Berthold and Julius, moreover, set a poor example for Ernst with their preference for sport and music over education or business.

Ernst was told in his late twenties that after eight years at university, he was to discontinue his studies. A minor managerial post in a bank was arranged for him by friends of the family. He was now in business, the domain that mattered most to his mother. My only photograph of Ernst shows him formally posed with his parents, sisters, and brother in the 1890s. Seated in striped pants, long coat, and white tie, his hands are placed uncomfortably on his thighs. Ernst smiles directly at the camera, while the others look proudly to their right as ordered—except for deaf Helene, lost in her silent world. Ernst is rather plump, has a small mustache, and is easily the most friendly in the group, although stiffly unsure of himself. Did he see winning a fortune by gambling as a last chance to prove himself? Early bets led to ever bigger stakes and the usual addiction. No record exists of the deceptive way that he tried to cover his losses and how his parents found out.

Two letters from Paul to Hedwig, dated July 14 and 24, 1904, refer to family arguments about Ernst. Paul defended his depressed brother against the outrage of his mother, while Heinrich made arrangements to settle Ernst's debts and to organize emigration. The earlier letter gives the flavor of those times: "I no longer worry about that discussion with Mother. It would have been more convenient for me and more useful if I had spoken bluntly against E[rnst], without insisting on any softening, thus gaining advantages for myself—like not repaying money lent for my clinic or insisting on a more severe formulation of [her] will. It would also have been more convenient if I had not ignored Frieda's financial problems. If Mother had any inkling of that! Perhaps she would not find that so inconceivable! I will just telephone her sometime" (July 14, 1904).

In his memoirs, Paul's nephew, Gerhard Masur (via Paul's sister Frieda), recorded the following:

> The second son, Ernst, was gifted and engaging in some respects, had charm, an excellent memory, and a gift for languages. He chose or was ordered to become another physician but never concluded his studies. Instead, he took up financial work but soon found the bourgeois life too boring. He started gambling, lost great sums, and covered his debts in a fraudulent manner. The bank fired him, and prosecution was avoided only when his parents offered to pay missing amounts. As was customary at the end of the nineteenth century, Ernst was then banished ... finally to Puntarenas, Chile, the hemisphere's southernmost port. In Berlin, Ernst's debts were paid by his parents only on two conditions: first, he should never return to Germany, let alone Berlin, and, second, his inheritance would be reduced to the legal minimum.[3]

Curious about the event, I called Masur in June 1975 and noted his answer:

> Oh, you've heard it mentioned that Ernst was the black sheep in the family. He was really quite gifted in many ways. Not in medicine, but in history or languages, I believe. But he had this problem with cards and gambling, even cheating, unfortunately. When they sent him to South America, they hoped never to see him again. He was a heavy cross for his parents to bear. One time he sold his ticket and all in Hamburg and came back, promising to reform. The next time, I don't know how long, he was in Puntarenas, Chile. I think he returned in 1911 and died in 1923. I don't know whether [Heinrich, Louise, and their children] were a happy family or not. I suppose yes. Very bourgeois, like the Treibels in Theodor Fontane's novel, *Jenny Treibel*. Before 1914, depleting family capital to cover a financial misdemeanor was looked on as a sin against the Holy Ghost. Especially his mother, the former Louise Levy, never forgave his transgression against bourgeois norms. His name could never be mentioned in front of the children. But I recall whispers about him. Who knows why there is sometimes a black sheep?

The first intended exile was to be the German colony of the Camerouns in Africa, and he was outfitted with missionary medical equipment. But at Hamburg, Ernst sold his ticket and his equipment and came home, promising to reform. Despite good intentions, the addiction to gambling got the best of him, and new debts led to new threats. Furious, Louise and Heinrich paid to avoid scandal, but another reprieve from exile was out of the question. Heinrich and Paul escorted their wayward son and brother up the gangplank of a freighter headed for Puntarenas. It was like sending Napoleon to Saint Helena.

More like Bonaparte after Elba, however, some eight years later Ernst baffled everyone by returning from Puntarenas with a substantial fortune. Heinrich had meanwhile died, but Louise was still alive at sixty-eight. My father, who was about seventeen at the time, remembered uncle Ernst giving lavish presents to everyone—brooches, earrings, cigarette cases, pins, and cufflinks, all of gold. He was the legendary triumphant uncle returning from America, rich. Everyone had misjudged him, he said. He claimed to have been a shrewd wool trader, but for all I know he made his money gambling, smart enough to outwit Latin high rollers but not Berlin crooks. Unfortunately, the Berlin crooks waited for him at the race tracks, casinos, and roulette wheels, and Ernst was quickly relieved of his fortune. Soon he was back in debt. The presents of gold had to be lent back to pay these debts. Just temporarily, he said. But it was permanent.

References to Ernst from then on are few in the remaining papers that have come to me. One occurs in a letter that his nephew Hellmuth wrote to his parents from the Spandau barracks of the Fifth Infantry Guards three months before World War I. In a postscript he reports that Uncle Ernst had been invited to play bridge with an old widow the previous Thursday. Ernst had told Hellmuth: "Wenn du ihr die Zehe wimmelst, hat sie schon gewonnen" (Tickle her toes, and she thinks she's a winner).

All his life Paul remembered Ernst when he read of conflict between an extravagant brother and a conscientious brother, for example, in Thomas Mann's *Buddenbrooks: The Decline of a Family*. An "E" for Ernst appears on page 554 of Mann's novel, where the older strict brother tells the younger: "Oh, you fool you! When you hear the will read, you will see just how much you are your own master! You won't get to squander Mother's inheritance as you have run through the rest already! I have been made the guardian of your affairs, and I will see to it that you never get your hands on more than a monthly sum at a time—that I swear!"

In the 1920s, Ernst could not gamble away his remaining capital—his knowledge of Spanish—and he spent his few remaining years teaching that language. He lived in a poor district and married a woman named Helene, whom the family, for reasons unknown to me, did not accept. In the late 1930s, Ernst's widow Helene was desperate for money and pleaded with Paul and his sisters for help. They paid a few hundred marks and later agreed to modest monthly contributions.

Ernst died around 1923 and was buried in a forest cemetery at the village of Stahnsdorf southwest of Berlin. On August 25, 1936, Paul wrote in his diary: "Ernst, my brother's birthday. Fate put fewer good gifts in his cradle. Peace be to his ashes." On May 10, 1938, Paul and Hedwig visited again: "The forest cemetery is extraordinarily tasteful…. We visit Ernst's grave where he rests with Mother [one illegible word][4] under a single stone. His nature differed from mine. Fate left everything good in my cradle, while he was their problem child [*Sorgenkind*]. What personal credit can anyone take for his own life?"

In June 2003 I visited that vast forest cemetery with our daughter Diana, her husband, Jeffery Smisek, and their sons, Julian and Patrick (both use Strassmann as a surname). We could find no one who knew how the grave of Ernst might be located. Buried in that cemetery among many others were the painter Lovis Corinth, the writer Theodor Fontane, the architect Walter Gropius, the composer Engelbert Humperdinck, the publishers Gustav Langenscheidt and Louis Ferdinand Ullstein, the industrialist Werner von Siemens, as well as Fritz Strassmann and his wife Rose, and the cartoonist Heinrich Zille, who symbolizes Berlin the way Daumier symbolizes Paris.

Frieda and Helene: One Musical, the Other Deaf

Two daughters were born after Ernst—Frieda (1869–1945) and Helene (1872–1942)—both in November, three years apart. Helene was beautiful and artistic but deaf (probably an Rh-negative blood type, which runs in the family including Antonie and myself), an affliction that Heinrich and Louise found as heart-rending as Ernst's misdeeds. The parents feared that deafness might be genetic and that children and grandchildren could be affected.

Helene was taught at home and learned lip reading, sign language, and even speech, together with drawing, painting, and academic subjects. Louise dedicated herself completely to Helene for two decades, never leaving her alone, traveling everywhere with her, and accepting no invitations that excluded her. According to Frieda's son, Gerhard Masur, this concentration on Helene cast a painful shadow over the other children, who were three, four, and six years old when Helene was born. Why had their mother time only for Helene?

Frieda, viewed as plain but strong-willed, in time concentrated on literature, especially Goethe, with more tenacity than talent, according to Gerhard, who believed that his mother could have flourished in a managerial office career, a role still unseemly for a woman in the Strassmann's new social circle of the high bourgeoisie, although a long way from selling cloth door to door as grandmother Judith had done in Rawicz. After a year at von Westhoven's finishing school in Meiningen, Frieda returned to Berlin and with zeal attended lectures, concerts, and exhibits. She played Schumann, Mendelssohn, and Mozart on the piano—a kind of shibboleth to her deaf rival. Her musical ability was Frieda's pride. Then, during a country hike, a bolt of lightning strafed her right arm, as if in retribution, and ended most of her music. Henceforth, she could play only short pieces.[5]

In June 1893, two months after Paul's wedding, Frieda, at twenty-three years old, married Emil Masur (1861–1933), a Jewish attorney, aged thirty-two, from Bernstadt, Silesia. He was the youngest of thirteen children, among them a coal wholesaler and a banker who supported Emil's studies of law at the universities of Breslau, Tübingen, and Leipzig. At a party in Berlin, Frieda struck Emil as proud and self-confident, traits that he lacked. Gerhard described his father as "a soft, almost sentimental person with a deep sense of justice. He spent sleepless nights because at times he acted against the letter of the law to save people from poverty and misfortune.... He knew Yiddish words, loved Jewish food, and had that unmistakable though undefinable Jewish sense of humor."[6] In his legal practice he counseled large firms and insurance companies and was executor in the divorces and wills of the wealthy.

The wedding of Frieda and Emil was elaborately held at an elegant restaurant at Unter den Linden. The menu was exquisite, an orchestra played, and a two-act play in verse of nearly six hundred lines was performed. Brother Paul Ferdinand had written the play, poking fun at bride, bridegroom, their friends, their taste, and Berlin society. Paul knew that his sister worshipped Goethe and his prophet, Erich Schmidt, so he composed and read a mischievous poem:

> Mornings, evenings, sooner, later,
> All one hears are words of Goethe.
> His sunsets, moonbeams are a pleasure;
> The poet's snot rag's worth a treasure.
> Frieda, once a timid toad,
> Feels a Goethe overload.[7]

As a couple, Frieda and Emil eventually grew apart, and they had problems with money. Frieda's dowry was 112,000 marks (an amount worth over half a million dollars of 1990), and she also brought a trousseau of hand-carved furniture, velvet curtains, porcelain, crystal, and silverware for twenty-four place settings. Being inept with money, Emil lost much of it trying to counter a brother's bankruptcy and doled out weekly sums to Frieda from her own inheritance in such small amounts that she pawned jewelry and silverware. She took up volunteer social work while he spent evenings dining and playing cards at a men's club. Emil and Frieda converted to Protestant Christianity around 1900, so all of their children—Paula, Heinrich, Charlotte, Gerhard, and Elisabeth—were baptized. In April 1933, the Nazi government decreed that such converts were too Jewish to practice law. A few days later, on April 19, 1933, Emil died of a heart attack.

Helene's husband was Max Keiler (1861–1924), who was eleven years older than Helene and, like herself, deaf. I have no further information about him except his birth at Schwerenz (Swasedz), a suburb of Posen, and his burial in the Strassmann plot at Weissensee. After her husband's death, Helene lived with Betty Leonhard, a niece of her mother. Some Levys had changed their name to Leonhard.

Heinrich's Last Days

One evening in early September 1905, Heinrich walked in pain to Paul's apartment at the Alexander Ufer and stayed for three days. Paul wrote:

> My wife allowed me to share a room with him day and night as in my earliest years. Full of humor, he played with the little girls [Gisela (8) and Antonie (4)] and checked on the homework of Hellmuth [11] and Erwin [10]. Then he entered the clinic of Prof. Klemperer, on Altonaerstrasse, where medicines helped for a while. His last note of greeting to me called off my visit since he was better. Unfortunately, the improvement did not last, and surgery on the blocked colon was urgent. On September 23 he resolved to be operated on for the third time, and in accordance with his wishes I took him to the clinic of Bergmann, where his faithful Prof. M. Borchardt operated the same evening. Father had left a citation from Leopardi next to his bed: "Thus my youth fades, the only blossom in the withered garden of life."
>
> On Monday, September 25, Mother's birthday, for him New Year's Day as well, at eight in the morning, his eyes closed forever with a last look past the meager flowers along the roof of the clinic into an immense distance. Without pain he passed away in my arms.
>
> According to his wishes, the cause of his final ailment [cancer] was determined scientifically. We consider it a mercy that he never knew the malicious nature of his illness.... For eternal rest we buried him [at the Weissensee Cemetery] next to his father!

Louise survived Heinrich by a decade and died in 1915. Gerhard Masur remembered his grandmother as a beautiful white-haired lady with lively black eyes, always well groomed and wearing Brussels lace over her blouses. Every Sunday, he and his sisters were invited to her apartment at Flotow Strasse 11, Hansa district, for an elaborate brunch, and he never left without a small present. He even accompanied his grandmother on vacations, once in winter for sledding in the Silesian mountains. A hired companion was always along on these trips to make all the arrangements. Writing in 1973, Gerhard concluded that Louise's characterization as a "hard, money-proud woman is something I only heard from my father. She always treated me with great love."

Early Medical Achievements

Paul worked at the University Women's Polyclinic of the Charité as assistant and chief of staff for eight years. While there, he earned his Habilitation to be a Privatdozent (adjunct professor) in 1897 with a lecture titled "The Appearance of Extra-Uterine Pregnancy." Altogether he published thirty articles while there.

In 1900, he founded his own polyclinic for a wide variety of women's problems at Luisenstrasse 45 in Berlin and two years later added larger quarters at Oranienburger Strasse 57 a few blocks away. In the late nineteenth century, better anesthetics and antiseptic practices made procedures possible that could not be carried out in private homes, as had been the custom for the well-to-do. Members of these social strata, however, preferred not to mingle with the poor in public hospitals, and so an economic niche for smaller private hospitals appeared. As a way of beginning and of maintaining adequate practical experience, private hospitals were often combined with small polyclinics.

Apart from first- and second-class rooms for wealthier patients, Strassmann's facility therefore had two large rooms with fifteen beds each for third-class patients. Their daily charge was the standard 2.50 marks if covered by insurance. Otherwise, patients paid nothing. Paul Ferdinand financed the equipment for all the premises with a loan from his mother. In 1903, the Strassmann Clinic treated 324 patients. Ninety percent of the patients were cured and 3 percent (nine) died, while the rest merely improved or stayed on until the next year.

From 1900 through 1909, the year he opened his larger clinic-hospital at the Schumannstrasse, Paul published fifty-six more articles and book chapters, about one every two months. Not all were technical. Among them was a eulogy for his Giessen chief, Löhlein, who died in 1906, an evaluation of Louise Bourgeois as the midwife of Maria de Medici around 1605, and an analysis of the positive effect of athletics on women's health. A twenty-two-page article of 1903 compared the evolution of the human fetus in detail with that of animals. "It would not be unfair," Paul concluded, "to designate him whose great vision gave us the laws of mankind's birth—Charles Darwin—as the Isaac Newton of the organic universe."[8]

Also in 1903, at a meeting of the German Society for Gynecology (Deutsche Gynäkologische Gesellschaft) in Würzburg, Paul gave a report about an operation on a double uterus and a split vagina. In 1907, he devoted a longer article in the *Zentralblatt für Gynäkologie* to the topic.[9] He wrote about this condition in several of his patients, cited literature, made phylogenetic observations, reported studies and findings of the pathological institute of the Charité, and presented a novel vaginal operating procedure—the unification of the two uterus halves. He concluded: "After giving its natural form to the organ, which had previously malfunctioned despite repeated beginning pregnancies, we can expect that our surgical efforts will be rewarded with the birth of a living child."

A first step toward such an operation had been taken by Carl Schröder (1838–1887) as early as 1882 and was acknowledged by Paul, but the idea of reconstituting the divided uterus was his own and therefore was associated with his name for decades. In 1926, he reported in the *Zentralblatt* that "the unification of a split or two-chambered uterus is still not routine among surgeons."[10] Familiarity with the technique was spreading, however, and the procedure can still be found in textbooks.

In the field of obstetrics, Paul discovered the "telegraphic signal" of a loosened placenta after delivery. In a lecture on postpartum treatment, given January 12, 1906, to the Berlin Society for Obstetrics and Gynecology, he said: "If you press or thump on the easily found fundus uteri, the hand holding the umbilical cord can feel a fluctuating wave in the vein, which is due to the transmitted external pressure through the thin division between the maternal and fetal blood vessels. If the placenta is loose, usually very shortly after birth, this sign ceases, and after slight pressure on the uterus, nothing can be felt on the umbilical cord. This signal rarely fails."

Paul's best-known book for physicians was titled *Arznei- und Diätverordnungen für die gynäkologische Praxis* (Medical and Dietary Prescriptions in Gynecological Practice). It first appeared in 1912 and came out in six new editions during the following twenty years. Organized like a dictionary, it described current diagnostic and therapeutic methods with reference to symptoms, clinical indications, general principles, rules, and experience. Every page had a "golden rule" that dealt with the ethical and psychological aspects of medicine.

His most popular book for the general public was *Gesundheitspflege des Weibes* (Women's Health Care). In the 1912 preface, Paul wrote: "Explaining scientific research and medical work to outsiders is something I consider useful and necessary for two reasons. First, teaching is a joy and a duty.... Second, for the sake of our profession and its goals. Health care and medical treatment, especially delivering babies, cannot be learned by any lay person from this book. But respect should be gained for the solid foundations, the serious work, and the responsibility of physicians."

Paul became secretary of the Berlin Society for Obstetrics and Gynecology in 1904 and retained that post until 1922. He was elected chairman of the organization in 1925 and 1926 and became a "perpetual" (*immerwährendes*) member. Throughout these years he enhanced meetings with lectures and comments. In 1906, he received the rank of *Titularprofessor* from the minister of education and the University of Berlin, but without formal teaching responsibilities until, in 1919, he became an *ausserordentlicher Professor*. During 1923–1925, he was elected to the Senate of the university. Meanwhile, the Shah of Persia awarded him the Medal of the Lion of the Sun, the Sultan of Turkey bestowed a similar medal, and the University of Birmingham in England gave him an honorary degree in 1911: "In the person of the eminent surgeon, Dr. Strassmann, we recognise another representative of a great and friendly nation ... the author of many monographs on various subjects in his department, and an accomplished operating surgeon ... a shining example of sterling ability in his branch of practice."

My grandmother recalled in 1941:

Father's medical activities began in the time of the *Junges Deutschland* [Young Germany] movement in literature and the arts. Since he was soon very well known, especially as an obstetrician, the young rebels often turned to him. They also knew that a picture or other work of art created by them meant more to him than money. On a medical basis we were thus friends with Corinth, Leistikow, Pfannschmidt, Zickendraht, the sculptor [Sandor] Jaray (who portrayed Erwin and Hellmuth together), and many others. The first assistance that Father rendered to this circle involved Gerhart Hauptmann [aged thirty-eight] in June 1900. "Rautendelein," as they called her [after one of Hauptmann's fictional characters], expected their baby "Benvenuto" out of wedlock in the village of Agnetendorf [in the Silesian mountains]. She was quartered with a peasant, while he lived in the loft of a cowbarn. A second boy arrived a few years later in the pompous "Villa Wiesenstein," unfortunately premature and dead after a few hours. In 1908 and 1909, we visited the Hauptmanns on New Year's Day with Hellmuth and Erwin.[11]

When in 1904 Max Reinhardt took over the Deutsche Theater, half a block from the later Strassmann Clinic on the Schumannstrasse, he produced various Hauptmann plays. As a result, the Kaiser canceled his subscription and warned military officers not to see such unidealistic, un-German trash.

Chapter 4

Golden Years of the Women's Clinic and of Forensic Medicine: 1909–1933

Paul's family usually vacationed together at the seashore or in the mountains, climbing peaks in the summer and skiing the slopes in the winter. One summer in 1904, after spending a few days together, Paul had to leave Hedwig and the children, aged three, seven, nine, and ten, in Giessen to return to Berlin. He took the occasion to write Hedwig a letter that summed up his life at age thirty-seven:

> I sat contentedly on the balcony and looked back and thought how lucky I am. I have a dear, faithful wife, intelligent and tender, four healthy children, radiant, carefree, and of beautiful character! One might almost fear the envy of the gods! But you know that I am free of theological seizures! The joy of seeing you even briefly is almost like awakening in the middle of the night and realizing one can go back to sleep.... I keep thinking of how Antonie wanted to travel with me and wept when I left! Hellmuth [felt lucky to be first].... Erwin was hanging on my arm, and good Gisela expressed all her devotion with a look that needed no words. Then I know what I owe to you, that the children have turned out as they have!... Yes, often I am not the way I want to be. I have the high-strung nerves of a descendant of that race that had to think and fight more to become the same as others. These nerves will gradually become more sensible and calmer, making fewer demands on the Eternal! May my children attain what they strive for! I resolve to steer the little ship into calm waters. And if life's May has not brought us everything, perhaps a beautiful summer will give us full joy. I thank you for much that was beautiful during recent days, and with sincere love and many greetings and kisses for our brood, I am your faithful,
>
> Paul, July 31, 1904

What did he lack amidst all that bliss? His reputation was at a zenith, money was no problem, and he had become a rising star of the family, matched only by his cousin, Fritz, the professor of forensic medicine. The best German physicians of those years thought of themselves not just as healers but as scientists and teachers, hence university professors. This role was invariably combined with directing government hospitals. To become a professor and director of a hospital, one had to have the respect of one's peers and the good will of the Prussian government, the Kaiser, his ministers, the City Council, and the university administration. Paul Ferdinand thought that he had earned such respect with his performance, yet he had not been appointed to higher responsibilities.

Invidious Comparisons

At his age, thirty-seven, others with no more accomplishments were already full professors (Ordinarius). In the 1860s, Paul's mentors, Robert Olshausen and Adolf Gusserow, had made it from their qualifying Habilitation lecture to Ordinarius in less than two years. Now his own Habilitation was already seven years in the past, and he had not even been appointed to the lesser rank of Extraordinarius. Ernst Bumm, aged forty-six, had just been appointed to the vacancy created at the Second University Clinic, the Charité, by the retirement of Gusserow. Bumm had gone from Habilitation to Extraordinarius in six years and to Ordinarius in three more. As his Charité associate, Bumm had brought Karl Franz along from Halle and had seen to it that this surgeon, aged thirty-four, would become an Extraordinarius a mere four years after his Habilitation. Soon Franz was working at the university hospitals of Jena and Kiel, and when Bumm moved on to the First University Hospital of Berlin, Franz took his place at the Second.

On August 3, 1904, Paul angrily wrote to Hedwig, still in Giessen on vacation, about the way some careers were unduly furthered while others were blocked:

> Today I was at a university ceremony. Baron von Richthofen, the former rector spoke.... The new rector is Hertwig. Since I came a bit too late, I spoke to none of these "anointed gentlemen." But I would have learned nothing that I did not know before. Namely, [Karl] Franz has now been called to Jena! A coronation for his services! I feel no envy if someone younger, *who can do more,* is preferred over others, no matter how deserving! But this one! What will Olshausen say, passed over with his suggestions! F[ranz] is surely a decent fellow and, I suppose, a good surgeon. But his publications lack a single new idea, not a single hint of progress! Who knows, but maybe God will grant him common sense together with his promotion!... In Baden, henceforth, only an Ordinarius professor will be allowed to found a polyclinic or any other! The way things are going, one has to expect that Blumreich will be promoted next and pass himself off as professor.... I really should pay no more attention to this cursed jockeying for position.

Medical promotions were determined by various prejudices, in addition to merit, and among the prejudices, anti-Semitism was clearly one. As mentioned in the introduction to this volume, at Berlin, 44 of the 113 low-level adjunct medical professors were Jewish in 1908, but no Jews were among the 19 Ordinarius professors, the highest-tenured rank. A journal dedicated to fighting anti-Semitism asked: "Is it really true that among so many Jewish unsalaried lecturers there is not one who could fill an academic position?" The case in their favor was strengthened by the fact that Jews were twice as likely to be specialists and hence technically more advanced than others. According to Efron: "The excitement of essentially creating new fields of medical research proved especially alluring to Jews ... [who] anticipated reaping the rewards of scientific discovery.... Specialists saw themselves not as university-based theoreticians but rather as a professional class of men who 'did not shy away from laying on hands.'"[1] In Berlin, the field of gynecology-obstetrics had been pioneered by Eduard A. Martin and was continued by his protégés, Ohlshausen, Löhlein, and Gusserow. All of these men welcomed and promoted the careers of both Heinrich Strassmann and his son, Paul Ferdinand. Anti-Semitism was not yet a monolithic phenomenon.

Paul Strassmann knew the outstanding German gynecologists and obstetricians well, and he compared the pace of their careers with his own. He thought he should have been granted more by now, but up to this point he had never identified religion or ancestry as the critical issue. He thought it might be merely personal animosity or perhaps envy of his record—nothing insurmountable. He thought his chance for advancement would surely come sometime.

The Great Disappointment

That chance did indeed come in 1906, when Paul was awarded the rank of Titularprofessor, a low rank without tenure or formal obligation, and when the city planned a large, new public women's clinic at the big Virchow hospital complex being built in the Wedding district north of the Berlin-Spandau Canal. Rudolf Virchow had died in 1902, aged eighty, and the City Council took pride in naming the new complex in honor of the man who had done more than any other for the sanitation and health of the city. Virchow had worked with City Council Chairman Wolfgang Strassmann during 1863–1885 and with Ferdinand Strassmann, the health magistrate, after 1889. These contacts should have helped Paul's quest to become the director of the new clinic. He applied for the position, submitting documents, forms, and letters of recommendation.

In his supporting letter, Professor Schaper of the Charité Hospital affirmed that "[Strassmann] proved himself to be excellent in all activities and gained the full confidence of his superiors with his prudence and his sense of duty." Paul summed up his own activities with the assurance: "Should I have the honor of being selected, I shall strive to fulfill all duties faithfully and with all my strength." To Paul's deep disappointment, however, the Berlin City Council voted against him, choosing instead Dr. A. Koblanck, a man now barely remembered. The 1994 history of the specialty in Berlin has an entire chapter devoted to Paul Strassmann, and eighteen other referenced pages refer to him. Koblanck is mentioned only once.[2] As the health magistrate, Uncle Ferdinand Strassmann might have exerted some pressure at least on the Jewish members of the City Council, but Ferdinand chose to play no part in the decision. As a Prussian bureaucrat, he said, he had to avoid all hints of nepotism. Besides, he had always abstained whenever a Jew, converted or not, was considered for any appointment.

After nearly a century, it is not possible to sort out just why Paul was passed over. Perhaps other candidates cultivated important contacts better. Maybe some potential supporters were hostile because they took him to be a Jew or a lapsed Jew. Although every account portrayed Paul as humanitarian and agreeable, industrious and brilliant, he had himself confessed to a tendency to be high-strung and authoritarian. These and other factors may have mattered in combination, or not at all, meaning that random events of minor importance could have led to the faster advancement of competitors like Koblanck.

Paul immediately sent Koblanck a congratulatory telegram, although he was privately upset about the decision and considered emigrating to the United States. An advance on his inheritance would have made the transition possible, and at age forty it was not too late. (His son Erwin would emigrate at exactly that age in 1936) After calming down, however, he chose instead to use loans from an insurance company and from his mother to build a large private research women's clinic of his own and to make it the best in Berlin. He already had the experience of operating the small clinics in the Luisenstrasse and the Oranienburger Strasse, and three years later, in 1909, his new clinic-hospital was opened. In its first decade, only the old university clinics at the Charité under Karl Franz and at the Artilleriestrasse under Ernst Bumm produced as many discoveries as the Strassmann Frauenklinik. Koblanck died in 1915, and Paul was asked to apply again for the Virchow position. He refused. Hedwig told me in 1949 that she had been apprehensive about going through such stress again, saying, "*Päpchen*, I won't allow it!" She added that it spared them from having the door slammed in their faces by the Nazis immediately in 1933.

The New Institution

Paul hired the creative Jewish architect Max Fraenkel (1856–1926)[3] to design and construct the new building after an older building on the site of Schumannstrasse 18 was demolished. Fraenkel's clinic structure was a gray, five-story building with a twenty-meter facade. The style elegantly balanced an Art Nouveau pattern of interlocking vertical and horizontal elements. Rough-hewn granite surrounded the entrance and the arched windows on the ground floor. Above them were (and are) three sculptures in bold relief by Sandor Jaray—a mother looking tenderly at her nursing baby, a convalescing woman supported by a nurse, and—modeled after Paul himself—an athletic scientist contemplating a book. Centered under the graceful curve of the eaves was a sculpted "1909." Above the gateway in a coat of arms, the letter "S" wound itself around a "P" like the snake around the staff of Asclepius, the traditional symbol of medicine. This "PS" was blasted away under Communist rule fifty years later, but its twin has remained above a similar entrance in the courtyard. The historical plaque of 2003 commemorating Paul Strassmann's career is now under the sculpture of the mother with her baby.

The hospital rooms, operating facilities, offices, and laboratories were mostly beyond the courtyard and in a connecting wing, while the Strassmann living quarters were on the second and third stories facing the street. The steel-beam-supported building had four stairwells, an elevator, ample corridors, and some two thousand square meters of directly productive space. Into the courtyard's formal garden, with benches and exotic plants, eventually came two storks in a large, fenced enclosure—suggesting the source of babies. In 1913, a larger-than-life, glacier-white marble statue of a graceful nude with a downcast expression was set up. A heavy chain went from one of her ankles to a stump, and she was handcuffed. The sculptor, Reinhold Boeltzig, called her, *The Sinner*, but Paul Ferdinand, less judgmental, changed that to *Woman in Chains* (*Die Gefesselte*). The chains to him implied some unjust fate. This statue was transferred to the garden of the suburban Dahlem house where Paul and Hedwig lived from 1936 to 1938. After the war, it was set up on the grounds of the Augusta Viktoria Hospital by Paul Meyer, who had been the first chief of staff at the Schumannstrasse clinic.

The street was not named after the composer Robert Schumann but after a local soap maker, who had a row of three-story houses built near his factory during the 1820s. In the eighteenth century, the Charité hospital complex (1710) and a veterinary clinic (1790) had already located nearby, and military barracks and parade grounds followed. Thus, the new district of the Friedrich-Wilhelm Stadt began in 1830 with housing for officers, soap workers, doctors, teachers, students, and office staff. Most were built in the austere Biedermeier style of Karl Friedrich Schinkel (1781–1841). Theatres and pubs appeared later, and for a while this area was Berlin's Latin Quarter. Karl Marx lived here as a student.

Operations

In 1910, the first complete year of the clinic-hospital's existence, 1,044 patients came and stayed an average of 18.5 days. Although 20 patients died, the clinic attained a reputation against mortality. People said, "Bei Strassmann stirbt man nicht" (You don't die at

Strassmann's). Paul had a talent not only for medicine but for organization, and he acted as his own business manager. Drawing on his experience in the Oranienburger Strasse, he made his hospital solvent, yet clinically and scientifically pre-eminent. It had chemical, bacteriological, and pathological laboratories, as well as an X-ray and radiation division, and physiotherapy. From 1909 to 1936, 15,000 babies were delivered there, and 25,984 gynecological patients were treated, usually operated on. In the polyclinic, up to 6,000 women were treated annually. Within a quarter century, Paul supervised 56 physicians on his staff, accommodated 99 volunteering doctors, and trained 344 graduate assistants. During these years, 2,183 students completed part of their training there, and 1,331 physicians were enrolled in postgraduate courses in gynecology and obstetrics. One doctor wrote in retrospect that the clinic was "appreciated as much by the inhabitants of Berlin's inner city and the poor north as by the wives of foreign industrialists and diplomats.... In the guest book of the clinic are entries by the most famous gynecologists and surgeons of the world, for example, the brothers Mayo of Rochester, Minnesota, who all came to study and marvel at the operative techniques of the director."[4]

In 1909, Paul organized something special for Christmas Eve. New mothers, with their husbands and older children as visitors, were assembled in the clinic's largest hall around a soaring spruce decorated with tinsel, stars, and burning candles. Gynecological patients were brought in as well, if necessary in wheelchairs. Paul said a few words of welcome, and Christmas carols were sung until a low-voiced nurse, dressed as Santa Claus, distributed apples and nuts. Paul's daughter Antonie, aged eight, appeared as an angel, with additional gifts for toddlers. Some older children recited poems, and visiting fathers brought presents for their wives. Windows were opened to hear carolers who had assembled in the courtyard. One of the patients described the evening in a letter to the *Deutsche Tageszeitung,* concluding: "Although I hope never to spend Christmas here again being ill, I am sure the day will never come around again without my recalling how genuine love once tried to spread the magic of Christmas in a hospital where one could easily feel abandoned" (December 28, 1909). These Christmas celebrations continued every year until the last, in 1935.

World War I

Five years after the clinic opened, World War I began, and Paul was appointed physician in charge of the second surgical division of the reserve military hospital at Tempelhof, Berlin. As the wounded came in from battles among the Masurian Lakes in East Prussia and the Marne in France, Paul volunteered to work late into the night, caring for injured soldiers, and was awarded the Iron Cross. He still found time to manage his clinic, to supervise research, and to publish an expanded second edition of his 187-page popular book on female health care, *Gesundheitspflege des Weibes*. The preface of the 1915 edition exudes patriotism:

> Who could take up a pen now that Germany's fate will be determined by the sword and be unaware of that goal?
> With the unshakable walls of its warriors, the German Army guards peaceful progress at home. Bold and courageous mothers have given us the best defense weapons—heroic sons to fight against an envious world!
> This work is dedicated to these women, mothers who see wealth, not burdens, in their children—the highest good of their fertility. You mothers of the last century are among the roots of German victory! Daughters, remember that!

Such enthusiasm was pierced by an agony shared with a million other German families when son Hellmuth, aged twenty-two, was killed in France. An infantry lieutenant and company commander in the Fifth Prussian Guards, Hellmuth fell on November 5, 1916, near Tilloy on the Somme. In his memory, a marble statue was erected in the entrance to the clinic. The preface to the 1918 edition of *Gesundheitspflege des Weibes* has a subdued tone. The book is dedicated to the women who replaced men in numerous tasks, suffering, working, and enduring: "Publication despite war is encouraging proof that women are seeking knowledge about health. For the nation's welfare and their own happiness, may German women soon be back at work next to their husbands."

Paul was now impatient for the war's end and the safe return of his other son, Erwin. The last of the nine Strassmann relatives on active military duty, and the second to be killed, was Paul's cousin, Martin Levy, son of his mother's brother, Julius Levy. In his copy of Erich Maria Remarque's *All Quiet on the Western Front,* Paul wrote: "In early November 1918, my cousin, Martin Levy, among others, was killed in the trenches. Uncle Julius received the fatal news on the same day as an official request to pay the customary subsidy for his son's lieutenant's commission!! Then came November 9!" On that day, the Kaiser abdicated. Two days later, Germany surrendered.

Hellmuth's loss meant relentless anguish to the Strassmann family, as they found themselves living in the chaotic capital of a nation of war-losers. Nevertheless, the Weimar Republic years were professionally the clinic's best. Paul Strassmann was at last appointed an Extraordinarius at the University of Berlin on August 31, 1921, and two years later he was the first such unpaid faculty member ever to be elected to the university Senate, where he served until 1925.

A Festschrift of the monthly, *Monatsschrift für Geburtshülfe und Gynäkologie,*[5] was dedicated to him for his 60th birthday in 1926. Contributions to the Festschrift came from friends and students. In the introduction, Paul Meyer wrote: "Your enthusiasm for teaching was transferred to your students.... Although attendance at your college, being a 'clinic,' is not compulsory, it is nevertheless crowded since students know what the Strassmann Clinic can give them.... And we also thank you for something else: conscientious thoroughness, self-criticism, and a sense of duty as a physician.... We can all learn from your indomitable optimism."[6]

The Ambience

The atmosphere at the clinic in the 1920s and early 1930s has been portrayed by Max Gutzwiller in *Das Büchlein mit dem Denkmal* (Little Book with a Memorial, 1942), honoring Paul and Hedwig's daughter Gisela:

The Strassmann Frauenklinik in the Schumannstrasse was barely a hundred steps from the Deutsche Theater and close to the Luisenstrasse with the vast grounds of the Charité hospital. Whoever entered this renowned site of medical exertions experienced a most striking first impression. A broad archway led past a bronze bust of Gerhart Hauptmann on one side and a memorial to the son killed in the war on the other, into a courtyard with a pergola. The courtyard connected the three main buildings, and at times harbored a pair of red-beaked, calm, philosophical storks. It served as playground and echo chamber for those steady companions of the chief, two or three brown dachshunds.

After a casual nod to the porter, a salty old Berliner, visitors climbed a flight of stairs to the right in the middle of the archway. The private quarters occupied two floors with all the stairs, halls, corridors, and rooms thoroughly covered with art: oil paintings, watercolors, etchings, painted glass, cabinets, bronze sculptures, precious crystal, porcelain, memorial medals, and curios. Notable among all this was a collection of seventeenth- and eighteenth-century Dutch masters—still lifes, flowers, landscapes, and interiors—and a few single works by Anton von Werner, Lovis Corinth, Walter Leistikow, Philipp Franck, and Lesser Ury.

Almost daily, after his 12–1 PM lecture in his own ground floor auditorium, my father-in-law's recreation was a stroll to nearby art dealers and galleries. He was thoroughly informed about the life stories, circumstances, techniques, and plans of each old master and had ideas about the provenance of unsigned works. From the terrain or buildings in a landscape, he meticulously tried to pinpoint the place or town that was portrayed. This research stimulated him, and if he liked a work in addition as a beautiful female portrait, as a fascinating event, or as a touching memento of Berlin, he would return to it again and again like a culprit to the scene of his crime. Sometimes we urgently pressed him to make the purchase.

These excursions were not pure joy for us of the younger generation. With his precious feeling of indulging himself only in these hours away from his demanding profession, he could stay away until 3:00 PM, while we had meantime been waiting for dinner since 1:30. The meals took place in a large dining room with many windows to the street and with an atmosphere of almost medieval closed culture and comfort. Afterwards came a nap at an hour as late as dusk in the winter. His consultation hours followed from 4:30 to 8:30 PM in one of those spacious "Berlin rooms" that opened to the courtyard.

In the back of this room, a secret door led into the clinic itself. Bookshelves were packed with journals, medical folios, leather-bound hospital records, and antique books. A narrow, winding staircase led straight up into his bedroom. In this study we occasionally talked after the evening meal of cold cuts served in the upstairs living room. I remember the room, with its enormous *Christ and Nicodemus* by Karl Gottfried Pfannschmidt and a glorious Madonna, as a site of profound creativity and difficult decisions that had to be reached there after physical examinations in the brightly lit neighboring room with all its instruments.

Dr. med. Paul Ferdinand Strassmann, Geheimer Sanitätsrat and Extraordinary Professor at the University of Berlin, had all the traits of a truly great physician. A broad-rimmed Italian hat crowned his tall figure, with its massive body, strong arms, and sensitive hands and fingers, and his fiery eyes under their bushy brows gave an affirmation of life and of faith in the grandiose rationality of nature. To a patient's bedside he therefore brought an immense gift for persuasion and encouragement. His memorial description of a famous Berlin colleague, Ernst Bumm, applied to himself: "A divine gift of artistic sensitivity was combined with a refreshing, cheerful, and healthy outlook." Everything about him was straightforward, uncomplicated, and natural in the best sense. Modest to the point of prudery, he could be indignant about a lack of suitable reserve in dress or manner in women, whom he regarded as the bearers of the most noble sentiments and of true human creativity. He was a brilliant surgeon, capable of the most rapid decisions even in the face of totally unexpected situations, and yet he exercised the greatest vigilance in his reconstructive—especially vaginal—technique, extreme observance of all safety measures, to whose development he himself contributed. For resident physicians, nurses, students, and patients, he was the complete teacher. It could be seen everywhere, even on the hospital walls, which were decorated by maxims he had chosen to inspire faith and courage.

The maxim in the delivery room read "Natura, artis magistra" (Nature, the master of art). "Only he who tries to do something never done before will do as much as he can," read another slogan in the lecture room between large portraits of Paul's uncles, Samuel and Wolfgang. Patients could also gaze at slogans such as "Hoffnung und Mut, bald wird es gut" (Hope and courage, recovery comes soon).

Max Gutzwiller went on:

> [Paul Ferdinand Strassmann] considered his main task that of putting the progress of scientific research ... in the service of a medical humanism. He set a good example himself, with his lectures about the Hippocratic oath and the moral duties of physicians (as he put it, "fundamentals that are unfortunately slighted in a purely scientific-technical education"), with his promotion of lifelong medical education, with his free care for needy mothers, and with his countless exhortations in his hospital and study. Although he was disturbed during hundreds of nights, and although daily operations, consultations, and a vast correspondence strained him, he read incessantly, dictated, published, and lectured. His list of publications considerably exceeds two hundred items. Among them are a discussion of feminine athletics, an analysis of the Frog King's fairy tale, and reflections about Goethe and Benvenuto Cellini.
>
> Numerous, often very short vacations, took him to the Arctic, to Spain and the Balearic Islands, to England, and to the United States. Above all, however, they took him to Italy and Switzerland, where even at the age of sixty-five he conquered a famous summit of four thousand meters. He kept himself informed about individual patients during these journeys and at times cut travel short instantly and without hesitation. Perhaps his best trait was the amazing and unerring simplicity with which he recognized the mutual interdependence of causes and effects and the social and psychological preconditions for diagnoses and clinical and personal treatment—all this with an aversion to anything unnatural and contrived.[7]

A great festivity was the celebration of Paul's sixtieth birthday on October 23, 1926, arranged in detail by his son Erwin, my father. The ceremony began at 11:30 AM with a presentation of the Festschrift, a 188-page special edition of the journal of obstetrics and gynecology, the *Monatsschrift für Geburtshülfe und Gynäkologie*, already mentioned, which contained a list of his publications and twenty-five contributions by others. After the presentation came sixteen speeches by his former students and assistants; current physicians at the clinic; the association of female doctors; clinicians; the clubs of Egyptian, Bulgarian, Persian, and Russian students at the university; the Masonic Lodge of Victorious Truth; the dueling fraternity Arminia; former classmates of the Friedrichsgymnasium; Berlin athletic associations; and others. When it was over, Paul thanked everyone by reciting a complex poem that he had composed for the occasion. It stressed that life had passed by quickly and that one could have accomplished nothing without a web of close friends.[8]

Scientific Work

In obstetrics, the doctrine and practice of Paul Ferdinand remained basically conservative. He considered pregnancy and birth to be natural physiological processes, which one should watch carefully without routine intervention. By the 1930s, in his clinic, contrary to prevailing custom, mothers were united in their rooms with their newborn children. His bibliography of 200-plus items includes five books, contributions to textbooks (among them Franz von Winckel's *Handbook of Obstetrics*), and articles on surgery, urology, and hygiene. He introduced lysoform for disinfecting hands and new ways of using boric acid. He was interested in medical aspects of sports and in medical history. He was an invited speaker at national and international medical congresses in the United States, England, Switzerland, Russia, Italy, Sweden, and Austria.

Among Paul's contributions to gynecology and obstetrics were several reconstructive surgical operations and the replacement of part of a bladder, the opening of a closed cervix, and the reconstitution of a fallopian tube. Especially significant were his corrections of malformed female genital tracts (metroplastic surgery in uterus septus, bicornis, and duplex). In recognition, August Martin, a senior colleague, closed the Festschrift as follows: "Your name will live in the history of our specialty because of your efforts to make congenitally malformed organs fertile."[9]

During those years of increasing popularity of abdominal surgery, Paul preferred the retention and improvement of the vaginal approach. In every case he asked, can we do it vaginally? Apart from hysterectomies, he operated vaginally to clear retroflexio uteri and to remove ovarian tumors. At the time, this was a major way of avoiding infections. In wielding scalpel, scissors, clamps, and needles, Paul combined audacity and speed with a perfectionistic control that showed a special feel for each physiological situation. Despite his speed, he was always on the side of caution. His hands moved gracefully in accordance with long experience and a sharp imagination about the pattern of nerves, arteries, and muscles. His son Erwin reported: "He loved to battle with large fibrotic uteri per hemisection and morcellement. His results were excellent. His fame as a surgeon came above all from his reputation for operating without incisions." He taught his students that they were treating an ill person, not a sick organ. He conveyed an invariable optimism and stressed uncompromising thoroughness. No effort would be spared to save a patient from death, and when all had been tried in vain, he expected the physician to stay and hold the patient's hand.

In 1935, its last full year, the clinic had 76 beds and 51 employees. The high ratio of employees to patients reflected a focus on performance, not profits. From January 1 to December 15, 1935, there were 26 first-class patients in single rooms, 109 second-class patients in double rooms, and 1,395 patients in large, third-class rooms. Among these, 39 paid nothing. Charges were levied not for an investment yield but merely to cover current expenses, to avoid layoffs of personnel, and to have funds for admitting indigent women. As Erwin summarized in a report to the Ministry of Interior, dated December 20, 1935: "This clinic is not the usual sort of private hospital but an enterprise in the style of a small university clinic, equipped for all the scientific tasks needed for studying and treating female afflictions and pregnancies. Only the director and his associates, not other doctors, can use this clinic for their patients."

No monetary income came from treating the wives of painters, sculptors, musicians, and poets, since Paul thought that a canvas or a concert was adequate compensation. Sometimes he went as far as treating the man as well as the wife, sitting up all night, if need be, with the severely depressed, as was the case with Lovis Corinth. A disturbed-looking self-portrait by Corinth, with a dedication of April 30, 1920, hung opposite Paul's desk. Käthe Kollwitz inscribed a copy of her woodcut, *The Mothers*, to "Herrn Professor Paul Strassmann dem Hüter und Förderer jungen Lebens, in Dankbarkeit" (the guardian and promoter of young life, in gratitude). Visiting the painters' studios and being allowed to select what pleased him, he sometimes went into backrooms and closets and came up with the unexpected. Thus, we have a gloomy Kollwitz etching of Death struggling to entice a dying baby from its mother's embrace, signed and titled *Unfinished Work*.

The First of Three Mothers: An Attorney's Wife

Of the thousands of patients who came to the Strassmann Clinic during these years, I will say more about only three of them, the wives of a lawyer, a prince, and a doctor. Records of the clinic's expenses are mostly lost, but I have the charges for the delivery of one child of Martha Stockfisch, the wife of an attorney living in Schulzendorf, a village northwest of Berlin. This case is special because it is the only one for which I have records of the charges made for the delivery of a baby. The event, which involved minor complications, took six hours and resulted in the customary clinic stay of twelve days. The clinic charged 416.60 marks in February 1926, as follows:

Physician's honorarium in marks	200.00
Days in clinic, twelve @ 12 marks per day	144.00
Child's eleven days of care @ 1 mark per day	11.00
Delivery room expenses	40.00
Laundry	5.60
Medicines, bandages, laboratory	15.80
Telephone	.20
Total Sum	416.60

Upon a request from the attorney, Dr. Stockfisch, Paul reduced his honorarium by 50 marks to 150 marks, an amount exactly equal to that paid upon admittance by Martha Stockfisch. The balance of 266 marks was paid in September 1926. This information came into my possession after the granddaughter of the baby born that winter gave the bill to a friend of mine, Dr. Matthias David, who photocopied it for me.

The Second Mother: Princess Hermine and the Hohenzollerns

The princess was Hermine von Schönaich-Carolath (née von Reuss, 1887–1947), whose five children Paul delivered, the first four at their castle in Saabor, Silesia, and the last, Henriette, at the clinic in Berlin on November 25, 1918, shortly after the armistice that ended World War I. The prince, who had been a diplomat at Bucharest, was then a house guest of the Strassmanns for three weeks before returning to Silesia. He died of tuberculosis in 1920. Hermine, a lively but fairly small brunette woman, was thirty-three years old at the time. Ambitious and rather talkative, she now determined to make a new life for herself.

In April 1921, one of Hermine's sons wrote a letter to the exiled and newly widowed Kaiser Wilhelm in Doorn, the Netherlands, expressing loyalty and devotion to him, no matter what happened. The Kaiser, who had met Hermine a few times before the war, was sixty-three years old and lonesome. He invited Hermine and her son to Doorn, his first such invitation. In the summer of 1922, he proposed marriage to her, and the two were wed on November 3. The Kaiser's daughter, Viktoria Luis e, who at thirty was only five years younger than Hermine, recorded that she and two of her brothers were "utterly dismayed" and refused to attend the wedding. Hermine, however, wrote: "I have decided to take this step because I never do things by halves, and besides, we are mentally compatible.… I shall do my utmost to see that the Kaiser never regrets the course we are taking."[10] With her encouragement, the Kaiser began to write his memoirs vindicating himself, as well as books about Corfu and ancient Mesopotamia. The staff at Doorn, including General von Dommes, his adjutant, now referred to Hermine as "Her Majesty."

Hermine left Doorn fairly often to visit her castle at Saabor and to be in Berlin, where she stayed at the Old Palais of the Hohenzollerns on Unter den Linden and socialized on occasion with the Strassmanns. Once she joined them on a trip to Greece and afterwards gave them a book of arty photographs, *Die Akropolis*, by Walter Hege, inscribing it, "In remembrance of our beautiful trip to Greece together," with a stamp, "Herminen-Hilfswerk, H" under an imperial German crown. Paul and Hedwig in turn visited Doorn. In 1941, Hedwig remembered that "the gratitude of this woman created a friendship, varied as the evening shadows until the sun of life sinks." Hermine kept up the contact throughout the 1930s, visiting the Strassmanns in Dahlem, and when Paul Ferdinand died, she sent a large bouquet of condolence flowers, as did the Crown Prince, together with the usual telegrams. The Kaiser said in 1938, after the *Kristallnacht* (Night of Broken Glass) pogrom: "For the first time I am ashamed to be a German." He died in June 1941. Hermine returned to Saabor in Silesia and saw the property given to Poland with the rest of Silesia when Russian armies marched in. Under surveillance, she lived in a house on the outskirts of Frankfurt on the Oder until, aged sixty, she died of a heart attack in August 1947.

The Third Mother: Another Ilse Strassmann

One Ilse Strassmann was my mother, and another (née Marwitz) married Georg Strassmann (1890–1972) in 1922 when she was twenty-seven, and he was thirty-two. Like his father, Fritz Strassmann, Georg was a pathologist and a professor of legal medicine (in Breslau). After their marriage, a year passed with no pregnancy, and Ilse became depressed, even suicidal. Their son—once Friedrich, now Fred—has allowed me to quote from his mother's diary.

> All my joy is gone, and tears come over and over again. I feel so lifeless and hopeless. All of Georg's love is no help. The world is so dull and monotonous.… Every little child I see pierces my heart like a dagger. I can't grasp that I shall never be allowed to call a little one my own. Isn't that my calling, to be a mother? Why is it not answered? What have I done to bear such frightful punishment? I never did anything except for love.… My life is pointless, superfluous.… Sometimes ghastly thoughts arise. But no, I love my husband too much ever to leave him. All I want is strength and the courage to face life and to make him happy again. (June 4, 1923)

Four years later, Ilse decided to let Georg's uncle, Paul Ferdinand Strassmann, examine her and perhaps try a corrective operation. On January 21, 1927, the operation was performed, and a week later Ilse wrote in her diary:

> They gave me a magnificent room. Uncle Paul himself brought me up. Georg stayed until after lunch and came back in the afternoon. My mother-in-law sent me a sweet little garden of cacti. In the evening they gave me morphine and I slept gloriously. I feared nothing, why should I? Uncle Paul is such a wonderful surgeon, and it was a harmless business to be carried out under an anesthetic. At eight the next morning they woke me. I fixed myself up, had another injection, and they brought me upstairs. I waited in a preparatory room for further developments. Uncle Paul finally came and said I had nothing to fear and held a mask in front of me.… I don't know what happened next.… I opened my eyes and was back in the bed of my room, a private nurse next to me.… There was nothing to eat, just a sip of tea now and then.… Georg sent a basket of hyacinths, Alpine violets, and lilies of the valley. Mother sent a velvet bathrobe, and Erwin came for a visit.… I felt as fresh as if nothing had happened. (January 28, 1927)

But the operation was of no avail. Ilse remained childless. Two years later, Paul resolved to arrange an adoption. In early 1929, a twenty-one-year-old baroness from Silesia, perhaps an acquaintance of Hermine, came to the clinic pregnant and wanted to give birth secretly, as if she had some major illness. I am told that her parents knew about the pregnancy but not her lover (see the epilogue to this book). Paul agreed to help feign an illness, and a healthy boy was born on July 19, 1929, weighing six and a half pounds. An adoption by Ilse and Georg was arranged after they saw the three-week-old baby for the first time in August. They named him Friedrich Werner Paul Strassmann after Georg's father, his late brother, and the helpful uncle directing the clinic. To minimize complications, the legal papers said that the adoptive parents and the mother were all inhabitants of Berlin when, in fact, all were Silesians. No father was listed, and Georg and Ilse had to promise never to inquire into the identities of the natural parents. They were told that one or both were aristocrats and that the father was highly musical. No more.

Back in Breslau, Ilse wrote:

> For four days, since Sunday the thirteenth of October, we have had our good little boy, our Friedrich Werner Paul here with us. I was with him for five days in the Schumannstrasse Clinic of Uncle Paul to be instructed in his care.... When I took the sweetie in my arms for the first time, he wet me as a greeting. I find that a good omen of friendship....
>
> Leaving the clinic was very hard. All the nurses were so fond of the little fellow that they came to say farewell. They had spoiled him quite a bit, each going into his room every morning and chatting with him.... On Sunday, October 13, at quarter of six in the afternoon we left from Bahnhof Friedrichstrasse on an express train to Breslau. Nurse Amalie and Grandmother Strassmann brought us to the station. (October 17, 1929)

Nine years later, in October 1938, Ilse, Georg, and Friedrich emigrated to the United States because the field of legal medicine was now forbidden to Georg and because they feared that their "Aryan" son might be taken from them, as had happened in similar cases. Their long-emigrated cousin, Antonie, met them at the New York docks and found an apartment for them at Waverly Place in Manhattan's Greenwich Village. Nearly sixty years later, Fred learned that his natural parents had married in 1930. Near Frankfurt, he met his three younger brothers and a sister, who all welcomed him with touching enthusiasm. That reunion will be related in the epilogue.

First Impressions of a Better Promised Land

Paul and Hedwig made a nine-week trip to the United States in the fall of 1927. They left from Cuxhaven near Hamburg on August 30, sailing first-class on the SS *Reliance*. They arrived in New York on September 8 and left on the SS *Hamburg* on October 27. Meetings had been arranged in advance in Asheville, North Carolina; St. Louis; Kansas City; Rochester, Minnesota; Chicago; and New York City. After friends brought them to the Waldorf Astoria Hotel, Paul wrote in his diary of the trip:

> Suddenly, through the haze, gleaming skyscrapers rise.... A news photographer has come aboard ship and takes our picture. We are already passing the Statue of Liberty. The skyscrapers are soaring like Babylonian towers, expected, yet very strange shapes. The great bridge to Brooklyn. I snap pictures, and in my excitement I reload the camera with already exposed film.
>
> In a stroke, I see that one small nation could achieve nothing after two and a half years of war against such power and might. I expected to see twenty to thirty skyscrapers. Instead, a forest of them is all around....
>
> Above Broadway lights are whirling.... Berlin is a dwarf! Each tower glows like the others, all seeming afire. It exceeds anything seen on the stage, all cubist pictures. Whoever has not been here cannot imagine it. Overwhelmed, I sink into bed and think of the insanity of declaring war against such power.

At breakfast the next morning, a Mrs. Röchling, a woman in her fifties, appeared with lilies. Paul had operated on her in Berlin before she emigrated, and that morning she had seen his and Hedwig's picture in the newspaper. She was now a cook, living with her daughter, and had taken the morning off for this reunion. Later, at Lennox Hill Hospital, he met a Dr. Arthur Stein, who had emigrated from Frankfurt around 1907 because he did not want to deal with German medical insurance. Now he had left Harlem Hospital because he refused to have Negro assistants. Among other New York sights, Paul Ferdinand visited Mount Sinai Hospital and found it marvelously neat and clean. There was no smell of ether or chloroform and no decorative picture of any type, as there had been none in the restaurants and the hotel. At Mount Sinai he learned that the poor were treated without charge since social health insurance did not exist. American capitalists were against it.

Eight weeks later, Paul Ferdinand and Hedwig were still enthusiastic about the vast country and its hospitality. On October 23, his sixty-first birthday, Paul wrote from the Blackstone Hotel in Chicago, describing more of their visit. Wherever he went, he had answered a hundred "how-do-you-do's" with a hundred "OK-I'm-so-glad-to-see-you's." He had been to the stockyards at Kansas City and had watched a beauty contest in St. Louis. At one grand dinner in Chicago with non-alcoholic beer, the diners had been entertained by a fine performance of arias from Mozart's *The Magic Flute*, with the best Queen of the Night whom Paul had heard in forty years. He and Hedwig admired much in America, including high shoeshine stands where the client could sit comfortably and the polisher did not have to stoop. "Again and again, the practical sense of Americans impresses us."

Last they visited Rochester, Minnesota, and the Mayo Clinic, a privately owned and funded, non-profit, socially oriented research clinic, much like the Strassmann Frauenklinik in Berlin. The Mayo brothers, Dr. Will (1861–1939) and Dr. Charlie (1865–1939), had made so many study tours to Europe that some dubbed them "the surgical travelers of the world." Dr. Charlie went first in 1889, especially to learn German antiseptic techniques. Dr. Will did not go until 1900, again beginning with Berlin, and then crossed the Atlantic thirty times in the next three decades. With such study trips to the world's outstanding medical centers, the Mayos gave a small and remote Minnesota town primacy in many aspects of American medicine, especially in surgery.

Very soon after the armistice ending World War I, Dr. Will cabled greetings to Paul Strassmann and other professional friends in Germany and Austria. Within hours, a Secret Service agent appeared at his office and asked why he had "communicated with the enemy." Astonished, Dr. Will said, "I thought the war was over!"

German and Austrian physicians had been expelled from the International Society of Surgery, and German had been replaced as the official language. Will Mayo took the lead in reinstating German scientists and told the press, "Medical science, like all science, has no country and no language…. To continue international rancor based on prejudice is unthinkable, justifiable in neither principle nor fact."[11]

In 1929, the two brothers, now in their sixties, traveled abroad together for the first time. They returned again to Berlin and visited with the Strassmanns. Apart from observing operations and seeing historical monuments, they went to the Luna Park in the suburb of Halensee to go on rides and to see the talking Turkish whale and the faceless woman. "Na, wer hat noch nicht? Na, wer will noch mal?" (Who's next? Who wants in again?), shouted the barkers. Lacking reservations, the Mayos and Strassmanns had to wait an hour to be seated at one of the restaurants. In response to Paul's death, Will Mayo recalled in a letter dated August 30, 1938: "I will never forget his inexhaustible friendliness toward us during our early visits to Germany."

Looking Backwards and Forwards

In 1930, Paul published an illustrated book, *Aus der Medizin des Rinascimento* (On the Medicine of the Renaissance).[12] He began this book with a discussion of the life and times of Benvenuto Cellini (1500–1571), perhaps the most skillful worker in metal—sculptures, medals, ornaments, jewel settings, vases—of Renaissance Florence, Rome, and Paris. In 1803, Goethe had translated Cellini's rather picaresque and brutally frank autobiography into German, including details of numerous illnesses, wounds, treatments, and doctors. Paul put these particulars into context and explained their significance in an oversized book of fifty-eight pages, with a scholarly footnote per page and twenty-two artistic photographs. Subjects dealt with included surgery, internal medicine, observation of pulse and urine, bleeding, prescriptions, poisons, syphilis, prostitution, courtesans, homosexuality, obstetrics, and children out of wedlock. The book's thesis was that after nearly two thousand years of blind adherence to Aristotle's and Galen's theories of health and disease, around 1500 a new era of curiosity and experiments had begun in which art and science reinforced one another, as they later would in the work of Goethe.

Paul stressed the wise tolerance during the Renaissance of matters that were later considered taboo. As early as 1501, the town of Ferrara had employed a physician to look after the health of prostitutes. Cellini noted that while courtesans might carry on loose affairs with bankers and cardinals, they nevertheless educated their own children sternly. In a postscript, Paul supposed that some preliminary, although surely not complete, insight into the state of medicine in the Renaissance and its cultural context had been gained.

> Discussing some topics might have been easier for Benvenuto Cellini than is true in our times!... On fallow terrain the first seeds of scientific medicine were germinating, straining toward light from intellectual darkness.... What the printing press did for the era of the Renaissance is the machine for us, as it moves into the terrain of intellect, of art, and of medicine itself.... Conquering the air is the apotheosis of the machine and stamps our era.... The globe has become a single unit, and nations are moving closer together. A new liberation and quickening of humanity—intellectual, economic, and physiological—will surely result. New life styles are appearing. A cosmic wave is rolling in, getting closer, we feel it inside.
>
> ... But the next revolution in medical science and skill—I dare to prophesy here—will follow new insights into the organic world on the basis of its *chemical* composition, of healthy and unhealthy secretions, and understanding the *chemical and physical connections of organs as a unit!*[13]

Not the direction but only the methods and details of our current molecular analysis of genes, synapses, and neurotransmitters would have surprised him.

Fritz Strassmann, Pioneer in Forensic Medicine

Paul's cousin, Fritz Strassmann (1858–1940), like other young Strassmanns, was enrolled at the Friedrichsgymnasium in Berlin (1866–1875), and went on to study medicine at the universities of Heidelberg, Leipzig, and Berlin. In 1879, Fritz passed his examination in anatomical pathology under the supervision of Rudolf Virchow at the Berlin university. "He became my patron," wrote Fritz of Virchow, "surely in part because my father and uncles shared his opinions and had been his students. Uncle Ferdinand even wrote his dissertation under Virchow."[14] After obtaining his medical degrees, Fritz spent his military year in 1880–1881 as a physician, with Prussian dragoons and the Hessian infantry.

Short and stocky, Fritz had scruffy brown hair, a bristly mustache, and thick, professorial eyeglasses. Samuel had insisted that his son take up anatomical dissecting late in his studies. He had feared that an earlier exposure to autopsies might have turned Fritz against medicine altogether. Instead, forensic medicine and analyzing cadavers became the young man's primary interest. Specifically, he wanted to further the application of medical science to legal problems, to study the behavior of cells to determine the time and cause of injuries and untimely death, and to use blood, sperm, and hair samples to identify the guilty. Among other tasks, he researched the physiological effects of alcohol, chloroform and other gases, explosions, and traffic accidents, as well as the psychological competence of the accused to stand trial.

Fritz wrote his dissertation and gave his academic inaugural lecture under Professor Carl Liman (1818–1891) on the topic, "The Appearance of Corpses in Water."[15] As early as 1833, Wilhelm Wagner (1793–1846), a professor at the University of Berlin, had urged the Prussian government to set up courses in the practical application of medical knowledge to legal questions, examining both living persons and corpses. The proposal was accepted, but new facilities—morgues, laboratories, and classrooms—were not provided. Johann Ludwig Casper (1796–1864), following Wagner in 1849 as director of the new Institute for Legal Medicine (Anstalt für die Staatsarzneikunde), put the emphasis on autopsies with standards amid reforms that earned him laurels as the "founder of legal medicine in Prussia."[16]

Carl Liman became Casper's successor in 1864. With the goal of coordinating the treatment of corpses for police, legal, and instructional purposes in a single institution, Liman organized the Berliner Gerichtlich-Medizinisches Institut (Berlin Institute for Forensic Medicine) in 1886. He had a larger and better morgue built, but his frequently tactless manner and tone limited his success otherwise. He also had an unfortunate prejudice against experimental research.[17]

An Ascent

After Liman's death in 1891, Fritz Strassmann became director of the institute, and in 1894 he expanded its facilities from two rooms to an entire building. His appointment became permanent in that year, and he acquired the rank of Titularprofessor, in part because the Austrian University of Innsbruck had offered him the even higher rank of Ordinarius. Fritz made legal medicine a fully recognized branch of medicine and a required field of study, one with its own association and journal, the *Zeitschrift für die gesamte Gerichtliche Medizin*, which he himself edited. He became a full professor (Ordinarius) at the University of Berlin in 1920, and the faculty elected him to its Senate.

Outstanding among publications by Fritz was his *Lehrbuch der Gerichtlichen Medizin* (Textbook of Legal Medicine),[18] with its seventy-eight illustrations. Originally published in 1895 and translated into Russian and Italian, it earned honors in Rome as late as 1928. In his 1933 memoirs, however, Fritz stated that his major professional disappointment was the limited success of this text: "I put my heart and soul into that book, my entire personality. Some friendly recognition did come my way and made me happy.... But I had to suffer malicious criticism, and sales were too few to justify a second edition."[19]

In 1898, Fritz visited the morgues and laboratories of some Balkan countries, operated by former students of his, and he found them well run. His itinerary had the advantage of "approaching Constantinople by ship via the Black Sea and the Bosporus, irrefutably the best first impression of that wonderful city."[20]

Among Fritz's duties after 1902 was the task of designating which pathologists of the Mordkommission would be available to the police on a twenty-four-hour basis each month, in case of murders. For this duty, a "murder car" with a searchlight and special tools was built.[21] In addition, Fritz organized a museum with 70 instruments, 300 photographs, and 1,500 specimens, including a variety of damaged skulls.

Apart from forensic medical research, teaching, and consulting, Fritz at first had an active practice among trade unionists in the north of the city. "Every morning when I opened the door to my waiting room," he recalled, "I saw fifty people sitting there. Meticulous examining and advising was out of the question with such numbers, and only with a standard routine could I cope with all of them.... Still I gained insight into conditions that would otherwise have remained alien to me."[22] Around 1900, Berlin was said to be the most densely settled city in Europe, and in its north and east infant mortality was two or three times that found in its western districts. Unemployment, prostitution, child labor, drug addiction, alcoholism, miscarriages, infant deaths, suicides, accidents, and murders were widespread. For dealing with all this, cooperation between the police and the medical profession, especially academic research, was crucial, and Fritz had partial success in promoting it. As summarized in his 1928 Festschrift, he "was among the few whom neither success nor honors could rob of his simple humanity, a man totally unpretentious, one who combined professional expertise with great erudition and interests. Perhaps a few abused his good nature, but many more experienced it gratefully and happily."[23] He was more *liebenswürdig* (tactfully amiable) than the norm.

In 1911, Fritz had begun to expand the institute's academic facilities for legal medicine, with larger lecture halls, better morgues, refrigeration, cages for animals, scientific equipment, and the like. Construction began in 1913, and in May 1914 an inaugural ceremony took place. The latest findings in related fields, including pathology, bacteriology, and X-rays, could now be applied. Compared with other branches of medicine, legal medicine had lately been deplored as lagging, but under new leadership it was thought to be catching up. Its principles were henceforth included in medical final examinations.

Fritz wrote over a hundred publications, including the textbook that had been translated into Russian and Italian. In 1928, the journal, *Deutsche Medizinische Wochenschrift*, said that "apart from their factual content, his writings invariably give aesthetic pleasure because of their polished, clear, economical style, always formulating new tasks in terms of practical problems.... The most valuable thing, however, that Strassmann has given his fellow workers is the example of a thorough sense of justice and devotion to duty combined with neutrality in testimony."[24] Fritz became an honorary member of several national and international organizations in his field, but he treasured above all a 1913 honorary degree from the University of Edinburgh. It annoyed him that his German compatriots invariably made the army's chief medical officer the head of their international delegations, thus reinforcing the country's ominous militarist image abroad.

Unloved by the Prussian Police

Fritz's autopsies showed how right-wing officers had murdered at short range the revolutionaries Karl Liebknecht and Rosa Luxemburg in 1919. His scientific report about it was ironically titled "Erschiessen auf der Flucht" (Shot While Escaping). Together with his son, Georg, a specialist in the same medical branch, Fritz also examined how Foreign Minister Walter Rathenau had been assassinated in a 1922 drive-by shooting. Fritz's 1933 memoirs described the incident:

Examining the condition of cloth fibers around the wound, dear Georg, you determined that the shots were fired from the right where the car of the perpetrators must have been. The traces of bullets showed clearly that the first shots were fired when the car was still behind that of the foreign minister, then when both were even, and finally as they passed ahead. Then the perpetrators turned back and threw a bomb into the car, shattering a foot and a hand of the unfortunate man. Even before the official autopsy, I was called to the villa of the deceased, where he had been brought, to analyze the event. I remember the attorney general (*Oberstaatsanwalt*) looking at the villa's décor and saying, "All this luxury doesn't bother me because it's so highly cultivated." Not in accordance with such high culture, the chief of police (*Polizeipräsident*) was chewing on a stubby cigar.[25]

These controversial reports did not ingratiate Fritz with the Prussian police, despite his honors and reputation. In 1926, the Prussian minister for science, art, and education dismissed Fritz, aged sixty-seven, from his position as director of the Institute for Legal Medicine earlier than Fritz had wished. His intended successor, Heinrich Zangger (1874–1957) from Zurich, visited and found that the relationship between the academic institute and the police was a "jungle of conflicting jurisdiction." Students were excluded from seeing autopsies performed, while the police let in lay persons with merely sensationalist curiosity. Strassmann had obtained indispensable resources only by begging for them from case to case in a humiliating fashion.[26] Zangger wrote a report outlining needed improvements for the Berlin institute, but he decided to remain in Zurich. The Berlin authorities pleaded with Fritz to resume direction of the institute in 1927, which he did until retiring two years later.

All his life, the personal code of Fritz Strassmann was one of uncompromising objectivity. He deplored the sensationalism of newspapers that thereby discredited their otherwise liberal editorial policies. He thought they should be cautious about matters that could not be scientifically and legally proven. His memoirs say nothing at all about Judaism, Christianity, assimilation, anti-Semitism, or political ideologies. Fritz's disinterest in converting formally to Christianity before his retirement (unlike his brother Walter and cousin Paul Ferdinand) was never mentioned as delaying any promotion, but perhaps it was a factor. After the death of her father, Gustav Borchardt, a physician who remained faithful to and active in the Jewish community all his life, Fritz allowed his wife Rose to have their sons, Georg and Reinhold, baptized in the 1890s.

Retirement and Restored Recognition

Fritz and his family moved five times during his medical career in Berlin, but they lived for the longest period (1895–1926) at Siegmundshof 18, a one-block street between the westernmost Tiergarten and the Spree River. After that came fourteen last years (1926–1940) in an elegant villa in wooded Zehlendorf at Ahrenshooper Zeile 35. In the autumn of 1933 with the Nazis in power, Fritz, now seventy-five and ailing, concluded his memoirs as follows: "The world of ideas and principles in which I grew up, and to which I held truly as an adult, the world of humane liberalism now lies shattered around me, although, as I confidently expect, not for all time. I can agree with old Attinghausen, who said, 'My time is already buried. Fortunate is he who need not live in the new time.'"[27]

During the years of Nazi power in Germany, Fritz had to fill out the usual forms about his ancestry and memberships. In September 1935, he wrote, among other reports: "I must have been dismissed from the Prussian Association of Medical Officials because my dues were returned to me as having been requested in error. When my dismissal took place was not told to me, so I cannot report a date."[28]

Fritz took comfort in the knowledge that his son Georg, another forensic scholar, and his wife and child had escaped Nazi persecution and were safe in the United States in 1938. When he died at age 81 in January 1940, Fritz still lived with Reinhold at Ahrenshooper Zeile 35. He was buried in the Christian cemetery of the village of Stahnsdorf south of Berlin. No obituary appeared in either newspapers or professional journals.

A Fritz Strassmann Medal has been launched in honor of the hundredth anniversary of Fritz's founding of the German Association for Legal Medicine (Deutsche Gesellschaft für Rechtsmedizin) in 1904. This medal is to be awarded each year for outstanding achievements in the field. The building where the Institut für Rechtsmedizin of the Humboldt University of Berlin was housed, Hannoversche Strasse 6, was renamed the Fritz-Strassmann Haus in 2002. Due to planned reorganizations of institutions of higher education in Berlin, its fate was uncertain five years later.

Chapter 5

Soldiers

Over the last two centuries, Prussia or Germany fought in six major wars, and the Strassmanns were inevitably involved, occasionally as army officers and often with doubts about the justification for combat. Thus, Heinrich remembered the onset of the Danish war of 1864: "Near the end of 1863, another contrived crisis in Schleswig-Holstein was rolled out to stir up emotions. We brothers participated in heated debates at the district club and in open meetings. As liberals, we were deeply suspicious of the ministry of Bismarck and wanted no part of any war launched by Prussia. On December 18, returning home with a heavy heart after one of those meetings, I found military conscription papers on my table. I was to be assistant medical officer in a light field hospital unit of the Sixth Infantry Division. I reported the next day and saw that military trains were already being loaded."[1]

Five years earlier, Heinrich had already had a stint with the Prussian military. In June 1859, Napoleon III sent his army into northern Italy and took Lombardy from Austria with victories at Magenta and Solferino—the high point of his reign. Many feared that further Austrian defeats would embolden the French to invade the Rhineland, so the Prussian army was mobilized. Medical personnel were lacking, and a call for volunteers went out.

Summer vacation had started at the university, and with little else to do, Heinrich volunteered for the apparently defensive cause of Prussia. He was accepted and given money for a horse, equipment, and uniforms for himself and an orderly. He borrowed Wolfgang's old uniform, removed the Holstein insignia, and pinned on Prussian devices. He had bought these, a helmet, and a formidable saber from an antiquarian's shop. "The outfit was hardly dashing," he wrote, "but in those days details did not matter."[2]

Heinrich was assigned to the main field hospital, Nr. V, in Posen, together with forty other young physicians, few of whom had passed their state examinations or had ever before owned hundreds of marks. He recalled:

> We had a jovial time, galloping through Posen, making the streets unsafe, or walking about letting the sabers rattle on the cobblestones, being saluted by enlisted men, and having an orderly at our disposal. It was novel, magnificent, truly overwhelming for us lowly students.
>
> I also took the occasion to visit my parents in nearby Rawitsch for the first time since going to the university in 1855. I still don't know who was more proud, my parents or I, crossing the market square on Sunday as the people streamed from church. I saw my sister in Posen daily, naturally arriving on horseback, my orderly riding behind.

July and August passed that way, and then Emperor Franz Josef and Napoleon III concluded the Peace of Villa Franca, letting the Habsburgs keep Venetia, Tuscany, and Modena, but not Lombardy. The Prussian army was demobilized, and Heinrich returned to Berlin, where he sold his uniform to a junkshop and resumed student life. "But the exalted vacation had smothered my diligence," he noted, "and I did not settle down to a strict routine until October."

Combat in Denmark

As the fabricated Danish crisis developed, Heinrich barely had a week to prepare for departure with the twentieth regiment of the Sixth Brandenburg Infantry Division.

> One may imagine how I had to rush about arranging things, buying equipment for myself and for an orderly, bidding farewell to patients, numerous relatives, and friends, and bringing order into my other affairs.... I bought a splendid half-blooded horse for 600 marks. His previous owner was relieved of a winter's worth of feeding costs. I had to pursue all this late into the night of the twenty-second [of December] and could not dwell on the melancholy aspects of this disruption of my career. Besides, most of us believed it was merely another demonstration, as in 1859, not a real war.
>
> The departure of our unit was scheduled for December 23, 1863, but the special train did not pull out until the early hours of the 24th. It took the entire field hospital, including horses, equipment, and a company of carriers for the wounded, as far as the village of Hagenow in Mecklenburg. Altogether, we were twelve physicians, two regular officers, two pharmacists, four inspectors of various sorts, the company of carriers, male nurses, two women—a cook and a laundress—plus wagon drivers and orderlies. On a road we stretched out a long ways. Because of the many horses, we were always quartered in villages. Now it was Christmas Eve, and everyone felt depressed, especially the married men, until glasses began to clink in the Hagenow Village Inn, reserved for officers. We began to feel like comrades....
>
> On the second of February, as I was writing letters to my parents and brother Ferdinand, a yellow Ulan suddenly rode into camp with immediate marching orders. At great intervals, as we approached Missunde, we heard light detonations, but no one thought a battle had begun. But, to horse! Mine galloped as if he were back in Berlin parks, heading for the Hippodrome, putting me in front. The detonations grew more frequent and louder. Unmistakably, cannons. A strange feeling—war, after fifty years of peace. Now was a time for doing one's duty. We already saw ourselves as heroes, revered and fêted like the freedom fighters of 1813–1815, with Iron Crosses on our chests.
>
> In this spirit we rode as fast as the horses could gallop, then dismounted, opened wagons, and prepared bandages.
>
> "What in hell are you doing here? Do you want the wounded to be hit again? Can't you see the Danes are bombarding our battery? In the name of the devil, go back five hundred yards!" In the same instant, a cannon ball crashed into one of our wagons.
>
> We moved back the five hundred yards, and the orderlies took the horses back even farther, while the carriers moved to the front line.
>
> Soon the first casualty was brought to me on a stretcher. It was Artillery Lieutenant Kipping with a bullet wound slanted through his head. He was dead. His cold hand still gripped a firing schedule. Just the day before, we had joked over a drink. Today the bullet, and tomorrow his cold grave.
>
> Deeply appalled we looked at the corpse. So here was the meaning of war: the sacrifice of young lives. I could bear the pain only by attending the wounded, now arriving in

numbers. In spite of the cold winter day, our faces broke out in sweat with the work of four hundred casualties. Firing ceased after sunset, blood red, and orders came to retreat....

[After the major victory at Düppel], I rode up to the bastion to look around. Blocks of concrete lay in erratic piles next to deep craters. I was scouting for souvenirs, perhaps a bullet, grenade components, anything. Near one of the less demolished ramparts, I saw a boot wedged under rubble. I pulled on it and discovered the bones of a human leg and a foot with its flesh partly decayed, partly dried up. At this gruesome sight, my admiration for the achievements of our artillery changed to horror. I left the site of our glorious victory with feelings rather inappropriate for a soldier of the king....

My last day in uniform was riding along with our victorious army through the Brandenburg Gate down Unter den Linden.[3]

Ten thousand soldiers marched or posted on horses down Unter den Linden to the imperial palace. General Friedrich von Wrangel and Prince Friedrich Karl were followed by regiments identified with Ruppin, Uckermark, Prenzlau, Oderbruch, and other places in Brandenburg. On his uniform Heinrich wore a prestigious medal for valor, the Order of the Red Eagle, with swords for distinction in wartime.

Heinrich did not march off to the wars of 1866 and 1870 that consolidated the power of Prussia and allowed Bismarck to proclaim Wilhelm I as German emperor at Versailles in January 1871. Heinrich was not called up because he had lost his hearing in one ear due to an infection contracted in 1864. He was limited to the care of those wounded who were evacuated from Bohemia and France to lodgings in well-to-do Berlin homes. At the same time, another cholera epidemic broke out in Berlin, and Heinrich volunteered to help in poor districts.

A Doomed Generation

After some forty years of peace but continuing militarization, Germans felt ready to defy any combination of other European states. A generation of young men born in the 1890s was thereby doomed to engage in combat and experience economic upheaval. Among them was Hellmuth Strassmann, born on January 21, 1894, nine months after Paul Ferdinand and Hedwig had honeymooned in Italy. A year and a half later, on July 14, 1895, came Erwin.

In 1894, the Reichstag building, designed by Paul Wallot, was inaugurated, as Kaiser Wilhelm with fanfare put the last stone in place. The city's most respected architect, Ludwig Hoffmann, however, commented: "[T]he result looks like a luxury hearse." In the same year, Gerhart Hauptmann's drama, *Die Weber* (The Weavers), moved from private performances to the Deutsche Theater despite police prohibition of public performances because it "incited class hatred ... through conspicuously one-sided, biased propaganda." The consequence was merely that the Kaiser canceled his subscription to the royal box. In 1895, the Kaiser Wilhelm Memorial Church on the swank Kurfürstendamm was dedicated by the emperor to commemorate the twenty-fifth anniversary of his Prussian grandfather's victory over Napoleon III. Social Democrats showed disrespect at the 1895 ceremony, so some of their organizations were dissolved that year: their meetings were banned, their publications confiscated, and their editors arrested. In the same year, one-fifth of Berlin women were paid cooks and chambermaids, and Max Sladanowsky demonstrated his motion picture invention at the Winter Garden Theatre with a film showing a boxing kangaroo.[4]

In 1902, when Hellmuth was eight years old and Erwin seven, the Strassmanns moved from Platz vor dem Neuen Tor 3 to nearby Alexanderufer 1, an apartment building along the tree-lined quay of the Humboldthafen, above the meeting of the Berlin-Spandau Canal and the Spree River. Tugboats pulled chains of barges through the confluence or anchored them to unload sacks and crates for transfer to horse-drawn wagons. The Alsen Bridge crossed the harbor from the Alexanderufer to the whitewashed Lehrter Bahnhof railway station. Trains from that station would carry Strassmanns bound for vacations, wars, and finally emigration. Just west of the Lehrter Bahnhof stood a curious, round baroque building, the Kolonial Museum or Panorama, containing a mammoth circular painting (115 meters long) of a North German Lloyd liner among tugboats and freighters, gliding past the Statue of Liberty into the glittering harbor of New York—Manhattan. In 1928, the Panorama building was demolished.

The Spree flowed past all this in a great bend, the Spreebogen, a loop well suited for architectural visions. Here Albert Speer cleared away elegant apartments in 1938 to construct Hitler's forum of greater Germany, including a never completed Great Hall, 290 meters high. Less grand, the Berlin Wall was erected in 1961 along the Humboldt harbor and the river, leaving the Spreebogen area an empty grassland except for one inviolable building, the Swiss Consulate. In the 1990s, the terrain became the site of a new architectural vision: the Federal Chancellery, transferred here from Bonn. The turreted and gold-leafed Reichstag building on the east side of the Spreebogen was gutted by the Nazis in February 1933 and sixty years later acquired a simpler glass dome designed by an Englishman, Sir Norman Foster.

At the base of the Spreebogen was the Königsplatz, a former parade ground landscaped into a formal park. In its center was the Victory Column, fifty meters high, decorated with gilded cannons captured in the Danish War of 1864 (but generally believed to be of the later Franco-Prussian War). Berliners called the column "the asparagus." Haughty statues of Bismarck, Field Marshall von Moltke, and War Minister von Roon frowned at the asparagus under its golden Victory Angel. In 1938, they were all transplanted a half-mile westward into the wooded Tiergarten, as if embarrassed by or hiding from Hitler. A new monument, the Soviet War Memorial, has appeared nearby, showing a metallic, solitary but fearless overcoated comrade between two authentic cannons and two tanks. Strassmann children of two generations, supervised by their mothers or nannies, once crossed the Königsplatz daily to play in the Tiergarten woods, respectfully, only on the paths where playing was allowed. Professor Paul Ferdinand Strassmann, however, let his dachshunds run loose, pretending that they had just twisted themselves off to dash away, dragging their leashes.

Two Valedictorians

In photographs Hellmuth looks seriously at the camera, his eyes very blue, like Hedwig's, his hair blond and curly, his height intermediate. His earliest pictures were his father's pencil sketches of him as a baby, followed by photographs of him in long curls and a dress. Then came sailor suits and lederhosen on vacation in the Alps, at the Baltic, or in front of Christmas trees. Hellmuth's expression never hints at the motto he formulated for himself: "Stets der erste zu sein und vorzustreben den andern" (Invariably to be first and outdo the others). With hard work and persistence, Hellmuth excelled at sports and scored highest on examinations among his Friedrichsgymnasium classmates. As was the Prussian custom, he was assigned the first seat of the first row. Like his father did in 1884 at the same gymnasium, Hellmuth graduated as valedictorian, *Primus Omnium*, in the spring of 1912. A teacher characterized him as "imperturbably modest and always friendly."

According to his mother, Erwin was shy as a small boy but then became a mischievous show-off, cavorting and joking with younger sister, Antonie. Although he was a less earnest striver than his brother or father, he also scored best in examinations in school year after year and also graduated first in his class from the Friedrichsgymnasium in the fall of 1913—another *Primus Omnium*.

After the Friedrichsgymnasium, Hellmuth enrolled in the Technical University of Charlottenburg, Berlin, to study machinery design. He joined Arminia, the dueling fraternity of his father; received practical training with the Borsig Corporation, leaders in steam engines; and did his year of military conscription with the Fifth Imperial Prussian Guards, an infantry regiment stationed in Spandau just west of Berlin. Hellmuth did not complete his internship at Borsig because his regiment joined the invasion of Belgium in August 1914, was shifted to Poland within a month, and in 1916 was back in the west for the first Battle of the Somme.

Erwin graduated from the Friedrichsgymnasium a year after Hellmuth in 1913, entered the University of Berlin for medical studies, and completed two semesters in medicine before Archduke Ferdinand was assassinated at Sarajevo in June 1914. Aged nineteen, he volunteered at once for the war, as virtually all students did, but his brother's Fifth Infantry Guards rejected him because of a heart murmur. As a medical orderly with the Red Cross, Erwin then served on freight trains in Belgium, bringing back the wounded from the front. Occasionally, the train stopped and corpses, now silent and still, were lifted off and laid beside the tracks for transport to military cemeteries. This was agonizing duty. Weekend passes to hostile Brussels were no relief.

A Glimpse of Combat

This is how Hellmuth reported an advance and retreat in November 1914 to his university dueling fraternity, Arminia:

> At 2:30 AM we began our march … without difficulty for three or four hours. Then the road went through six kilometers of forest occupied by Siberian sharpshooters.… From time to time, a shot hit someone in our rows.… At dusk in a clearing we encountered a railway embankment said by prisoners to be manned by two regiments with machine guns. We could not worry about that. Only one thing to do. In the twilight we moved on, myself ten paces ahead with revolver in one hand and saber in the other. At any moment I expected barbed wire, exploding mines, or rattling machine guns. Thirty meters before the tracks, we rushed the embankment with deafening "Hurrahs!" and found no one.… That night in two large villages we caught about two hundred Russians, sleeping peacefully.… We had been at it for twenty-two hours, but the main task still lay six kilometers ahead, the town of Brzeziny.… At 3:30 AM, we twelve thousand unloaded our rifles and mounted bayonets on the orders of Lieutenant General Karl Litzmann. We encircled that town and entered quietly.
>
> Altogether, we captured two hundred Cossacks and two hundred fifty infantry soldiers in Brzeziny, as well as the headquarters of a corps.… After marching or fighting for twenty-five hours, I was happy to stretch out on a leather sofa. They woke me after twenty minutes: "Regimental orders, have your company fall in. Russians have sprung a trap and are on our heels." Now we had to attack through the same terrain as the previous night, but in the opposite direction. We took another six thousand prisoners, and during the next night all our baggage and cannons followed. None fell to the enemy. This retreat was the greatest achievement in which I participated.[5]

For moving in and out that way, General Karl Litzmann earned the title, "Lion of Brzeziny," and received the highest decoration, the *Pour le Mérite*, from the Kaiser. Litzmann was sixty-four years old in 1914 and incredibly had already won an Iron Cross in the Franco-Prussian War of 1870–1871. In his dotage, Litzmann was the oldest member of the Nazi Party, and when he died at age 87 in 1936, Wilhelm Frick, the Nazi minister of the interior, sent a telegram: "As a leader of German soldiers in the world war and as a fighter for Adolf Hitler, our old Party comrade, General Litzmann, served the German people passionately, and his simple loyalty became a model for many."[6]

During World War II, the Nazis renamed the Polish city of Lodz "Litzmannstadt." About one-third of the population—220,000 people—were Jewish, fewer than in Warsaw but more than in Berlin. They did hard labor at starvation wages in local factories or were deported to Chelmno or Auschwitz. Only 887 Jews had survived in the ghetto when the Soviet army arrived in 1944. The Poles renamed the city "Lodz."

A Bullet Ends All

On July 1, 1916, a British-French army launched the Battle of the Somme with an attack northeast of Amiens, partly to take pressure off the fortress of Verdun, which was under siege farther toward the southeast. Over the next five months, three million men from both sides fought along the Somme, and more than a third were killed, wounded, or captured. As a result, the Allied front bulged only seven extra miles eastward for a gain of two hundred square miles of French territory. The British concluded that the main benefit of the battle was training for the rest of the war. They learned how the Germans fought, and they introduced a novelty, tanks. Allied casualties were 750,000, while the Germans lost 500,000, plus 80,000 taken as prisoners.

At the center of the Allied front along the Albert-Bapaume road were a British Midland division and an Australian division. Records of the Fifth Guards for November 5 state:

> Great battle. At night English artillery launches a strong bombardment of our trenches and beyond.... At 9:30 AM Australians attack in three close waves, followed by columns. Our machine guns suffer heavy losses, so that defense depends on sharpshooters. Storming Australians penetrate with 150 men into the 10th Company and with 40 men into the 11th. They also position machine guns.... Since the 11th Company has heavy losses, the entire 9th Company is pulled forward. Their brave, often tested commander, Lieutenant Strassmann, falls.... At night an encircling trench is dug around the nest of Australians. Heavy enemy losses! The Fifth has 79 killed, 111 wounded, of whom 10 died later.

Ten days later, on November 16, Erwin Strassmann as an aviation officer came to Beugny and heard more from Hellmuth's companions. He wrote home:

> When [enemy] soldiers jumped out of their trenches in front of Hellmuth's sector, they received such fire that they had to take cover in open terrain. From there they occasionally shot back. Throughout that time, Hellmuth watched across the ramparts. Then came the bullet straight through his helmet and skull. Without a word he sank into the arms of his messenger and had the shortest, best possible soldier's death. They brought his body here to Beugny, 6 kilometers east of Bapaume, and buried him in the German military cemetery.... Do not weep.... The myriad of crosses in enemy territory will be the basis of our people's peace and future.... Today at the cemetery, in the midst of all these emotions,

I nevertheless smiled. Hellmuth's grave is first in the first row. Even here he is true to his principle, "to be invariably first, to outdo the others."

In writing this now, I am reminded of the scene in Erich Maria Remarque's *All Quiet on the Western Front,* where Paul, on leave, falsely tells Kemmerich's mother that her son died a painless death: "I tell her that he had a bullet in the heart and was dead at once … he felt nothing. His face was calm.… She moans and cries. I should tell her how it really was, she says, and I invent a story that I now almost believe myself."

Erwin did not quite have his brother's feelings about the war. In the same letter of November 16, he wrote:

> Today in my balloon I floated above Hellmuth's grave, above the trenches where he fell, where comrades fall steadily, and above the enemy. Seeing it all makes one doubly conscious of one's duty. This may now be the best place for me.
>
> Here in the continuous thunder of the battles it is some consolation to know that he is outside, where grenades no longer annoy, for without interruption the murdering goes on.… Here life and death are a community separated by no barrier. I wish you could picture the rows and rows of graves that are being dug, and the numbers daily laid in them.… I wish you could also see the survivors of the Fifth Guards who head back to the trenches in the evening. They are such quiet transfigured boys with a peaceful, otherworldly infinity glowing in their eyes. They come and visit their fallen comrades one more time. It restores them to stop at one cross or another and to speak of him who lies below. The thought of soon joining them confers a quiet bliss, for they long for sleep. But we have to keep awake! Eyes open! Look ahead to survive attacks.[7]

On the day of that letter, November 16, the Australian pocket was finally wiped out while freezing rains turned the land into cold, muddy slime. According to the daily report: "Digging now useless." The British across no man's land likewise reported that "King Mud has commanded an armistice." During the past month, the Fifth had lost 141 men, including 6 officers.

On the first Sunday of Advent, December 1916, Erwin answered his mother's letter about Hellmuth's death, admiring her composure. He added: "Just how is it possible that humanity should succumb to such insanity, this ghastly murdering of one another by the thousands? And that has gone on for months, years!… Leaving [Hellmuth] that day, I had an awful premonition and felt the sun had vanished, and the world was dark and cold." In an earlier letter about that meeting with Hellmuth at the front, Erwin had quoted his brother's comments about the chance of a fatal bullet or grenade: "Any such end can't be the worst. Look, so far my life has been undisturbed and full of joy. It was a steady ascent, and now the war is its high point, sure to be followed by decline. I'm sure I'll accomplish something after the war, no matter what I do. But it will never come up to who I am and what I am achieving here at the front." Hellmuth's obituary in the Berlin papers began with his Iron Cross, listed his family as survivors, and in closing stated: "May those who loved him not mourn but confidently join us in the hope that this sacrifice will be another blessing for our Fatherland."

The Fifth Imperial Prussian Guards returned to Berlin on December 11, 1918, exactly a month after the armistice, and marched through the Brandenburg Gate down Unter den Linden. A newspaper, the *Deutsche Abend Zeitung*, the next day noted that many marching officers wore *Pour le Mérite* medals. Killed in battle had been 4,085 soldiers of the regiment, including 79 officers. Within a month, some surviving officers led the street fighting against the Marxist Spartacus uprising in central Berlin. Their brutality matched anything in German history. Even after the fighting on March 11, 1919, they lured two hundred fifty unarmed sailors who had sympathized with the uprising into the courtyard behind Französische Strasse 32. Lieutenant Otto Merloh of the Freikorps had promised them back pay. Instead, twenty-eight of them were executed. Seven were identified in the official morgue as having been massacred.[8]

When Paul Ferdinand had to sell his clinic and move to the Dahlem suburb of Berlin, the statue of Hellmuth came along and was set up among palms in the winter garden of the new house. Eventually, it was moved to the Strassmann grave in Wannsee, where it seemed to peer across the cemetery wall near the Saint Andreas Church. Neighbors on the other side of the Linden Strasse objected to the steady, wary gaze of Hellmuth's militarist and anachronistic visage. Its removal from a grave designated as "honorary" was impossible, but a solution had to be found. A substantial hole was dug, and the statue was sunk into it, low enough to put the steel-helmeted head below the top of the wall. I last saw it there in 2006, just like that.

A Combat Observer in Balloons

With his heart murmur reappraised as negligible, Erwin became a soldier in the new air force. As an artillery observer from late 1915 to 1918, he floated 487 times in baskets hanging from balloons to observe French and English trenches from on high and to report the accuracy of German artillery. He could observe action within a sixty-mile radius and correct faulty shelling with a telephone call via miles of cables to the ground or with carrier pigeons. Erwin was promoted to First Lieutenant in 1917 and was awarded the Iron Cross, Second and First Class.

Erwin's enthusiasm for the war was less than that of Hellmuth, as is reflected in his letters about his brother's death. Anticipating a French offensive across the Aisne River in April 1917, Erwin wrote:

> To sing "the Month of May has come"
> Is joyous after winter's thaw;
> But by then we'll be overcome
> And lie in coffins packed with straw.

A letter home on June 9, 1918, showed that some optimism was restored by early German successes in the second Battle of the Marne. It was General Ludendorff's third and last attempt in the spring of 1918 to defeat the French and British before millions of American soldiers arrived.

> Our balloons, three kilometers behind the front, were equipped with new wires and ample messenger pigeons.... Hundreds of our photographs were distributed to the troops, so that everyone knew not just from maps where to attack.... On May 26, all troops moved into the farthest front lines, and suddenly the battle was on. The balloons rose half an hour after midnight while all remained quiet. At 2 AM, the artillery barrage broke loose. All things up to fifteen kilometers behind the enemy's front—road intersections, villages, camps, airports, gun emplacements, and trenches—were to be devastated with explosions and paralyzing gas.... Paris is the goal of these preparations and receives a "praline" every few minutes from Big Bertha. At dawn, shortly after 4:30 AM, our infantry moved out while the artillery continued, setting off explosions ahead of the troops. The front line was overrun.

Hardly any combat took place. Enemy artillery emplacements and troops were soon in our hands: the front was broken....

Here on the right flank we swung around to maintain contact with the immobile western line, and remain north of the Aisne, while the middle corps from the Ailette moved across the Chemin des Dames and the Aisne, making a north-south salient.... Enemy artillery shooting from the flanks bothered our advance, as did their rapidly mobilized reserves. Our brave Brandenburg infantry regiments had to leave fallen comrades behind.... Our balloons followed a few kilometers behind the infantry, keeping their staff officers informed. Thus, galloping enemy cavalry and treacherous machine guns quickly received effective fire, reducing our losses. The weather was so favorable that balloons could hang in the sky from dawn to dusk, earning thanks from those below. The enemy also noted the effectiveness of balloon observation and set their fighter planes on us. A row of balloons was shot down, but with few exceptions our parachutes saved the baskets' occupants. Every balloon shot down was replaced within a few hours by another hanging in the sky. Soon we were so far forward that even enemy machine guns could shoot at the balloons.

Soissons fell, although the enemy remained in the southern outskirts. Under flaming roofs, wine cellars were meanwhile plundered, slaking the thirst of many a warrior. Droves of prisoners streamed back from the fighting almost unguarded. Now the battle is west of the city, and the infantry is again digging into trenches.... Being early, we commandeered three villas that had been least damaged by infantry passing through. It took hours to put the houses in order, but with furniture, beds, and dishes, we live like nobility. Most appreciated are the splendid gardens with vegetables of all types. But I hope we move on soon. Warm greetings and thanks for Mother's cookies.

The Defeat

The German army did indeed move on for another sixty kilometers, taking fifty thousand prisoners in the most rapid advance of the entire war. On May 30, they reached the Marne River for the first time since 1914 and occupied Château Thierry. But here and at Rheims the attack bogged down. On July 18, the army of French Marshal Ferdinand Foch, supreme commander of the Allied forces, counterattacked. In their first major engagement, American troops dislodged the Germans from Château Thierry. A million Americans had arrived in France by now and were overrunning the Germans from Cantigny to St. Mihiel, positions once thought impregnable. After two weeks, the Germans were thrown back across the Aisne River, where the offensive had started. Ludendorff's army could not attack again. With the war lost and revolution seething in Berlin, Kaiser Wilhelm finally abdicated on November 9 and fled to Holland. The armistice was signed two days later. Since rebellion was underway throughout Germany, the retreat of the army from France was delegated by generals Hindenburg and Groener to elected councils of soldiers. Enlisted men were usually chosen, but Erwin's unit of balloons elected him, a lieutenant, to their *Soldatenrat*. He saw to it that during their retreat through Westphalia and other German provinces, his men slept not in stables, like troops of other regiments, but in the guest rooms of inns. In one village, he told me later, a baker's daughter offered tender consolation for the lost war.

On December 20, 1918, Erwin's battalion of balloons was back in Berlin, and his discharge papers were signed, not by officers, but by the enlisted men now in charge, members of the *Soldatenrat* in Reinickendorf. Meanwhile, sailors of the imperial navy had captured the royal palace and held Berlin's commander as a hostage. Other revolutionaries later occupied the telegraph office and a variety of publishing houses and newspapers. The aim of this "Spartacus rebellion" of Communists, led by Karl Liebknecht and Rosa Luxemburg, was to forestall the election of a constitutional convention set for late January. On January 5, 1919, they called for a general strike to establish a "dictatorship of the proletariat" in place of the provisional socialist government of Friedrich Ebert.

Near the Schumannstrasse clinic, soldiers set up machine guns and barricades of barbed wire to protect not the hospital or the Deutsche Theater but the barracks across the street. Erwin took his steel helmet, uniform, and pistol and joined the volunteer company, Oranien, of the Reinhard Brigade. Reinhard had been a major in Hellmuth's Fifth Infantry Guards. In later life, Erwin recalled riding toward the shooting at the Belle-Alliance (Waterloo) Platz in freezing streetcars occupied by couples in tuxedos, evening gowns, and furs, headed for the opera or concerts. Among the performances was Beethoven's *Egmont*.

After a week, the rebellion was defeated by some four thousand returning soldiers volunteering in these Freikorps units haphazardly led by the civilian, Gustav Noske, the provisional Social Democratic minister of defense. On January 15, Rosa Luxemburg was arrested, clubbed to death, and thrown into a canal. In the Tiergarten, Karl Liebknecht was shot in the back after surrendering. Fritz Strassmann's official autopsies showed how these murders took place. Thus began the Weimar Republic.

That January, Erwin, now twenty-three, wrote in a guestbook:

> By starving and outnumbering us,
> the enemy has won the day.
> How we would have laughed at him,
> had victory come our way.
>
> Now disappointed and half-crazed,
> we tear ourselves apart.
> Hope is gone and all are dazed;
> Gone from our sky is the last star.
>
> So here I come to visit you,
> shattered by war, we falter.
> But friendship is a granite rock
> that storms and floods can't alter.

Chapter 6

Stage and Sky: Antonie I

Whoever knew Antonie was certain to have found her enchanting, for she concentrated on her present companion—whether lover, relative, or friend—affectionately and intensely. Neither superficial nor deeply intellectual, she immersed herself in the project of the moment in an invariably sporty and zestful way. Fame in acting, sports, and aviation came her way in the 1920s. She had a temper and could scold with ironic slang, but usually she was quick and witty without being contentious, ambitious but not inconsiderate. It was a joy to be with her.

Does Antonie fit into the Strassmann story of frustrated assimilation? Perhaps she illustrates its very opposite by assimilating successfully over and over again—first into the exclusive world of theatre folk, then the international circle of aviators with their cherished novelties, and after that the wheeling-dealing negotiating of business—and by finally making her wisecracking Berlin celebrity self into a cosmopolitan, seemingly "dyed in the wool" New Yorker. Could only she have done it, being somehow a unique woman? Or does her case warn us against oversimplified generalizations about insiders rebuffing outsiders? Let the events of her life speak for themselves.

To the Stage

Antonie Strassmann was born on April 14, 1901, the youngest and most flamboyant of the four children of Paul Ferdinand and Hedwig Strassmann of Berlin. That a Strassmann daughter would think of an acting career is hardly surprising. Berlin's best stage, Max Reinhardt's Deutsches Theater was a few doors to the east, and the Lessing Theater under Viktor Barnowsky was about a block to the west. Antonie saw Friedrich Hebbel's play, *Judith und Holofernes*, during the war in 1915, and later she recalled: "After that evening I … had only one wish, to be an actress, and at least once in my life to play Judith opposite Paul Wegener. My parents said I was insane. If I merely said the word 'theatre,' a torrent of hard words engulfed me and disarmed me. But I tore myself away, took lessons, and appeared on the stage."

Aged sixteen, Antonie was bored with gymnasium studies and believed that waiting three more years would be fatal for a stage career. The actress Maria Frei, whom she had seen as Judith, was a family acquaintance, and Antonie wrote and telegraphed her for advice about approaching the Deutsches Theater for training. As a result, she had a meeting with the actor, Eduard von Winterstein. Born in 1871, von Winterstein was now forty-six. In 1905, Reinhardt had founded an acting school for his theatre and used von Winterstein as one of the instructors and also as Iago opposite Paul Wegener as Othello. Lessons were supposed to be two hours long, beginning at 4 PM, but could last five to six hours if von Winterstein was not performing that evening. The focus of his teaching was that a student should not merely "learn a role, a scene, or … recite a speech more or less well, but should *live* the part. *Living* alone is the core of acting, truly living the part, not just imagining and pretending. He should not *act* angry, but *be* angry!… Acting angry only strains the voice, but being angry strains the heart.… All acting depends on the heart, not the voice."[1]

Antonie wrote to Erwin, who was on duty in France, about her meeting with the celebrated actor on December 5, 1917. She had recited the "Call to Arms," by Joan of Arc from Schiller's play, and the rather melodramatic prayer to God in Act 3 of *Judith*. When she finished, von Winterstein stood next to her and said: "I am happy to have heard you, and I now realize that I can only encourage you." In twenty further minutes of discussion, he agreed that delaying her training for another three years until she had her Abitur and was nineteen would indeed be too late. Antonie told him she could not bear that anyway. That evening she broke the news to her parents, and the next day she wrote to Erwin:

> Erwin, my happiness hangs in the balance.… No one can stand in the way of another's career. I believe it's asking too much if I ask for your support. All I want is to end school at Easter and to study elocution. I beg you, Erwin, don't make it harder for me. It pains me enough to let them know.
>
> Forgive the confusion of this letter, but it's understandable when I feel so disturbed. I hope you know what I mean, nevertheless. I don't want your help, just don't oppose me and make things harder. You know how much Father will rely on you. But you also know that I cannot be held back.… I have risked much and am prepared to risk more.

Paul was, of course, entirely against these plans. He told Antonie that he would do everything to stop her. Not yet seventeen, she had to conform to his will. When she told him it was her life, not his, "he became quite vehement and said I had to live the way they wanted and they were absolutely against it."[2] Antonie thought the opposition was so intense because her father already feared it was in vain. She was relieved that at least attending the theatre was not forbidden to her: "After all, I learn the most there."

The day before, on December 12, 1917, Paul had indeed written to Erwin:

> Surprise: Antonie plans to study acting and has talked to von Winterstein and Berthold Held! I respect her energy! But—I don't see the stage as a goal in life for any of my children, and now a daughter is turning toward that. She recited a poem for us, then Saint Joan, and Judith with feeling but a voice that has never been quite right.… I don't rate the occupation of acting as dignified.… I gave no veto but said clearly that this path suits neither Mother's nor my wishes. Shall I pave the way for a 16-year-old? I have fewer reservations against oratory and elocution than against acting. But that's just the first step! Tell me frankly what you think. You are old enough to know what is at stake! How few women [can have such a career] and still manage their full-time roles as happy women and mothers.

Erwin, however, supported Antonie, and Paul gave up. Antonie reported that he had said to their mother: "You led [Antonie] in that direction, so now you can lead her back." But Hedwig answered that her family had the tradition of never making anyone a martyr.

So for Christmas they gave her luggage and tickets to twelve lectures at the Deutsches Theater. Antonie concluded: "Things are going smoothly, almost too smoothly." She remembered reciting in front of von Winterstein: "As I stood there, cause and consequence were suddenly clear! Now all depended on me alone. I felt for the first time: I'm alive! That awareness made me strong and happy, joyously ready for every battle!… It's beautiful to be so young and enthusiastic!"

The Beginning of a Career

Antonie's first professional role over a year later was Puck in *A Midsummer Night's Dream*. This play was Reinhardt's personal favorite since he thought it completely embodied all aspects of theatre. Later in 1919 came a contract in Stolp, Pomerania, in *Die Fledermaus*, although Antonie was no singer. Her next play, in the Berlin suburb of Steglitz, was Moreto's *Donna Diana*, about a princess who defies and then succumbs to love, somewhat like *Much Ado About Nothing*. One critic thought that the sparkling dialogue called for greater freedom from earthly cares than Antonie conveyed. Another wrote: "Still young but already mature, she has a tragic voice that is alien to comedy. But she captivated me with her artistic self-assurance and competence."

Her first great success came in the city of Magdeburg, west of Berlin, as Maria Stuart in Schiller's play about the Queen of Scots. Performances began on May 5, 1920, and Goethe's *Iphigenie auf Tauris* followed in repertoire. A reviewer wrote: "Antonie Strassmann's voice did full justice to a most human Iphigenie, seeking Greece with her soul, yet a virgin priestess. She seemed released from earthly cares by the transcendental visions of Goethe's verses, an artist who used her own experience and intense study to absorb the spirit of this poetry. No wonder that the other actors were swept along by her self-assured and perfect expression."

Now nineteen years old, Antonie had the great chance to compete for the role of Judith opposite Paul Wegener, aged forty-six. She won. Opening night was Tuesday, January 4, 1921, in Magdeburg, after hardly any rehearsal before Christmas.

Nearly the End of a Career

During these months in Magdeburg, Antonie fell in love with a tenor at the local opera, who rejected her when he learned she was not a virgin. On Saturday, January 12, 1921, Antonie in despair went into a city park and shot herself. How she obtained a pistol is unknown. The bullet hit a rib and moved around to her back, where it remained all her life. Neither heart nor lungs were hit. A guard in the park had noticed the distraught young woman, heard the shot, and called the fire department. An old man guarded her until the firemen came and took her to a hospital. Antonie had left a letter to her parents and a last will in her room. I have no copies.

Paul, Hedwig, and sister Gisela, a trained nurse, came at once from Berlin. Paul wrote to Erwin at Freiburg University in Baden on January 13:

> This time no theatrical performance brought us here. Antonie is unfortunately in a hospital but in satisfactory condition. She turned a weapon against herself…. We came fearing the worst and without hope…. X-rays tomorrow. We met Dr. Eilman's wife at the station, and she relieved our hearts in a small way with news about the favorable prospects for the

injury.... The doctor said that A. did it because she could not face having lied to someone. Only now have we learned what you have known all along ... the exertion of being on the stage with Wegener and an "unhappy" love affair.... For me, she is now my sick child.... I hope to write to you more comprehensively on Thursday. Events and sorrows, body and soul are now in action. At least we are not without hope. It is painfully disturbing that the career of an artist and daughter has led to this. Your presence here is not sought or needed. You will get a daily letter and, if need be, a telegram. Berlin is told pneumonia and influenza.

Starting Over

After convalescing in Berlin, Antonie looked for new theatrical roles. A possible contract with the State Theater of Stuttgart seemed promising, and a decision was expected in early May. Now twenty years old, she was still set on her career but was uncertain about making it acceptable to the family. On April 26, 1921, she wrote to them from Baden Baden.

> Still no news from Stuttgart, and I pass my days with steady hoping. Tomorrow will be the fifth day since being there, and they promised a decision in five or six days. So tomorrow a rising anxiety will creep in....
> Vis-à-vis you, I have many thoughts. But a "Father, I have sinned" is always hard to put on paper, especially since I will not return to the parental home but will keep on my own path.... Of course, it pains me to have lost your confidence in various ways. That's bitter—especially for you but also for me. Don't think that I can carry on without your trust, just like that. I have the determination and hope to reach a high level of humanity and artistry, but it will be a struggle. I learned what my goal is, not because of philosophy, ethics, and calm inner growth, but because of human and artistic needs and deep experiences, happy and unhappy....
> Bear with me, despite all the bitter things I did to you and to myself, a poor return for your love, until I find myself and your love again—like Peer Gynt—and will then remain ever the same.
> The caring hands of parents cannot clear rocks and menacing obstacles to life out of the way. I have to do it myself and am glad of it.... My effort will not be lacking. And if I have lost it, I will thereby recover your trust!

The telegram from Stuttgart came with good news, and before the end of the year, Antonie appeared in minor roles in Goethe's *Götz von Berlichingen* and Schiller's *Jungfrau von Orleans*. Other small roles followed the next year in *Faust*, parts one and two. Then came major roles as the Amazon, Penthesilea, in Kleist's play by that name, and as Lady Macbeth. A reviewer said: "Above all, Fräulein Strassmann should be singled out as a Lady Macbeth with everything demonic in the character, especially the horrible grandeur of the mad scene. Straying through the night, arms stretched out, holding a lamp, she was somehow grisly and mythological."

The First Willy

A Stuttgart romance began with a handsome curtain manufacturer, Willy Joseph, and was followed by marriage in Berlin on January 25, 1923, barely two weeks after brother Erwin's wedding. Willy was thirty, a veteran of the war, and Antonie was twenty-one.

Erwin was the first to hear about Antonie's engagement, as recorded in a letter penciled on a November evening:

My dear Friend and Brother!

As a sign of our ancient and close friendship, be the *first* to know: I am engaged! Yes, my little one, that's life! To my profession, to celebrity, to everything else, farewell!

I love Willy so much with all my heart, and since June I have weighed everything that might disturb our marriage in later years, and all that will be sacrificed for *him* in advance! I am aware that true mutuality makes one human and that together we can build our own world!...

I know *what* I'm giving up. But I also know for *whom* and *why*! I am so filled with happiness that I keep smiling and thinking, is this reality? Oh, such inner peace! Actually nothing has changed, except that being together is suddenly a mission for eternity!

Please prepare the parents for what is coming, perhaps *not mentioning* this letter and its contents!

But no pregnancy came from this paradise at Kanonenweg Nr. 4, Stuttgart, and Antonie, aged twenty-two, was restless. Her brother Erwin's wife, Ilse, was expecting a baby within months of their wedding (although it was stillborn), and another came in November 1924. Her sister Gisela delivered her second in September 1923. Paul Ferdinand demanded that Willy have his semen checked in a laboratory and apologized when the sperm count proved to be adequate. Eager to have children but frustrated, Antonie told me once:

I didn't mind darning socks, cooking preserves, and washing dishes. One could go out in the evenings. But in April 1925, we traveled to America, and only business and curtain factories interested Willy. I had to drag him to Chicago, Washington, and Niagara Falls. Then on the way back in London, he just cared about Wimbledon and shops, not Buckingham Palace, Westminster Abbey, and the Tower. But Paris really was the end of our marriage. He was just interested in the Champs Elysées and the night life. I had to go to Versailles, the Louvre, and Notre Dame alone. Then I knew I could build no marriage on that.

I met him at his peak—a cavalry officer, attorney, and factory owner—well-read and good-looking. I thought he would develop further, but he was finished, self-satisfied, and that did not suit me for the long run.

Willy suggested that Antonie should go back on the stage, since he had to travel more than ever. Antonie told him that she had quit the stage for him once, and now he was asking her to go back. She would not quit a second time. Willy agreed, but when Antonie scored a major success as Joan of Arc, he became jealous and demanded that she retire after all. In 1949, she could act out the scene that followed:

Willy: "Perhaps you don't mind if I talk to your father about a divorce?"
Antonie: "No, not at all. I think it might be very intelligent of you."

Willy began to sob, but Antonie arranged the divorce anyway, returned to the stage, and became involved for a year with the former crown prince, Wilhelm von Hohenzollern.

The Next Willy

Gerhard Masur recalled that what Antonie called her "Crown Prince Year" was reported in all the scandal sheets. The prince sent her poetry that he had composed. One twenty-four-line poem was titled "Die Stunde vor Tag" (The Hour before Dawn) and came with a warm dedication referring to the room in a little house that had inspired it. The first verse reads:

Awake not! Thoughts are ready,
like hungry dogs to ambush you,

when you stir. They're all around you;
hatred against you flashes in them all.

After a year, Antonie dropped the prince in favor of the actor Rudolf Forster (1890–1968), now best remembered as Mac the Knife in the film version of Brecht and Weill's *The Threepenny Opera*. Right-wing radicals had earlier thrown stink bombs into a theatre where he played in Arthur Schnitzler's *Reigen*, known in the United States as *La Ronde*. After seeing him as the King of France in Shaw's *Saint Joan*, the drama critic of the *Berliner Tageblatt*, Fred Hildenbrandt, wrote: "Rudolf Forster conclusively proved himself one of the greatest actors of our generation.... [Later] I caught on why this actor ... had such a bewitching effect on women. In no way was he enticing, nor charming, nor bubbly, nor witty, nor temperamental, nor aggressive, nor even especially polite or pleasant, and never forthcoming. He made no effort. He remained uniformly calm, serious and alert, yet somehow distant, morose, and distracted although wide awake. And extraordinarily virile."[3]

For the rest of his life, however, the Crown Prince wrote occasional letters and sent photographs. He regretted not having seen Antonie on her final visit to Germany in 1936, and he wrote about it in a "charming and faithful" way, she told me. He also sent books about himself, including his memoirs with a penciled dedication to Antonie: "Youth and beauty fade, passion vanishes, but true, deep friendship outlasts all fateful rolls of the dice."

At one point, Wilhelm donned a swastika and tried to cooperate with the Nazis. But they never trusted him, so he went his own way. In one letter to Antonie, he wrote, mixing metaphors, "in every respect the outstanding characteristic of this century is the way life and death, the cheerful and the bitter march oddly next to one another at lightning speed into a grinding mill (*Zwickmühle*) that makes one's hair stand on end, raising one's hat" (May 25, 1937). Without hostility, Antonie always referred to him as "her little Willy of Potsdam."

A Changing Berlin Stage

In the mid-1920s, some German expressionist playwrights were still creating strident plays to stir the masses, but against this came a new vogue for realistic objectivity, called *Neue Sachlichkeit*. Then the public shifted its interest to easy entertainment and revues. Some dramatists, like Bertold Brecht, hardly compromised with these changing tastes, but others, including Georg Kaiser, Paul Kornfeld, Walter Hasenclever, and Carl Zuckmayer, now wrote light comedies.

Neither the experimental theatre of protest nor featherweight comedies suited Antonie. She was best at portraying rather exotic but powerful women in classic dramas, such as Desdemona in *Othello*. Among her roles from 1926 on were two at Jessner's Staatstheater: Salomé in Hebbel's *Herodes and Mariamne*; and Sittah, the Sultan's sister, in Lessing's *Nathan der Weise* (Nathan the Wise Jew). She also played Hippolyta, Queen of the Amazons in *A Midsummer Night's Dream* at the Bülowplatz; and Joan of Arc in Schiller's *Jungfrau von Orleans* at the Schiller Theater. She had roles in two films, in some radio dramas, and in plays by Heinrich Kleist, Georg Kaiser, Hermann Sudermann, Carl Sternheim, George Bernard Shaw, and more by Shakespeare.

On Tour

In 1928, Antonie joined Paul Wegener's ensemble and toured Germany and Eastern Europe with them for two years. She told reporters:

> Wegener is … a friend like no other. He is good, gentle, imaginative, and astonishingly magnanimous with suggestions, money, and soul. He is a great actor, but his humanity overshadows his art. On the road, when time drags on drearily, he has stories to cheer us to the point of hysterical laughter.
>
> One has to live life with intensity: feel it in all pores. One has to relish all joys and laugh at all stupidities and enjoy oneself forever.

Paul Wegener was present at that interview on April 8, 1928, and said: "Look at this woman, not just a first-class actress, but Germany's pride as a pioneering aviatrix. What a splendid woman, a true comrade, a delicious partner. Antonie Strassmann will always be my ideal of an energetic, sporty, working woman."

Reviews of Antonie's acting until 1930 remained awestruck and adoring, at least those that survived in her scrapbook. In Berlin, as Hippolyta, Queen of the Amazons in *A Midsummer Night's Dream* (1926), she was "noble and refined in bearing, performance, and language," according to one critic, and "most worldly and modern like a tennis champion," according to another.

Partial List of Antonie's Roles

Playwright	Drama	Role	Place and Year
Friedrich Schiller	*Maria Stuart*	Maria	Magdeburg 1920
J. W. von Goethe	*Iphigenie auf Taurus*	Iphigenie	Magdeburg 1920
Friedrich Hebbel	*Judith und Holofernes*	Judith	Magdeburg 1921
G. Engelke	*Die Kugel*	Various roles	Magdeburg 1921
M. Moreto	*Donna Diana*	Diana	Berlin 1921
J. W. von Goethe	*Götz von Berlichingen*	Helfensteinerin	Stuttgart 1921
Friedrich Schiller	*Die Jungfrau von Orleans*	Queen Isabeau	Stuttgart 1921
Heinrich Kleist	*Penthesilea*	Penthesilea	Stuttgart 1922
J. W. von Goethe	*Faust I*	Evil Spirit	Stuttgart 1922
J. W. von Goethe	*Faust II*	Five roles	Stuttgart 1922
William Shakespeare	*Macbeth*	Lady Macbeth	Stuttgart 1922
G. Kaiser	*Zweimal Oliver*	Colleague	Berlin 1926
Friedrich Hebbel	*Herodes und Marianne*	Salomé	Berlin 1926
Gottfried Lessing	*Nathan der Weise*	Sittah	Berlin 1926
William Shakespeare	*Midsummer Night's Dream*	Hippolyta	Berlin 1927
Friedrich Schiller	*Die Jungfrau von Orleans*	Saint Joan	Berlin 1927
Heinrich Sudermann	*Stein unter Steinen*	Lore	Berlin 1927
Heinrich Kleist	*Käthchen von Heilbronn*	Kunigunde	Berlin 1927
T. van de Velde	*Die Ehe* (A Marriage)	Wife	Film, 1929
L. Stein	*Scheidungsreise*	Trude	Berlin 1929
G. B. Shaw	*Saint Joan*	Saint Joan	Stolp 1929
Gottfried Lessing	*Minna von Barnhelm*	Minna	Stolp 1929
William Shakespeare	*Merchant of Venice*	Portia	Stolp 1929
C. Sternheim	*Der Snob*	Sybill	Frankfurt 1929
S. Guitry	*Jacqueline*	Mme. Villeroye	Tour 1928, 1930
L. Andrejew	*Der Gedanke*	Tatjana	Tour 1928, 1930
A. Strindberg	*Ghost Sonata*	Alice	Berlin, tour 1930
A. Strindberg	*The Father*	Laura	Berlin, tour 1930
Friedrich Schiller	*Kabale und Liebe*	Lady Milford	Chicago 1930

In Strindberg's *The Father*, an authoritarian but brilliant cavalry captain has become a scientist obsessed with the future. The captain opposes his wife's ambition to bring their daughter up as a painter. He wants her to move in with distant friends to train as a teacher. The conflict escalates until Laura, the wife, ridicules his assumption that he is actually the child's father and destroys him. A critic in Bonn found that Antonie as Laura was "a total Strindberg woman, a python, wild and dangerous, but too slippery to be captured. She insists on victory, this feline. A mother's love turns into a triumphal scream." In Frankfurt, another wrote: "Fräulein Strassmann is razor-sharp as Laura. A slim, controlled appearance, slowly turning her profile with a murderous cold glance, cutting with words, testing the reaction, a Satan in ambush." The critic in Aachen said he calmed down with difficulty after the play: "Such hours with Strindberg—and Wegener! And what a Laura!… Is this Laura still human, a woman with soul and dignity?"

Antonie's formal acting career ended in the winter of 1930, partly because the economic depression was closing theatres in Berlin and partly because her interest in aviation had become paramount and brought her to the United States in March 1930. We now go back to the beginning of that interest in 1925.

Sports: Medals and Records

Actually, an interest in sports came before aviation. In interviews, Antonie always traced that interest to family vacations on the shore or in the mountains, with swimming and climbing, skating and skiing. But athletics became her major obsession after the separation and divorce from Willy Joseph. She trained intensely to receive first the bronze and then the silver Deutsche Turn- und Sportabzeichen medals of distinctive athletic achievement. To qualify in mid-1927, she swam 200 meters in 4.58 minutes, cleared 1.15 meters in the high jump, ran 100 meters in 15 seconds, threw a five kilo shot put 6.63 meters, and cycled 20 kilometers in 43 minutes and 42 seconds, a world record for women. Six years later, aged 32, her performance remained comparable—for example, cycling the 20 kilometers in 48 minutes and 43 seconds. Cycling was her main passion, and for that she trained with Walter Rütt at the cycling tracks in the wooded Grunewald outskirts of Berlin. She claimed that during those years, no six-day bike race by men ever happened without her being enthusiastically and loyally at her place. I have some ancient home movies of young Antonie at an empty stadium, high jumping, shot-putting, and running, her tousled hair blowing in the wind.

Into the Clouds

Erwin and a cousin took Antonie on her first flight in a basket hanging from a yellow canvas balloon at dawn in May 1925. During the war, Erwin had been an artillery observer in balloons, and the experience had become a hobby. That spring morning, the three left from Bitterfeld about sixty miles south of Berlin and flew two hundred miles westwards, landing fourteen hours later in Marburg, Hessen. Antonie said it was magic "to glide over the landscape on a festive Sunday and hear the church bells far below. Otherwise, all is quiet, no sound, not even wind" (May 6, 1928).

After two more years of weekend ballooning and acquaintance with aviators, one flier, C. H. Edzard of the Junkers aircraft factory and a world record holder, invited her to fly in his rickety two-seater plane. They flew to the Frisian Islands in the North Sea and dropped sacks of mail, sometimes at night. Thus began a long association with Junkers. Antonie said that it not just awakened her to the joy of flying but created a veritable thirst for it: "You can't control a balloon, but one has the feeling of mastering an airplane, steering it wherever one wants to go." So in September 1927, Antonie enrolled for flying lessons at the Bornemann school in Staaken, a few miles west of Berlin.

At the time, she was playing Queen Hippolyta in *A Midsummer Night's Dream* at Berlin's Bülowplatz Theater, a three-hour performance that never brought her home to the Schumannstrasse before midnight. Yet every morning Antonie rose at 5 AM to drive to Staaken for five hours of flying and related lessons. Near that village, next to a rudimentary hangar, was a small brick house with a sign outside that read "Lernt Fliegen!" (Learn to Fly!). Inside was a room with a long table holding maps, airplane models, and instruments. Another room had bunk beds, so pilots could relax or sober up before a solo flight. Students learned not only the theory of flight but also how to dismantle and reassemble engines and mechanisms.

After ninety-eight flights with an instructor, Antonie flew her first solo on Friday, October 13, 1927. She summarized the experience as follows:

> It was true fairy-tale solo weather, no hint of wind.... For a few seconds my heart beat strongly, but at the signal to start I was entirely calm. When the machine lifted off the ground, I was unspeakably happy to fly alone at last. I banked slowly over the field and saw old things with new eyes. The shadow of my tail assembly zipped over my slanted wings, and I saw people on the ground! Had they known a woman was up there doing her first solo, they would have fled in panic! I thought of my parents away in America with no inkling of their daughter's latest enterprise!... I saw Spandau, the Heerstrasse of Berlin, and the Havel Lakes, and wheeled around back to Staaken.
>
> Now I had to concentrate on the most difficult part—landing! I knew everyone standing on the field below followed such a first solo with expectation, worry, interest, and curiosity! Above all, keep calm! I told myself once more that this joy of a first solo flight would never return. I decelerated, adjusted the stick, and moments later I brought the machine safely and almost softly to the ground. Happy and proud, I heard everyone's congratulations, and, already considering myself a veteran, I was at once ready for three or four additional flights.[4]

On awarding Antonie the license, the school reported that her reactions were unusually fast and accurate in the air, that her grasp of theories was especially good, and that she participated in repairs with "the greatest interest and energy.... Her friendly and helpful character was appreciated by the entire school.... We have already recommended her for acrobatic training."

Acrobatics in the Air

In the summer of 1928, Antonie went to Würzburg to learn acrobatic flying. "I had no intention of stunting," she told Charles Renshaw of the *American Weekly* two decades later. "But we had so few instruments in those days, I decided I ought to know what to do if my plane ever came out of a fog upside down" (April 24, 1949).

Antonie wrote in 1928:

> Acrobatic flying is first learned by flying with an instructor in a two-seater. Theoretically, one should have grasped all steering and maneuvers with a model and removed all uncertainty. But in execution, sensitivity is decisive. Flying is not a matter of intellect but of accurate feeling.

After I had familiarized myself with the new type of Flamingo, one morning at six o'clock I flew solo into a radiant blue sky above Würzburg. As the altimeter approached 1,000 meters, a boxing match began between courageous joy and a bit of cowardice that we honestly have to admit comes at certain moments. It was knocked out, KO'd, and I climbed, accelerating the machine to 120, 130, 140, 145 kilometers—then pulled it up more, rising softly but steadily—more—still more—now upside down for a moment—I pulled more—and saw the earth swing back into place—I decelerated and relaxed—my first loop was a success. Although still concentrating like iron, I felt like somersaulting for joy! Right away, I looped again, then tried rolling. With sharp banks to the right and left, I ended my first acrobatic solo.

Before the flight ... an expert in parachutes had again explained to me the technique of bailing out. It created such an odd impression that while flying, I felt strongly that I owed it to him to parachute out. Comrades later told me they felt the same compulsion.

It's peculiar how fast the body adjusts to all positions: head down, quick turns in all directions, fast loss of altitude, etc.... Now flying calmly without a few stunts is no longer fun at all. Once you're a novice acrobatic flier like me, and that's all I am, you can understand the extraordinary skill of a Udet or a Fieseler.

Aces and Jokers

In 1930, Ernst Udet (1896–1941) became Antonie's great romance, displacing the actor Rudolf Forster. A flying clown, Udet would perform with top hat, wig, and false beard as the "flying professor." He was also the top surviving flying ace of World War I, with sixty-two victories (compared with eighty for the "Red Baron," Manfred von Richthofen). Undoubtedly Germany's most popular aviator, Udet taught acrobatic flying and co-starred with Leni Riefenstahl in adventure movies directed by Arnold Fanck. Ernst Heinkel, the German aircraft designer and manufacturer, wrote that "Udet was the friend of every good bottle of wine or cognac ... and his attraction for women matched the strange charm of his entire personality, although the legends told about him far exceed reality."[5]

To novice acrobatic fliers like Antonie and Elly Beinhorn, Udet would say: "I saw your program, sweetheart, and find it ambitious. If you crack up, the public will be charmed, but for oneself it's actually quite unpleasant!... Don't fly too high either. People want to see your silly face as you skim over them upside down." Unlike other Germans, Udet believed women pilots were as suitable as men because they were just as likely to have calm nerves, technical gifts, and the right kind of sensitivity. In a joint interview, he singled out Antonie as being in better physical shape than himself and even doubted that he could still pass the physical. He insisted that flying was already safer than driving and regretted the spread of bureaucratic controls.[6]

Udet's first impression of the Nazis was that of "a comical background noise." But Hermann Göring—a comrade from Richthofen's squadron in the past war and, after 1933, minister of aviation—urged him to become director of his Office of Technology. Udet said he knew nothing about large airplanes and mass production, but Göring replied, "For that we'll hire as many people as you want. It's your name we need above all." So Udet accepted. "For the sake of aviation, one had to make a pact with the devil," Udet later told Heinkel, "but he mustn't devour one." He thought Göring was basically "a sneaky cur posing as a man of iron."[7]

In 1938, Hitler believed that British and French inaction against his Austrian and Czech annexations was due to hysterical fear of the new German air force. A still greater Luftwaffe would keep them from interfering with the conquest of Poland and Russia. Hitler therefore demanded vastly accelerated aircraft production, costing billions. The Air

Ministry's general staff and Office of Technology agreed unanimously that such a rapid expansion was physically impossible. Yet no one dared to tell the Führer.

The demand for sheer numbers could be met if no four-motored bombers were built and if fighter plane production also avoided delays by settling for shorter ranges and slower speeds. The Junkers Ju-88 became the Luftwaffe's standard bomber and the Messerschmidt 109 the standard fighter. As an economy measure, technical development of other new models was stopped in 1940, since the war was thought to be almost over.

The air battle over Britain was then lost not just because of heroic Spitfire pilots, radar, and the breaking of the Germans' secret code. The capacity and range of Luftwaffe planes was too short to reach either the ports on the British west coast or distant aircraft factories with adequate bomb loads and fighter protection. In 1940, the British produced 9,924 planes or 23 percent more than the Germans. The Luftwaffe never fully recovered from the bombers, fighters, and pilots lost over England.[8]

At the Ministry of Aviation, Göring and Field Marshal Erhard Milch decided to put the blame on Udet. According to Heinkel, as early as October 1940, Udet looked pale, confused, and on the verge of collapse. A desperate attempt was made to produce stronger but potentially four-motored He-177 Heinkels. Many crashed and burned. During the Russian campaign of 1941, the Luftwaffe almost collapsed for lack of spare parts. Udet, looking ill and shaken, asked Heinkel: "Why did that happen with the 177? Everything goes against me.... Milch dishes everything out to the Führer, every mistake I ever made. I can't cope anymore. These gusts are too many and too much for me."[9]

In the night of November 17, 1941, in his bedroom, Udet shot himself. He was only forty-five years old. In her memoirs, Leni Riefenstahl wrote: "Udet must have suffered greatly because of that situation. In earlier times we had known him only as a cheerful man, bubbling with life." The night he killed himself, Udet telephoned Leni saying that it was Erni—that he was calling about "nothing special, I just wanted to hear your voice again."[10]

The newspapers reported that Udet had died in a crash for the Fatherland. He had bailed out a number of times from crashing planes, sometimes in the last seconds, once with a shoe remaining stuck behind in the fuselage. Another time, he was really hurt upon landing and had to be wheeled into a hospital emergency room. "Better X-ray my pants," said Udet. "I was really scared that time. Maybe I unloaded."

Bella Fromm Welles, the former Berlin society reporter and longtime friend, was in Antonie's New York office when someone called with the news that Udet was dead. Antonie turned pale. "They rubbed him out," she said, tears shining. "He hated the Nazis same as I did. He was just a pilot, nothing else." Udet was later portrayed in Carl Zuckmayer's *The Devil's General*.

But in 1930, all that was eleven years in the future, and Ernst Udet was Antonie's great romance, displacing a crown prince and an acclaimed actor. Erni gave her one of his pilot's jumpsuits, and she used it for years.

Criss-Crossing America

For a trade promotion of German airplanes, Gimbels department store of New York City, the Airplane Model League of America, and the German Ministry of Transportation brought Antonie to America on March 29, 1930, on the SS *Albert Ballin*. To help exhibit a collection of large, precisely built model airplanes, another celebrity, Baron Koenig von Warthausen, followed Antonie on April 9 on the SS *St. Louis*. The baron had recently flown around the world and had thereby won the annual Hindenburg Pokal prize for the year's best achievement in motorized sport flying. Warthausen had made his twenty thousand mile impromptu flight in 1928–1929 in a mere 20 horsepower, 586 pound Klemm airplane that was carried across two oceans by ship. He was twenty-one at the time.

With photographs and interviews, newspapers reported the two arrivals, and Gimbels advertised that every noon, for ten days, the two would lecture about thirty-five models of German airplanes, gliders, and balloons on display on the sixth floor. The exhibit opened with a ceremony attended by flying notables such as Amelia Earhart, Eddie Rickenbacker, Clarence Chamberlain, and Frank Hawks, who had made a transcontinental glider flight.

"A Flier, Actress, Writer, and Auto Racer: German Girl Says There's Time for All," was the headline in the *New York Telegram*. One reporter wrote: "Of a slim, straight build, there is a distinct freshness about this dark-eyed versatile young woman. Her voice is deep and rich with the emotionally husky quality of Ethel Barrymore." Another reporter wrote that he felt grateful for that "rare bit of luck, to meet a true personality, to see her intense manner and expressive gestures, the way she reports plans and describes impressions," and he could "wish her nothing better for her twenty-ninth birthday, today, but that she should always remain as she is." A Milwaukee reporter wrote about "this vibrant dark-eyed girl whom it's almost impossible to imagine ever growing old" (May 23, 1930).

From New York, the model airplane exhibit moved on to Gimbels-affiliated stores in Philadelphia, Baltimore, Boston, Washington, Pittsburgh, Chicago, Milwaukee, Detroit, Cleveland, Columbus, and Akron. In most cities, Antonie and Baron von Warthausen arrived by air in their own planes and were greeted by the mayor and a delegation of celebrities. Antonie knew how to flatter them. She told them that "America is far ahead of all other nations in feminine flying." In the United States, 203 women had licenses, compared with only 18 in Germany. Antonie did not think women pilots should have a separate club: "We are much stronger to go with the men. Men are such very nice comrades."

During these months, Antonie was accompanied by a white canary named "Okay," a gift from her father. Antonie entertained audiences by describing the canary: "You wonder about his name? That is the first American slang I learned, so I called him that. He got dirty like that in Chicago! He hopped about on the molding outside of the hotel, and when he got down he was all coal dust…. As a solo flier he is not so hot, but he bursts into song whenever I open the cockpit. He has outflown the greatest eagle that ever spread a wing. He travels in a special little wicker cabin with me, so he flies in fine style. His flying hours are about 150, so he is almost ready for his transport pilot's license."

Baron von Warthausen also traveled with a mascot, a white Siamese cat, named Tamina. "I feel so badly," said Antonie. "We are such good friends but we can never fly together. He must take his cat, and I must take my bird. The cat would eat the bird. Is it not a very difficult situation?"

In June, Akron, Ohio, was the last stop for the model planes, and Antonie was in charge of packing them for shipment back to Germany. She then had a chance to fly blimps and to learn gliding. Americans, she reported, seemed to believe that all German pilots were expert in gliding, so she felt compelled to give it her first try, solo.

Air Races and Tournaments

After the model exhibits, Antonie remained in America for nearly a year, visiting airplane factories, making business contacts, and flying in air shows. Outstanding among these were the National Air Races in Chicago in August 1930 and the All-American Air Races in Miami in January 1931.

Participating women in Chicago included Amelia Earhart, sole female transatlantic flier and president of the Ninety-Nine Club of Women Fliers; Eleanor Smith, holder of the altitude record and perhaps the best female pilot; Blanche Noyes; Ruth Nichols; Betty Lund; and Louise Thaden, winner of the 1929 "Powder Puff Derby." They all flew in a "dead stick contest," in which a plane had to glide to a landing close to a mark after its engine was switched off in mid-air.

For Antonie, the best thing Berlin could still offer was an acceptable glass of beer. She repeated that comment in articles and lectures about her American trip. At the Aero-Club of Germany in October, her audience included her parents; brother Erwin; Ernst Udet; Elly Beinhorn; the Zeppelin maker, Hugo Eckener; the airplane manufacturer, Ernst Heinkel; Erhard Milch, then director of the Lufthansa; and other industrialists, fliers, and foreign observers. An article in the *Berliner Zeitung* said: "She drove her audience of German airplane builders wild with envy. She depressed listening engineers, and among German sport fliers she aroused a longing for that country of still unlimited possibilities. Such an attentive audience must be rare at the Aero-Club where Miss Strassmann told of flying in America in a charming manner, brisk and entertaining, stimulating, amusing, knowledgeable, warning, and encouraging. Everything was splendidly observed and analyzed. Thundering applause afterwards. Well-deserved, to say the least" (October 7, 1931).

Among other things, Antonie reported:

> What was I up to over there? Can't be said in just one word.... All I planned was to stand on my own two feet, holding my canary, and to not make too bad an impression … and not cook up a manuscript, *Myself and America*.... I plunged right into the stream of life … to learn American habits, characteristics, and the mentality.... The generosity of Americans allowed me to fly twenty-eight types of airplanes, blimps, and gliders and to participate in air races and tournaments … and to make a thorough study of airplane and engine factories. Some even thought I was a spy.... Chicago is especially fascinating and full of life. The whole atmosphere reminds one of Berlin.

Three weeks later, Ernst Udet spoke at the Aero-Club about his recent flight to Africa, and it was Antonie's turn to write about him in the *Berliner Zeitung*: "An unprecedented success of a lecture!… One did not know what to admire more: his bold flying, the masterful photography, or his modest yet humorous commentary. Whenever the tone lapsed into seriousness because of all the danger and beauty, Udet switched to a Saxon dialect.... Udet is a great aviator, an artist with a camera, a humorist, a unique, very great personality" (October 28, 1931).

But Antonie's choice between the chaos of Germany and returning to America was easy. She wrote her mother not to worry about the end of her affair with the actor, Rudolf Forster. Some journalists like Fred Hildenbrandt saw Forster as an incredibly positive personality, who "quietly realized himself with purity and clarity, without scars or fissures."[11] But Antonie saw him differently:

> Forster is weak and cowardly.... He is a monstrous mixture of refinement, on the one hand, and most vulgar compulsions, on the other. His relations with women are most peculiar, and the length of our friendship is astonishing since I'm anything but his type. He was great friends with that Valetti and with Lydia Wegener—his physical deficiency results in a kind of depraved eroticism. I knew that all along and thought it explained his devotion to me, because I never wanted anything from him and never aroused his unhealthy, low instincts.... Forster is basically stingy and much too great an egotist for devotion to others.... This man will walk over cadavers if he considers himself psychologically threatened.... I liberated myself from Forster through Udet! I know that you're averse to him,

but he meant more to me than he suspected. He saved me from the abyss of filth toward which Forster was dragging me.... With my new interests in flying, etc., Udet let me displace Forster! Today I look on both without sentimentality, considering just what role they could play in my life. But I owe more to Forster, not because he deserves it, but because I truly loved him! Now I'm left only with the beauty of our relationship, and I know that I benefited more, although—or because—I gave more and suffered more! He is a carnivorous orchid, and orchids are the only horny flowers! (February 25, 1932)

Emigration

Before the end of 1931, Antonie had her visa and quota number for emigrating legally to the United States, and she took the first liner that sailed after New Year's Day in 1932, the SS *New York* of the Hamburg-America Line. She arrived on January 8, and her picture appeared via Associated Press in newspapers in New York, Washington, Chicago, Dallas, Wilmington, Louisville, Columbus, South Bend, and other cities, along with the headline: "German Woman Flyer, Pioneer of Air, to Make Her Home in America." Some captions identified her as "Germany's leading woman aviator" and as an alien quota passenger who planned to make her home in America after flying at Lake Placid on a plane mounted on skis.

The previous spring, Antonie had already told the *Milwaukee Sentinel* that she would come back to stay. She stated: "Back in 1925 I sensed the stimulation and knew how many chances America held.... In Germany I was disconsolate. There is not the same pride in accomplishment there.... Anyone trying to make a success of her life is helped here on all sides. In Europe, they make the very devil out of life for someone trying to get ahead. 'Why do you do all these things,' they ask, 'why not live quietly?' I work because I like to—I have more ideas here in an hour than I ever had in Germany in a week" (May 23, 1931).

Now in 1932, in her New York hotel, the St. Moritz, she told Evelyn Seeley of the *New York World Telegram* that one great thing about America, that ultimate Promised Land, was not being stared at when you smiled. Germans were too grim-faced.

> Am I going to become an American? You bet I am! America opened my eyes to what life can be.... You who live here cannot realize what it is you have. You say it is not democracy, but to me it seems to be. You complain it is not freedom, but *ach!* how you are free!... Germany is not only broken financially but spiritually too. She is all in. My people have known no let-up since 1914. They have gone through the meat grinder again and again. There is no reserve—financial or spiritual—left in the closet. There are twenty suicides every day in Berlin—the old and the young, parents and children, who cannot fight any longer.

Among her ideas were to represent the Junkers and Siemens corporations in patent negotiations, to become a flying instructor in Cleveland, to help fly the twelve-motored Dornier Do-X seaplane back across the Atlantic, and to report on winter sports at the Olympics in Lake Placid. She told the *New York Herald*, "As a regular immigrant, I no longer have to worry about extensions of a visitor's visa and have five years to think thoroughly about my plans" (January 9, 1932). The Nazis coming to power a year later made the decision easy.

But first came the third Winter Olympics, on February 4–15, 1932. Two weeks before opening ceremonies, Antonie reported that Lake Placid had record temperatures of 67 degrees Fahrenheit, blue skies, and no trace of snow or ice. It looked bad for her plans to fly stunts with a plane on skis. According to the Albany weather bureau, the winter was the warmest in 147 years, and for the first time the Hudson River had not frozen. Snow had to be brought in from Quebec on trucks. One could count most on hockey and skating in the new ice arena. There Sonja Henie won the gold medal in figure skating for Norway against two eleven-year-old English girls, among others. Sonja also won gold medals in 1928 and 1936.

Do-X: Twelve Motors, 53 Tons

In August 1931, the giant Dornier Do-X seaplane had landed on its belly in New York waters after a long and problematic flight down the west coast of Europe and Africa to Dakar, then across the Atlantic to the Cape Verde Islands and to Pernambuco in Brazil. With a variety of technical and financial problems, its crew of fourteen flew down the South American east coast to Buenos Aires and back up and then stopped in Venezuela, in the West Indies, and at a number of East Coast American cities. After obtaining massive subsidies from the German Transport Ministry and making a few overhauls, raising engine capacity by 600 horsepower, the return flight across the Atlantic began on May 19, 1932, in New York, continued from Newfoundland on May 21, and ended on the Müggelsee Lake east of Berlin on May 24. Seaplanes like Claudius Dornier's spectacular Do-X were really flying boats, with a hull-fuselage strong and buoyant enough for water landings and take-offs.

Antonie persuaded the German consul and the airplane's commander, Friedrich Christiansen (another war hero, aged fifty-two), to let her fly along as assistant pilot and purser. Two years earlier, she had exhibited a model of the Do-X in America as part of her commercial tour with Baron von Warthausen. As a celebrity known from air shows and tournaments, her participation now gave "the return flight a special flair … sensational for the press on both sides of the ocean."[12] The worldwide economic depression had lowered the commercial promise of the Do-X, including the demand by tourist passengers for flights around New York City. Something special was needed, and perhaps Antonie's name filled the bill. Mayor Jimmy Walker sent a book, *Legendary Germany*, by Regina Jais, to Germany's President Hindenburg and wrote: "Permit me to make use of the welcome opportunity of the America-Germany flight of the Dornier X to send you, through the German girl flier, my most sincere greeting. This flight shows again that the time has come when the spirit of invention and enterprise has brought even the air-ocean as a link into the chain which forms closer ties among the people."[13] Antonie officially signed up on May 6. "Kids, I was overjoyed!" she wrote on a postcard to friends. It made her the second woman after Amelia Earhart to fly across the North Atlantic. For her second flight, Amelia left Newfoundland on May 20, 1932, and flew alone, non-stop, to Ireland.

The aluminum 53-ton plane could only carry enough gasoline for flights of about 2,400 kilometers at speeds somewhat above 160 kilometers per hour and at altitudes as low as 10 meters. Climbing higher was possible but would consume too much extra fuel. The twelve American Curtiss engines of the Do-X used 1,700 liters of gasoline per hour, generating 8,000 horsepower. On top of the wings, six engines were oriented forward and pulled, and six had the propellers behind and pushed. The tanks could hold some 27,000 liters, enough for 16 hours of flight. Stops for refueling at Newfoundland, in the Azores, at Vigo in Spain, and near Southampton, England, were mandatory. To conserve fuel to reach the Azores at all, the Do-X landed on a calm, moonlit Atlantic Ocean and taxied nearly four hours at sea for the last six and two-thirds miles to Horta.[14] Transatlantically, the Do-X could carry the ceremonial letters to President Hindenburg of Germany and to Mayor Heinrich Sahm of Berlin, along with several thousand other letters, but no commercial cargo. The only non-crew passenger was Elmer M. Applegit, whose Vacuum Oil Company supplied the fuel at Newfoundland, the Azores, and Vigo, Spain.

Now as a journalist, Antonie kept a log and published it in the *Berliner Illustrierte Nachtausgabe.*

> Thursday, May 19 ... Moonlight. 3:30 AM the anchor is raised. One motor after another starts: 10, 11, 12.... We sail quietly as a board. No vibrations.... Everyone aloft is cheerful and animated. Shocking good appetites. Icy cold despite sunshine. Altitude only three meters.... I catch a little nap....

> Saturday, May 21 ... Behind the machinery cabin I crawl through a little door into the radio room. Kiel, the radioman, has earphones on his boyish blond head.... He pushes buttons and turns dials. Needles swing and lights glow. Telegrams and weather reports come from Hamburg and New York in fractions of seconds.... Our record pace is the talk of the crew. Joyfully, I give everyone an extra banana. I believe they consider me horribly stingy.... With tension it's easier for the stomach to cope with small amounts. As medical officer I have to tolerate their complaints. We all want to land in good health.

> Monday, May 23. Spain is now behind us, 10:45 AM, and we're heading across the Bay of Biscay to England. A storm is raging below with 70 kilometer gusts, and I'm glad not to be on a ship climbing mountainous waves and disappearing in valleys.... At 6:30 PM we land at the seaplane station of the Royal Air Force.... One of our crew falls overboard while anchoring.... On May 24 we pass the light ship at Terschelling. Everyone sees it, Germany's first greeting. We're home!

The last lap crossed the Straits at Dover, then the Do-X flew along the coast toward Hamburg and for two hours followed the Elbe and Havel Rivers to Berlin. Antonie later recalled how it felt looking down:

> After Brandenburg, I know every nook and cranny of the Berlin region. Friends, Werder is over there, see, with its famous orchards now in bloom! We fly right above Cäcilienhof and Nikolskoe. Reminds one of plum tarts with whipped cream. Sunday excursions. Pichelsdorf. Green eels with sour pickles and Pilsener beer. Over there, the Kaiser Wilhelm Memorial Church. We're already above the Great Star confluence of roads in the Tiergarten. I wonder what my pals, the cops, looking up down there, are thinking? One respectful circle around the Victory Column of 1870 slings us over my parents' house. My Schumannstrasse. I see doctors in white coats racing outdoors.... Here is the Reichstag ramp that I sped down on roller skates as a child. There the house where I was born—do my eyes feel tears welling up? That I should ever come to Berlin like this!... A circle above the suburban Müggelsee Lake is followed by our usual smooth landing.

The southern half of the Müggelsee was left empty for the Do-X, but the other half was crowded with hundreds of boats, while thousands watched from roofs and along the shore. For Germans, it was like Lindbergh's landing in Paris.

My father, my older sister, Renate, and myself, five years old, were in the crowd, but my memory is mainly of the blurred black-and-white home movies filmed that day, all now on videotape. On tape, the Do-X approaches from afar, circles above the lake, lands, and floats up close, surrounded by all those small boats.

Rabid Politics

In covering the return of the Do-X, Goebbels's virulent Nazi newspaper, *Der Angriff* (The Attack), assailed Antonie as a Jewess, with the headline, "Who Invited Her?" During the coming Nazi years, Antonie, once hired for her name, was henceforth never to be mentioned or pictured as a member of the Do-X crew. But seven years later, the flight's commander, Friedrich Christiansen, recalled an inspection of the airplane by Hitler at Warnemünde in July 1932 as "the greatest experience, for we met the Führer—already *our* Führer because, from captain to the last machinist, the entire crew of the Do-X were National Socialists."[15] All her life, Antonie believed that another well-known flier, Thea Rasche, had brought her ancestry to Goebbels's attention, but it might also have been the Do-X *Flugkapitän*, Horst Merz, second in command, who had been a hard-line Nazi since 1922.[16]

That same day after the Berlin landing, other newspapers reported a shoot-out between Nazis and Communists, in which one Nazi was killed and several men were wounded on both sides. Within a week, Chancellor Heinrich Brüning resigned under pressure, and Hindenburg appointed the right-wing Franz von Papen in his place to rule by decree while the Reichstag was dissolved. New elections were scheduled for July. Thirty-eight more Nazis, thirty Communists, and eighteen others were killed during street battles that month.[17]

So far, not all Nazis were Antonie's enemies. The airplane manufacturer, Ernst Heinkel, recalled that in the summer of 1932, Antonie, "an extraordinarily intelligent and engaging woman," was his guest at the Warnemünde factory when Göring showed up by surprise for afternoon coffee at Heinkel's residence. Antonie knew Göring as an aviator, a friend of friends. With Göring was his fiancée, Emmy Sonnemann, who had acted with Antonie at the Stuttgart Landestheater. Antonie rushed over and embraced Emmy with enthusiasm. She called out, "Göring, what the hell are you doing with such a gorgeous woman? She's much too good for you!" Göring replied, "Soon I'll be minister of aviation. Then you'll see here the largest aircraft factory in Europe."[18]

In postwar letters, Heinkel asked Antonie, "Do you still think of those splendid times ... which we Germans will never see again?" (November 6, 1946). Antonie answered, "Those weeks at your hospitable house remain unforgotten. What cheerful, harmless, and happy times those were" (May 25, 1947). She wondered whatever happened to Hanns Klemm, another aircraft manufacturer and "one of the few from whom I have heard nothing. Do you remember his famous dictum [in dialect] that, compared with our times, Tannhäuser's Venusberg was sheer trash?" Heinkel answered, "Klemm still lives and is the same crazy fellow as before" (July 6, 1950).

South American Journey

Antonie's last major flight, along the east coast of South America, from Pernambuco (Recife) to Buenos Aires, spanned over two thousand miles and took more than two months. Major stops were at Bahia, Victoria, Rio de Janeiro, Sao Paulo, Montevideo, and Buenos Aires. She flew a small open-cockpit, Klemm-Hirth Moth from its factory at Böblingen near Stuttgart to Friedrichshafen on Lake Constance. There, Hugo Eckener (1868–1954), the colorful chief of the Zeppelin enterprise (and once a potential president of Germany), allowed her to load it disassembled aboard the airship, Graf Zeppelin, for a flight across the South Atlantic on September 12–15, 1932.

In Pernambuco in 1932, no one but herself knew how to uncrate and reassemble the Klemm aircraft, so she did the job alone with laborers on the field where the Zeppelin had landed, a space too small for an airplane to gather speed for a take-off. She hired fifteen Brazilians to carry the Moth on their shoulders twelve miles along a jungle path to a regular airport. Articles about Antonie appeared in Brazil, describing her as "um belo tipo de mulher morena, transpirando energia y simpatia. Afabilissima, a sua palestra encanta pela modestia com que narra a sua intensa vida de aviadora" (a beautiful type of dark woman, revealing energy and friendship. Her most courteous talk charmed us by the modesty with which she told of her intense life as a flier).[19]

From Pernambuco, it took a week for Antonie to fly to Rio de Janeiro, where she was met by officials, journalists, and members of the German colony. She thanked airmail officials for the use of their facilities along the route and told everyone: "Land of sun and light! Brazil is simply enchanting. I have never glimpsed a panorama so infinite and meaningful and of such natural beauty. All sons of this privileged land, and especially the daughters, should see Brazil from above through the windows of an airplane.... I have crossed part of the state of Rio and am ever more enthusiastic about what I have seen. All this thanks to my airplane, which is of absolute perfection and when aloft responds to all my demands."[20] With an inscribed map, the journey is commemorated on a silver platter given to Antonie by Hanns Klemm, the designing engineer and industrialist. I never heard if any Klemm planes were sold as a result of her flight.

Arriving back in Berlin, she found a new Reichstag had been elected with fewer but more desperate Nazis as still the largest political party. Göring was the Reichstag's presiding officer. General Kurt von Schleicher was the new chancellor and clearly too weak to hold back the Nazi tide. He also antagonized President Hindenburg with proposals to take over bankrupt Junker estates. Antonie's decision to emigrate to America looked more sensible than ever.[21]

Fritz Strassmann (1858–1940) around 1925. He played a leading role in making forensic medicine a separate scientific discipline.

Georg Strassmann (1890–1972) around 1925. Like his father, he specialized in legal medicine and until 1935 taught at the University of Breslau. In 1938, he emigrated to the United States.

Paul Strassmann's family in 1907. From the left: Hellmuth, aged 13,
Antonie aged 6, Hedwig, aged 38, Paul, aged 41,
Erwin, aged 12, and Gisela, aged 11.

In a trench near the Somme River, France, where Hellmuth Strassmann was stationed in 1916.

Hellmuth's monument at the Wannsee cemetery. Originally it stood at the entrance of the Strassmann Frauenklinik, Schumannstrasse 18.

Hellmuth on his last furlough in Berlin, 1916.

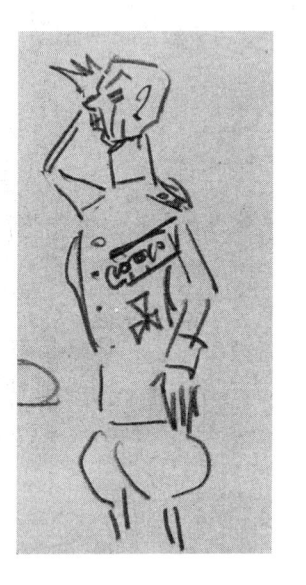

Erwin drew these sketches in the Somme-Aisne region of France,
where he was stationed as a balloon observer in 1917.

Four Strassmanns in the war, 1915. From the left: Erwin, Paul, Hellmuth, and Gisela.

Lieutenant Erwin Strassmann in the basket of a captive balloon at Marle, France, 1917.

Erwin Strassmann as a balloon observer in World War I.

Gisela Gutzwiller (née Strassmann) on March 27, 1942, at Locarno, shortly before her death.

Max Gutzwiller, Gisela's husband, around 1940.

A New Year's concert at Fribourg, 1940. From the left: Marianne, Hellmy, Martin, Ruth, Ursula.

Antonie Strassmann.

Antonie in her first major role as Mary Stuart in Schiller's drama in 1920 at Magdeburg.

Paul Wegner was Antonie's partner in various dramas, beginning with Hebbel's *Judith and Holofernes* in 1921 and concluding with Strindberg's *The Father* in 1930.

A photograph from the winter of 1925. In the back, from the left: Erwin, Antonie, and her husband, Willy Joseph. In front: Ilse with Renate, Hedwig, and Paul Strassmann.

Antonie exits from the Do-X, Müggelsee, 1932.

Reception for the crew of the Do-X after arriving from New York on Berlin's Müggelsee, 1932.
From the left: Flight Captain Christiansen, Antonie Strassmann, Dr. Dornier,
Ministerial Counselor Mühlig-Hofmann.

Antonie and Fritz Lohse. She noted: "With Fritz Lohse during the National Air Races in Chicago with the 'Bird' that I flew."

The flying ship Do-X circling New York.

Antonie arriving with the Hindenburg, May 20, 1936.

Antonie (far right) on the beach of Martha's Vineyard with Robert L. Hague.
He was vice president of Standard Oil.

Antonie in 1948 in the Empire State Building directing the East Coast Hearing Aid Division of the Zenith Radio Corporation.

During World War II, Antonie taught women how to run machine tools at the Delahanty Institute, New York, 1942.

Chapter 7

A Zenith in Heidelberg with a Bitter End: Gisela and Max

This chapter is one of several that are not about medical affairs and politics in Berlin. Instead of physicians, we deal here with lawyers, and the place is Germany's premier university town, Heidelberg. Here was Paul Ferdinand's alma mater, and here Nazi persecution was especially vehement. The similarities and differences are significant and fit into the story because Hedwig and Paul Ferdinand Strassmann's third child, Gisela, who was born on October 23, 1896, is involved. My chief source, apart from postwar conversations with five cousins, are the published memoirs of Gisela's husband, Max Gutzwiller (1889–1989), especially a 169-page memorial, *Das Büchlein mit dem Denkmal* (Booklet with a Monument), written within three months of Gisela's death and published privately on July 10, 1942.[1]

A Postwar Romance

When World War I began, Gisela was seventeen and had not yet finished her gymnasium with the Abitur examination. She is remembered as a thoughtful, quiet child, invariably serious and conscientious like Hellmuth, not restless, conspiratorial, or mischievous like Erwin and Antonie. She became a nurse at military hospitals, mostly in Berlin, and did not resume her formal education until 1919. Gisela then concentrated on Greek philosophy with Ernst Hoffmann of the Mommsen Gymnasium.

Max Gutzwiller, an attorney from Basel, was appointed legal attaché at the Swiss Embassy in Berlin in 1919. He remembered first seeing Gisela at a reception. Radiating an inner glow, she was walking alone toward a window. Her dress had a bodice of brown-gold brocade so reserved and unstylish that Max thought only someone with bold convictions could wear it. Max now went to all parties and country excursions if he expected Gisela to be there. Soon they were together at museums, concerts, and lectures. Max tried to enroll in her Greek tutorials with Dr. Hoffmann, who asked, "How can I analyze philosophy with Fräulein Strassmann while teaching you to spell?" So they studied Greek separately.

The Swiss Embassy at the Königsplatz in the Spreebogen area was a short walk from the Strassmann Clinic. One afternoon, Gisela persuaded her father to invite Max to Schumannstrasse 18 for a Beethoven commemoration. A renowned, white-bearded violinist flamboyantly launched into the Kreuzer Sonata with theatrical gestures. Gisela felt embarrassed and thought that her brother Erwin could have played just as well. Max sat next to her and shared her disdain.

In late April 1921, Gisela learned that Max was being transferred to Bern in May. The two met in the Rembrandt room of the Kaiser Friedrich Museum, and Max asked without preamble, "How would it be if we became engaged?" Gisela agreed, but it was somehow unromantic, a decision burdened with responsibilities. Max recalled that it felt as if the greatest task of his life now lay ahead, and he walked back to the embassy, both excited and troubled. His friend Ethe from Bonn had told him that he might look on his friendship with Gisela as merely a gallant adventure, but that breaking it off on the pretext of separation might irrevocably damage his character. On the other hand, marriage to a citizen of a great power was impossible for a Swiss *diplomate de carrière*. Max and Gisela resolved to keep their engagement secret.

Meanwhile, Gisela thought about her future and concluded that she was not up to an academic career with its demands, especially the time-consuming preparations for examinations. She needed activity and breathing space. She wrote, "So there I am with my fantastic intellectual capacity and hunger for knowledge, on the one hand, and a heathen compulsion to enjoy life, on the other." Should she become a scientific academic or take on the duties of a woman—scrubbing, cooking, and all that—or perhaps even athletics? She discussed it all with Dr. Hoffmann, who laughed and told her, "The best thing is to marry a young professor without a penny in his pocket. Then you'll be challenged with as much housework as you want!"

Max was welcomed back in the legal department of the Foreign Office among colleagues who noticed that he had a new self-confidence. Perhaps, some jested, he merely had an admirable new tailor. But before the end of the first month came an inquiry from the University of Fribourg about his availability as professor of Roman law. He was to replace Professor Peter Tuor, a Romansch Swiss from Grisons, who had been Max's teacher ten years earlier and who was moving to the University of Geneva. Max had never given a lecture, nor had he published anything, but he was considered brilliant. He took the Saturday night train to Berlin to discuss the possibility with his fiancée.

Gisela was at the Anhalter railway station early that Sunday morning. After hearing the details about the alternatives and asking questions, she suggested that perhaps the time had come to tell her parents about the engagement. Max agreed, went to a telephone, and talked to Hedwig, who wrote a note to her husband: "Dear Paul, Dr. Gutzwiller has just called and will visit! I'll let you know when he's here. Reason is obvious. Your Hedwig." All her life Gisela carried that note in her purse.

As a foreigner, a Catholic, and, worst of all, not even a physician, Max Gutzwiller was not the son-in-law that the Strassmanns had hoped for. Paul came in a surgical gown and talked at length about the practical considerations of any marriage. He insisted that Max would have to ask his own parents as well. Hedwig said both young people had her unconditional trust. Max stayed for Sunday dinner and took the overnight train back to Switzerland. Gisela wrote to him on June 7, 1921: "It's touching to see how relieved my parents are, almost grateful to know what we are about, and they wish us the best with all their hearts, and—as you, dearest, have perhaps noticed?—have taken a great liking to you, but understand that it may be a problem for your parents."

A Definite Conversion

For Max's mother, Emilie (Meyer) Gutzwiller, the wedding plans were a heavy blow. She was rooted in Catholicism with all her being and had even been president of the Swiss

League of Catholic Women. She was devoted to her eldest son and looked on the intervention of a foreigner, and a Protestant at that, as the collapse of her most beautiful hopes. Max's cold determination to proceed no matter what struck her deeply. But after meeting Gisela and Erwin on a trip to Freiburg im Breisgau, she wrote to Max in Bern, "Your Gisela has won my heart." Of course, Gisela had to convert to Catholicism. For the time being, Max's father, Carl Gutzwiller, was not informed at all.

Contrary to expectations, Carl was not upset by the news of Max and Gisela's engagement. From his point of view, anyone from a family that had already converted from Judaism to Lutheranism was ready for the next step to Catholicism. In mid-summer 1921, Paul Ferdinand and Hedwig Strassmann were invited to Basel for a "meeting of the clans." Max reported that his father, "with his unfailing ability to assess people, declared the prospective in-laws to be sharp and elegant persons."[2] A festive dinner was arranged, and the place cards for Gisela and Max read "Bride" and "Bridegroom."

The couple had seldom discussed religious problems in the preceding two years. For Max, Gisela was the embodiment of pure thought and unconditional morality. Her family surroundings, classical schooling, Lutheran catechism, and wartime service had fully prescribed an elevated life. Max wrote after her death that she had never become a typical Catholic but that their "common sympathy for everything truly essential in Christian faith had in the long run added depth to our religious lives."[3] Gisela was revolted by moral lapses and could confront them with an uncompromising severity that would astonish anyone used to her normally tender manner.

Wedding and Emigration

Back in Berlin, during the autumn of 1921, Gisela, now twenty-five years old, finished her religious training and prepared for the wedding on December 29 and for the subsequent emigration. For all three steps, forms had to be filled out and notarized. Even export and import permits were needed. A Prussian official warned Gisela of the peril of losing her German citizenship. But she wrote to Max:

> Separation from you grows ever harder! I already belong to you so absolutely and live only through you, so that I no longer understand anything else. Why am I still here, instead of there with you? Why do I walk where you are not along and sit at tables without you next to me? How can I go to sleep without first telling you "good night," whispering tender words, and enjoying your nearness? And how can I awake in the morning disappointed to see you absent?... I am grateful for every experience of my life, happy or sad, that was a seed now ripening—all for you, a way to bring us together....
>
> I am happy that you are enjoying your work. Just wait! When we are finally together, I shall keep everything secondary out of your way, so you can devote yourself entirely to your work, our work! Life will be beautiful![4]

First Spell in Fribourg

In 1922, Fribourg, Switzerland, was a town of about twenty thousand inhabitants and was capital of the canton with the same name. The Sarine (or Saane) River flows through the middle of both town and canton and is the language frontier, with German Swiss on the eastern right bank and French Swiss on the left. The town is also known as Freiburg im Üchtland, to prevent confusion with another university town, Freiburg im Breisgau in Germany.

A medieval duke, Berchtold IV of Zähringen, founded Fribourg in 1157 as a rocky fortress above a tight loop of the Sarine, a strategic location for controlling the trade route. The canton joined the Swiss Confederation in 1481, but under the influence of the Dutch Jesuit priest, Peter Canisius (1521–1597), it avoided the Reformation and became, in effect, the Catholic capital of Switzerland. It was an Episcopal residence where Cistercians, Capuchins, Franciscans, and Jesuits had their churches, monasteries, and schools. Fribourg's Catholic university was founded on October 1, 1889, the day Max Gutzwiller was born in Basel.

Fribourg's medieval walls, watchtowers, Romanesque and Gothic churches, monasteries, fountains, patrician mansions, and little squares all looked enigmatic under heavy snow when Gisela and Max arrived on January 7, 1922. For Gisela, the forested white valleys descending toward the Sarine, as viewed from the passing train, already felt cozy. A horse-drawn carriage took them first to their hotel to leave luggage and then up to their empty apartment in a house on the Avenue Moléson, with its view of the Kaiseregg mountain, the Körblifluh, the Moléson, and, far away, the Mont Blanc. They had no telephone. While their furniture and household goods were being delivered and arranged, Gisela and Max lived in the hotel for five days. A following diary entry reads: "Married for fourteen days! We have come a long way and are fine! Our first supper here together, and for the first time we sleep at home."[5]

According to Max, writing twenty years later, Gisela was a conscientious and frugal housewife. She seldom bought new clothes or accessories unless Max urged her to do so. Taking her mother as a model, she treated all hours that Max spent in his study as sacred and inviolable. But whenever he felt frustrated by slow progress or dead ends, she thought of something encouraging or diverting.

In twenty years, Max wrote in 1942, they never grew bored with one another. All their trips were like honeymoons—perhaps less fiery, but ever deeper. Citing the writer Gottfried Keller, he recalled the importance of simply enjoying Gisela's gestures and face, the delicately expectant eyes and the pleasing voice. She treated works of art, not with historical pedantry as he thought he did, but only in terms of their integrity and emotional effect. Her favorite painters were Giotto, Mantegna, Peter Vischer, Dürer, and Altdorfer. The two read and reread old and new classics of literature together, not just the Germans—Goethe, Schiller, Lessing, Mörike, Rilke, Stefan George, Gerhart Hauptmann, and Thomas Mann—but also Balzac, Stendhal, Shakespeare, Ibsen, Strindberg, and the great Russians. She played the piano well enough to render pieces by Schubert, Brahms, and Beethoven tolerable for visitors, with Beethoven's Sonata No. 12, Opus 26, her favorite. Her performances always began with apologetic disclaimers.

Academic Beginnings

As a thirty-two-year-old new faculty member, Max was at times taken for a student by both his colleagues and other students. "Sit down, young man," said one influential professor peremptorily as Max entered his office to introduce himself. Another time, a student asked him in the corridor, "Is the old man in a bearable mood?" Upon entering, he found that Max was the "old man."

Every afternoon, when Max climbed up the narrow streets from the university to their abode and then to his study, he found fresh flowers on his desk. Gisela did not attempt to learn jurisprudence and viewed Max working at his desk like a friendly dog "gnawing on his bone." But every new published article called for celebration. Looking back, he found it hard to believe that he had time to publish anything at all in those early years, with his lectures on Roman law in two languages and some optional courses in international and Anglo-Saxon civil law.

During the four years in Fribourg, Gisela gave birth to four children. Hellmuth, born on September 28, 1922, was named after her older brother, who had been killed in the war. Ursula came almost a year later, and the twins, Marianne and Martin, arrived in October 1925. All were delivered in the small Basel hospital of Max's uncle, Dr. Karl Meyer, Emilie's younger brother, who had spent months assisting at the Strassmann Clinic in Berlin. A journal was kept of the daily progress of the first two babies, but the book for Marianne and Martin remained empty, except for an introductory quotation from Goethe about twins.

Heidelberg Looms

In December 1925, during a visit to Heidelberg, Max was invited to the office of the eccentric, old professor, Otto Gradenwitz, who began an inquisition about technicalities in ancient Greek law and the Justinian Code. The discussion turned into a heated argument, and finally Max stood up with an exclamation. He knew that a vacancy in Roman law existed because of the retirement of Professor Friedrich Endenmann and thought that his chances were now over. But white-bearded Gradenwitz changed his tone, stood up, and extended his hand, saying, "Shake that, colleague! I daresay, you're a character!" As they walked outdoors afterwards, Gradenwitz asked Max what he thought of his overcoat. "Frankly, a bit shabby for a Heidelberg professor," said Max, and Gradenwitz nodded with satisfaction. He wanted an implacably honest colleague, not a toady, even about trivia, and Max would prove that implacable.

On Christmas Day, a special delivery letter arrived in Fribourg offering Max the chair in Roman and German civil law at Heidelberg. At the same time the death of Professor Andreas von Tuhr at Zurich created a similar vacancy, but Max and Gisela preferred Heidelberg. As the train pulled into the station in late March 1926, they came to a town that was the idyllic answer to all their dreams, a vision that was celebrated in German literature and that Gisela had known through her father's reminiscences about his student years in the 1880s. On display in the Schumannstrasse home were several Heidelberg mementos, especially the Arminius beer mug that Paul's father, Heinrich, had given him, one with a pewter eagle on the handle, an elaborate black-red-gold coat of arms on the cover, and six notches commemorating saber duels. Max always remembered that Gisela's happiness was indescribable; she was fulfilling her father's "secret wish to somehow return to this beloved site of his student years." Max recalled: "With bliss in our hearts, we took our first walk along the famous Philosophenweg, high above the Neckar River, orchards in bloom, the old town on the other shore below thickly forested hills, the famous bridge celebrated in songs of Hölderlin and Gottfried Keller, the agreeable slate-roofed university, sunshine on the mighty red-sandstone palace above, and in town the good spire of the Heiliggeistkirche."[6]

The Premier German University

The University of Heidelberg, formally called Ruperto Carola, was long thought to be the quintessential German university, the most ancient and scenic, populated not just with uniformed students dueling and singing about their wine and lost sweethearts, but also with a faculty more learned, demanding, and yet more accessible than any other. It was indeed the oldest in the country, founded in 1386 by Prince-Elector Ruprecht I of the Palatinate with thirty-nine faculty and four hundred fifty students recruited from the still older but strife-torn universities of Paris and Prague. The next prince-elector, Ruprecht II, a nephew, assumed the throne in February 1390 and eight months later expelled the Heidelberg Jews, whom his uncle had welcomed a generation earlier. The confiscated synagogue and Jewish houses became Ruperto Carola's first buildings.

When World War I began, of the 2,700 students enrolled at Heidelberg, many volunteered or were drafted for the conflict. About 480 were killed, as were 14 faculty members. The faculty generally supported the war but not the planned expansion of the German empire. After the war, enrollment at Heidelberg fluctuated from semester to semester between 2,000 and 4,000, with one-fifth female students. Outstanding in the faculty of law when Max Gutzwiller arrived were Gerhard Anschütz (constitutional law), Karl Heinsheimer (civil procedures), Otto Gradenwitz (Roman law), Richard Thoma (public law), Alexander Graf zu Dohna and Gustav Radbruch (criminal law), and Heinrich Mitteis (legal history). By the end of 1934, none of these were left.

A joy for Gisela and Max in Heidelberg was that Ernst Hoffmann, their former Greek teacher, was now professor of philosophy and pedagogy at the university. Ernst and his wife Dorothea had no children and lived on the Ziegelhäuser Landstrasse. Born in Berlin in 1880, Ernst had studied there and at Heidelberg and Göttingen. From 1907 until 1922, he taught at the Mommsen Gymnasium in the Charlottenburg district of Berlin and worked on his history of Greek philosophy. Its publication was sufficient for his call to the university in 1922 when he was forty-two years old. During their decade at Heidelberg, Max and Gisela saw the Hoffmanns often. As they made their rounds at the first large social gathering, an old professor of medicine looked at Gisela, winked at Max, and whispered banally, "If only all new faculty brought along such wives!"

Heidelberg University still had a mystique matching that of Oxford in England or Princeton in the United States. Viewed not just as a fairytale music box or elite spa, it was seen as a "Noah's ark with a mission to preserve everything sublime in the human spirit," according to Max's colleague, Gustav Radbruch, who had been minister of justice under the Social Democrats. Radbruch remarked on something called the *Heidelberger Geist* (spirit of Heidelberg): "At no other university did the brightest communicate with one another so intensely ... such ceaseless discussion ... including the active participation of wise and educated women."[7] During the stable last years of the 1920s, such groups feared bourgeois philistinism more than Nazi fanaticism.

Max recalled:

Everywhere one sensed movement and a corresponding receptivity, elasticity, and versatility; [there was] imagination, of course, a graceful artistry, and generally courteous behavior. Every Sunday at Marianne Weber's at the Ziegelhäuserlandstrasse—in front of the large fountain among old trees opposite the castle—a circle of men and women listened to the report of some master, mulling over their incisive questions. At the Bayerschen Garten, young people might stage a Shakespearean comedy. At the Egyptologist Hermann Ranke's, someone might give a lecture about antique poetry.... Radbruch and his wife might have organized a concert in the vaults of an old *Refektorium* on the Friesenberg ... and at a single reception given by the chemist Friedrich Bergius, one could encounter Gerhart Hauptmann, Thomas Mann, Rudolf Binding, and Friedrich Gundolf....

The Heidelberg decade [began as] the unequaled zenith of our life together—its spontaneity, rich diversity, and deep feeling of joy cannot be described.... Gisela was entirely fulfilled and, at age thirty, somehow magical.... Anyone sitting next to her at dinner might begin with modest exploratory remarks and be amazed at her energetic response, probing some deep issue. The more condescending the gentleman's initial comments, the less likely was he now to leave Gisela's side for the rest of the evening.[8]

Gisela gave birth to their fifth child, Ruth, on December 19, 1928. Everything went well in the small private hospital on the Zähringerstrasse, and Gisela said she was exhilarated to be nursing another baby. An acquaintance once spoke to her of the opportunities that women missed because of their nursery duties, and Gisela answered that she could not imagine "what beauty the world might offer better than the inexhaustible wealth of these golden children."[9] Max believed that for Gisela in Heidelberg "every day was Sunday."

Max on the Job

During the Heidelberg years, Max gave eight lectures weekly, usually between 6 and 8 PM. In the summer of 1927, he became dean of the law faculty, a one-year rotating position. It was the senior faculty's custom to vote unanimously on all important measures, so one had to be skilled at accommodating nine temperamental antagonists. In tense situations he sanctimoniously referred to their lofty duties and the challenging principles of their immortal predecessors, whose portraits hung above them in a row. In the fall of 1933, Max was scheduled to become Rektor of the university for a year; but with Nazis now in power, he was told that the times were inopportune for an outspoken Swiss married to a woman with regrettably Semitic ancestors. Max agreed.

When Max was dean, Gisela did not mind entering the decorated ceremonial hall third in rank in the academic procession while the orchestra played Brahms's *Gaudeamus Igitur*. Max wondered later if her joy in these years had perhaps been a small advance compensation for the bitter times that lay ahead.[10]

Paul Ferdinand Strassmann was filled with radiant nostalgia for Heidelberg through this new association through Gisela and Max. He longed for his student past and for a future in this picturesque and historic town on the Neckar River below the Königstuhl hills. In October 1931, he composed a twenty-eight-line poem for Gisela and Max. The third verse read:

> You land of Baden at the Königstuhl
> Among German lands, the crown,
> And Heidelberg its diamond:
> Lord, make it my home town!

The Nazi Takeover of Heidelberg

Nazis pretended to be dominant among Heidelberg students by 1931, although no more than a third of the students ever voted that way in secret ballots or joined the party.[11] Only one of the fifty-nine regular (*ordentlicher*) professors was an outspoken Nazi supporter and anti-Semite: the Nobel Prize–winning physicist, Philipp Lenard. In August 1933, however, the national regime introduced the authoritarian *Führerprinzip* to the university and vested all power in the Rektor. The historian Willy Andreas was Rektor at that time, and he stated rather boldly that he preferred the existing democratic procedures. From then on, the academic Senate could only advise.

In every faculty except that of law, the opponents to the Weimar regime—who were not Nazis but still nationalist and authoritarian—had already been in the overwhelming majority. It was close only in the faculty of law: nine for, nine against, and three undetermined. As the economist Alfred Weber, brother of the sociologist Max Weber, wrote later: "Wasn't all that Heidelberg spirit nothing but a masquerade?... How could one have been so carried away by otherworldly, romantic dreams of heroism when a totally different hero was about to kick in the door?"[12]

Rektor Willy Andreas, aged forty-nine, bravely wrote a fifteen-page memorandum to the education minister of Baden, stating that the *Führerprinzip* was not applicable to universities because science depended on the free exchange among equals and because bureaucratizing universities would stifle creativity. As a result, his salary was cut sharply when his term was over in October 1933, but he was not dismissed.[13]

By 1937, 40 percent of the regular professors of 1932 had resigned or were fired for racial or political reasons. Some of the remaining professors joined the Nazi Party and made speeches praising Hitler and condemning Jews. Student enrollment fell from 3,687 in the summer of 1933 to 1,815 in the winter of 1937–1938, and the number of certified professors declined from 59 to 32. The number of uncertified faculty rose from 34 to 49, and among these, Nazis were conspicuous. For "Aryans" to remain on the faculty, however, they only had to be silent about National Socialism; they did not have to support it actively.[14]

Wilhelm Groh, forty-three years old, a specialist in labor law, became the new Rektor (and university Führer) in 1933, and he stood to be re-elected in 1934. On that occasion, he appeared before the faculty in his brown storm trooper's uniform and shouted, "No more silly secrecy! German men vote openly!" He was also the only candidate. Many faculty members accordingly handed Groh their ballots unfolded with one hand and gave a Nazi salute with the other. Max Gutzwiller fixed Groh with a hostile stare and handed him a folded ballot with a write-in candidate and no salute. The philosopher Karl Jaspers had tried to dissuade Max from this gesture, but Max asked how else he could express his contempt as one lawyer to another. As a result, his salary, like that of other dissidents, was reduced.

As soon as he heard about the pay cut, Max telephoned the Rektor and asked if Germany still had a government of law. "Is that supposed to be a criticism?" said Groh in a self-assured manner. "As a lawyer, you should understand my meaning," replied Max. Two hours later the dean of the law faculty heard about the incident and called Max to tell him he must be out of his mind.[15] In Groh's view, every professor was either a comrade or an enemy of National Socialism, and he regretted that "the number of responsible fighters" on his side was "quite small." An "iron broom" would be used to cleanse the establishment, and untouchable "islands of bliss" would not be tolerated.[16]

No iron broom was actually needed because most remaining faculty members had little difficulty in making what is nowadays called a paradigm shift. Eugen Fehrle said his relation to Hitler was a matter of "the heart, a feeling in the German soul, based on the fact that once we were governed, but today we are led." Hitler was like a physician who "had to make an incision to remove pus to prevent fatal blood poisoning." The swastika was "like a star that shows us the way ... toward hope." A legal scholar, Heinz Hildebrandt, saw National Socialism "as permeated by the highest ideals" and "illuminated by a heroic point of view." Another former legal expert, now a brown-shirted storm trooper, said: "Justice is what serves the German people, and unjust is what hurts them." The military historian, Paul Schmitthenner, a later Rektor, saw the Weimar Republic as a "world of insanity, crime, and shame ... the Germany of heroic pride turned into one of subordination, reeking like a cadaver." In repeating these and many more citations, historian Christian Jansen notes that virtually every National Socialist cliché had been taken up by some Heidelberg professor.[17]

The only professor who stayed on throughout the Third Reich and openly defied National Socialism was the conservative geographer, Alfred Hettner, who published a journal. He mocked the new belief in miracles and transcendental ideas and rejected unclear holistic notions. Accused of having ignored the "young generation," he asked every challenger for his credentials as an expert, besides youth. When his own approach was labeled as "liberal," he asked his antagonist to demonstrate the superiority of any alternative approach in practice. Hettner was never punished. Instead, he showed that dozens of his colleagues had overdone their silence, opportunism, and duplicity.[18]

Nazism as Seen by Gisela and Max

Gisela and Max at first saw Nazism as an inept proletarian copy of the French Revolution. The emancipatory events of 1789 had been made possible by long decades of cool thought that overcame tradition. Abstract theories in physics and astronomy had explained the mechanism of the cosmos, and, as Descartes had foreseen, philosophers would similarly try to deduce human behavior from simple premises. Their lofty cerebral exercises laid the foundation for 1789.

By contrast, wrote Max, the "uprising" of 1933, if it could be called that, and its ideology came from "hundreds of hazily smoldering heads who mistook their intellectual puberty for political visions" that were actually based on the "clever hypnosis of barely a dozen slogans." Its foundation was lame, inarticulate, and oriented toward the "most primitive mass instincts." One could not respect phrases such as "diseased plutocracy," "swamp of business corruption," "folk-devouring rabble Jews," or "international asphalt intellectualism." Max found ludicrous the way that Nazis praised their pretense of superlative masculinity, eternal youth, and the providential creativity of Germans, while scolding the rest of mankind as inferior subhumans "whose only hope for dignity was to voluntarily subordinate themselves to the master race."[19]

Writing while German armies were at their zenith in Egypt and the Caucasus in mid-1942, Max explained the Nazis' rise to power as follows:

> First came the uncompromising impudence of the leaders ... who had nothing to lose and who sensed the irresolution of the newfangled [Weimar] government of party secretaries, lawyers, gymnasium teachers, and professors.... Second, the Nazis knew how to rally all losers—the demoted, the failed, and the bitter—around its flag, a symbol to all who nursed grudges: the anti-Communists, anti-Catholics, anti-Semites, monetary heretics, racial and agrarian reformers, folklorists, devotees of the deposed Kaiser, and adherents of Nordic heathenism.... Finally, brown-clothed storm troopers noisily terrified an insecure bourgeoisie with well-timed atrocities, so dim-witted industrialists considered it wise to buy friendly neutrality with support of all types.
>
> All of that was insufficient for a complete assumption of power and suppression of all resistance, yes, of all criticism and every warning. As the victory of the "movement" grew more likely, however, it was joined by widespread layers of opportunists, cowards, insensitive snobs, and the naively hopeful, who wanted to share in the booty, to be on the winning side, and perhaps to have some constructive influence.[20]

Anti-Semitism

On the Heidelberg faculty in 1932 were twenty men who identified themselves as practicing Jews and fifteen others who were converted Jews, a combined 15 percent. Of these thirty-five men, eleven, or nearly a third, had supported the Weimar Republic, while only two had identified with the conservative opposition, which was authoritarian but not National Socialist. Of the rest of the faculty, only 10 percent supported the republic, and many more were opposed.[21]

Although authoritarian nationalism and conservatism were widespread in Heidelberg in the 1920s, racial anti-Semitism was at least not rampant. Fifty members of the community, including ten professors, had signed a declaration in 1919 condemning the "spiteful fight against our Jewish fellow citizens ... blaming them for military, political, and economic misfortune.... We protest against these one-sided generalizations."[22] But when the German League for Human Rights circulated a similar petition in 1930, only one professor, Martin Dibelius, a theologian, chose to sign. Nevertheless, until the Nazi takeover, written anti-Jewish statements by the Heidelberg faculty, excluding those by Philipp Lenard, were almost non-existent.

Like all Germans in 1933, the faculty of Heidelberg University had to fill out forms about the religion and ethnicity of their parents and grandparents so that expulsions could begin. The medical faculty expressed its doubts about the prospects in a letter to the Ministry of Education on April 5, 1933: "We cannot overlook that German Jews have participated in scientific achievements and have produced great medical personalities. As physicians, we feel obligated to express our misgivings when responsible convictions are in danger of being displaced by emotions and force."[23]

In 1933, Max had an offer to take the chair in civil law at the new University of Istanbul, Turkey, but Gisela thought it meant impossible school problems for the children, so Max declined the offer. However, that year Gisela accompanied him and friends to Greece, fulfilling her fondest dream. They took a ship from Venice to Corfu, then traveled by car from Olympia over the mountains to Sparta, and with another ship went across the Aegean Sea to Smyrna, Ephesus, Pergamon, and Troy. Finally, they crossed the Hellespont and concluded their voyage in Athens and Delphi. Everywhere she stood in front of statues and temples that had been imprinted in her mind for decades. Among olive trees and cypresses at the Creek of Ilissos, she happily identified the place where, according to Plato, Socrates must have talked to Phaidros. The last entry in her Greek travel journal reads: "Anyone who has experienced this will never be entirely miserable."

Actions against Max Gutzwiller

The Nazis' case against Max Gutzwiller was special. Not only was he a foreigner, being Swiss, but (like seven other professors) he was reprehensibly "clanned up" with Jews (*jüdisch versippt*), being married to Gisela. Although no national regulations had yet been issued for dealing with the "clanned up," Max was barred from participating in examinations. He reported:

> Near the end of 1934, a few circumspect colleagues began to avoid me. An oppressive silence reigned in the faculty lounge. But from time to time I boiled over, and vehement quarrels took place.
>
> At the beginning, Gisela resigned herself with a certain equanimity, as I also tried to do, especially since we still had a good circle of steady friends. The removal of more and more trusted associates from the faculty caused her the first wounds. Others followed, such as having to avoid all university functions to escape insults. The many difficulties her father had with his clinic ... heavily burdened her spirits....
>
> Month after month, the humiliations of "non-Aryan" fellow citizens were exacerbated in the most cunning ways, severely testing marriages like ours. The more decisively as

"unaffected" partner I repelled this cowardly abomination, the more my very indignation seemed to hurt the already deeply wounded spirit of my life's companion. But we survived this heavy burden, which actually deepened our mutual affection."[24]

Among his colleagues, Max noticed that quite a few were intimidated by the aggressive behavior of students who menaced and stigmatized anyone unsupportive as "rotten, senile, and from the day before yesterday." One colleague of the legal faculty told Max frankly that he would "find it simply unbearable to no longer be in the ruling class." It took uncommon courage to oppose the shameless claim that Nazism was the sole repository of genuine patriotism. Endless speeches and tasteless propaganda poisoned the atmosphere, and the feeble warnings of the few about rapidly sinking academic standards came much too late, recorded Max. Loyalty to the university changed to contempt and corruption. Unlimited press attacks had to be swallowed silently. Even the most justified doubts unleashed persecution.

> Students who styled themselves as "fighters for the national revolution" were granted all sorts of exemptions in examinations and were elected to leading positions by means of unbearable pressure. Those who rose in this manner were mostly the ones who had previously been in the shadows because of inadequacy and who now thought of themselves as misunderstood geniuses. Safe from consequences, they used their unfamiliar power for personal gain. Whoever tried to assess historical conditions accurately in lectures was certain to earn the gratitude of the decent majority but would therefore be labeled as a secret "saboteur" by the cadres of the Nazi Party and find himself in a hopeless cul de sac. In discussion periods these Nazis asked the instructor cleverly contrived but ensnaring questions so that they could later use the answers in public accusations. At university ceremonies, more and more professors wrapped themselves in the protective disguise of brown party uniforms, so that in this military scene the few remaining in academic robes embodied a lost epoch.[25]

On May 21, 1935, storm troopers posted themselves at the doors of Max's lecture hall and blocked anyone who approached. They said that his disparaging comments about National Socialism had gone too far. It was the beginning of a permanent boycott that was also applied to his Jewish colleagues, Walter Jellinek and Ernst Levy, and to four others. Max immediately took a train to Berlin and with the help of the Swiss ambassador, Paul Dinichert, arranged a meeting in the Ministry for Culture. He was told by an official in an SS uniform that spontaneous boycotts had not been authorized and that the dean of the law faculty would receive instructions in writing to unblock the lectures. They were issued, but Rektor Groh, who hated Max and feared a confrontation with Nazi students, did nothing.

The boycott was reported in the Swiss press, which asked how such disturbances could take place and why students had not been punished for the disorder. Rektor Groh replied on October 23, 1935: "In the summer semester, students declined to attend the lectures of professors who are Jewish or who, like Professor Gutzwiller, view National Socialism with aversion. Student leaders tell their comrades clearly that these professors are unacceptable as teachers and educators. There was no occasion for me to oppose their justified aspirations. My only concern was to make sure that the orderly routine of the university would not be disturbed. That has happened, and the conduct of the students provided no occasion for disciplinary action."[26]

The Baden and Reich ministers of science and education agreed with the university's Führer that the time had come to Nazify the law faculty and that Jellinek and Levy should be dismissed. As a Swiss, Gutzwiller was to be chastened and transferred to another German university to make a fresh start. Max, however, resolved to "emigrate" back to his homeland, a decision that could mean a devastating loss of savings and property. It led to "a wholly incredible number of applications, depositions, trips to Berlin and Karlsruhe, presentations, interviews, and scenes ... a [fight] that took brains and tenacity that would have been more appropriate in the service of some higher task." The final document relieving Max of his duties, the *Entpflichtungsurkunde,* had to be signed by Adolf Hitler himself. The Führer wrote on June 9, 1936: "Ich spreche Ihnen für Ihre akademische Wirksamkeit und dem Reiche geleisteten Dienste meinen Dank aus" (I declare my thanks to you for your academic efficacy and your service to the Reich).

This document was also signed by the minister for education, science, and culture, Bernhard Rust, and transmitted by Rektor Groh. No further words of thanks were added by Groh. He merely wrote: "For the minister, I transmit to you the document of June 9, which relieves you of your official duties at the faculty of law." Without that document, the Gutzwillers' Heidelberg house, insurance policies, and other assets could have been partially confiscated as the penalty for "fleeing the Reich." The document arrived on July 3, 1936, but earlier in April the family had already settled in St. Gallen, Switzerland, just in time for the new school year.[27]

Heidelberg and the Holocaust

Two Heidelberg professors were deeply involved in research that entailed killing children deemed mentally defective in a euthanasia program that began in 1938 and continued until 1943. The two professors were Carl Schneider, director of the Clinic for Psychiatry and Neurology, and Konrad Zucker, professor of psychiatry. Heidelberg thus became one of Germany's two principal training centers for the scientific murder of children that went on at thirty killing clinics for three years.[28] The other center was at Görden. The professors' findings were applied on an industrial scale at all the extermination camps.

In 1933, some 1,100 people in Heidelberg were Jewish by faith (1.3 percent of the population of 84,600). But the Nazis also classified 600 others as Jews. Of the combined 1,700, only 23 survived in Heidelberg. Fourteen committed suicide, and 879 (51.8 percent) emigrated. The remaining 780 (46 percent) were mostly murdered in the Holocaust, although the fate of many cannot be traced. The main deportation took 309 people to the concentration camp of Gurs in the western foothills of the French Pyrenees on October 22, 1940. At 4 AM that morning, SS troopers and Gestapo agents broke into people's homes and ordered them to pack no more than fifty pounds. The victims were taken in trucks to the railway station, where a train had been stealthily prepared. After four days, this sealed train reached Gurs by way of Mulhouse, Dijon, Lyon, Avignon, and Toulouse. About 7,000 other Jews from southwestern Germany were also deported to Vichy France and Gurs that October.

The camp at Gurs had once served as a shelter for refugees from the Spanish Civil War and seemed to have room for 15,000 inmates. International relief agencies had access to the camps, and a few of the Heidelberg deportees managed to get affidavits to emigrate to England, Switzerland, the United States, or the rest of Vichy France, which took some of the aged and most of the children. About 86 of the 309 Heidelbergers died in epidemics that swept the camps. More than 100 were eventually shipped from Gurs to Auschwitz for industrialized murder. Together with 6,000 other Jews, they were shipped first to the transit camp at Drancy near Paris and from there to the killing centers in Poland.[29]

Some very young children and sickly old Heidelbergers had been exempted from the Gurs transport in 1940 but were shipped directly to Auschwitz in 1942–1944. Sixty-five others were in hiding by now, but of these forty-two were tracked down in the city by the Gestapo, who were helped by denunciations. Thus, only twenty-three people survived. Fifteen "clanned-up" people or "mongrels" were shipped to the Theresienstadt concentration camp as late as February 1945 but were liberated at the end of the war three months later.[30]

During the war, the Allies never bombed Heidelberg, viewing it as a symbol of salvageable German culture. In 1945, it became the US Army's headquarters for the American zone of occupation.

Return to Switzerland

Six years of life remained for Gisela in 1936, two in St. Gallen and four in Fribourg. The two boys, Hellmy and Martin, were enrolled in the Cantonal Gymnasium of Trogen, Appenzell, near St. Gallen, so the family settled there in the spring of 1936. In accordance with then prevalent European values, the boys' education seemed to have higher priority than that of their three sisters. Both Gisela and Max felt relieved to be back in a land they considered "gently wholesome and modestly practical," compared with Germany. They knew that Switzerland also had Nazis, under a *Gauleiter* (regional chief) who ranted about Jewish and Communist conspiracies and who led marches carrying swastika banners and singing hoarsely about a better Europe. Terrified conservatives typically pondered the benefits of giving local Nazis some power. For the time being, though, the difference from Nazi Heidelberg was vast and refreshing.

The five Gutzwiller children could readily speak Swiss dialect at school since Max had always spoken it to them at Heidelberg and on vacations in the Alps. Even Gisela was thoroughly used to it and could adapt. Soon, a few of their inflections and idioms were those of St. Gallen, rather than Basel.

For Gisela, as the most tenderhearted of the Strassmann children, the unjust wreckage of her father's lifelong work and hopes in Germany caused a deep depression. An aggravating circumstance was that Max had no sympathy for the old man's urge to find some ray of hope, some mitigating rationale for reconciling his own tragic fate with alleged patriotic sides of National Socialism. To a democratic Swiss attorney imbued with ideals from ancient Greece and the French Enlightenment, the old man's efforts to see redeeming qualities in Nazism were ludicrous. Decades later, when I asked Max what to do with the Paul Ferdinand's diaries, he told me that they were hopeless because Paul was so "falsch gewickelt" (deluded, or off the beam).

As best he could, however, Max tried to ease Gisela's pain with the standard remedy of vacations—to Samedan in January 1937 for winter sports and to Lake Como in April. But when he began commuting back to Fribourg in late April, to the professorship that he had given up ten years earlier, it left Gisela alone with her thoughts, Tuesdays through Fridays, when the children were at school or in bed. It was too much. She had a nervous breakdown.

To cheer her up, Max made plans to build a new house in Fribourg. With a hundred thousand inherited francs, he bought the site of her choice and hired an architect. Nothing worked. A case of sciatica aggravated her condition. Then their Heidelberg dachshund, Moki, died of an illness on Sunday, July 13, 1937. The little fellow, who would no longer amuse Gisela, had been with them for five years, perhaps barking too much, begging too hopefully, digging stubbornly where he should not have been, and following the children to school and coming home alone. On future walks, no passerby would again say how droll Moki was in Swiss German: "Nai bischt du aber en härzige!" (Aren't you a darling!) or "Lueg doch, Mamme, das nuggisch Daggely!" (Look, Mom, a cute wiener dog!). Max quoted these comments in a commemorative booklet for Moki.[31]

So in late July 1937, the five children were sent to the Berlin grandparents in Dahlem, and Max took on the housekeeping in St. Gallen. With their servant on vacation, he learned how to make breakfast, even coffee. The other meals were delivered twice a day from the Rotmonten pension where they had first lived in St. Gallen. Max and Gisela were now continually together, usually reading outside as in the old days. Max summarized the results five years later: "The heavens were radiant day after day, and this time the convalescence was complete, notwithstanding a few later relapses."[32]

On March 11, 1938, Max gave Gisela a book that had become a best seller throughout the world, *Gone with the Wind*. That day, the Nazis marched into Austria. Max had been working on a lecture for a conference of the Legal Society of Vienna, a group with many Jews. This occasion itself was now gone with the wind.

Somewhat later Max participated in the Congress of the International Law Association in Amsterdam and had his first chance for an all-out confrontation with Nazis on neutral terrain. The German delegation sought to remove a Jewish delegate from a major committee and put the right to discriminate against Jews into the draft of an international resolution. In both cases, Max defeated the Nazis, although he found that British support for his position was lax, in his view because "the English clearly had no sense of the threatening catastrophe." The British delegate told him privately that he agreed with the former foreign secretary, Lord John Simon, that "as long as not a single hair of any Englishman was pulled, Mr. Hitler's movement was not his concern."[33]

Meanwhile, the last dabs of paint were applied to the new house in Fribourg, Praz de Riaux 4. It sat high on a hill at the southern edge of town opposite an old farmstead. Beyond ranges of Alpine foothills they could see the Moléson and the distant icy dome of the Mont Blanc. With both boys in the Trogen Gymnasium in Appenzell, Gisela rose every morning at seven to have breakfast with the girls, who were in school locally, and went shopping daily for fresh groceries. She planted, watered, and weeded flowers and herbs, especially dill, sage, and lavender. In the afternoons she monitored the music practice of her daughters, and after dinner, if weather allowed, came a stroll with Max through nearby meadows. The evenings were spent reading, writing letters to Berlin and Trogen, mending clothes, checking homework, and listening to bedtime prayers. On Sunday afternoons, the family usually stayed together and played duets, trios, and even quartets for one another on cello, violin, piano, and flute. Max wrote four years later that Gisela "was the uncontested center of our family circle, set the tone, showed a mother's pride, and was simply happy."[34]

Catastrophes

By early June 1940, Poland, Denmark, Norway, and the Low Countries had all fallen to Nazi armored divisions; an outflanked British army was being evacuated at Dunkirk; and, unlike 1916, a German army was crossing the Somme in a massive drive toward Paris. Gisela wrote to Erwin in Texas on June 3, 1940: "I suppose I don't have to say that I've long wished to write to you, and that everything happening has led to moods that have kept me from doing so!" She went on with a response to Erwin's letters and then told about each of her children. Max was busy preparing a number of publications and arranging the opening of a major new university building. "There is little satisfaction in lecturing about law in these times, and lawyers in general are doing badly and are under new pressures. Max has often wished that he had chosen some other branch of knowledge."

An aunt from Basel was living with them, the letter continued. She had "evacuated herself" since Basel, right on the frontier, was too disrupted by the war. Much worse was Gisela's worry about Gertrud Nothmann, once Gertrud Bernard, who had been Erwin's beloved around 1915. She had fled Germany to The Hague and had been waiting for her papers to emigrate to the United States. With Holland invaded, everything looked grim for Gertrud. Gisela would inquire about her soon.

Forty days after Gisela's letter, Max wrote to Erwin, bringing him up to date about his unsuccessful efforts to have the inheritance from Paul transferred out of Germany. By now, July 13, 1940, France had fallen. Hitler was photographed at Napoleon's tomb in Paris, and an invasion of Britain, called "Operation Sea Lion," was expected. The semester at the University of Fribourg had just ended.

> We are also trying to bring up our children to be self-reliant as a counterweight to whatever we may have to put up with.... My brother Ernst, looking worn out, has driven here from southern France and reports that there they blame the Freemasons, the Jews, and the lawyers, whom they consider all one and the same.
>
> You are right: the last months were sickening. We kept hoping for a miracle, lightning striking German headquarters. The fate of France moved us almost more than our own, the collapse of our prototype culture. By the way, Basel looks like a French-German combat zone. Concrete barricades and barbed wire are everywhere. A row of steel and cement tank traps runs straight through the garden of my sister Charlotte. My brother Ernst, claiming to be an expert, dismissed them: "Worthless. Too high. A 70 ton tank can break them like matches." The village of Haltingen, 4 kilometers north of Basel, where we children always went on Sundays, has been shot to ashes by Maginot Line cannons. The nights must have been ghastly.

Two single-spaced pages follow about complex negotiations with respect to the inheritance and about confused correspondence with Berlin and New York.

On January 7, 1942, Gisela was examined by a gynecologist, Dr. König in Bern. Max was asked to return alone, and the physician told him that a growth on the ovaries was malignant. The report from the pathology laboratory about a biopsy was devastating. It was hopeless to treat a cancer so far metastasized. Max was told the phases in the deterioration of Gisela's body that were coming. "I often asked myself," he wrote later, "what might have possessed the man to treat me so inhumanely. My primitive conclusion was that he wanted to impress me with the accuracy of his diagnosis." They resolved not to tell Gisela.

Hospital rooms in those days had no radios or intercoms, and Gisela heard no music until a former patient came to give a concert on the institution's piano. She told Max, "To hear music again after such a long time, was very special. Of course, it made me cry at first. But then I felt a deep peace, the heavenly peace that comes from music."

During those weeks, Max sat for hours at his desk, unable to work on anything. A leaden weariness overtook him. After taking care of routine tasks at work and home, he traveled to Bern to hear the contrasting opinions of doctors, then pretended to be carefree at Gisela's bedside before catching the train back to Fribourg. Waking up was the worst time, having to face everything once more. He tried intense prayers and told himself that dreams were not a question of time—that the remaining weeks could outdo the preceding years in meaning.

Nightfall

On March 18, 1942, Gisela and Max took a train over the Alps to Locarno and checked in at the Park Hotel for two weeks, a golden sunset. The almond trees were already in bloom, and yellow butterflies were busy among the camellias. Gisela and Max wandered among the spring-green meadows to ancient hamlets with arcades and down to the docks for a boat ride to Ascona. Some tourists mistook them for late honeymooners.

Gisela received the last communion in April at the Clinica Santa Agnese in Locarno. Medications for sleep and against pain were injected during the afternoon of April 14 as Max sat there reading *The Imitation of Christ*. Waking up later, Gisela said, "My darling, all of you should enjoy a good life." She woke up once more, and a nurse took her temperature. A doctor came and went. On the verge of sleep, Gisela smiled at Max.

The next morning, April 15, Max was called to the hospital at seven and found the head nurse waiting at the entrance. "But she's still alive?" The nurse shook her head.

Max went to the room and saw Gisela's face, "no longer the familiar features, but something without life ... and the recognition hit me like devastating lightning that something ultimate had happened, frightening and ultimate beyond all I had imagined ... a ghastly silence reigned on the bed. A new absence forged our loving, natural, and indispensable union into something past.... How should I now carry on my life apart from her—not caring about her, not accompanied by her, not guarded by her, not elevated by her, not charmed, not enriched?"[35]

In Fribourg, Max went with Ursula to select a burial site under a chestnut tree in the cemetery. The coffin bedecked with flowers was set in the parlor, and the children sat around it for hours, looking at photo albums and saying prayers. The funeral service was held on April 18 at Saint Peter's Church, crowded for once. Not many people followed to the cemetery. Ruth gave each one there a red rose to toss into the fresh grave.

By now, most of Gisela's relatives had left Europe for the United States, Latin America, and Australia. The war was at its low point with the watershed battles of Midway, Stalingrad, and El Alamein still months away. Hedwig, Antonie, and Erwin would learn about Gisela's death by black-bordered airmail sent via Lisbon. We all received copies of *Büchlein mit dem Denkmal* and saw a picture of Gisela's tombstone. Above her name, "Gisela Gutzwiller, born Strassmann," is the biblical passage, "The Truth Shall Make You Free."

Chapter 8

Stalked by Nazis in the Schumannstrasse: 1933–1936

The loss of the Strassmann Frauenklinik in all its glory and the worldwide dispersal of family and colleagues are told in this chapter mainly from the point of view of the clinic's founder and director, Paul Ferdinand Strassmann, and his wife Hedwig (née Rosenberg). When the Nazis took power in Germany, they classified Paul as a Jew, questioned his right to operate a hospital, and forced him out of his profession.

Questionnaires and Decrees

In Berlin on March 15, 1933, Julius Lippert, the leading Nazi member of the City Council, was appointed as a novel *Staatskommissar* by Hermann Göring (the Prussian minister of the interior). Now entrusted with great powers to "cleanse" the city of "Marxists, corruption, and Jews," on March 17 he ordered the dismissal of all Jewish physicians from public hospitals. Non-Jewish physicians swearing allegiance to Hitler were eager to take their place.

Doctors, like other Germans, conformed obediently to Nazi demands, sending forms to one another about their ancestry and nervously filling them out. In April 1933, Dr. Beckmann of the Berlin Chamber of Physicians (Ärztekammer für Berlin) sent everyone a single page inquiring about the ethnicity (*Stamm*) of their parents and grandparents, their religion, and their military service and decorations. A second one-page form came in May from a Dr. Claus of the Greater Berlin Society of Physicians (Ärtztebund). He warned "with collegial respect" that wrong or incomplete answers would mean the loss of all medical rights and licenses. A third questionnaire sent by the government's health insurance company was six pages long and had to be returned within a week. Not ethnicity or race, but religion and conversions had to be reported this time, under the rubric "*Konfession (auch Wechsel)*." A fourth, similar questionnaire was sent by the University of Berlin.

New decrees specified that "non-Aryan" physicians could not be paid with government health insurance funds and could not employ other physicians with such funds. Paul and Erwin applied for an exemption from the rule but were informed five months later that the request was denied. They were given one week in May 1934 to prove that they no longer employed health insurance physicians. The notice was signed, incongruously, "Mit kollegialer Hochachtung" (with high collegial respect).

Numbers and Proportions

In 1925, according to the last pre-Nazi census, Jews so classified by religion constituted only 0.9 percent of the German population of 62.7 million, that is, 564,400 people. Of these, 172,700 or 30.6 percent lived in Berlin and made up 4.3 percent of Berlin's population of 4.4 million. Even in the elegant western districts of Charlottenburg and Wilmersdorf, Jews composed only 9 and 13 percent of the population. According to data of 1910, some 15.8 percent of Jews had come from abroad, especially Poland and Galicia (which were Russian and Austrian). Another 27.5 percent had migrated from former German provinces in the east, such as West Prussia and Posen, the homeland of the Strassmanns and the Levys in the past century.[1]

Some believed that the 1925 tally of 172,700 Jews residing in Berlin was low and suggested that many Jews had denied their religious affiliation or were living there illegally. After a thorough investigation, Hubert Pollack concluded in 1931 that estimates of the number of Jews could not be raised above 179,000, meaning an underreporting of only 3.5 percent. In May 1939, a Nazi report said that the number of Jews by "race" was 4.8 percent higher than the number by religion.

While Jews were relatively few in percentage terms, they were conspicuously successful, making up a quarter of the enrollment of gymnasiums in Berlin in 1933. Twelve percent of university lecturers were Jews by confession, and another 7 percent had converted to Christianity. All were equally "non-Aryan." In 1933, Jews made up 48 percent of Berlin's attorneys and 52 percent of the city's physicians (compared with 13 percent in all of Germany). In five years, from 1934 to 1939, the number of gynecologists and obstetricians in Berlin fell by 89 doctors, or 37.9 percent, from 235 to 146.[2] Accurate data do not exist, but since the number of "Aryan" specialists increased during these years, the number of expelled or emigrating gynecologists and obstetricians must have approached one hundred.

By early 1939, over half the Jews from all of Germany had emigrated. Some 130,000 (including Austrians) went to the United States. Eventually, 170,000 German Jews were killed in concentration camps, including 51,000, or 30 percent, from Berlin. The Jewish population of Berlin in 1939 had fallen by over half to 78,700. A further 20,000 still managed to emigrate, but over 50,000 were sent to extermination camps. By the end of the war, a mere 4,700 Jews in mixed marriages lived in the city, and 1,400 others survived "underground."[3]

In this industrialized murder, physicians played a leading, almost proprietary role. Soon after Hitler came to power, a law for promoting hereditary health (*Erbgesundheitsgesetz*) was enacted on July 14, 1933, and physicians under the Reichsärzteführer (Reich Physicians' Führer), Gerhard Wagner, were put in charge of organizing some 400,000 sterilizations of the deformed and mentally retarded. Doctors were told that such sterilizations provided an opportunity for research in the use of radium or X-rays. The influential professor, Rudolf Ramm, of the University of Berlin, wrote that physicians were "biological soldiers" who had a duty to the nation to "keep our blood lines pure," not just to keep patients alive regardless of merit. Wagner was the first to whom Hitler told in 1935 that the time had come to move on from sterilization to killing undesirables, those with "lives not worth living." First to be killed was a blind boy from Leipzig, who lacked a leg and part of an arm. Other children followed, and, using the war as a cover, adult killings began in October 1939. The physicians who organized this secret "euthanasia" program for adults—with its six killing clinics, which used carbon monoxide—were assigned two years later to the genocide program of killing Jews. Meanwhile, 45 percent of German physicians joined the Nazi Party, a higher percentage than in other occupations. Hitler's biomedical vision for German regeneration flattered doctors, and the elimination of Jewish competition was remunerative.[4]

Paul, a Slow Learner?

In 1933, however, the crimes of the future seemed beyond the imagination of both Nazis and Jews. With his uncomplicated patriotism, Paul Ferdinand Strassmann could not understand the pressure to give up and get out. He was devoted to Germany, Prussia, and Berlin, took pride in medical science, and had compassion for his patients. Who could doubt that he would fulfill all of his duties cheerfully? He was a rather authoritarian, patriotic optimist who expected harmony, not malice. In the early 1930s, he could not picture the evil of Hitler, Goebbels, Streicher, Himmler, and their loathsome cohort. If the new government overreached itself with mistakes, that had happened before in history and would not last. Paul's illusion came from a disposition too sunny and humanitarian to detect evil. He could not envision prominent German compatriots behaving monstrously.

Thus, Paul remained unrealistically hopeful from mid-1933 to mid-1935 despite all that had happened, including a failed attempt by a subordinate, Dr. Martin Jung, to take over the clinic-hospital. During this period, the war hero, General Paul von Hindenburg, was still president; radicals among Ernst Röhm's storm troopers challenged Hitler from the left (until they themselves were murdered on July 1, 1934); and from the right, army generals were expected to oppose anything too unconventional. Would not the wind go out of the Nazis' sails and make them sensible and constructive? Had they not already relaxed the one-Jewish-grandmother standard?

The Failed Coup by Martin Jung

Dr. Martin Jung, a contributor to Paul Strassmann's 1926 Festschrift[5] and his chief of staff during 1924–1932, in June 1933 openly denounced the Strassmann family as Jewish. One morning, Jung appeared at the clinic wearing a swastika, and he remained seated, reading the Nazi newspaper, *Der Voelkische Beobachter*, as Paul entered his office. Paul had told Jung on January 1, 1933, that since Erwin was now a professor and returning to the clinic from a research leave, Paul could no longer let Jung work in a position superior to someone who had higher qualifications. So Erwin replaced Jung as chief of staff of the clinic. Jung believed bitterly and erroneously that Paul had used connections to obtain the professorship for Erwin and that he had not lifted a finger to advance Jung's career. But if the Strassmanns were Jews, perhaps the Nazis would now put Jung in charge.

Jung made his move when the new regulations forbidding the treatment of health-insured patients in non-Aryan clinics were instituted. On June 24, 1933, Erwin wrote to Ilse (who was summering with the children in her hometown, Bad Nauheim) that without health-insured patients, the clinic could not be maintained. It was close up shop or let Jung take over. Paul decided, nevertheless, to let Jung go: "Parents are calm, although they realize that the end of the clinic is in sight."

Meanwhile, a group of American physicians was visiting the clinic, and Erwin wrote that it seemed like the good old days, perhaps a last glow. His father had performed three major operations in their presence, had given a lecture, and had hosted a luncheon for forty guests with speeches and toasts. Erwin wrote: "We were ashamed to admit to being already dead, threatened with closure now for three days. Our response is under way, at the moment through Antonie [who notified her aviation acquaintance, Hermann Göring]. An appointment has been arranged. Today Antonie and I saw a movie, yesterday chess with Father, Sunday cards. Family life blooms.... As in all fateful times, we are calm. Among the employees, however, one feels apprehension.... What is life worth without respect? Nothing" (June 27, 1933).

Facing insolvency and political threats, the clinic was to dismiss all fifty-eight nurses, workers, and physicians on August 1, 1933. The visiting Americans invited Erwin and Paul to a farewell dinner at the Adlon Hotel, and the problem was finally discussed. In a letter, Will Mayo asked: "Can I do anything for you?"

On June 30, 1933, Erwin wrote that Antonie had met for half an hour with Göring. She later sent him the book, *Kriegsbriefe Gefallener Studenten* (Combat Letters of Fallen Students),[6] which contained letters from Hellmuth and Erwin. Erwin wrote to Ilse: "He [Göring] is completely informed about Father, myself, and the clinic.... Of course, no final approval was given [to Antonie]. But he noted everything and will make a decision. More could not have happened" (June 30, 1933). On July 5, 1933, Erwin telegraphed Ilse: "BARRIERS DOWN AND DISMISSALS CANCELED." Personnel of the clinic were exhilarated and almost daily reported outrages committed by Jung that they had not dared to report before.

A few days later, Erwin and Antonie saw a play, Bjornson's *When the Young Wine Blooms*, in which Emmy Sonnemann, Göring's fiancée and Antonie's long-time friend, acted. They saw Emmy after the performance, and she told them that she had cried and cried when Göring showed her *Combat Letters*. But Erwin wrote: "Main thing for me now—to learn English." He felt he could trust neither the government nor "Aryan" physicians. According to a historian of German medicine, "it was clear that the ongoing arrests and condemnations of Jewish doctors were in no small degree the result of the German physicians' collusion and outright cooperation with regime authorities."[7]

After the war, Erwin received a letter from Martin Jung, dated December 4, 1946:

Most honorable Professor:
... As a former member of the SS, I am still in a British concentration camp and unable to contribute any [family income] support. They are employing me in a medical capacity but without compensation.

I therefore turn to you, Professor, in memory of your father, who like you experienced injustice but who escaped this last most bitter fate that we must experience, and ask you respectfully to send us a Care Package and me a pair of striped pants that I could use for a position with the occupation authorities.

Erwin answered the letter in mid-January 1947:

Dear Sir:
You speak of the "collapse of an idea proven to be erroneous." It was your SS which eradicated entire villages and towns and which murdered over six million innocent human beings—all for the sake of your "idea."

What you and your family are experiencing ... cannot be compared to the continual, systematic degradation my father had to suffer....

In all probability, as long as the SS was the most esteemed organization, you were proud. I do not know whether or not you had to do things in Norway while wearing the black uniform which your conscience as a doctor should have prohibited. The point is you did wear it. You are therefore responsible and guilty, and you have to bear the consequences.

Two Deceptively Calm Years

Until the summer of 1935, calm seemed to return. To celebrate the twenty-fifth anniversary of the opening of the clinic, on July 4, 1934, the entrance to the courtyard was decorated with hundreds of intertwined blue cornflowers shaped like the number 25. Everyone was assembled in the auditorium at 9:15 AM as Dr. Zimmer played "Praised be the Lord" on the harmonium. Erwin presented his father a collective gift in the form of a porcelain coffee service decorated with Alpine flowers. Paul replied by commenting on twenty-five years of birthing, healing, and research. He stressed the contributions of all nurses and associates and gave golden rings to two co-workers who had been with him the whole time.

The guestbook of the clinic was filling up with poetry, photographs, cartoons, and other expressions of gratitude, not just in German and European languages, but also in Arabic, Hindi, and Chinese script. Some poems were over five pages or more than a hundred lines long. A verse of sixteen lines was composed by an elderly husband, Julius Zielenziger, for his much younger wife, Charlotte (née Neugebauer), and their nine-pound baby girl. Here is my translation in part:

> 74 years old I am, I tell you true,
> My little woman is just 42.
> We have stayed happy all our days
> Because we love each other in many ways.
> We owe that to Geheimrat Strassmann,
> A man who can do all and then some.

Misleading straws in the wind made Paul feel secure enough to undertake a second voyage to America, not to emigrate but rather to enjoy an excursion. Since 1930, he had been an honorary member of the American Society of Obstetricians, Gynecologists, and Abdominal Surgeons, and now he was invited to lecture at the meetings of the affiliated Interstate Postgraduate Medical Association of North America at Philadelphia. The Prussian minister for science, art, and education considered the voyage "urgently desirable for science and the Fatherland." Meanwhile, Paul learned that using radium could be safer than operating on a tumor to extend a patient's life and to lower her agony.

Pursuit Resumes

In June 1935, however, vehement persecution of Jews resumed, and in September, extreme anti-Semitic decrees were promulgated at the Nuremberg Nazi Party rally. In October 1935, Paul was informed by the Rektor of the Friedrich-Wilhelm University that he was immediately suspended from teaching, since he had replied to an inquiry in 1933 that his "four grandparents were of Jewish descent and members of the Jewish religious community." On December 31, 1935, Paul Ferdinand Strassmann and his son, Erwin, thus lost their licenses to teach at Berlin University "on the basis of Paragraph 2 of the National Citizenship Law and Paragraph 4 of the Directive of November 14, 1935, implementing that law." Both Strassmanns, father and son, lost their titles of professor.

It was at this time that Dr. Gerhart Zimmer, who had been on the clinic's staff for over a decade and had contributed to Paul's 1926 Festschrift, warned a new colleague, Dr. B. Schürmann, and his wife against accepting dinner invitations from the Semitic Strassmanns. When the new physician went anyway, Zimmer reported this to Goebbels, now the *Gauleiter* of Berlin. Although Zimmer in time reversed his course and tried to identify with the Strassmanns, my father, Erwin, often said that this treachery firmed up his decision to emigrate. He let his father write to Will Mayo in Rochester about emigrating. Steps for leasing or selling the clinic began.

Paul faced this persecution with calm despair. A friend, Ellen von Siemens-Helmholtz, convinced him to start a new diary. He began with these words:

> On Sunday, March 8, 1936, Memorial Day [*Heldengedenktag*], the statue of our son, Hellmuth, who fell November 5, 1916, was decorated in the entrance of the clinic, our home. Laurels were twined around his steel helmet. Across the passageway burned two large candles. Between them was the green marble head (by Klimsch) of the playwright Gerhart Hauptmann. The poet's large eyes seemed to regard the pale visage of the warrior asking why this life had to be sacrificed.
>
> We are not allowed to display the colors of the old or the new Reich.
>
> > Du fandest wozu Du ausgesandt
> > Den Weg zur Höh' für Dein Vaterland.
>
> > [You found the path toward destiny,
> > Scaling heights for your Fatherland.]
>
> Thus it is written on the pedestal [from "Drei Kreuze," a poem by Paul Strassmann]. And we, who are no longer to be regarded as Germans, seek consolation in these words!
>
> Outside we hear jubilation and see banners waving because yesterday the radio told everyone—including us assembled in the clinic auditorium—that the Versailles Treaty has been repudiated and that the "demilitarized zone" of the Rhineland has been reoccupied.
>
> We parents, Erwin, brother of the fallen one, and his wife feel as never before the might of this hour. We are facing a farewell. The second son will move out, away from wife and children, away from his old parents, giving up his father's legacy.
>
> His decision was free, and I could neither promote nor oppose it. He is 40 years old, educated as a German and Christian; and as a combat officer, physician, and young professor, he has been hard-working and flawless.
>
> Nothing matters anymore. He is no longer regarded as a German physician. Like me, according to the Law for Protecting "Blood and Honor," he had to dismiss his young secretary and the children's nanny. The university has withdrawn his teaching qualification. As "fully Jewish," he is bound by ever tighter restraints. All organizations (the student association, the athletic club, medical groups) are treating us as ordered. The Aeroclub that he belonged to as an aviator dissolved itself "according to the wishes of its members."
>
> … I am facing the biblical age of 70. Already ghosts are fluttering around the clinic. Erwin, well-meaning relatives, even children and friends would consider it a mercy if I could sell the clinic to the state! Preliminary conversations have been under way ever since Erwin determined to go to the United States.

Paul and Hedwig felt isolated, and on March 12, 1936, he noted: "Quiet evening! Yes, the physicians and assistants no longer associate with their non-Aryan boss. I don't resent that. Their orders are thus, and they don't want to burden their careers." On March 14, he wrote: "Without participating in the intellectual life of my specialty, I feel like a camp-following mechanic. I am forbidden to take part even in postgraduate medical education—actively or passively."

Until September 1938, however, Jews were allowed to treat "Aryan" patients. On March 15, 1936, the diary records: "Today is Army Day. We enjoy this accomplishment. Twenty-seven members of our family [including cousins] served during 1914–1918. A third failed to return! These nine were lucky." A day later, Paul wrote: "Relations with colleagues have changed greatly. 'Aryans' may no longer consult us; 'Jewish physicians' cling together. We non-Aryans are between both groups.... A new ethic exists. A colleague is no longer a colleague.... What is the use of protesting? I am thinking of E. M. [unknown] ... who languishes in jail! 'Taking arms against a sea of troubles' ... is not an option. 'For thine is the power....' Protesting against the victor would be in vain and would not serve the general welfare." He recalled the Sermon on the Mount: "Blessed are they who are persecuted for righteousness' sake: for theirs is the kingdom of heaven" (Matthew 5:10).

Here and there in the diary he reflected on the new ideology:

> The word "race" has been hurled at the German people. It is a "new faith" and very powerful. There is something to it in a limited way. The "Jewish race"—the only one involved—has been a tributary flowing into the mainstream of the nation, surely not for its destruction. Making waves, yes, but also productive and adaptable. This confluence could have been accepted easily, for they were Germans who sacrificed in the war, like all others, who felt German, and who worked for their Fatherland. They were ambitious, of course, but they sought to merge with the nation, and many—like our family—showed with baptism where they belonged.
>
> The non-Aryan grandmother caricatures the tragedy—nothing can portray how it looks in the hearts of those who are suddenly shut out because of innocent ancestry. Many of these—Jews as well as non-Aryan Christians—would have gone along waving flags. Granted that the political wish for a "homogeneous nation" is a forceful concept; but the counterforce against Germans abroad in Austria, Switzerland, the Baltics, etc., may destroy any hoped-for gains....
>
> Penitentiary and jail for "racial shame" [intermarriage] is a rule that can be imposed for a time but cannot be maintained.... This forced march sees us as rubble! May God be with us and grant us a glance into a hopeful era! (April 11, 1936)

Negotiations Begin

On March 24, two weeks after Erwin's departure, Paul met with Dr. Kuhnert, the managing director (*Verwaltungsdirektor*) of the Charité, to discuss the possibility of leasing the clinic to this large enterprise. In light of Erwin's decision to emigrate, exclusion from postgraduate contacts, and the loss of health-insured patients, Paul had already broached the subject informally. He had always operated his clinic as a research and teaching institution affiliated with the university, so the loss of that role was devastating. With no diary before March 1936 and few surviving letters, we cannot follow step by step the development of Paul's plans. At first, he thought of merely leasing the clinic, rather than selling it, perhaps to resume operation if government policies changed. Paul dictated four pages of notes as a record after the meeting with Kuhnert:

> K. received me in a very friendly manner.... I told him that he should understand that we had to proceed rather carefully because if I gave up the clinic in any form, E[rwin] would have to explore other possibilities for himself. He was now on leave until May 1, visiting his sister in New York and looking around. K. said, "After his return, your son can see for himself how things are going."
>
> I then mentioned that I had offered to lease the clinic for 22,000 marks annually [$70,000 of 2000] ... based on a rental value of around 19,800 marks and the tax estimate of our apartment at 4,800 marks.... If the apartment were converted to hospital use, an additional 20 beds could be set up, making a total of 95 to 100. I asked if the Charité were interested, and he answered, "Of course, we are eager." ... But after the expiration of the lease, they would not wish to be evicted. I answered that I would look on a transfer of the

property to my old training institute as a vindication of my life's work. I mentioned no sales price, but that the initial appraisal [of Nr. 18 alone] was 631,000 marks [$2 million dollars of 2000] ... and that I would turn over the inventory at a moderate price. K: "Your beds are said to be good." I agreed.

... I said that if the premises are not to be used as a women's clinic and hospital, they would be suitable for surgical cases. K. said: "[Ferdinand] Sauerbruch is interested in these premises." ... We exchanged high praise for this generous man. I said that he and I had become fairly close, which he seemed to know. He asked about our rate of occupancy that I had reported for 1935 and if he could send an accountant to examine the books. I agreed.... That mention of Sauerbruch should be helpful (given the weight of his position). I therefore need not hurry to make any special offer.

A Charismatic Colleague

Ferdinand Sauerbruch, director of the Surgical Clinic and the Cancer Institute of the Charité, was perhaps the most famous surgeon in Central Europe, a man whose achievements gave him almost royal prestige. He was most famous for innovations in chest surgery—on the esophagus, the heart, and especially the lungs. He could try novel operations because he had found a safe and simple way of maintaining respiration while the chest was wide open and the lungs were exposed to atmospheric pressure.

Sauerbruch was one of 960 prominent German professors who had vowed their support for the Hitler regime in the autumn of 1933. Although he never joined their party, he accepted medals and honors from the Nazis. Yet he soon complained about their interference with medicine. At a 1934 meeting of scientists and physicians, he insisted on the autonomy of universities, saying: "Science needs no cleansing by outsiders. It has itself always been most revolutionary and has always known how to free itself with its own strength from errors and mistakes." In 1936, he warned colleagues to stay with proven concepts and values "since history teaches that abandoning exact scientific methods easily leads to chaos and mysticism." When programs to kill the mentally deficient "as unworthy of life" were launched in 1939, his anti-Nazi skepticism turned to active hostility, and he became loosely associated with Paul-Gerard Braune, Klaus von Stauffenberg, Karl Bonhoeffer, General Ludwig Beck, and Hans von Dohnanyi, all of whom were opposed to Hitler. Sauerbruch was part of the first Berlin government appointed by the Soviets after the war in May 1945.[8]

Inspection

On April 7, 1936, the delegation of physicians from the Charité that was to inspect the premises for purchase consisted of Director Kuhnert, Professors Sauerbruch, Hans Auler, and Erwin Gohrbandt, and a few others. Auler was already Hitler's favorite cancer fighter because he equated excising cancer from the body to cleansing Jews from Germany. Auler made medical education films in which cancer cells were described as "revolutionary" in the Marxist sense.[9]

That day in April 1936, all Charité representatives came properly dressed in dark suits except Sauerbruch, who arrived without a necktie and in a medical gown spattered with blood. Like Paul, he had operated that morning. In the stained glass window of the large dining room, he saw not only the scouts from the Promised Land but the inscription of a family slogan, "Honor without Work Is Useless." (In the German mantra, each word begins with a different vowel: "Ehre ohne Arbeit ist unnütz.")

Sauerbruch said: "It's true, your slogan. But so is the reverse. Work without honor is also useless. It's a scandal that they don't let you carry on. Such a complete all-around enterprise! You know my attitude, and I can understand yours. If you need working space later, it will certainly be available." Paul added in his diary: "Sauerbruch is a warmhearted man, the first to find the right words of support.... But he sees my giving up this house as a foregone conclusion! If inevitable, let it be for this man as the best! He will raise its fame! But I shall not accept his working space."

Three months later, on July 13, 1936, Director Kuhnert of the Charité did indeed offer to buy all three Strassmann properties, Schumannstrasse 17 and 18 and Luisenstrasse 49, and to make the complex a center for cancer research and treatment. Further bargaining could involve only details.

Medical Events

Paul operated often during the clinic's last seven months; he thought his assistants might learn more that way than by muddling through on their own. He had always insisted on iron discipline in administering anesthetics and never had an anesthetic fatality. If pulse, breathing, complexion, and pupils were continually monitored, nothing need ever happen. For secondary cases, Paul relied more and more on Dr. Emil Häfeli, a reserve major in the Swiss air force, who had come from Basel in 1934, leaving behind his wife and children and a private practice for an extended time. Paul was pleased that all patients were doing well this spring and summer and had touching confidence in Häfeli's skill. Indeed, on March 26, 1936, he noted in his diary: "Complications have become quite rare ... and since I started with radium in 1913, even cancer deaths occur seldom." Yet he was often called from his morning bath to resolve an operational complexity that daunted Häfeli or Schürmann. Nevertheless, Paul believed that a physician's or nurse's first responsibility was not dedicating oneself to science but rather showing humane love for another person: "Rule one is that we are facing a wounded soul, hungering for consolation and love."

Paul wrote that he always had to make the most important decisions in haste. More than the difficulty of technique, the need to be decisive created the principal strain of operating. Of course, with obstetrics one was never master of one's schedule: "And yet I would not have chosen any other branch of medicine. This is the one with the most responsibility and the most gratitude! I am still enthusiastic about the work and will never stop being amazed!" (March 30, 1936). An effective obstetrician, Paul noted, needed a wife like Hedwig who could tolerate an irregular, tense life. He felt that he could keep on operating, or at least advising others, until the end came—"hopefully without pain and not too late!"

In early April 1936, Forester Berthold from Schorfheide delivered the two storks as usual for the clinic's courtyard. Sometimes people asked why storks stood on only one leg, and Paul would tell them: "That's easy. If Bubi tried to tuck up his other leg, too, he'd plop down on the ground, wouldn't he?" Every month some fifty babies were born.

In early June 1936, a patient came from out of town who had had a premature birth but no release of the placenta. A major operation was necessary, and the husband told Paul to "do whatever is necessary." He was a physician himself and a Nazi Party member. Another Nazi official said that he had boldly told his superior that his wife would have her baby at Strassmann's and was told, "Good, you chose the best." Still another patient was afraid that if she delivered again at the Strassmann Clinic, her husband's job could be in jeopardy. Paul told her to be considerate of her husband and go elsewhere. A fourth woman told him that if she could not deliver at Strassmann's, she would rather have no more babies. The wife of a pastor had six children, all born in the clinic.

On July 27, 1936, Georg and Ilse Strassmann came by from Breslau, where Georg was pensioned off as a pathology professor and now spent his time gardening. Suffering from insomnia, he rose as early as 5:00 AM. His prospects for emigrating seemed poor for his specialty, pathology, and he was considering Colombia with the help of Gerhard Masur, Paul's nephew via his sister Frieda. Georg discussed his fear about trying to emigrate with an adopted "Aryan" son.

Paul and Hedwig sometimes visited Paul's cousin Fritz, Georg's father, the retired professor of legal pathology, aged seventy-eight, now in a wheelchair at Zehlendorf near Dahlem. Paul wrote in his diary: "Conversations with Fritz are always pure and intellectual. He and [his son] Reinhold, who is still employed, are faithful Christians of the sort found especially among descendants of Jews" (August 27, 1936).

Milestones

On June 20, 1936, baby number 15,000 was born in the clinic on a hot Saturday. After a one-hour delivery, a thirty-five-year-old mother, Frau Dräger, welcomed her firstborn son. Meanwhile, a younger mother had been in labor for twenty-four hours, and the birth finally had to be brought about with drastic intervention. So both mothers and their babies were honored, exactly as had occurred in August 1928 with babies number 10,000 and 10,001. In their honor, all patients, nurses, physicians, and employees were given whipped cream, cake, chocolate, and lemon sorbet, all very special in that decade. Around the neck of Stork Bubi now hung a sign, "15,000!" It should have read "15,001!"

In September, Paul delivered a woman's first baby by Caesarean section, using a novel regional anesthetic injected near the lumbar part of the spinal cord, so that the patient did not lose total consciousness. She was forty-six years old, lost hardly any blood during the operation, and laughed in happy anticipation of the first cry. It was Paul's third Caesarean that week. He dictated an article about performing Caesareans through an appendix scar. As September 1936 came and went, he wondered who would be his last mother and when his last operation would take place. He found that operating was still no strain, performing sometimes three in a day.

Chemotherapy, a novelty in those days, was being advocated by a Professor Hilgermann. Paul had already tried it with success in one case. In a letter, he suggested that Erwin should mention this new approach to the Mayos (July 26, 1936). His own curiosity and drive to improve never let up.

The 1936 Olympics

Antonie's friend, the American asbestos heiress, Sunny Manville, who was in Berlin, invited Paul and Hedwig to the opening ceremony of the Olympics, which took place on Saturday, August 1, 1936. Before leaving for the event, Paul showed his collection of odd specimens, preserved in alcohol, to Dr. Stassny, a visiting pathologist from the Mayo Clinic. By 1:00 PM, he was in the crowded elevated train with Hedwig, heading for the Reichssportfeld stadium. He wrote in his diary that evening:

I admire the facilities and the order—everything in military precision. After 3 PM, no more admissions. By 2 PM, we are sitting in our places—stairway 5, bench 22, seats 36, 37—prepared for a hint of rain. Without concrete, building such a structure so quickly is unthinkable. It replaces the old stadium dedicated in 1910 by Wilhelm II, when I marched in with the dueling fraternities.… Instead of herons, the airship Hindenburg is drifting above the vast stadium. At 3 PM, music plays, and a peasant farmer, "Louis," marches in with the olive branch from Olympia. Ushers and officials wear blue coats, white pants, and white caps, as once did the Garde du Corps. The Führer arrives through the marathon gate at 4 PM with a large entourage, who descend to their seats. Few soldiers are with him, but members of the Comité appear in their black robes with gold chains. At the side of their loge are the Olympic flag and a flag with swastikas and four golden eagles. All around are the flags of fifty nations. As bells ring, the athletes march in, first the Greeks, then alphabetically down to the United States, and last, Germany, the two strongest teams.… A Swiss throws his flag in the air and catches it. Many march with a Nazi salute, others remove their straw hats. The women are very attractive. A runner comes with the torch carried through seven countries by three thousand others, one per kilometer, circles the stadium, and lights the fire.… Adolf Hitler declares the Olympics open, artillery is heard, doves from all countries fly away, and the Olympic hymn is conducted by [Richard] Strauss.… The Olympic oath brings the crowd to its feet, then Handel's "Hallelujah" chorus (which I sang in church for Heidelberg's anniversary in 1886!!). It is 6 PM. The impact is grandiose. A German triumph. "Ave Caesar, moritutus, te saluto." The crowds flooding out are also well-ordered.

A surging host from all nations is here seduced by the splendor of the games—and tomorrow, and tomorrow! Without pity, the iron wheel is crushing us. Woe unto me, grandson of Jews!!

Final Negotiations

Apart from the Olympics, the final negotiations for selling the clinic took place during these first two weeks of August 1936. Paul insisted on a stipulation that all his employees should find work with the Charité or receive a generous payment from it. At noon on August 7, 1936, Paul drove to the *Schatzkammer* (Treasury) together with Hedwig and her brother, Ernst Rosenberg from Giessen, the lawyer who had drawn up the sales contract. In room 53, with its two great Romantic paintings that had once hung in the imperial palace, they met with Ministerial Counsel von Krücke, Procurist Guloff, one attorney named Zimmermann, and another named Schultz, the only one wearing a swastika. Paul wore a small replica of his Iron Cross. He read the documents carefully and while signing said, "My clinic was intended for Germany's welfare, and I worked for that. I am happy that the premises will continue to have that dedication."

That night he added in his diary:

Strange, a few strokes of the pen, and now everything, everything is gone!! Surely, I had other wishes, but once ceding was inevitable, giving the property to the Prussian state is the best solution. Its medical tradition continues, and it joins the great hospital complex where I worked in 1892–1900. A 4 percent mortgage on bonds that amount to only two-thirds of what I paid is not much, but it is the most secure value that we could get for our children. Some will say, "Strassmann was lucky again, getting his head out of the noose," etc. But I do not feel satisfied or grateful.… Muttchen was in the Ministry's garden while all this went on. Then we exchanged a depressed kiss.… Certainly, it was Sauerbruch who put these proceedings into high gear. Perhaps I did manage to grab Fortuna's robe at the very last moment. The future will tell.

The clinic was almost full, and four daily operations and four deliveries were not unusual. Paul noted: "Prosperous patients often check into the cheaper second class, calculating that they might still be alone, thus saving money off the physician." The anti-Semitic state insurance now owed him thousands of marks, and he had to pay salaries and wages out of personal savings. His income was only half as much as was needed. He remembered that in 1933, one of the clinic's chief nurses, Amalie Mücke, had offered him all her savings, if ever needed. But he would never accept that. For the furnishings and the medical inventory of the clinic, the Charité's representatives offered a mere 30,000 marks, claiming most of it was not useful for a cancer institute. It was an opening move of a bargaining process, but Paul had no time for such maneuvers, writing that "haggling is one thing I'm not suited for" (October 5, 1936). So he accepted the price. The library collected by his father, Heinrich, contained dozens of volumes from the sixteenth century, and two from 1493. For these volumes, another 30,000 marks would be absurd, but it was eight times as much as he would actually get.

A note came from Sauerbruch. He wanted to keep the last stork, but Paul sent Bubi away with a fisherman who lived near Berlin. Schlorchi, the other stork, had already gone with Forester Berthold. In his diary, Paul wrote: "With [Bubi] a symbol vanishes. Many enjoyed him, especially children. I showed the fellow to every visitor, and when I saw him in the courtyard, I went about my business cheerfully! Forester Berthold, whose wife and child I saved, brought him when he heard my wish for a stork. Our concierge Fuchs built a house, pond, and cage for him. He was our lucky mascot" (October 27, 1936). After Sauerbruch took charge of Schumannstrasse 18, storm troopers came with the intention of hoisting a swastika flag on the roof. Sauerbruch forbade them to do so in the magisterial manner that these men could best understand.[10]

More Decisions

On July 8, 1936, Paul had written in his diary: "More than in earlier years, the ceaseless tension of obstetrics and all the inquiries and decisions involving insurance—all who seek information and hope here—take all my strength. How vigorously I once tackled problems, gave lectures, and organized courses! How happy I was when some tiny discovery surmounted the hurdle of the [main journal] *Zentralblatt*." Now state health insurance no longer allowed patients to go to this "Jewish institution." One of his staff, Dr. Schürmann, told Paul that he had to send a young woman who had previously delivered at Strassmann's to a neighboring clinic. This place sent her home too early with a high temperature, and she died of an embolism.

The last baby born in the clinic was baptized by Pastor Johannes Küssner on October 22, 1936, the day before Paul's seventieth birthday. Twenty-nine people were present. Küssner spoke simply and referred to the fifteen thousand babies born there: "I bless you, so may you be a blessing."

A new concern was that on October 8, Paul's deaf sister, Helene Keiler, had attempted suicide in Dresden by slashing her throat and wrists. When Paul arrived at her hospital room, she told him that panic about religious and political persecution had been the reason. A Dresden doctor had already stitched her up, but too late to make the right arm normal. Paul had her transferred to a first-class room with an extra nurse. Helene survived for six more miserable and terrified years, only to die in the concentration camp of Theresienstadt on November 19, 1942. Paul wrote, "A tragic victim.... Good that I have my loyal Hedwig at my side." They were like Philemon and Baucis, he penned, the ancient Greek couple whom Zeus spared from a punitive flood and turned into trees with intertwining branches.

The leading Nazi physician, the Reichsärzteführer, Gerhard Wagner, had just written in the *Deutsche Ärzteblatt*: "To those who think that the Nuremberg Laws have finally disposed of the Jewish question, I say: The battle continues." As of October 1, operating a pharmacy was forbidden to Jews. Paul asked Erwin to picture having no passport and hence no permission to return to America. One Jewish or "non-Aryan" clinic after another was being sold, although for another two years Jews were allowed to keep their medical licenses.

In the next letter to Erwin, Paul explained in detail how the contents of the clinic were to be divided. From the laboratory he would himself keep the best microscope and perhaps a centrifuge, as well as the most striking specimens. Other collections of value would go to Erwin. Equipment from the operating and the delivery room would be left for Charité officials to fight over, "like hyenas for the skin of a lion."

Three Birthday Celebrations

Hedwig's birthday—her sixty-seventh, not a big round-numbered one—came first on September 30. Paul described her as "the best, most pious, most devoted being" and gave her a necklace and a brooch, engraved, "Hedwig Strassmann, my beloved wife, the best supporter of the work of the Frauenklinik P. Strassmann, 1909–1936." In his diary, he asked himself, "Who could have earned it more than she, the beloved, the faithful, happily enduring one?" Flowers, letters, books, and other gifts were spread about on a table. Among others, Dr. Schürmann came with his one-year-old son, born in the clinic, again defying Dr. Zimmer, who by now seemed remorseful. In the evening, they met Gerhart Hauptmann and his wife at the neighboring Deutsches Theater and saw a performance of Hauptmann's *Hamlet in Wittenberg*. Paul wrote: "A worthy conclusion for our high holiday! The poet's words lend an eternal glow to our present affliction." The next day, Paul and Hedwig visited the Hauptmanns again just before that couple departed for Dresden.

The double birthday of Gisela and Paul began at 8:30 AM in the Schumannstrasse residence on Friday, October 23, 1936, with presents, letters, and roses from family and friends on two tables in the music room. Among the mail were telegrams from Erwin, Director Kuhnert, Ferdinand Sauerbruch, and the Mayo brothers, but nothing from anyone with an official title, such as Walter Stoeckel, the chair of gynecology at the university. "Empress" Hermine sent a sympathetic letter and a copy of Alfred Schweitzer's book about Johann Sebastian Bach. Hedwig had a seal made of the Strassmann symbol of the scouts bringing giant grapes from the Promised Land. My parents, Erwin and Ilse, gave an elaborate shortwave radio, and my own contribution was a drawing of the ship elevator (*Schiffshebewerk*) at Niederfinow, north of Berlin. At 10:00 AM, over a hundred guests assembled in the auditorium of the clinic. Ilse described the occasion in a letter to Erwin, who had earlier that year emigrated to the United States:

> Herr Fuchs [the concierge] had made a large wreath of pine twigs and decorated it with seventy candles. Looked very pretty. A trio—flute, violin, and piano—played too long with Nurse Ulla Meyer's fingers striking a few sour notes [of a Stamitz piece]. Then Zimmer read his speech fairly well but without much warmth, which was just as well, given everyone's emotions. Pastor Anton was the opposite and read a poem composed by himself about Päpchen's career, making our dear father unnecessarily nervous about possible topics, but they were avoided. Nurses Hedwig Schulz, Gladow, and Meyer sang a Mendelssohn hymn, "Lift Thine Eyes to the Mountains." A silent movie, *Unsere Klinik*, followed, made by H. Pfannkuch and Dr. Zimmer (!) with skill, humor, and much effort—truly charming

and for us all a memento of inestimable value. While the movie went on for at least three quarters of an hour, Fräulein Gladow played an accompaniment on the piano in the dark, very musical, going fluently from one melody to another. We never knew she had such talent. The event concluded with a humorous parody of "Max and Moritz" sung by Nurses Hedwig and Ulla, accompanied by Fräulein Gladow.

Paul himself thought Zimmer's talk showed "grateful recognition," for a change, and awareness of the painful circumstances. He found Pastor Anton's interjection too fanciful and "shattering to the eardrums." The movie was "witty and had everything from my morning gymnastics to Schürmann puffing forbidden cigarettes with the night nurses."

After nearly two hours of all that, Paul thanked the guests and blew out the seventy candles. He had theatre tickets for every employee and recalled that such had also been the gift twenty-seven years ago when the clinic had opened in 1909. Now he invited everyone to join him in the large family dining room for a buffet catered by Kempinski. Naturally, the painters Franck and Zickendraht were there. Paul democratically seated himself between the concierge's wife, Frau Fuchs, and Frau Schnalle from the fish market. Ilse made a point of saying nothing to Dr. Zimmer. Why had Zimmer been selected to give the speech after the trio? Instead, she chatted with Dr. Häfeli, who had given a nut tree and had written a charming poem for Paul. A Dr. Schneider brought a second nut tree. Another old friend came disguised as a white-bearded peasant and amused the guests by presenting Paul with a large pitchfork for respectable composting in suburban Dahlem. She was Fridel Marie Kuhlmann, who had once been the girlfriend of Hellmuth. She recited her nineteen-verse poem in Berlin dialect. Here are two verses, followed by a rough translation:

Und weil nu Dein Jeburtstag ist,
So bring ick Dir 'ne Fuhre Mist
For Deinen neuen Jarten an.
Da draussen steht mein Ochsjespann.
…
Und dat Du mir nu nich verjisst
Nimm diese Forke for Deen'n Mist
Mit dem Jeburtstagswunsch entjejen:
"Wo Mess is, da is Jottes Segen."

[Celebrating your big birthday,
I hope you think manure's okay.
For your new garden I impart
The contents of an old oxcart.
…
So you will never forget me
This pitchfork's for your jubilee.
Sing as you spread dung on your sod:
"Where there's manure, there is God."]

Three old drinking chums from Paul's Friedrichs Gymnasium days, Anton, Knaut, and Prager, appeared and asked for beer, offering to pay for it themselves. Walter Strassmann, the gourmet architect and cousin, said he was so moved that he lost his appetite for an entire fifteen minutes. Antonie (back again from America) had the task of dramatically reading letters and telegrams from celebrities—Gerhart Hauptmann, the Mayo brothers, Ferdinand Sauerbruch, a number of painters, and many others.

Hauptmann, who was now seventy-four himself and had in June already invited Paul and Hedwig to visit him in Agnetendorf, wrote: "We are happy that your daughters are doing well and that your son is firmly on his way. God is my witness that I know no family more truly German and willing to sacrifice than yours! No word or letter would be needed to make me realize that you could never separate yourself from the solid German core of your being."

After two hours of festivity, the rooms were still crammed with people. I myself remember the crowds among dozens of bouquets of flowers, everyone talking. It was important to sign the guestbook, and to this day I recall, with embarrassment, misspelling my own name (as "Woflgang") in the confusion. My mother told me later that I had asked her: "For your seventieth birthday, will you invite this many people?" She consoled me, then ten years old, by saying that it was still a few years away. In her letter to Erwin, she listed the many friends and relatives who were still there for late-afternoon coffee, and how they had all asked to be remembered with greetings. Ilse knew that she herself was seeing many persons for the last time. She concluded her letter by reporting: "School questions are to be clarified by Easter. Jewish children will have to leave the upper grades, but the fate of children with mixed ancestry is not yet set. These questions no longer disturb me.... Every evening your letter accompanies me to bed like a precious jewel. The time of our separation is now in its declining phase."

That night, Paul wrote in his diary: "A splendid day, a final chord. And giving was more blessed than receiving. One should have such celebrations, if for no other reason than to avoid slinking away quietly, looking beaten. This day will prove unforgettable to all, and the gloomy backdrop made the colorful images sparkle all the more. We only miss our poor son in the United States. Without bitter feelings we retire. And the Spirit of Dreams keeps the images alive."

Three days later, on October 26, Paul performed his last operation in the clinic. The patient was the wife of a colleague, and the procedure went well. "Sie kommt leicht davon [Got off easily]," says the diary. Her husband asked, "Couldn't your son carry on with the clinic?" Paul answered, "He was a combat officer but is no longer a citizen. He had no future here!"

The last three patients who signed the guestbook were named Elsa, Elise, and Else. Elsa Niequisch wrote on October 30 in verse, concluding: "Herr Geheimrat artfully achieved once more what none will ever copy." Elise Honwald wrote in November: "This thick book testifies to much love and gratitude, but now you have to experience that mortals get no unmixed joys." Finally, on November 6, 1936, Else Heinrich wrote that she was thankful to be healed through the Geheimrat Professor's great art: "May the love that he gave to suffering people be rewarded with a healthy and happy life's evening!" A breech delivery of a baby for Frau M. Rundlandt by Dr. Häfeli made her the clinic's last patient. Dismissed at 9:30 AM on November 8, she wrote nothing in the guestbook.

A final page in the guestbook was headed "die letzten Getreuen" (the last faithful ones) and was signed with addresses by thirty-one men and women. Gerhart Zimmer signed first, followed by Emil Häfeli, Fritz Ade, Günther Brehster, Alfred Schick, Marianne Rudeloff, Amalie Frieda Mücke, Ilse Dürselen, Dorothea Gladow, Geraldine Effenberger, Maria Mummert, and twenty others.

Sale and Farewell

A notice was tacked on the front gate: "Die Frauenklinik wird endgültig am 10, XI. geschlossen" (The Women's Clinic will be shut once and for all on November 10). The family walked past that notice dozens of times daily on the way to their private apartment. The clinic beyond the courtyard was closed, dead without lights in the windows and with no clatter from the kitchen. Moki stood there and barked. There was no one to let him in.

Paul sat at his desk and wrote six hundred thank-you notes, responding to every greeting. He heard the old Bechstein grand piano being tuned a few rooms away. In 1893, it had been the wedding present of the Rosenbergs, Hedwig's parents.

On November 10, 1936, the transfer of the clinic took place. Paul gave Dr. Kuhnert, Professor Adam, and Professor Auler a two-hour tour of the premises, blueprints in hand. Documents were signed in his study, with its clutter of books, paintings, and memorabilia. Paul wrote that evening:

> Earlier I had brought over a volume of Schiller (*Wallenstein*) and the large Luther Bible made of parchment. We needed a support, and so we signed—myself first—on the Bible! Hedwig wore black with Hellmuth's Iron Cross, First Class. Today, twenty years ago, we were informed by his commanding officer, von Ratwitz, of his death.
>
> Head Nurse Marianne [Rudeloff] and Dr. Häfeli had tears in their eyes. But I said loud and firmly: "The Frauenklinik is dissolved. May the new medical institute be established within the framework of the Charité and flourish—like the old one—for the welfare of the German people and our Fatherland, with God's blessing!"
>
> And now even this moment had been overcome! All participants shook hands with much emotion. Hedwig gave me a kiss in front of all. Then began the prosaic payment.

During the following week, sounds reverberated in the empty halls as in vaulted tombs. Moki barked at the echoes. Hellmuth's statue was lifted and carried to a truck headed for Dahlem. "He was our beloved oldest, the child of sunny Lugano 1893," wrote Paul in his diary on November 11. "Shoving us faithful citizens aside in our old age is just monstrous!"

The final exile from his life's work took place a week later. Packers arrived in the early morning, hammering up crates and wrapping cabinets in thick padding. Patients who came had to be referred to other clinics. Dr. Gerhart Zimmer arrived to take his leave, and finally Paul spoke his mind about the treachery of his denunciation of Schürmann for visiting Erwin. "How that helped to ripen our plans!"

"All around me is a frightful wasteland," Paul wrote on November 19, 1936, the last day. "Finally, I take leave of my most loyal helpers. Head Nurse Marianne Rudeloff has been at my side for thirty-four years! Thus, one person melts into another.... After Hedwig, she was closest to me. Yet Erwin has a bigger burden than we do.... For a last time, Moki barks his way around the block: Albrecht—Marienstrasse—Luisenstrasse—Schumannstrasse! We see the electric sign of the Deutsche Theater and prepare ourselves for the last night in the house at Schumannstrasse 18. I am unable to write more."

The next day, the last movers came at 8:00 AM. When every room was empty, Paul went around and locked all of the doors. In the corridor stood the head nurse and a few others, including Frau Stalinski, the laundress, all in tears. At the last minute, the automobile racer, Bernd Rosemeyer, showed up and asked about an antique automobile painting that had belonged to Hellmuth. Paul maintained his composure and said, "Bless them that curse you!" Into his car Paul carried paintings attributed to Jacob Van Ruisdael, Adrian Brouwer, and (falsely) to Rembrandt. Moki was already at his usual window spot. Hedwig carried the canary named Schrilpifex. They said nothing during the long ride to Dahlem. It was a gray November day.

Chapter 9

Inseparable despite Emigration: Erwin and Ilse

From 1921 to 1922, Erwin had an interlude of medical studies in the German southwest of Baden, not at Heidelberg, like his father, but at the University of Freiburg. There he was affiliated with the Pathologisches Institut of the university. Founded in August 1883, this institute had attained distinction under Professor Ludwig Aschoff (1866–1942), who had joined the university in 1906. During most of World War I, which he opposed, Aschoff was the leading pathologist for the German army and served on both fronts.[1] In 1934, he had the courage to call for international cooperation in medicine because diseases were "not contingent on individual, cultural, or political circles."[2]

One day, after calling Erwin into his office, Aschoff said:

> Strassmann, you want to become a gynecologist. You know that everybody who is connected with my department has to write an Arbeit. I want you to find out why the Graafian follicle ruptures. Everybody takes the rupture of the follicles for granted, thinking these are cysts that have to reach a certain size until the intrafollicular pressure becomes too great. If this is all there is to ovulation, how can pathologic cysts of the ovary reach the size of a fist, a man's head, or more and yet hardly ever rupture? The ovary is the only gland in the human body with external secretion that does not possess a permanent duct system and outlet for its products, like the testicles, the salivary glands, the kidneys, etc. Granted that there is some endocrine stimulation, there must be a definitive mechanical process through which these hormones accomplish their task. I cannot tell you what it is and how to find it. That is your job. Now go to work and keep me posted. Good luck.[3]

After examining more than eighteen thousand slides of human and animal ovaries over the course of twelve years, Erwin showed that a "theca cone" formed within the ovary, leading the way for the Graafian follicle, which contains the maturing egg in all mammals. As the follicle ascends, conical theca layers appear, growing eccentrically to form a cone that drives like a wedge to the nearest ovarian surface. The enlarging follicle follows this line of least resistance. At the surface, the follicle expands, ruptures, and gently releases the egg as a last step in the chain of events. Without slides showing sections perpendicular to the ovarian surface and cutting through its axis, this phenomenon could not have been detected. It was Erwin's most significant discovery and led to a professorial appointment in Berlin, fifteen publications, and the 1940 Foundation Prize of the American Society of Obstetricians, Gynecologists, and Abdominal Surgeons.[4]

Apart from work and study, Erwin was elected chairman of the medical students of the University of Freiburg. He was also a member of Arminia, the same dueling fraternity (*Burschenschaft*) that his father had belonged to in Heidelberg and his brother in Berlin.

Ilse Wens from Bad Nauheim

One morning in October 1921, a tall and elegant but shy young woman, Ilse Wens, was shown the premises of Aschoff's institute. She had been engaged as a laboratory technician, an appointment arranged by Dr. Walter Koch, who was a first cousin of Ilse's mother and Aschoff's associate director. Ilse had studied the piano for years but faced the improbability of ever giving concerts. Nor did she want to teach beginners.

According to family legend, Erwin approached Ilse that first morning and said briskly, "Miss Wens, we welcome you to the Institute of Pathology and want you to feel at home here. If there is anything you need, contact me." Ilse asked a secretary who that authoritative but very young man was. "That's Strassmann," was the answer. "Just a student from Berlin. He arrived only yesterday." Seventy years later, on December 4, 1991, my mother recalled those times: "Yes, he was interested at once, and until much later I had no idea how many other little girlfriends he had then. But never in my life was I jealous, fortunately. At Aschoff's institute they had cultural evenings every Wednesday, and someone had to perform—sing, play, declaim, anything. Erwin suggested that we play a duet, violin and piano. He wanted to get it just right, so we had to practice a lot. It was his way of getting to see me often. I don't remember what we played in that duet, something easy, of course, maybe Kreisler."

The two were married in Bad Nauheim, Hessen, Ilse's hometown, on January 7, 1923. She was the daughter of Ferdinand Wens, a native of Bielefeld, and Käthe Luise (née Schwarze) from Diepholz near Bremen. Ferdinand and Käthe came from musically active families but had met playing tennis. Ferdinand was a physician specializing in cardiovascular cures at the spa of Bad Nauheim, where he had moved in 1903, at age thirty-six, to cure his own heart ailment. Besides Ilse, they had an older and a younger son. The older son, Ulrich, was studying commerce in 1914 but was killed in 1915, aged twenty, at Tschermysch-Kolki on the Russian front. The younger son, Gerhard (1900–1997), studied cardiovascular medicine, like his father, at Tübingen. When Ferdinand Wens died in 1929, aged sixty-two, Gerhard took over the practice.

Medicine, Jews, and Bad Nauheim

The village of Bad Nauheim became a spa in 1835 when some of its hot mineral waters were diverted from salt making to a bathhouse for curing rheumatism under the direction of a Dr. Friedrich Bode. Its international reputation was established after the Jewish doctor Isidor Mayer Groedel (1850–1921) came to Bad Nauheim in 1875 and wrote numerous scientific reports while successfully treating German and foreign industrialists and aristocrats, even royalty. Controlled hot mineral baths, Groedel claimed, provided exercise for deficient hearts through the effect on the capillaries of temperature, pressure, and carbon dioxide bubbles.

Groedel was made an honorary Nauheim citizen in 1920. Later, his baptized son, Franz Groedel (1881–1951), was considered "without the least doubt the most outstanding physician in the history of Bad Nauheim."[5] Franz wrote over three hundred medical papers, was professor at Frankfurt, had William Randolph Hearst and the Roosevelts among his international patients, and organized the large Kerkhoff Research Institute with a million dollars from the widow of an American patient. One German-American industrialist named Oberlaender made a trip to Berlin to ask Hitler to "Aryanize" Groedel—in vain.

When he left for the United States in 1933, at first temporarily, Franz Groedel hired Gerhard Wens (Ilse's brother) to direct his sanatorium, which Gerhard did after getting permission from Berlin. As a teenager, Gerhard's best friend had been a Jew, Emil Grünewald, but Gerhard wanted no further risks with Jewish affiliations other than his brother-in-law, Erwin. The sanatorium was nevertheless closed in 1936. Other Nauheim physicians proposed that Groedel should resign from the Kerkhoff Institute "since an institution led by a non-Aryan is now unsuitable for our meetings." Feeling hopeless under the Nazis, Groedel's sister Frances committed suicide in 1935. Franz wrote that "masks fell off the faces of some traitorous colleagues who had feigned friendship for years and had fattened themselves at my table. Only a few previously underestimated persons stood by me."[6] Groedel emigrated to the United States, settling in Warm Springs, Georgia, where he occasionally treated Franklin D. Roosevelt, who died there in 1945.

In the 1920s, however, Jews still played prominent roles in the public life of Bad Nauheim. Sally Schoenewald (1871–1939) was the long-time chair of the Bad Nauheim Physicians Association. Emil Rosenthal (1872–1937), a businessman, and Arthur Stahl (1869–1929), an attorney, were community leaders with many functions, especially on the City Council. Few Nauheim Jews were deeply religious, several had converted, and almost no enterprises were closed on Saturdays. So in the early 1920s, marriage to a Jew, converted or not, was seen as quite acceptable.

After a honeymoon in the Harz Mountains, Erwin and Ilse moved into two rooms at Schumannstrasse 18 that teenage Strassmanns had occupied before the war. After a spell at suburban Wannsee, they moved to Luisenstrasse 47 near the Frauenklinik. A baby, Erika, was stillborn in late 1923. She was followed by Renata ("the reborn") in November 1924, Wolfgang in July 1926, and Angelika in April 1930.

Erwin spent four more years becoming a specialist in obstetrics and gynecology, first in 1923–1924 with Ernst Bumm[7] and then in 1924–1926 at his own father's clinic.

Erwin's First Trip to America

In the winter of 1929, Paul sent his son Erwin, now thirty-four years old, on a medical study tour of the United States, as he himself had done in 1927 or, before that, the trip to England in 1891. Erwin arrived in New York on the SS *Albert Ballin*, Hamburg America Line, on January 21, and sailed home on the SS *Deutschland* on March 23. Ten days were spent in New York, followed by two weeks in Philadelphia, Baltimore, Washington, and Chicago. Then came two weeks at the Mayo Clinic in Rochester, Minnesota, and on the way back, Detroit, Cleveland, Buffalo, and Boston.

His first letter home was written a week after landing in New York: "Whoever has not been here cannot grasp it. Here is not just a new, young continent. Here is a new century, a realized Utopia! We poor Germans: Fine installations, bad prospects." From Rochester, Erwin wrote that Americans had better luck at aging. For example, Charles Mayo, aged sixty-four, had just performed six major operations in a single morning. Both Mayo brothers invited Erwin to farewell luncheons. On March 1, 1929, he wrote to Ilse:

> Often people have asked me, "Why are you devoting as much as two weeks to Rochester?" But with awe I can now attest to the accomplishments of two truly great men. At the same

time, the modesty and simplicity of these brothers Mayo is indescribably touching. By comparison even with men like Bumm and Aschoff, these two are fully absorbed in their work, and not a word or gesture projects a personality. They are 100 percent matter-of-fact, genuine, and of unfathomable greatness.

I wish we had a house and garden like all young doctors here. For Americans, America is a paradise. A promised land.

Stressing the higher status of women in America, Erwin wrote to Ilse on March 6, 1929:

That would make you happy here, the acceptance of women's roles by all social classes. I wish we had that over there. It explains why women here see their own obligations so differently.... This clean atmosphere is fundamental to the young country, and it quickly converts everyone who arrives here. For example, nurses and doctors don't flirt in hospitals but are friendly and matter of fact....

An ethical strain characterizes the entire nation—trust in business and honest, open, simple competition. No slandering of opponents, just efforts to outdo them. Among physicians, I heard no slurring comments about others, just friendly observations. Perhaps it was not always sincere, but one has to appreciate the style.

Competence and achievement are what count. That makes leaving this country hard for me. There is something fascinating about these healthy inner and outer constraints. The leading continent! Unfortunately! But deservedly so.

University Appointment

Erwin was appointed a titular professor at the University of Berlin in December 1932. In the history of the university, this was but the second time that a father and son were awarded professorial positions simultaneously on the same faculty. Professor Walter Stoeckel told Erwin that to get the appointment, his research had to be so outstanding that it would be inexcusable not to take him. He had to overcome the opposition of Paul's old enemies and of those who on principle were against father-son appointments.

So Erwin set about making his eighteen thousand slides of the ovaries of cattle, carnivores, rodents, and humans. Working with his assistant, Erika von Moellendorff, he discovered that hardening and mobile theca cones help guide follicles containing the maturing eggs to the surface of mammalian ovaries, displacing the previous theory, universally held, that the growing egg and follicle simply burst out through sheer force.

On December 17, 1932, Erwin gave his inaugural lecture in the large university auditorium at Unter den Linden. By then he had a completely new topic, fetal electrocardiography, a procedure never before attempted.[8] Students, friends, and relatives were in attendance, and a champagne party followed. The Nazis came to power forty-four days later, but Erwin believed that he had won the race.

Nazis Closing In

As anti-Semitic decrees and regulations were issued one after another in early 1933, Erwin, like others, was stunned. In late June, while on summer vacation with the children in Bad Nauheim, Ilse heard about Dr. Jung's attempted takeover and the imminent closing of the clinic. She wrote to Erwin:

> One really had believed that all insults had reached their limit, and now comes this most bitter blow.... I am totally convinced that no matter what fate is on the way, you will master it somehow and prevail with your tenacious energy. If such a blow would hit Gerhard [her brother], I would worry more because he is no fighter like you and Päpchen [Paul Strassmann]. (June 28, 1933)
>
> I cannot imagine that these regulations will remain.... I cannot believe that such an obvious injustice will stand.... Dr. Jung's departure is unsettling. Will you two control yourselves? He should not be dignified with words but deserves a kick in his Aryan behind. (June 30, 1933)

Erwin replied on July 7, 1933:

> It depresses me to be dragging you and the children down into this whirlpool. An undeserved barrier appears, and suddenly one no longer belongs where one belongs. It is hard to leave and hard to remain. Should one be poor but respected abroad or well-off but despised here? Meeting anyone is an agony. What is worse—the secret sympathy of some or the secret distancing of others? Everywhere suspicion! A basically cheerful, carefree person can't breathe in this atmosphere. In the war, one learned to endure everything, and that helps; but these insults wear one out. Then I was young and without cares, but now my life is half over and I am responsible for five people, for whom I had hoped to shape a happy future.... One learns to love all the more when one has to suffer. (July 7, 1933)

Ilse replied, "I am calm and will accept whatever comes and consider it my role to strengthen and to help you.... How happy we could have been now! But I am not afraid and will feel cozily safe with you" (July 10, 1933).

For Erwin's thirty-eighth birthday, Ilse reminded him that the past year had brought him his hard-won goal of a university professorship, adding: "It also brought much affliction, doubly bitter because of utter innocence. Yet this affliction has had its good side. For me, the clear awareness, never before felt as strongly, is that in hard times I am twice as united with you. It is a great happiness to know that one has chosen correctly in life" (July 12, 1933).

Two years later, on June 24, 1935, Erwin wrote to Ilse (again on the annual Nauheim vacation) that in the general atmosphere, "one has to recognize clearly and soberly that one has to make a fundamental change. The dogs will bite those who leave last. In the long run there is nothing here for us." Antonie was returning to New York on business and was going to explore possibilities on his behalf: "For the time being, just information, where to train oneself." Added to these worries, he wrote to Ilse, were heated disputes with his father about managing the clinic, even scheduling vacations. Ilse answered, "What a nuisance, new squabbles with Päpchen. Let it go and tell yourself one can't change old people. Remember his happy face when you toasted his health" (July 3, 1935).

Erwin's relations with other staff members during those years may be illustrated by a letter from his colleague, Dr. Häfeli, written in early 1936 after Erwin had emigrated:

> Rather proud and conceited, I may report to you that in the past month we delivered an astonishing number of eighty babies! The obstetrical consultations are overbooked, so we are threatened with further blessed infants. In obstetrics we are so overworked that to my joy and Schürmann's annoyance we have to encroach on his domain.... Nurse Ruth has defected to the paradise of matrimony and been replaced by an apparently competent little blonde with a don't-touch-me air about her. Not to be misunderstood, may I report that I have thoroughly reformed ... and have energetically begun to restore my decent repute.... I shall

be totally annoyed with you as a dyed-in-the-wool American, whom Uncle Sam does not deserve, a view shared by a certain bosomy proportion of Berliners.... Nobody can really deal with our Berliners in the polyclinic as well as Strassmann junior.... Your absence and our clumsiness makes Strassmann senior sigh in the course of every surgery, that I know definitely.... My misfortune was a complication during a Caesarean, a premature rupture of the water sack, a problem resolved only with the help of God and all the saints.

In Berlin, meanwhile, Jews were assaulted on the Kurfürstendamm, at Wannsee, and in the Hansa district, where the children's Kritzinger School was located. On July 29, Ilse wrote to Erwin in Berlin: "What is happening? I am upset because I am completely uninformed. We have only the local newspaper, which reports nothing unusual. I heard from Gerhard that [something is happening] because of the Jewish question. Please send me newspapers right away. In such days it is an agony to be apart. Everything had been so beautiful! Now one almost fears to spend any days festively or cheerfully."

The Decision

No replies came to requests from the Strassmanns for official clarification of their status as militarily decorated and baptized non-Aryans of Jewish descent. As a result, during the Christmas holidays of 1935, celebrated with the Wens family in Bad Nauheim, Erwin resolved to emigrate. How could he stay in a country where he would eventually be forbidden to practice medicine? His preferred new country was Switzerland, where many friends as well as the Gutzwiller relatives lived, where the mountain scenery was incomparable, and where no language problem arose. But the Swiss wanted no medical immigrants, so the United States was chosen as next best, a country that both Erwin and his parents had visited with enthusiasm in recent years and where Antonie had already settled. "We saw it as friendly and the land of the future," Ilse remembered in 1973.

On December 29, 1935, Erwin took the night train back to Berlin and had breakfast with his parents the next morning. All decisions were now clear. On the evening of December 30, Erwin wrote to Ilse:

At breakfast with the Parents, I noticed at once that they have crossed an inner threshold, the decision to lease the clinic, possibly as early as April 1. A definite, though tragic, peace envelops them. Their thoughts have already turned toward details: where to go, what to do with furniture, etc. The outcome of the citizenship affair seems to them (and to me) no longer all that important....

The weapons in this hopeless battle are put down. We did all we could to defend the ramparts to the last. Now is the time for an honorable retreat. The Parents will find peace with dignity, although bought at a bitter price. Well-timed arrivals are clever, but knowing when to go is even smarter.

Our destiny may be hard, yet it is also great. We have to prove ourselves worthy of it. As sorrow is a greater teacher than joy, so we may gain in strength and grow with all this.... We shall enter the new year with resolute hearts and a calm spirit. An ocean may separate us for a time, but we are now welded together more than ever.... A richer harvest of love can be reaped when it is not just the best but the only thing we truly possess. May heaven grant us health until these storms have passed. For the New Year we beg for that.

In the course of that first day in Berlin, Erwin was at once called in to help Dr. Schürmann "with a difficult operation that he nearly muddled." He also found that "a surprising number of private patients" had called for appointments, so there was hardly time for a haircut before rejoining his parents for supper. Hedwig's brother Ernst Rosenberg and his wife were also there and talked of following their children, Erwin's cousins, to Australia.

From Ilse came a letter written on New Year's Eve:

> Perhaps the most decisive year of our lives begins now, so my wishes for you, darling, are twice as deep and tender. That we belong together for all time is a trust, solid as granite, so a temporary separation cannot affect us. You will create a new existence, I am certain, and I shall do my utmost to deal with unfamiliar circumstances. We have to keep telling ourselves how lucky we are to have been spared the worst deprivations. New demands over there will divert you, while the children will help me. Actually, right now they are a nuisance because they are supposed to write their letters, and it doesn't suit them.

To Erwin's letter of December 30, she replied on January 2, 1936:

> You know superbly well how to dress feelings and thoughts in words, and that makes me feel twice as united with you in everything that fate has in store. The decision does seem rather abrupt, but better like that than a slow disintegration. I hope deeply that your parents will survive this great sorrow and can manage to live on under such different conditions....
>
> A girl next door said she wouldn't play with Renate anymore, "She's a half-Jew." Renate [aged eleven] came to me indignantly. That was the moment to tell her everything. She kept repeating, "But aren't we all evangelical?" Then she asked, very concerned, "Does Daddy worry about it? And you?" It was something of a blow to her, and she was consoled that the Reis's [Eva and Hans Reis, close Kritzinger School friends] and the Friedländers were also hit. I see clearly how they discriminate in this little town where all know one another: "That is a Jew, and that is none." In Berlin, people may think just like that, but they keep it from you.... One has to face how the soul of a child suffers.

Because of this incident, Ilse decided to spend the year or two of separation not in Nauheim but back in Berlin. It meant continuing to rent the expensive Luisenstrasse apartment. Her mother, Käthe Wens, promised to stay with her in Berlin, a city neither of them really cared for. In the dozen years of living in Berlin, Ilse had never taken to the city with all its confusion and the Schumannstrasse household with the continual company and parties and baffling intellectual talk that made her feel provincial and uncultivated. "I couldn't feel at ease there," she told me once. "They'd work themselves up into a state for reasons I could not fathom." She had learned that if she said little or nothing, others would speak to her very respectfully. She recalled even a hint of awe in the way Paul spoke to her, calling her "Ilschen." She and Erwin mutually called one another "Patzi," a term coined in Freiburg whose origin I do not know. Perhaps it is a diminutive of *Spatz* meaning "Sparrow," a common endearment. Letters often began, "Mein geliebtes Patzilein."

Another element in the decision to emigrate—perhaps a rationalization—was Erwin's occasional apprehension about taking over the clinic. Medicine might be at a stage where new discoveries and innovations could never match the pioneering of his father's generation. For them, novel anesthetics and antiseptic methods had allowed decades of surgical innovations. Erwin wondered if he could ever attract as many wealthy patients and charge them enough in first class to finance hundreds of poor women annually in third class. If he succeeded, it would seem like a set-up, while failure would invite unfavorable comparisons. "He's not cut from the same cloth as the old man," people might say, or, in the words of an old adage, "Never succeed a legend." At Rochester, Erwin would learn that young Charles W. Mayo, about his own age, had the same apprehension about taking over from the famous brothers, Dr. Will and Dr. Charlie (Charles W.'s father). In America, however, like millions before him, Erwin would have an opportunity to prove his mettle independently. Emigration had already occurred to him as a tempting step after his first American visit in 1929. What appealed to him most about American medicine was the open, fair, and friendly relationship among people with different responsibilities. American doctors never shouted at nurses and assistants the way his father and others did daily in Berlin.

Preparing to Emigrate: Letters to the Mayos

Within a month of the September 1935 adoption of the Nuremberg Laws, Paul Ferdinand Strassmann wrote to his Minnesota friends, the Mayo brothers, about possibly employing Erwin in their clinic. They had already offered to help in 1933. Concerned about censorship of the mail, the letter was carried out by Antonie, and Paul requested that the answer be sent to her at her suite in the Hotel St. Regis in New York.

William J. Mayo, aged 74 and already retired, replied to Antonie on October 16, 1935:

> My brother and I are very much grieved to learn of the conditions of which your father has written us.... I am taking the matter up with Dr. L. B. Wilson, who is the Director of the [Mayo] Foundation in Rochester, hoping that we may be able to secure some opportunity for your brother to come here as a fellow of the Foundation. While the stipend is small, it would at least support your brother himself and would afford him a breathing space while he adjusted himself and made plans for the future....
>
> My brother joins me in sincere sympathy with your father and his family in the troubles they are undergoing, and we assure you that if there is anything we can do to be helpful to our friends, we shall have the utmost satisfaction in undertaking it.

Dr. Louis Wilson was a research pathologist who had worked for the Mayos for thirty-one years after a brief period with the Minnesota State Board of Health. In Rochester, he organized the Mayos' first repository of pathological specimens and introduced them to medical photography, to freezing cells for fresh-tissue diagnosis, even to basic research itself, using animals for experimentation. During World War I, he was assistant director of the American Expeditionary Force Division of Laboratories and Infectious Diseases with nearly a hundred facilities overseas.[9]

In 1935, he refused to proceed with Erwin's case, as the brothers had wished. He wrote Antonie on October 23, 1935, that Erwin qualified neither as a graduate student, being too far advanced, nor as a faculty member, since visitors had to come with a guaranteed possibility of returning to their home universities. Moreover, the clinic had no vacancy, and even if there were one, only physicians with a year of residency in the United States could obtain a Minnesota license. "It would be practically impossible for us to be of assistance" and any aid given "would almost certainly in a year or two result in a worse complication."

On receiving this letter two days later, Antonie replied at once and sent a copy of the reply to Will Mayo. She thanked Wilson for his thoroughness and asked his pardon for not taking his letter as a definite "no." She stressed the momentum that a year with the Mayo Clinic would give Erwin and his enthusiasm for becoming American: "My brother certainly would have stayed in this country after his first visit here in 1928 [actually, it was 1929], and it is not only the urgent necessity to secure a peaceful future for his family that makes him emigrate to the United States, but to a very large extent admiration and a warm, honest liking for the United States. These two factors made me come over four years ago."

Fearful of postal censorship, in reporting the bad news to Erwin, Antonie pretended to be writing about a mutual friend who was trying to emigrate:

> A letter of rejection has arrived from Dr. Wilson, infuriating in tone and content. It had erroneous facts and assumptions, so I wrote to him at once correcting them and have sent a copy with another letter to Dr. Will Mayo. If he has any sense of honor, he cannot accept these proceedings because he had been entirely supportive. I imagine Dr. Wilson took me for a dumb goose that would quietly go away.
>
> … Nevertheless, tell your friend to come at any time, that he can stay with Mother L. [Johanna Lewin, a long-time friend of Hedwig Strassmann] and that he can count on some pocket money from me.… Assure your friend that I shall remain in New York until this matter has been settled.… If you advise your friend to emigrate without R [Rochester], come hell or high water, that really should be feasible, given his many connections over here. But he has to face one very hard year! Above all, his English must be so advanced as to risk no failure in an examination.… Apart from that, he should not lose his nerve, and while speed is appropriate, one still has to proceed step by step.
>
> I regret sending your friend this disappointing news, but as I said, no reason to lose hope! Above all, I reacted vigorously and immediately! Wait and see! (October 28, 1935)

To Will Mayo, Antonie wrote how "terribly embarrassed" she was to approach him again "with my grief," but she had already wired her parents, "REPLY VERY POSITIVE. DETAILS BY LETTER," and they had answered back, "SO RELIEVED. THANKS FROM OUR HEARTS." Did Dr. Mayo believe her reply to Wilson was now enough? "I beg you, dear Dr. Mayo, to believe that … more than anything else, the urgent desire to ease my mother's sorrow makes me impose on your valuable time and your friendship for my parents once more." The Mayo Clinic was by then nominally independent of the family, and after 1932, neither Dr. Will nor Dr. Charlie ever attended another meeting of the Board of Governors of the Mayo Foundation (incorporated in 1915). Nevertheless, in something of an understatement, Dr. Will replied that he and Dr. Charlie, although retired, still had "a certain representation" on the Medical Graduate Committee.

Unpersuaded but forced to cooperate, Dr. Wilson wrote to Antonie in November that Erwin could come for one year as "an *observer* of American methods of diagnosis and treatment" and would "be presented by the Mayo Clinic with an honorarium of $840.00 in twelve monthly allotments of $70.00. During this period he must not expect to do any clinical work," since he would lack a license. Wilson wrote that it was illegal to employ any alien before arrival in the United States. He repeated that there was "no probability of your brother ultimately obtaining a remunerative position in Rochester" and suggested fourteen other states and the District of Columbia, where a prior year of US residency was not required before granting a medical license, as better alternatives.

After he arrived in the United States, Erwin was shown all this correspondence by Antonie, and he thanked Dr. Will for his "very, very kind letters. The possibility to go to Rochester is a great honor for me and … is sunshine breaking through dark clouds. As you commented in your letter to Antonie, it is not easy to leave one's native country.… But there was no alternative" (April 6, 1936). After his arrival in Rochester in June 1936, Erwin and Louis Wilson became good friends, and no obstacle to clinical work arose, provided no fee was paid.

On to the Ocean

On March 9, two evenings before sailing, Erwin, his parents, and Ilse ate their last supper together at Schumannstrasse 18. Erwin gave his father copies of his publications and said that a complete set of surgical instruments had been packed. Everything was discussed one more time. Paul wrote in his diary that evening, March 9, 1936: "Enough depression. All sails aloft! He'll make it. We old ones have lived. Erwin will carry out what I gave up thirty years ago because of patriotism! I will not operate tomorrow morning and have asked the night nurse to call me only in emergencies!"

The next morning, on March 10, 1936, they met at the Lehrter Bahnhof, across the Humboldt Harbor from the Alexanderufer, where the family had lived thirty years before. Paul and Hedwig arrived by 10:30 AM and recalled how Hellmuth's train had moved out from here in 1914. Erwin, Ilse, and their three children came somewhat later, just minutes before the train, a silvery dragon, Paul thought. In the final moments, photographs and last-minute wishes were exchanged. Ilse joined Erwin on the train and both waved as it pulled out. Afterwards, Renate, Angelika, and Wolfgang went with their grandparents to the Tiergarten, passing patriotic statues decorated with wreaths for Memorial Day. Most had swastikas, but one without them came from the exiled Kaiser, and some had only a few violets from passers-by.

Erwin and Ilse had dinner aboard the SS *Manhattan* in the harbor of Hamburg that evening with Willy Küper and his wife, their oldest friends from Freiburg. With much banter, the four of them inspected the ship from one deck to another—from Erwin's cabin to luxurious salons and to the lifeboats. Saying farewell to one another was not as heartbreaking as they had feared. Suddenly, bells rang and announcements bellowed commands about the gangways coming down in minutes. Their final moments together brought last, confused good-byes, kisses, and forgetting to say what had been thought out before. After disembarking came farewell waves and a bit of mischievous mugging from the ship's railing by Erwin to those far below on the pier.

Actually, the ship did not glide out of the harbor until 4:30 AM when Ilse was trying to sleep at the Küpers'. The next day at Luisenstrasse 47, she found an entire bed of spring flowers from Erwin and a note, "Mein liebes Herzchen, my life without you is *nothing*, with you *everything*. The physical separation binds us more closely than ever."

"Don't be angry about the flowers," Erwin wrote to her from aboard the ship. "Just one more time I had to express all my feelings. You are a treasure of happiness that makes up for all one has to endure." He also wrote: "Saying good-bye, we panicked a little. Although they threatened to remove the gangway to cabin class, and did, the one for tourist class stayed, and most visitors poured out much later. Still, it was good like that, quick and painless.... Now we are in the North Sea. The ship vibrates, but the sea is calm. No rocking at all. I am happily waiting for lunch. I am alone at my table but hope for nice English-speaking partners from Southampton."

Ilse's first letter, dated March 15, 1936, agreed about the departure:

Maybe it was all right that our farewells had to be said so fast—how many feelings were stirring inside of us! May all our hopes and wishes be fulfilled!... The Küpers were kind and loving to me as we drove to Altona. They proudly showed off their children, the house, and I even had to admire their garden, but my heart was not in it....

Shortly before 1 AM we heard a liner's foghorn. Willy said, "That's him." Then I realized clearly what they mean when they say happiness can float away. Darling, now I know more than ever how much I love you, and I think I never showed it enough....

In Berlin I first visited Muttchen [Erwin's mother] to tell her everything. Then I entered our apartment. It's good that I was alone because your greetings totally overpowered me. All your love spoke to me with that bed of flowers, made me happy, but doubled my boundless solitude. How empty the apartment is and how miserably neat is your desk....

Our three little imps are trying hard to be good. I overheard Renate telling Angeli, "You must behave very well now." "Why?" "Because if the ocean liner sinks, we'll have no more Daddy, and Mom will have to be a laundress to earn bread for us."

On March 18, 1936, six days after leaving Bremen, Erwin wrote:

New York is a few hours ahead. The passage was smooth. Calm ocean, much sun.... In the daytime, ping pong, gymnastics, swimming. I studied English and tried to get pronunciation from the movies. Altogether, the voyage seemed brisk and short.... False political rumors were very unsettling one day, but things turned out well. The critical point seems to have passed.

I am eager to know what Antonie will have to say, where I will stay, etc. I'll write as soon as possible. How are you managing everything alone? Is Mutter [Wens] marching in? Make sure that the principal rooms are photographed by Dürselen [the Strassmann Clinic X-ray specialist and photographer] before changing anything. One wants to preserve something, somehow. Above all, watch your health, and don't let them crap on you in business affairs, taking advantage of a straw widow, causing panic. Greet Parents and kiss the children!!

On into the new country!

Chapter 10

Transatlantic Tensions in New York: Antonie II

After 1932, Antonie ceased acting and flying to become a businesswoman, negotiating patent and technological license contracts between American and German airplane manufacturers. She lived in the luxurious St. Regis Hotel on Manhattan's Fifth Avenue and crossed the Atlantic two or three times a year. Some newspapers wrote that she "shuttled." On both sides of the ocean she helped her family and others to resist Nazi persecution and finally to emigrate. When Antonie acquired American citizenship in 1937, this goal was made easier. Romantically, she was committed to Robert L. Hague, president of the Standard Oil Company's tanker fleet subsidiary. They could not marry until his divorce became final, and he died before this happened.[1]

Antonie had acquired some business experience by promoting German airplane sales in America with models in 1930 and by marketing the Klemm monoplane in South America in 1932. Arranging sales and exchanges of production machinery, gadgets, know-how, and patents now became her primary occupation, and she enrolled in business courses, earning the equivalent of a Master of Business Administration degree. Tight German exchange control exacerbated commerce between the two countries, and barter-like contracts often had to be worked out. Among her American corporate clients were Bendix, Budd, Fleetwing, Glenn L. Martin, General Tire, and Goodyear. To their factories she brought representatives of German companies such as Klemm, Focke-Wulf, Messerschmitt, Bayerische Flugzeugwerke, Siemens, and, above all, Junkers. Some of these buyers were friends who had learned to fly with her at Staaken in 1927 or had been aboard the Do-X in 1932. During these years, Antonie promoted her business by lecturing to groups such as the Society of Automotive Engineers, New York University's Men in Finance Club, and others.[2]

At the beginning of the 1930s, only Junkers and Heinkel had anything like American assembly line production in airframes. Air-cooled engines were a particular bottleneck in cost and quality. Some foreign buyers of German airplanes specified that the engines should be American. Americans also led in the early 1930s in developing controllable-pitch propellers, retractable landing gears, wing flaps, and air pressure systems.

A Confused Memory

Every three or four months until 1939, Antonie was herself in Europe, spending weeks in her old abode at Schumannstrasse 18 until late 1936. I remember a room with strange souvenirs—a silver-studded elephant-hide hassock, a yellow straw Mexican horse and rider, a large Popeye the Sailor doll, pilot's caps with goggles, ashtrays mounted with model airplanes, and silver trophies. In that room Antonie showed us children how she could juggle five Ping-Pong balls in a great circle. We could barely manage two, but we were good for laughs. Dreams of an exotic life in deserts and jungles beyond the seas began in that room. Aunt Tony never visited Berlin without taking my older sister Renata and me, from the ages of six to twelve, to Kranzler's Konditorei on Unter den Linden for an orgy of ice cream, a delicacy that we otherwise had only two or three times a year. It was just a six-block walk, but there was always much to show and tell.

In March 1933, we were eager to show Antonie an exciting store window selling Flit insecticide with marching grenadier figures carrying sprayers. It was on the Luisenstrasse just before the Marschall Bridge over the Spree River. Under radiating lights near the grenadiers, baby chicks had hatched for Easter! We had watched the eggs for days, and now broken shells were lying about with tiny chicks staggering nearby. A crowd had gathered, staring.

My sister finally said, "Aunt Tony, did you know the Reichstag building burned? We saw it from our attic! They say the Communists did it!" It was three blocks away on the opposite embankment of the Spree. I had heard differently and, being six years old, liked to contradict my sister. I said, "No, those Nazi swine did it themselves." All we knew about Nazis was that they marched with swastika flags and wore brown uniforms and that an ominous secret about them lurked.

What made the incident memorable for decades was that Aunt Tony suddenly yanked us by the arms out of that crowd and said loudly, "Yes, it's disgusting how those swine litter the streets! Look at that!" The street was shabby but quite clean—no paper or banana peels lay along the streetcar tracks or in the gutter. Perhaps no hoarsely singing columns of brown-shirted storm troopers had marched this way. Or they had not littered. What did she mean? We could not fathom what had agitated our aunt, and she did not explain. Many years later she remembered the incident, recalling her fear of denunciation by strangers.

Counterespionage

In 1936, Antonie crossed the Atlantic five times, twice by air on the *Hindenburg*. After she boarded the SS *Europa* in Bremerhaven to return to the United States in October 1936, four Gestapo agents brusquely entered her cabin to search her person and her luggage and to confiscate documents. The departure of the ship was delayed for hours. A month later, her papers were returned by the HAPAG shipping line under German government orders without explanation. Antonie wrote her parents from Southampton that the Bremerhaven departure could best be described only in person, adding: "From yesterday until today I have gained 100 years in maturity and age! It was a peculiar, incomparable farewell at Bremerhaven! Beloved parents, find peace and the meaning of your lives, knowing that Father's work is complete and your children are secure.... Father should forget the defunct furnishings from his parents and treasure Mother's devotion of 43 years!" (October 30, 1936).

The phrase "defunct furnishings" was Antonie's way of scorning the futile ambition of nineteenth-century German Jews to be accepted by a nation run by overbearing bigots. One had to assume that letters were being opened and read by the Gestapo. She notified the FBI about the incident, and two agents were assigned to protect her while others investigated the case. The British MI-6 sent evidence of German plans to obtain American codes, maps, and defense designs, especially for the Panama Canal. The FBI investigated and indeed uncovered a substantial network of Nazi spies along the East Coast of the United States. Agents had been recruited at a number of military bases, at naval shipyards, and among such aviation manufacturers as Seversky and Curtiss. Using couriers on German ships, these agents reported to the German intelligence-gathering organization, the Abwehr, directed by Admiral Wilhelm Canaris. Specifically, they reported to Dr. Erich Pfeiffer, head of the Marine Nachrichten Stelle (Naval Intelligence Service) in Bremen, who directed Nazi espionage in the Americas.

Directing German espionage in New York until he was trapped by the FBI was Dr. Ignatz Griebl, a surgeon and obstetrician, who revealed much about his subversive work, including the pursuit of Antonie. His medical office was located at 56 East 87th Street in the Germanic Yorkville section of Manhattan. Griebl had emigrated to the United States in 1925, had become a citizen in 1930, and was a founder and president of the Nazi-oriented Friends of New Germany, later the German-American Bund. Reporting to Pfeiffer in Bremen, Griebl was in charge of everything except for the local Gestapo office, which was headed by Karl Friedrich Wilhelm Herrmann, a waiter at the Longchamps Restaurant on 59th Street at Madison Avenue. But Griebl continued to be important and traveled to Berlin in June 1937 for further personal instructions from Pfeiffer and Admiral Canaris. Griebl's pay was to be accumulated in Germany, and he was promised access to confiscated Jewish property in Giessen. Trapped by the FBI, however, Griebl became a double agent and FBI informer until he reversed himself again, warned the Nazis, and hurriedly left on the SS *Bremen* in May 1938 as a stowaway. The FBI pursued him with a seaplane, but Captain Ahrens of the *Bremen* refused to turn him over. Griebl opened a medical practice in Vienna, where the banning of Jewish doctors after the Anschluss gave him lucrative opportunities.

The ships of the North German Lloyd and the Hamburg America (HAPAG) lines were constantly used by the Nazis as a cover for espionage agents and secret police to obtain inventions and military plans and to spy on others, especially fellow Germans. Someone who alarmed them was Valerie Claire "Sunny" (Mrs. Thomas) Manville, who was in her seventies. This society matron had inherited an asbestos fortune after her husband died in 1925, and she now gave lavish presents and invitations to stewards and hairdressers after transoceanic trips. Befuddled by this generosity to some of their espionage couriers, other German agents wondered if she and Antonie were trying to recruit their comrades for counterespionage.

A close friend of Sunny, Antonie was involved in exchanges of aviation technology and was thus thought to be a logical agent of counterespionage. She was known to be a legitimate, principal proponent of bringing German automatic pilot technology to the United States. The New York Gestapo agents, Karl Herrmann and Fritz Ewald Rossberg, a mechanic with the Silverton Process Company, had orders to abduct Antonie and send her to Germany for interrogation and punishment for "treason." Abduction meant being forced aboard one of the German ocean liners for the trip back.

To build a case against the German spies, the FBI used lie detectors and then had some of the Germans testify against others in exchange for leniency. Once the trial was under way, the defense lawyer, George C. Dix, two US attorneys, and an FBI agent, J. T. McLaughlin, traveled to Berlin to examine Dr. Griebl, who now claimed to be an abductee himself. In his seventeen-thousand-word statement, Griebl said that his principal accuser lacked credibility because he was a radical and a Jew. The agent in charge of these investigations was Leon G. Turrou (a Gentile), who resigned from the FBI afterward and wrote about the case.[3] McLaughlin said that in Berlin, Griebl told him off the record: "You can understand what would happen to me here if I did not say that and did not contradict the things I told the FBI.... Personally, self-preservation has always been my god."

On June 20, 1938, eighteen people were indicted by a US federal grand jury, primarily for conspiring to steal military secrets. The trial took a month and a half and on December 2 led to guilty verdicts for all eighteen, although only four of the accused were actually in police custody. John C. Knox, the judge in this case, had been in charge of spy prosecutions during World War I. Now he told the court: "In some countries spies are given a secret trial and shot immediately. A few months later an announcement is made of their death, and that is all we hear about it. I am certain that foreign countries were represented in this courtroom and knew what was going on daily. I am convinced some of the daily spectators at the trial were spies for those countries. I believe I could point them out. [I want] other nations to know that America provides a fair and humane trial for all, regardless of nationality or the offense charged."[4]

The sentences were rather light. Johanna Hoffmann received four years, Otto Voss, six years, Erich Glaser, two years, and Guenther Rumrich (an American), two years. In the following year, everyone involved—spies and FBI agents—achieved Hollywood immortality in a melodramatic movie, *Confessions of a Nazi Spy* (1939, 102 minutes), directed by Anatole Litvak. Edward G. Robinson starred as the fearless investigator together with Paul Lukas, Henry O'Neill, Sig Ruman, George Sanders, and James Stephenson.

Antonie herself thought the whole affair had an element of personal vendetta, inspired by the well-known yet envious German aviatrix and Nazi Party member, Thea Rasche. As long ago as 1932, after the Do-X flight, this woman had set the "Who Invited Her?" article in Goebbels's *Der Angriff* newspaper "on my neck, and then, much worse, set the Gestapo after me on the SS *Europa* in 1936 …. and had them hunt me down here in 1938." Thus wrote Antonie on May 25, 1947, to the German industrialist, Ernst Heinkel, adding: "Should I ever encounter this vile creature, I'll slap her ears right and left so that for a while she can't appear in public." Antonie either did not know or did not care that Thea Rasche declined further work for Goebbels in the 1940s.[5] On February 23, 1951, Heinkel wrote to Antonie, "I don't know what Thea is doing and how she supports herself. In any case, in her denazification hearings, she behaved oddly."

Business as Usual

Immediately after her return to New York on the *Europa* following that Gestapo search in October 1936, two Junkers representatives came from their engine factory, including von Brauchitsch, the director. Antonie wrote home that this man behaved unpleasantly, tossing a letter across her desk. She then treated him so icily that he apologized, "but I refused to accept that apology! I heard nothing! Two days later he wanted to make up with friendly grins and invited me to lunch with his wife. I remained businesslike but absolutely icy and did not even ask about her children!" The Brauchitsches became increasingly obsequious, and a week or so later, Antonie forgave and invited them to a Christmas Eve party.

Meanwhile, two others had come from the Junkers airframe plant. After Christmas, Antonie took them all to Washington, DC, to meet senators, an assistant attorney general, and even a son of President Roosevelt. It was export promotion but required licenses. On New Year's Eve, they all took the train back to New York, and en route Antonie received a telegram from Senator Robert R. Reynolds, chairman of the Committee on Military Affairs: "HEAVENLY TO HAVE BEEN WITH YOU TODAY. WILL CALL YOU TONIGHT. HOPE YOU HAVE A PLEASANT JOURNEY TO THE METROPOLIS. AS FOR THE NEW YEAR, MAY EVERY DAY BE ONE PROVIDING AN ABUNDANCE OF SUNSHINE."

The delegation from Junkers seemed astounded, she wrote home. In Manhattan that evening, she took them to Times Square at midnight, then to Maxl's German restaurant in Yorkville, and to other night spots until 5:00 AM. She slept until 10:00 AM and then joined them again to show them the Statue of Liberty, the Empire State Building, and the Brooklyn Bridge. The next day she translated and typed nine letters of introduction for the Junkers representatives, arranging an itinerary to aircraft factories in Pennsylvania, Maryland, Kansas, and California. Meanwhile, Senator Reynolds called several times from Washington.

Robert L. Hague, the Romance of the 1930s

Antonie met Robert L. Hague (1880–1939) at a party on an ocean liner in 1933. He was traveling with an entourage of twenty people, some in show business, and he had reserved an extra cabin to serve as a private bar. As vice president of the Standard Oil Company and president of its shipping affiliate, his objective was to get oil tankers built with German marks that were now no longer convertible into US dollars. Antonie told me that one such deal amounted to $27 million (equivalent to $340 million of 2000).

Hague's career started in shipping in San Francisco after he had quit school at age fourteen in 1894. During World War I, in his thirties, he worked for the national shipping board, coordinating schedules. Afterward, he joined Standard Oil and moved up through the ranks until he was head of its shipping subsidiary, the Standard Shipping Company, operator of the world's largest fleet of tankers. Without including the crews of these ships, Hague's office had about two hundred fifty employees. As an ardent Democrat, Hague was Standard Oil's contact in Washington during the Roosevelt years. His hobbies were theatre, watch collecting, and sailing. Bob's own sailboat was seventy feet long and had bunks for sleeping four passengers and a crew. Antonie learned how to sail it from Long Island Sound to Martha's Vineyard.

Hague had thus become rich and was a patron of the theatre, backing shows and supporting the charitable Lambs Club for stage folk. With annual contributions of $25,000 to $50,000, he kept that club from bankruptcy, and each year he bankrolled the Lambs Gambol Ball at the Waldorf Astoria Hotel. In the 1930s, Hague was married to Metropolitan Opera soprano Mary Lewis (1901–1942). Born in Dallas, she had made her singing debut at the age of eight in a Methodist Church choir. After contracts with the Greenwich Village Follies and the Ziegfeld Follies in New York, Mary's grand opera debut came in Vienna in 1923 in Gounod's *Faust*. She then toured Europe giving concerts and made her Metropolitan debut in 1926 as Mimi in Puccini's *La Bohème*. A 1927 marriage to the basso Michael Bohnen lasted only a few years. In the mid-1930s, she still gave concerts but had become an alcoholic. Antonie never referred to Mary by name, but only as "Madame" or "She," for example: "'She' is coming back on the 14th. Who knows what will happen then? But since I can do nothing about it, I don't feel disturbed! I shall see my friends and do my work, and have so far neglected or given up nothing, unlike my past record. So I'm moving ahead in every way! It will be harder for him! Under no circumstances will I spend the summer in New York" (March 5, 1935).

Mother Hedwig worried that Mary Lewis might physically assault or shoot Antonie, who wrote back again not to worry. Mary had started meeting her husband daily for lunch and remained in his office all afternoon. She had stopped drinking and making scenes. Antonie wrote to Bob that he could do whatever he pleased, that he had no obligations to her. To Mother Hedwig she wrote that it was puzzling what captivated her so much about this man. In his absence she had no urge to flirt with anyone else. If she had not seen the Crown Prince for weeks back in the 1920s, that would have ended that. This man, however, "is closest to me in personality, vitality, generosity, and character, and that almost outweighs sheer passion." Antonie tried to explain: "I don't know what it is, Mother, but this man fascinates me so much! Besides he *truly* worries about me, and that matters! When this man says, 'I love you more than anyone in the world,' he means it, I know! He just works insanely!... Obviously, his contacts are professionally immensely valuable to me and Erwin! He even offered me a position with Standard Oil, which I declined, not needing it yet! I promise you, this time reason will prevail! Too much is at stake! I'm in no hurry, thank God!... But when I saw him again, I confess I 'broke down'" (undated letter, fall 1935).

In early March 1937, Hague told Antonie that he would take the initiative to obtain a divorce without waiting any longer for Mary. Everything was proceeding smoothly, and Antonie resolved not to push him. She suspected that Hague felt insecure about her. Apparently, he had heard that Senator Reynolds had given instructions that he was to be informed immediately whenever Antonie called, even if he was on the floor of the Senate. Antonie occasionally took advantage of that. Once she went to Philadelphia to hear Reynolds speak and then drove him back to Washington the next morning. She wrote that Rhett Butler in *Gone with the Wind* was that sort of man, incredibly charming. Reynolds hoped to be the Democratic nominee for president in 1940, assuming that Franklin Roosevelt would not run for a third term. When Roosevelt's re-election ambitions became clear, Reynolds aimed at the vice presidency instead. In either case, he could not burden his chances as a divorcé by marrying a former alien, or so he said. Antonie wrote to Berlin, "It would be just like me again, to pick someone like that!"

If Antonie was less than farsighted about some of the implications of her work, in retrospect she looked better than Senator Reynolds, the member of the Senate's Foreign Relations Committee who was also chairman of the Military Affairs Committee. In 1934, he had been a strong supporter of naval construction, but as early as 1935 he had (unsuccessfully) opposed American adherence to the protocols of the International Court of Justice at The Hague. He was one of only twelve Democrats in October 1939 who opposed repeal of the arms embargo to help the Allies.

By that time, however, Reynolds and Antonie had parted company. On May 22, 1939, Antonie wrote to Erwin that Reynolds "didn't care a damn" about his isolationist pronouncements and was even ashamed of them, "but only does all that to become vice president in 1940." After he failed with that ambition (Roosevelt chose Henry A. Wallace instead), Reynolds continued opposing the president's warlike support of transatlantic shipping to Britain, saying in 1941: "If we continue to look for trouble, the probabilities are that we will eventually find it."[6]

Actually, Reynolds never had a chance against Bob Hague. As Antonie wrote her mother, "No one matches [Bob Hague] as a personality" (March 16, 1937). On April 1, 1937, she wrote home: "Madame is off to Europe, which eases the situation." After the divorce, thought Antonie, Bob would have to let a year go by "before he recovers his faith that living with another person is possible! I'm in no hurry, have enough to do, and things are further along than I expected."

American Citizenship

Throughout the 1930s, when she was not traveling, Antonie typed a two-page letter home once or twice a week, especially to her mother, recounting all events, visitors, impressions, plans, and emotions. She commented on everything mentioned in letters from her parents and timed correspondence to match the schedules of ocean liners. Without those letters, rescued from flames, this chapter would have lacked the best details.

In 1937, Antonie said in a letter to Erwin that she worked with the German aircraft companies *"without any* enthusiasm whatsoever, just with the sober objective of earning a living! Changing flags has totally transformed me without any pain! I am counting the months until I take the oath. Stars mean more to me than the swastika!... As an extremely vulgar expression has it here, 'They can kiss my ass in Macy's window at high noon!'"

A great party celebrated Antonie's American citizenship on June 14, 1937. Twenty-six guests met on the Viennese Roof of the St. Regis Hotel. From the terrace, one could see Manhattan's sea of lights glimmering in the spring evening as yellow roses and blue delphiniums were spread around an American eagle made of ice, and as flags and bunting fluttered all around. Dinner consisted of salmon, Westphalian ham, white asparagus, and pineapple. The wines were a 1929 Chateau Latour and a 1933 Erdener Treppchen. There were toasts and speeches, and Bob gave Antonie a silken star-spangled banner and ten dozen roses. A singer and a violinist entertained for over an hour. Senator Reynolds and Jimmy Walker (the former mayor of New York City) could not make it, but Antonie's other best friends were there, especially Dr. Bishop, Sunny Manville, and Vincent Bendix, among others. Some of the guests remained until 3:30 AM.

A week earlier, on June 9, Antonie had written her parents about the moment that she took the oath of citizenship on the previous Monday: "A decisive and deep change took place! My hand trembled more than at my wedding! I did not dare to telegraph you because ... people exist who cannot forgive one for behaving decently, for thinking of more than one's own fate! It's tiresome to defend oneself continually. Until lately I subconsciously kept hoping that life would calm down for you, for me, for all of us! But that doesn't seem to be in the cards for our generation, neither here nor over there, and we have to stick it out! Whenever one problem is solved, another turns up!"

Athletes and Actors from Abroad

A stream of German visitors to New York included celebrities from sports, aviation, and theatre, such as Max Schmeling, Helene Mayer, Rudolf Forster, Fritz Kortner, Elly Beinhorn, and Bernd Rosemeyer. She found the former world heavyweight boxing champion, Max Schmeling, someone who was "always polite, refined, and tactful," not at all the arrogant Nazi of later legend who deserved to lose to Joe Louis in one round in 1938. Actually, Schmeling had a Jewish manager and was dismayed that his 1936 twelve-round knockout of Louis was puffed up as a racial triumph in Germany.

Helene Mayer, the Olympic gold medal fencer, had emigrated to Los Angeles but, although classified as "half-Jewish," returned to Berlin to win a silver medal for Germany in the 1936 Olympics. Back in America, she came to New York in April 1937 for the National Fencing Tournament and stayed with Antonie. Helene won the tournament and as thanks, according to Antonie, "left the most touching letters in my apartment, one in every drawer, and others pinned to my dresses!"

On August 22, 1937, Rudolf Forster sailed for America on the SS *Berengaria* and that day wrote a last note to Hedwig Strassmann: "I'm traveling a bit to America to play a bit of theatre, a play called *Tovarich*. In the last two years I have experienced so many unattractive and disagreeable things here that I have decided to go to America. Unfortunately, I have heard nothing from Antonie ... but I shall be extremely happy to see and greet her." Most disagreeable for him, apparently, was that certain scenes had been cut from a film in which he had acted. Antonie wrote her mother: "Reading that, I know why I left the theatre—such overestimating of one's own importance together with total naiveté may be good for success, but I never did it! A nervous breakdown because a few scenes were cut! Of course, I can understand it, but still such a narrow horizon is too much!"

One evening, in a Chinese restaurant, Antonie met by chance a celebrated actor of the 1920s, Fritz Kortner (1892–1970), who had played Gessner in Leopold Jessner's path-breaking expressionistic *Wilhelm Tell* and Herodes in *Herodes and Mariamne*, with Antonie as Salomé. Antonie was ecstatic:

> He looked very good, and from the depths, a whole past existence suddenly bubbled up, my stage years that had been discarded in 1930.... Nothing before in New York life could have reawakened that time. Seeing Forster again was only personal. Now all at once *Herodes and Mariamne*, those evenings at Schwannekes,[7] etc., were resurrected! He also seemed enormously happy to see me [and said] I never looked so fantastically good, which did please me. He no longer acts but writes and directs. His wife and children are still in London, but here an old gang suddenly finds itself together again. Thus, nothing in life is ever totally lost! Old times and a life that seemed sunk away were really just in mothballs in the attic! (November 30, 1937)

In the spring of 1939, Antonie heard from Forster that Kortner, other actors, the playwright Ernst Toller, and even famous directors, including Max Reinhardt, Leopold Jessner, and Erwin Piscator, were all in Hollywood. Toller, however, committed suicide, fearing that what had happened in Germany would be repeated in the United States. Forster returned to Germany and after the war asked Antonie to send him silk underwear.

Elly and Bernd

On a rainy morning in June 1937, Antonie stood at Hudson Pier 86 and waited for the racing driver Bernd Rosemeyer to come down the gangplank. "You can't imagine my indescribable joy, suddenly seeing Elly Beinhorn!" reported Antonie. Elly, her flying friend and Bernd's wife, looked as charming as ever and said not a word about the perennial worry over Bernd's perilous occupation. He was trying to break the 400 kilometer-per-hour barrier. For days, Antonie spent every available moment with them. The races were postponed from the Fourth of July because of rain, and then Rosemeyer won. This victory, the Vanderbilt Cup, was considered by Elly his greatest. The racers had to circle the Roosevelt Race Track ninety times, and Bernd in his Audi came in ahead of Richard Seaman (in a Mercedes), Rex Mays, and Ernst von Delius. On their last day, July 6, 1937, Antonie wrote: "Tomorrow it will seem unreal to me that they were ever here and have departed loaded with fame and foreign exchange.... Yes, the days with Elly were beautiful but much too short ... and, my God, it's not easy for her! I could not bear such worries anymore! If you could have seen how they raced yesterday, three and a half hours, and that every week, plus training in between!"

Von Delius was killed later that fall in a collision with Seaman. Death on the road was ahead for Seaman as well and for Rex Mays. On January 28, 1938, on the Autobahn near Darmstadt, Rosemeyer, the last of the four, was killed losing control in a gust of wind. Two months earlier, on November 12, Elly had delivered Bernd Junior and had written to Antonie, who reported: "A wonderful letter came from Elly. What a magnificent woman! She is deliriously happy with her baby, yet so elegantly simple" (December 7, 1937).

On February 1, 1938, Antonie's father in Berlin wrote to us in Rochester, Minnesota: "Preserving our good humor is not easy, since our mood is shattered by Rosemeyer's accident. Not long ago he sat at our table with his wife Elly. Another evening, he returned, rather unsettled, due to a diet for his stomach. Today is the funeral in Dahlem by invitation only. We have not yet seen the poor young woman, a two-month-old fatherless child in her arms. Her husband has entered immortality like a knight. Her happiness is gone."

The *Hindenburg*

The greatest disaster of 1937, however, was the explosion on May 6 of the airship *Hindenburg* when it touched its mooring mast at Lakehurst, New Jersey. With Hugo and Fred Stinnes (sons of the late Ruhr steel magnate, Hugo Stinnes) carrying wine and money, Antonie drove to the Lakewood Hospital the next morning. As she visited two friends, the airship's captain, Ernst Lehmann, died in the next room, having muttered something about sabotage and the fate of passengers. Although he had not been a Nazi Party member, he was hated by Antonie as a collaborator who, unlike his chief, Hugo Eckener, played the Nazi game and was paid a "high Judas price." Ten years later, on July 22, 1946, she wrote to Eckener: "I was in a side room when he died—it left me more than cold—the destruction of your proud child was partly his fault. And we often said here, 'It never would have happened, had the Old Man (you) been aboard.' They would receive you here with open arms, since no one ever associated you with those monsters."

One friend who did not burn up in the *Hindenburg* was the boxer, Max Schmeling. He had changed his itinerary at the last minute.

The End of an Era

Bob Hague died of a heart attack on March 8, 1939. Antonie wrote to Erwin on April 1 about the anguish she felt, especially when "La ci darem la mano" from Mozart's *Don Giovanni* was played on the radio. Other friends had committed suicide or died in Germany of obscure causes: "One after another, comrades from those times have gone. And that swine Hitler and his cronies live. What kind of leader is that, orating behind bulletproof glass and traveling in armored trains? How safe does he feel, this 'beloved and honored' leader of the German people?"

With World War II unleashed later in 1939 and Bob gone, Antonie had to reorganize. Even before Poland was invaded and war was declared, it was clear that contracts for technical exchanges with Germany would end. Siemens and Junkers withdrew in May 1939, but Antonie's contract with Bendix lasted until January 1941. Erwin regretted the financial strain caused by the German firms' withdrawal but supposed that "inside you must feel relieved to no longer work for them over there despite continued good personal relations. How often did you say you were fed up and kept on mainly to raise funds for us?" Actually, Antonie did not believe that airplane technology would be critical for winning the war, and she considered the Germans still inferior in engine design, workmanship, access to materials, and fuel supply. These could not overcome their advantages in skilled labor and plant capacity, she told the Men in Finance Club of New York University on November 22, 1939.

Money was now too scarce for helping as many refugees as before. Above all, Antonie had to find a job and a place to live with her mother, who was due to arrive on the SS *Champlain* on August 17, 1939.

A Surprise

Antonie considered joining Silas Newton, a Texas oil man and an old friend of Bob Hague, "somehow in his business, since things here [in New York] are too dubious without money from abroad" (May 9, 1939). In mid-July 1939, she traveled to Colorado Springs where Si happened to be, but a letter to Erwin gave no hint of an imminent wedding. Si was a stocky, short, widowed Texas millionaire who had studied at Baylor, Yale, and Berlin before founding his Newton Oil Company in Denver. For Christmas 1937, he had given Antonie a matching set of jade earrings, a ring, and a bracelet set with diamonds. Antonie had written her parents on December 15 that Si had said "he was just waiting for the day when I say 'yes,' and would meanwhile be patient. That's touching because with various rivals, the odds are against him."

A civil wedding with Si did take place at Castle Rock, Colorado, on July 16, 1939, but Antonie returned to New York the following day. She thus left Si after a single night and immediately considered having the marriage annulled, as she later told her cousin, Gerhard Masur. They never lived together, and Si contributed nothing to the household. At first, Si refused to cooperate with a divorce and kept seeking a reconciliation, but Antonie thanked him and told him it was too late for that. To Erwin she wrote, in an undated letter of early 1941, that she sought "a quiet, quick, and decent divorce. Annulment unfortunately is impossible.… One can divorce legally in Mexico in a single week. I just have to go there, establish residence in a day, and it's valid if he is considered represented.… I'm hoping he'll agree. If only he could briefly get to the point. I can no longer abide his yard-long letters."

The marriage ended on March 2, 1942, with a decision in Chihuahua. Antonie's 1950 passport application says no more about him than "last known residence, Denver, Colorado." In her will, she bequeathed "unto Silas M. Newton of Denver, Colorado … all interest in an oil lease owned by me on property in Ness City, Kansas." While she lived, I never heard his name and can only wonder about all the details.

Arrivals: A Mother and Some Inheritance

Returning to New York from Denver in July 1939, Antonie moved from the St. Regis Hotel to an eight-room apartment overlooking Central Park at 1158 Fifth Avenue. That much space was needed for all the inherited furniture that had been loaded aboard ship on June 27 and was due shortly. A cousin's wife, Käthe Posner, came to help open all the crates and to set up the familiar cabinets, chairs, and beds from the Schumannstrasse and Dahlem residences. Exciting, yes, but the steamy morning of August 17 was more exhilarating: Antonie's beloved mother and confidante, Hedwig Strassmann, known as "Muttchen," arrived on the SS *Champlain* with an immigration visa.

Two years later, in June 1941, Antonie and Hedwig moved from Fifth Avenue to a house they had built on a hemlock-forested promontory above a small lake in Westchester County at Croton-on-the-Hudson, a few miles south of Peekskill. Antonie's physician and old friend Ernst Mueller and his wife, Rosel, had bought a house on the shore of that lake the previous summer. Antonie built her chalet among three acres of trees high on a neighboring hill and called it Hemlock Hague. A lengthy access road wound up steeply through the woods from Croton Avenue, RFD-1.

Most distinctive were a great stone chimney, a carved double front door above a grand outside stairway, and rustic-patterned iron grillwork protecting a large picture window facing the lake, far below. The door, grill, and dining room furniture all came from the Romanian

Pavilion of the 1939 World's Fair in New York. Blasted into the rock under the living room was a bunk room decorated with portholes and other marine paraphernalia. Visitors slept there on a bigger than king-sized built-in bed. Above Antonie's bed in another room hung the impressionistic Philip Franck painting of the tip of the Fischer Insel in central Berlin showing a bridge, tugboats, and great-grandfather Joseph Bender Levy's mansion. Above a fireplace was the luminous Van de Velde seascape with Dutch square-riggers. Antonie's daily commute to the Empire State Building took an hour in her convertible.

War Years

During the war that for the United States started officially on December 7, 1941, with the attack on Pearl Harbor, Antonie and Hedwig lived in two-room apartments in Manhattan during the winters to save on rationed gasoline and heating fuel. In the summers, cucumbers and other vegetables were planted at Hemlock Hague in a small "victory garden," and a shed was built for ten chickens. The worst year was 1942, made personally tragic by the news of Gisela's death from cancer in April. Hedwig reported that Max had written touching letters, already hoping for a reunion with herself and Antonie. These letters have not survived.

Seeking new employment, Antonie studied shorthand in night school and volunteered for the Red Cross two or three days a week. She wrote to Max that it felt "weird" to be driving around in a uniform. She drove vehicles for the Red Cross and taught a course in first aid. In addition, she donated pints of blood for the British Red Cross, although she was classified as somewhat anemic with a tendency to go into shock. As mobilization gathered momentum, Antonie found a job as an instructor at the Delahanty Institute, teaching prospective workers, especially women, how to read blueprints and to operate metalworking equipment, such as lathes and drill presses.

In 1943, Eugene F. McDonald (1890–1958), founding president of the Zenith Radio Corporation, gave Antonie a chance to organize sales for inexpensive hearing aids. She had met McDonald when she participated in the Chicago Air Races in August 1930, and the two had been friends ever since.

McDonald was born in Syracuse, New York, attended Syracuse University, sold Franklin automobiles, and became a US Navy lieutenant commander during World War I. Afterward, he founded the Zenith Radio Corporation and joined exploratory voyages to the Arctic and the South Pacific. He became devoted to aerial gliding as a sport and wrote a book about it, *Youth Must Fly: Gliding and Soaring for America*. He believed that the Germans had an enviable head start in gliding, which explained their "mighty corps of pilots." He wrote that he had no intention of becoming an authority on aviation: "My business is manufacturing radio receivers, which is similar to aviation only in being a young industry with unpredictable developments constantly on the horizon.… When any man says to me that a mechanical job … is perfected, he is only telling me that he, himself, is finished." New devices, McDonald added, should be hopelessly obsolete in two years.[8]

The Zenith Hearing Aid Division

In the 1940s, Commander (as he always labeled himself) McDonald still personally controlled the Zenith Radio Corporation. On October 24, 1943, in Chicago, he launched with great fanfare a "Crusade to Help the Hard of Hearing." A thousand people, including

Antonie, were there to see the first Radionic hearing aids, which would sell for $40 instead of the $200 charged by the established firms, Beltone and Accousticon. There would be no more profiteering in hearing aids, said McDonald, neither in America nor abroad. Six weeks later, on December 5, 1943, Antonie and seven other Zenith employees opened the Hearing Aid Division for the East Coast with only two dealers, one in Manhattan, the other in Brooklyn. Fifty-seven units were sold, one for a nine-year-old girl who had never heard a sound before.

A hearing aid has a tiny microphone, a battery-powered radio receiver, and an amplifier that magnifies sound before it reaches the tympanic membrane and auditory nerves of the inner ear. In 1943, their cost of manufacture was about $25 per instrument, making $40 a reasonable retail price. The markup to $200 by Zenith's competitors allowed enormous profits behind a façade of pseudo-medical appointments, diagnoses, and showmanship. Zenith's problem was convincing buyers that a cheaper, over-the-counter hearing aid could be just as good.

Antonie loaded cartons of them into her convertible and with a sales pitch drove to optometrists and department stores in sixteen states. Within a few years, she had five hundred dealers from Maine to Florida and served them with a staff of forty employees in the Empire State Building. Others worked in a warehouse on the waterfront, including myself in August 1946—after two years in the navy and before returning to college. On drives between Manhattan and Hemlock Hague, I heard about conflicts with inventors and competitors alleging infringement. If you did not lose 2 percent annually, you were not a good credit manager. Antonie said it was as exciting as aviation or a stage career.

When I returned to New York in 1949 to study at Columbia University, I saw Antonie (Aunt Tony) often and heard more about the hearing aid business. I recall her telling me:

> At the office I could be the mother of any of my boys. And that's the sort of relationship I want. I never make bones about my age. I'm forty-eight, and I'll tell anyone who wants to know. But I can still wear any of them down, go biking with them, and go along on a joke. With the boys it's important to know baseball more than superficially. I swear and say "son-of-a-bitch" when I mean it. Makes them feel less bad working for a woman. Still, I always try to act my age, though it doesn't look like it in this outfit. All day long I've got to work and think like a businessman, then there is the drive back and forth, and when I come home, I've got to do all the things a woman has to do. Every age has things you can do. At any other time they're absurd because they're unnatural. Why can't people grow old gracefully?

Gene McDonald allowed Antonie to run her office with much authority, for example, letting her determine the salaries and raises of all employees. Any famous person who sought a hearing aid was certain to be visited by Antonie personally. Among them were Eleanor Roosevelt, Charles Edison (son of the inventor, secretary of the navy, and governor of New Jersey), and Rupert Hughes (playwright and composer). These three allowed their names to be used in Zenith advertisements in major magazines, saying that they, "who can afford any hearing aid at any price, wear Zenith."

In 1951, an elderly foreigner with a hearing problem came to the New York offices of Zenith but had trouble making himself understood. He seemed to be German. Antonie was called out of her office to help. She recognized him from three decades earlier and immediately presented two hearing aids as gifts. The old gentleman was Ernst Reuter, the mayor of West Berlin, celebrated as the leader against the 1948–1949 Soviet blockade, which was broken by a massive airlift. Antonie had known Reuter thirty years earlier in Magdeburg, where she had been a young actress and he an urban official.

Antonie and I

Antonie's flying, traveling, and even juggling had fascinated me as a boy in Berlin. I remember her welcoming our family when the SS *Bremen* docked in New York in 1937 and showing us around Central Park and Rockefeller Center. The only time she and Grandmother Hedwig visited us in Houston was Christmas 1939, when I was thirteen. She gave me a subscription to the *New Yorker* magazine, partly because of the cartoons. She had always liked the sketches that I enclosed in letters. I have kept up my subscription since then—for over six decades. When I was in the navy in 1944, I sent her a photograph of myself as a sailor at the Great Lakes Naval Training Center in Illinois. Antonie wrote to my parents in Houston, "I feel sorry for the girls whom this Seaman First Class is going to turn down!" (August 17, 1944).

Later I spent summers at the National University of Mexico. Antonie wrote to a friend, Paco de la Macorra, the chief General Motors distributor, asking him to introduce me to a Mexican girl "who was a good kid and knew about life," so that I could break her heart. I remember meeting Paco and nineteen-year-old Gloria at Ciro's Bar on the Paseo de la Reforma. She said in Spanish, "What gift are you bringing me now, Paco?" All that broke that summer was my budget. She was a general's daughter and loved horses—but that is another story.

After two more years, I enrolled at Columbia University in 1949 for graduate studies, lived on 119th Street, and drove to Hemlock Hague about every other weekend. At other times, Antonie and I met in midtown Manhattan for lunch or supper, sometimes even meeting up at a nightclub. She evaluated performances with Berlin slang, saying one crooner sounded like someone coughing into a flower watering can ("hustet in 'ne leere Gieskanne"). I thought she was so concerned with immediate objectives that she could not understand inner conflicts and hesitation by others, considering them a weak waste of time. Nevertheless, she seemed to relish whatever I told her, laughing and countering with anecdotes about people she had seen recently, like the journalist Dorothy Thompson, the labor leader John L. Lewis, Ben Grauer of television, and more durable icons, such as Eleanor Roosevelt and Marlene Dietrich.

At Hemlock Hague much fuss was always made over the three black dachshunds. Moki presumably did not like other dogs because he did not consider himself a dog. He could not understand why anyone would want animals in the house. He did not like to be laughed at, although occasionally he was drunk on beer and once passed out in the snow. Mickel was a dumb goose but very conceited. She fell in love with any visiting young man. But she had to be admired and told she was "beautiful, a good dog, a poor unfortunate little Mickel, but so intelligent and with a conscience." She liked to chase bugs but was afraid of the lake, thunder, and automobiles. Chickie was "just a plain good dog who thought he was entitled to special privileges." He liked to be addressed with "thee" and "thou," so one said "lie thee down" and "shake thy hand" to Chickie. One of the dogs died, I forget which, and was replaced by another named Pinkernose. Everyone agreed that the dogs were spoiled rotten, sitting on dining room chairs during meals, begging for scraps. Antonie asked visitors, "You wouldn't mind taking the place of one of these dogs, would you? You'll have to get on the waiting list!"

I will relate only one other incident. One Saturday afternoon in spring, I drove to Hemlock Hague with a girl named Laura, a student of English at Queens College who had won a few literary prizes and had even published some poems, one dedicated to me. The dachshunds heard the tires on the gravel and charged out of the woods, barking fiercely. Antonie came around the house with a rake and said she had been burning leaves, the first cleanup since October. Laura and I should go in and make ourselves at home, and she would be with us shortly. Muttchen was taking a nap.

So we sat on the couch in front of the Dutch marinescape over the fireplace and were shortly doing what infatuated people are likely to do on couches. Antonie came in sooner than expected. "Am I interrupting something?" she said. "Maybe I should have knocked before interrupting this terrific conversation."

Muttchen came in later with some sewing, and coffee was served. She asked some questions and then mentioned a book about Babylonian history. Antonie became restless and got up to rearrange a long bookshelf, which then collapsed. "Someone has fooled with this! Now they're really out of order!" Muttchen apologized for dusting them too thoroughly. "People judge you by your book collection," Antonie said to Laura, who helped pick up the fallen jumble. "Look at these, mostly autographed. More than half of them. From these, *Iphigenie, The Father, Egmont*, I learned plays years ago. Can't give them away. But Paul, you can have these about skiing." She reshelved them, however, and I never saw them again.

"Enough of this," said Antonie. "I don't want to be an old dragon." A new conversation started about wars and "lost generations" afterward. Antonie doubted there was such a thing, even after World War I in Germany. She reminisced about her acting career and going to Schwannekes café with Kafka, Werfel, Paul Wegener, and Max Reinhardt. Her father had said 1914–1918 was just the first of three wars, so that was why she came to America, the only place where democracy, a constitution, and free enterprise meant anything. One had to be a pioneer, whether in flying, acting, or choosing a country. One had to take a stand and declare oneself. But publicity was not the point. For that, one could go down Fifth Avenue doing handstands on a bicycle.

The doorbell rang, and in came her neighbor, Dr. Ernst Mueller, bringing mail from the aluminum box at the end of the road. He looked like a pink lizard with mumps, I thought, and I introduced Laura. "Young lady, I have to know your last name," said Dr. Mueller, meaning he could not tell by sight if she was Jewish. The dogs barked at him.

After a supper of open-face sandwiches, we put our coats on to leave. Laura said that she had a dachshund made of seashells and would bring it next time. "That's very cute," said Antonie. "Very highbrow. Moki will be jealous." She gave Laura a kiss and said, "New York gets lonesome on weekends. Just give me a ring some Friday afternoon and come on out with me by yourself. But don't expect to be entertained. You can do as you damn please, watch television, swim, paddle the canoe, play with the dogs." As far as I know, Laura never came and never handed over that seashell dachshund.

Catholic Conversion

Before severe abdominal pains came in the spring of 1949, Antonie had little interest in religion. She never mulled over philosophical problems in talking to friends and relatives and did not go to church. A feature article about her, titled "Lady with Wings," by Charles Renshaw, Jr., which appeared in the *American Weekly* on April 24, 1949, does not mention any religious concern. But one Good Friday she had an inspiration while in a taxi on Fifth Avenue passing St. Patrick's Cathedral. She saw a long line of worshippers, four or five deep, extended almost around the block, waiting to enter. From loudspeakers came prayers, hymns, and the voice of Monsignor Fulton J. Sheen. Antonie left the cab and joined the line. Two years later, she recalled the event in a talk at a Communion breakfast in Philadelphia:

> A little embarrassed at first, I joined the line. The sermon and the hymns came to me from far away—as I stood outside the Church—body and soul. I really did not "belong"—yet some strong force compelled me to stay, and to wait until I could walk into the church—into the Faith.
>
> I did not realize that it was the voice of Grace that commanded me—I simply obeyed—and yard for yard, for two hours, I inched my way toward the steps that would lead me to the foot of the Cross....
>
> From within St. Patrick's came the words of the last prayer: "Into Thy hands I commend My Spirit. Lord, receive my soul."—The Three Hours had ended. And within my heart I said "Amen," as I slowly walked against the stream of worshippers leaving the Cathedral, and went up the steps to enter the Church—body and soul. I was baptized three months later.

Antonie had already been baptized by Pastor Scholz in Berlin as a Protestant baby in 1901, but in 1949 it seemed like a good idea to do it again. The priest in charge of her conversion was Father John M. Oesterreicher, a forty-five-year-old immigrant to the United States. He was born in 1904 in Vienna to Jewish parents and studied medicine; but after reading the New Testament, he enrolled in a seminary and became a priest in 1927. After the Anschluss, he moved to Paris and made broadcasts and wrote articles against Hitler. When France fell, he escaped to Portugal and in time reached New York. Oesterreicher's parents were killed in the Holocaust.

An acquaintance, the exiled Prince Otto von Habsburg, brought Father John Oesterreicher to the chancery of the Archdiocese of New York. "Here was I, a simple priest, unable to speak English, being escorted by imperial royalty," he recalled later. He was given a parish, Old St. Peter's Rectory, on 16 Barclay Street on the West Side of Manhattan, and there he met Antonie.

Converting people of Jewish ancestry like himself was Father Oesterreicher's specialty, and he wrote a pamphlet, "The Apostolate to the Jews," about this mission. In the course of the 1950s, however, the convert lost his mission, and Oesterreicher rejected the "Jews for Jesus" movement, saying that "their evangelical piety is not my piety.... The only real dialogue is between real Christians and real Jews, not between those who have a rather suicidal attitude toward their beliefs."[9]

Eulogies

On January 9, 1952, my father Erwin called my Washington office from New York and with a shaking voice told me that Antonie had died of colon cancer the previous day. He was uncertain whether I should come or not, but perhaps Muttchen expected it. Hedwig had now lost three of her four children. Only Erwin remained. I left at once and made the familiar drive up the New Jersey Turnpike.

The church of St. John the Baptist on West 31st Street was crowded. Perhaps Antonie was the most outstanding person that everyone here had most proudly felt admired by. That's how she was. With charm she had accepted them all as they were. Four pallbearers brought in her casket with its wilting roses on top. Erwin and I followed slowly and sat in the first row. From there, unfamiliar with the complex and uninspiring mass, we had trouble knowing when to stand, sit, or kneel. Eulogies were read about Antonie, how she really knew the city, took it in her stride, typified New York.

Finally, we were told to "take leave of the body," all that was left now, the mouth fallen, the hands ghastly, holding a rosary. I thought of the weeks and months of agony, the tubes, the injections, the struggle. The real mystery was not death but life. Suppose she could jump up now and say, "The hell with all this, it makes no sense!"

Afterward, we drove in my Chevrolet up Tenth and Amsterdam Avenues, endlessly north, through the Bronx, to White Plains, always behind the hearse limousine. Numerous cars were behind us with pennants on their fenders. The rain turned to snow. Most of our conversation seemed inappropriate and irreverent. Finally, the procession arrived at the Gate of Heaven Cemetery at the Community of (would you believe it!) Valhalla, New York.

At the cemetery gate we had to wait until the flowers were properly arranged at the grave. Then my father walked in first, next to Gene McDonald. I followed through the mud with a crowd of others. In a strong wind it was snowing hard now, and snowflakes accumulated on shoulders, in the beards of the monks, and on the flowers. Father John Oesterreicher conducted the rites under an umbrella and mumbled things about Antonie's soul. Two or three people were crying.

At Hemlock Hague, Muttchen met us in tears. My mother, Father Brady, and Father Didacus had spent the day with her. The house had its familiar sweet, musty odor, and I wondered if that would stay when everything was sold, broken up, and shipped away. Who would get Chickie, Mickel, and Pinkernose? The dogs seemed sad and were not barking. About ten people had gathered, a group that Antonie would easily have spellbound as the center of attention. Now McDonald dominated with cheerful but condescending anecdotes. The Dutch marinescape over the fireplace would soon be his. Someone brought in Antonie's two suitcases and reported that it was snowing really hard outside. Anyone leaving would have to shovel a lot.

Antonie's obituary in the *New York Herald Tribune* that day, January 10, had a picture and the headline, "Antonie Strassmann Dead at 50: Pioneer German Woman Flier." Kurt Pinthus wrote an obituary for the January 18 issue of the New York German-language newspaper, *Aufbau*. He concluded: "Antonie Strassmann loved remarkable people and knew a countless number of them—poets, actors, inventors, nobility, industrialists, little people, officials; and they all admired this remarkable, beautiful woman, who always glowed and sparkled with life, intelligence, bold enterprise and energy." In her syndicated newspaper column, "My Day," on January 21, 1952, Eleanor Roosevelt remembered Antonie as "a very ardent admirer of my husband and his policies. I found her a very lovely and inspiring person and was always glad when something brought us together. She was only 50 years old and that seems so young an age to be called to death." To Hedwig, she wrote from Paris on January 15, 1952: "I read in the New York paper of the death of your daughter, and I must write to you just a line of sympathy. I always admired your daughter greatly and felt she had such a remarkable personality. I am deeply grieved that she should have died so young."

It all happened five decades ago. One June afternoon some years ago, I drove back to Hemlock Hague, expecting it to be enlarged or renovated and repainted in a depressing way and enclosed by witless gardens. Unbelievably, house and woods looked the same, brown and green, the scraggly rhododendrons blooming. A small modernistic metal sculpture had replaced the saints—no other changes. No one was there. All was silence, except for the wind in the trees. If Antonie had suddenly appeared with a rake, welcoming me and saying Muttchen was taking a nap, and telling the dogs not to bark, it would have seemed normal. And when I attend a performance of *A Midsummer Night's Dream* with a good Hippolyta or when I see three black dachshunds cavorting or when I am in a small propeller plane bouncing through clouds, I sense a hidden presence—Antonie.

Chapter 11

Old Trees, Transplanted: Paul and Hedwig in Dahlem

Paul Ferdinand and Hedwig began their last twenty months in Berlin with the convulsion of the move to Faradayweg 14 in the wooded suburb of Dahlem in November 1936. Twenty months later, in July 1938, they boarded a train for a Swiss vacation, and on that same day Hitler ordered Jewish physicians to stop treating "Aryan" patients within two months. No scientific works by Jews could henceforth be published or even cited. Paul Ferdinand Strassmann, like many others, was thus separated from the three elements of his life that mattered most to him: family, Fatherland, and profession. As a Promised Land, Berlin was a defeat and a failure. On August 15, Paul died of pancreatitis in Gstaad, Switzerland. Hedwig returned briefly to Berlin with the body to have Paul buried at Wannsee. She then spent a year with her daughter, Gisela Gutzwiller, and her family in Fribourg, Switzerland. As World War II loomed, she sailed for New York to live with Antonie for thirteen years, followed by eight years in Texas.

Moving In

After that taxi ride with three paintings, Moki, and the canary, life at Faradayweg 14, Dahlem, began with a lunch of boiled cod, a dish called *Kabeljau*. Soon trucks came with furniture, and nine workers spent three hours lifting, dragging, shoving, and positioning. When the harmonium was set up, Paul played a melancholy song about the end of things. Oddly, he slept well that night, perhaps due to exhaustion or the unearthly silence of Dahlem—no honking, no streetcars grinding around the Luisenstrasse corner, no bellowing drunks. But the next day it felt strange not seeing any patients, and he had to remind himself that he had none. Should he install water in the room next to his study, or would he never use it for treatment? In his diary he wrote: "We old trees are not for transplanting." Water was later installed.

The second day at Faraday was a Sunday, and Paul Ferdinand spent hours with his stamp collection, "a beloved sticky microcosm." Stamps of German principalities before Bismarck's unification were his specialty. The doorbell rang: "Flowers from Herr and Frau Dr. Zimmer!" Amazing! "Now all of a sudden!!" he wrote in his diary. In the evening, he observed through his telescope constellations in the heavens, so much clearer than in the smoky city center.

On Monday, three women telephoned and came as patients in the afternoon, so perhaps he was not finished after all. One was afraid of cancer, another worried about sterility, and the third suspected a pregnancy. Paul compared himself to an ancient digger who kept plodding away, unwittingly shoveling his own grave. A modest brass plaque with his name and usual office hours had been nailed to the gate, but Paul thought it might be provocative and had it removed.

Resumption of Routine

By the middle of January, life had settled down. At 8:00 AM they were awakened by Hellmuth's old alarm clock and by Moki barking at the bedroom door. Gymnastics as directed by a radio impresario came at 8:20, and by 9:00 breakfast was set up by Wally, the cook. Afterward, crumbs of toast, cheese, and sausage were fed to blackbirds on the terrace. The rest of the morning was spent with paperwork—taxes, finance, and correspondence. "How the hours drag. I could never be a bureaucrat. Instead of forceps and knife, now ink and accounts." Once or twice a week, Paul returned to the Schumannstrasse basement to check records for insurance and other claims. In the Dahlem basement, he perused old family papers: "Here is the clear handwriting of father, carefully scrutinizing my studies; there the delicate lines of Mother that accompanied gourmet packages to Heidelberg, my joyous years as a student … our engagement in Giessen, the travels … the first scribbles of our little ones … the clinic, the world war … much accomplished, often in vain! Life's storms tear families apart."

In a letter of January 16, 1937, Paul spoke of a visit to the Frauenklinik to search files and accounts: "As I walked through the Karlstrasse [one block from the Schumannstrasse] yesterday evening, every stone, every sign was deeply familiar, while here everything feels like a temporary vacation resort. Perhaps all life on earth is but a vacation, though no doubt our only time of consciousness. The Creator needs to reuse, reshape, and transform all mass with its inner soul."

One day, however, Paul saw something that did not fit. Above the entrance of Schumannstrasse 18 fluttered a swastika flag. Hours later, he had a nightmare that he was back at the clinic, which strangers were bombarding with a hailstorm of stones. Ferdinand Sauerbruch, the new director of the oncological institute, had the flag removed without a word from Paul.

Not until April was the white marble statue, the *Chained Woman*, from the courtyard of the clinic set up toward the left of the Dahlem house. Herr Bauer, the gardener, had to clean her. No problem, he said in Berlin dialect: "Koof mer Persil, waschse ab, zwo Eimer ha'k jebraucht" (Bought soap, washed her, took two buckets). Once again the statue exuded beauty and lent charm to spring nights, often enhanced by the flute solo of a nightingale.

The Thielpark snaked by the Faraday neighborhood as the "Schwarzer Grund" and was often crowded with laughing, scrambling children, in the winter, sledding and throwing snowballs. In their first winter there, Paul and Hedwig tried on their old skis, long wooden specimens with leather straps. Cakes and sausages were sold at two outdoor market sheds, one at old Dahlem and the other in Lichterfelde. Three saleswomen at these markets identified themselves as former Schumannstrasse patients.

My memories of Faradayweg 14 are vivid but surely incomplete. The two main stories had seven rooms that were bright with the light of enormous windows. Two small, dark rooms belonged to Wally, the cook, and to Old Minna Mohnke, who had begun working for the Strassmanns thirty years ago at the Alexander Ufer, when Antonie was still a toddler. In the basement lived the gardener, Herr Bauer, and his family. Carpets were spread everywhere, not just on floors but also on the piano, on sofas, on walls, and even along the balustrade of the main stairway. Opposite Grandfather's messy desk hung a Gobelin tapestry, showing swans among reeds. Here and there were exotic plants, bronze bowls, a variety of clocks, busts of family members, and religious figures on pillars. Only Antonie's room was restrained and modern with some white porcelain, two photos of the Do-X aircraft, and a small watercolor by Paul Signac showing the Pont des Arts in Paris. Had her other memorabilia been shipped to New York?

Every night the Blaupunkt radio, a gift from my parents, Erwin and Ilse, played concerts. In his diary, Paul wrote that the heavenly sextet (Opus 20) by Beethoven transferred him to a better world, that Schubert's Trout Quintet flooded the room with beauty, that his two-cello quintet had the healing and consoling power to dispel all sad thoughts. If a pretty guest was present and the Blaupunkt played a mazurka, Paul would ask her to dance and twirl her about the room. His voice was still that of a tenor, and he began singing lessons with a Frau Schmidt at the Holsteinische Strasse. In June 1938, he dared to put on a small concert with Schubert and Beethoven songs. He was especially fond of songs by the now banned Felix Mendelssohn, of whose work he said, "He is a splendid composer of songs. One cannot picture German music without him" (February 6, 1938).

Two Sad Days

In February 1937, two sad events took place—losing pictures and losing a favorite cousin. First, on Friday, February 12, at 4:00 PM came the sale of eighty-six good pictures at Lepkes auction house in the Bülowstrasse. These pictures had been the source of a thousand joys, and Paul could not bring himself to consign them to some dusty attic. Not sold were a few dozen of the best paintings that now decorated the Dahlem house, among them unframed pictures, reproductions, and portraits of family members. Someone asked, "Do you really want to sell? What can you do with the money? Isn't any investment just speculation, no matter what you do?"

Paul and Hedwig sat in the first row and saw picture after picture set up on an easel in a beam of light. The auctioneer was a friend from a gymnastic club, and at his side stood Heinrich Unus, an expert whom Paul had long known and trusted. Two ladies were there to levy taxes and maintain decorum. Most pictures went for a quarter or half of what Paul had paid. For example, a large Brueghel that he had bought for 7,000 marks sold for 2,650 marks. From all over Germany, art dealers, museums, and a few private collectors were bidding. All but ten pictures were sold, and others—an Ostade, a Bril, and the delicately painted king with his ornamental medals (Master of Utrecht?)—Paul bought back for himself, trying to avoid outrageously low prices. Unus passed him a note: "Don't bid too high for inferior pictures." Poignantly, *Moses Seeing the Promised Land* failed to sell. Two years later, of all the paintings, it would be used as a bribe for Nazi officials to let other unsold ones be packed for shipment to Switzerland and America. In his diary, Paul wrote:

> So even this feared event has passed.... The old elevator operator congratulated me, saying things had not gone this well in a long time. So now they journey away, they who had brought us so much joy and relaxation! But what does it matter when one's own children have been forced abroad! So journey away and find new homes, you paintings, you who allowed me to live and work night and day in the service of pain and suffering! At least, a few beauties remain with us.

No palpitations, no agitation. Another voluntary experience, no compulsion! It was the first auction I ever witnessed! Indeed! I always employed an intermediary. (February 12, 1937)

Except for some drawings, etchings, and woodcuts—mostly unframed—Paul Ferdinand Strassmann did not own post-Impressionist modern art, and what he had was not part of the auction. In his diary he wrote: "With all my passion for painting, I get nothing from this art. A decline cannot be denied." Nevertheless, he was distressed that some of his friends and patients—Ernst Barlach, Lovis Corinth, and others—were included in the exhibit titled "Degenerate Art," which opened in Munich on July 19, 1937. He was alarmed to see Otto Dix, Emil Nolde, and Karl Schmidt-Rottluff included, among many others. Seven of Corinth's pictures had been confiscated and were in the exhibit, exceeded in number by few other artists. Paul doubted that art would march in a new direction, as ordered by the government. In his diary he wrote: "Corinth remains great! Should they not have spared his memory? Art is an expression of the times.... With free expression, art will find its way best, choosing (according to its aims) what is most lofty and harmonious for the community. History shows the mistakes of interfering (see Rembrandt's *The Night Watch*)" (July 25, 1937).

As it turned out, two million visitors went to the "Degenerate Art" exhibit in Munich over the next four months—five times as many as passed through a large exhibit of Nazi-approved German art just across the park, which had been inaugurated by Hitler himself. Of the one hundred twelve "degenerate" artists, only six were Jews. A committee was empowered to confiscate sixteen thousand pieces of modern art from museums, parks, and public buildings. Some paintings were sold abroad for foreign exchange, and others were burned.[1]

Adieu, Henni

The other sad event that February was the suicide of the artist and poet Henni Lehmann-Strassmann, Paul's cousin and the daughter of Uncle "Dicker" (Fat One) Wolfgang, who had been chairman of the Berlin City Council sixty years earlier. One child of hers had already died, and two had emigrated to the United States. She ended her life to avoid an agonizing cancer death. Everyone attending the funeral service on February 26, 1937, was in black mourning, but the lilacs on the coffin were white as the new snow outside. An organ played Mozart and Bach. Henni had wanted no cleric to officiate, so Paul spoke the eulogy:

> For your last journey, precious departed one, a word of accompaniment and thanks! *Not farewell:* your image *remains* with those who loved you, who looked up to you, and who grieve at your departure!...
>
> Your last words were, "Do not unsettle the children with my illness!" ...
>
> A benevolent Creator laid great gifts in your cradle. Proud of your family, you were conscious of the *duty* to pass on its values. Working hard for others, blessing them with your poetry and your artistic craft, that was your deepest urge.
>
> In the spiritual center of Germany, Weimar, you worked and helped with your *social and patriotic* outlook....
>
> As you pass on through that dark portal, Henni Lehmann-Strassmann, you prove the poet's words: "The highest good of life is reputation. The body turns into dust. The great name lives on."

In his diary he wrote: "She cut short her final worries and agonies with Veronal. Years ago I refused to prescribe it for her, so she obtained it in Weimar. She was the brightest head in our clan: a worthy *Strassmann*!"

Visiting and Visitors

Several times each month, Paul and Hedwig visited Paul's deaf sister, Helene, who had moved from Dresden to Berlin and was now living in the Sanatorium Berolinum in the suburb of Lankwitz. Her right arm never recovered from her suicide attempt in October 1936. The right wrist was stiff, and the fingers could move only minimally. A scar was on her neck.

On June 6, 1936, Paul wrote: "Ernst and Elisabeth Keiner and their well-brought-up daughter, Annemarie, are our guests for coffee." Elisabeth and Annemarie were the daughter and granddaughter of Fritz's younger brother, Walter Strassmann, a retired architect once employed by the City of Berlin. Within a decade, mother and daughter were to avoid the war and the Holocaust by hiding in villages, while racially acceptable Ernst Keiner kept teaching Latin in Berlin.

A group of twenty-five British gynecologists came on May 29, 1937, led by Dr. Henry, a Scotsman from Glasgow, and a Sir Berkeley, whom Paul described in his diary as a "hungover Falstaff." They wanted Paul to introduce them everywhere, so he met them at the Adlon Hotel at 8:00 AM. Wherever they went, he met former students from the Strassmann Clinic who were delighted to have a reunion but were well aware of Paul's predicament.

Paul stayed with the British group on a bus ride to the new Institute of Heredity Studies on park-like grounds. The Reichsärzteführer, Dr. Gerhard Wagner, and his wife were there to receive them. In 1935, Wagner had been at the forefront, clamoring for a harsh "Law to Protect German Blood," and, according to British historian Ian Kershaw, his hours-long repeated urging in Hitler's company at Nuremberg was "instrumental in the decision to bring in the long-desired law there and then." The drafters were unclear about which unwritten instructions had come from Hitler and which from Wagner.[2]

Wagner had lately written again that mixing Jewish and non-Jewish blood was spreading the "diseased genes" of "bastardized" Jews into "relatively pure" European stock.[3] For him, a single Jewish great-grandparent was fatally polluting. Paul had the impression that even the "Aryans" were avoiding this Nazi. In Berlin in 1937, only a quarter of non-Jewish physicians were Nazi Party-affiliated, compared with about half elsewhere. Twenty-six of the thirty-two German *Gaue* (provinces) had a larger proportion of Nazi doctors than Berlin, whose population was "long notorious for giving the Nazis more trouble than that of any other German city."[4] Nevertheless, that evening Paul had no urge to "choke down a dinner with [the British] and to fake joviality when [he] had to bear the emigration of [his own] children."

On Saturday afternoon, December 4, 1937, Arnold Strassmann, a physician, came for a visit. His grandfather, Chune Strassmann, was the brother of Paul's grandfather, Heiman, of Rawicz. One of Chune's sons was Arnold's father, Ephraim, a merchant and civic leader in Raszkow, sixty kilometers east of Rawicz. Arnold himself did not know that his own stepson (possibly his biological son; see chapter 15), Ernst, was organizing an anti-Nazi resistance movement, the Robinsohn-Strassmann-Gruppe or *Widerstandsgruppe* (described in chapter 15). Here with Paul, they discussed whether the proliferation of loose icebergs that season could mean a harsh winter. Paul said that "such forecasts are very uncertain, nothing but luck if it turns out that way." In his diary he added: "Arnold Strassmann, very vigorous at 76 years, with a physique like Uncle Ferdinand, is a second cousin [*Grossvetter*] of my father. At last I know that we come together in my great-grandfather

[Schmuhl Molower Strassmann]. In any case, our name is unusual and therefore well-chosen. 'Strass-' might mean 'street,' 'jewel,' or, in Polish, 'guardian.' ... For over four hours we had a lively conversation. Advent candles flickered and, despite differences of opinion, we had a congenial sense of family."

Three days later, Paul met a truly non-related Strassmann, the chemist Fritz, a student and assistant of Otto Hahn and co-author of the articles about splitting the atom for which Hahn was awarded the 1944 Nobel Prize in Chemistry. Since the bombardment of uranium with neutrons led to ever greater emissions of neutrons and energy, physicists abroad realized that a chain reaction and an immense atomic explosion were theoretically possible. Thus, Hahn's discovery led to the atomic bomb in America. Paul wrote in his diary: "I bring a mistakenly delivered manuscript to the Chemical Institute in the Thielstrasse to Dr. Fritz Strassmann, a young chemist from Allenfeld, who works with radium. He has a Strassmann forehead, but no relationship can be ascertained. His brother is the judge Paul Strassmann in Berlin. The institute's director, Professor Hahn, greets me. He had a relative as Erwin's patient in Schumannstrasse 18. Strange meeting."

On December 18, 1937, Paul met another Helene Strassmann, the widow of his brother, Ernst (once exiled to Chile), in the center of town near the Anhalter railway station in the presence of a lawyer named Lignitz. She was in financial difficulty, so Paul gave her a check for 320 marks and assured her that he and his sister Helene would each send her forty marks monthly. Ernst had died in the 1920s and was buried in the wooded Stahnsdorf Cemetery. I do not know why, but no one in the family had approved his marriage to this other Helene (last name "Stang" or "Streng," illegible in Paul's diary). In the elevated train on the way to and from the meeting, Paul read works of Goethe, and that night he recorded in his diary: "He will remain a miracle, a god. For me, he is religion itself."

Paul's Religious Views

After more reading, Paul occasionally summarized his views on religion.

> No "sinful fall from Grace" or "descent to Hell" exist for me. If they're just figures of speech, they need further development. Religion is subject to evolution like everything else. If "faith" means "considering something to be true," one should not be puzzled by current [skeptical] trends. If "faith" means "attaining a reassuring concept," to "hope for consolation in the midst of human misery," and "to bring people around to that," then it can all be accepted. Otherwise, here, too, the good must be replaced by the better. But it will take centuries to replace Christianity with something stronger and more supportive. I find it hard to deal with such spiritual issues. But the times force one to think about this. I distinguish only "religious" and "irreligious" feeling, whether or not a higher power exists. Religion is man's deepest emotion. Labels are noise and smoke. Religious conflicts have concerned themselves only with [superficial] forms. (October 5, 1937)

In Paul's view, truth in life was relative. Only laws of physics involving gravity, the conservation of energy, and the like were untouchably true. What was otherwise true was revealed by life itself as it called on people to make decisions. Paul decided to reread all of the Bible, the basic root of events in recent millennia, but he wondered if he "could not spend the time better analyzing great current questions. It is as if I look at ancient paintings while the fanfares of Judgment Day are sounding outside" (August 7, 1936).

When it came to "loving my enemies, my oppressors," he wrote, "no, I cannot manage that, but I am actively trying to understand them" (September 4, 1936). He found consolation knowing that life would continue when he was gone, carried on by those whom he had brought to life or kept from death. He pondered death and wondered if a longing for rest from turmoil was not as natural for old age as the urge for life among the young. Some of Paul's diary entries were thus gloomy. On March 12, 1937, he thought about its general tone and accuracy:

> Whoever someday glances at these diaries will not enjoy their mood. But I would be deceptive if I wrote as if I had much zest for life. I feel as if I—the Paul Strassmann of long ago—were walking next to some strange being, a demon, that wrestles with me, and I keep it from overpowering me. I am still the stronger! And a wife is at my side, clear-headed and good, like the foundry wife in the poem about the sunken bell [by Schiller].... I have the feeling of a shaking, endangered, decaying life. I envy only those whose battle is over. Could I stand it in a monk's cell? I observe myself in a clinically dispassionate way. I wish to keep going! But the burden grows heavier.

A month later, the exuberance of spring blossoms in the garden cheered him: "I should write my daily notes in the mornings when I have more zest ... everywhere juicy colors are bursting forth ... miracles within miracles. Why should pantheism—seeing the divine in every fiber—be less than acknowledging 'a personal God'?" (April 16, 1937). He summarized: "Life ends with death. Immortality is what was accomplished, the best consolation. It is impossible for me to believe in life after death, actually a ghastly thought.... My last wish is no long pain and no harmful events for my house and my homeland!" (September 12, 1937).

The Nearby Church

On a Sunday morning in November 1937, at the nearby Faradayweg church, the Strassmanns heard Pastor Eberhardt Röhricht as usual read the names of one hundred arrested pastors, among them Martin Niemöller and a Vicar Strassmann from Tiemendorf (probably not a relative). Niemöller (1892–1984) had become one of three pastors at the Dahlem church in 1931. The others were Eberhardt Röhricht and Fritz Müller. Until March 1933, Niemöller had voted for the Nazi Party, believing Hitler when he said that the churches had an important part to play in "the moral and ethical renewal of the German nation [against] international atheists."[5] Under the influence of Karl Barth, the Swiss theologian, however, he became an opponent of Nazi methods, specifically, the "Aryan paragraph," which would have kept converted Jews out of the Lutheran Church organization. Against Nazi plans for an intolerant "German Christianity," he formed the Pastors' Emergency League. By 1934, 7,036 of 18,000 Protestant pastors had signed a pledge that their allegiance was only to the Bible, that they were against any "Aryan paragraph," and that they were in favor of protecting the persecuted. An eight-member Council of Brethren met in Niemöller's Dahlem home to lead the new organization. Their opposition to the majority of Protestants under Reich Bishop Ludwig Müller was declared illegal, and many pastors were jailed.

Niemöller was dismissed from his post but reinstated by a court when a dispute about his pay came up. Soon, the protesting pastors reorganized themselves as the Bekennende Kirche (Confessing Church), a synod that rejected the totalitarian xenophobia of the government. This group was the only major open opposition in the early Nazi years. Niemöller expected it to become a church of martyrs and catacombs, given the despotic brutality of the government. Eventually, seven hundred ministers were imprisoned or under house arrest for days for reading a manifesto that declared the racist, nationalist religion spread by the Nazis to be a "deadly danger." When he read the manifesto in August 1936, Niemöller added that he did not wish "to have it said of us before God's judgment seat: 'When the gospel of Jesus was attacked in Germany, you were silent and, without resisting, left your children to an alien spirit.'"[6]

On Good Friday in 1937, the young and amiable Pastor Franz Hildebrandt calmly preached at Dahlem that Pontius Pilate's unprincipled "Take him and crucify him" was the sort of cynical condemnation still used by governments nowadays. Everyone in the congregation understood. In his diary, Paul wrote: "A good sermon can awaken lofty thoughts and feelings and make it easier to cope with life's agonies" (March 26, 1937).

Two days later, the church was overcrowded for Easter, and in his sermon Niemöller boldly called for the release of the imprisoned pastors. Later, on May 2, he said not to despair, that something wonderfully devastating was in the wind. Paul thought he was unnecessarily harsh, but no one challenged the pastor that day. Perhaps as a sop to the government, Niemöller had said that two thousand years ago Jews were the crucifiers. Too pointed, Paul thought.

These events reminded Paul of the Sermon on the Mount, and he looked at it again, concluding: "It truly led to a new insight for humanity. I can understand how people ran away because it was mighty, not bookish. In the light of our times, it takes on new meaning. What effect had these words when first heard? They are still fighting words—as four more pastors have been arrested for reading the names of those who have been ousted" (June 25, 1937).

Two days later, Niemöller preached about Gamaliel, the Jewish leader who had taught the law to St. Paul before his conversion and who had advocated Jewish tolerance of Christians. Niemöller spoke of the early martyrs and related them to recent events in Germany:

> We have no more thought of using our own powers to escape the arm of the authorities than had the apostles of old. Nor are we more ready to keep silent at man's behest when God commands us to speak. For it is, and must remain the case, that we must obey God rather than man.... [The Sanhedrin] accepted Gamaliel's advice as regards freedom of conscience and released the prisoners—though not without beating them and renewing the embargo on their speech.... In Germany neutrality is impossible. Persecution has begun. I think, for instance, how on Wednesday the secret police penetrated the closed church of Friedrich Werder and arrested at the altar eight members of the Council of Brethren.... I think how yesterday at Saarbrücken six women and a trusted man of the Protestant community were arrested because they had circulated an election leaflet of the Confessing Church.... And we recall today how the pulpit of St. Anne's Church [in Dahlem] remains empty because our pastor and brother, Fritz Müller, with forty-seven other Christian brothers and sisters of our Protestant church, has been taken into custody.... It may still be a long road until we are truly glad ... like the apostles, who were counted worthy to suffer shame for Jesus's name.[7]

Paul wrote that evening: "Niemöller is the last of them.... So many others have been arrested, even women. Three young Nazi officials were there today as he preached, 'Today I beg for the church, for we have nothing left.' A shudder went through the congregation. How will this fight end? Outside the sun shone on worried faces.... But how can dynamite and gas overcome this?" (June 27, 1937).

It was Niemöller's last sermon in Dahlem until after the war. He was taken to Moabit Prison by the police four days later, on July 1, 1937; it was his sixth arrest. Otto Dibelius took his place until he was arrested for preaching about St. Paul's persecution, actually meaning Martin Niemöller's. The names of the arrested were read every Sunday until the end of the war.

Niemöller was not tried until February 1938 and, surprisingly, was acquitted with only a 500 mark fine and the prison months he had already served. Hitler was enraged by this news and called his cabinet for a meeting that afternoon. He told them, "This man is my personal prisoner, and that is the end of it." So Niemöller was taken to solitary confinement at the Sachsenhausen concentration camp and then to Dachau in 1941, and was kept there until 1945. When the war started in September 1939, he volunteered to serve Germany "in any capacity" but was rejected. Later on, in the atomic age, he became a pacifist. I heard him speak in East Lansing, Michigan, in the 1960s.

On Sunday, August 8, 1937, three days before our departure to Bremen and the United States, we visited our grandparents in Dahlem and by chance witnessed events at the church across the street. Several thousand people had come by train and bus from all over Berlin and the surrounding province of Brandenburg for the religious service but found the church locked by the Gestapo. Their indignation was obvious, and after a while they marched off singing Luther's "A Mighty Fortress Is Our God." They headed for the nearby St. Anne's Chapel but found it locked. The police arrested many of the demonstrators and brought them to police headquarters at the Alexanderplatz. Such demonstrations were rare in Nazi Germany.

Grandfather wrote in his diary: "Around six in the afternoon, the service pleading for Niemöller is broken up. Police—crowds of people are pushed back—one hears Luther's hymn from side streets. Shy faces." Shortly afterward, we eight assembled grandchildren sang the ABCs with our "innocent children's throats." Then, having only four nights left in Germany, we four Strassmanns (including our mother, Ilse) returned to our nearby pension. Grandfather's sisters, Helene Keiler and Frieda Masur were visitors later that evening.

Faith and the Bible

By January 1938, and in accordance with his resolve to do so, Paul had finished reading the Bible again from Genesis to Revelations, usually at night in bed after writing in his diary. He found almost nothing unknown, but seeing it all connected together amounted to more than the separate rules, insights, and experiences:

> It is a mighty compilation of thousands of years of human struggle to the divine understanding of Christianity, from the Creation to the apocalyptic vision—that fantastic end when the old earth is replaced by a new one. Think what you will. A God exists, a divine will lives, no matter how humanity wavers. High above time and space, the highest thought is living and weaving. And in the Bible it has its highest expression. It is a "Revelation." (January 9, 1938)

> Ultimately, everything is atomic or electrophysics and chemistry. But ultimately precisely these become the force of life and remain just as unintelligible in their basic principles as simple events. I follow Goethe more and more, absorbing everything that I can reach with the senses.... But I can achieve that with only part of my life—my profession. I am not strong enough to influence history in the least way. (March 24, 1938)

Politics and Nationality

Why should innocent people like himself be punished, Paul asked, as was now happening? The Strassmanns were not only innocent but positive contributors to the welfare of all. When passing City Hall in Central Berlin, Paul always remembered how in 1885 the great funeral of Uncle Wolfgang, chairman of the City Council, had started here. Paul had been nineteen at the time. Half a century later he wrote: "The German heart is surely something independent of race and territory, but how can one reconcile a decent heart with end-justifies-the-means politics? Frederick the Great outdid Machiavelli by writing against him yet skillfully using his principles. Was it heroic to go against humanitarianism, liberalism, and tolerance, or merely authoritarian? Even mighty intellectual spirits like Mommsen [historian] and Virchow [physician-politician] were tyrannical in their spheres" (November 4, 1937).

If only Kaiser Friedrich, the son-in-law of Queen Victoria, had lived to reign for a normal period, Paul thought, the last war with its unfortunate consequences for Germany might have been prevented. Once the war was on, Erich Ludendorff as dictator had to be held responsible for inciting American entry. That killed off Germany. Ludendorff then joined Hitler in the 1923 Beer Hall Putsch. "His literary-religious scribblings after the war were only self-salvage attempts. But one should not torture oneself with conditional 'if's, could's and would's'" (December 12, 1937).

Now rearmament was speeding up everywhere in a divided Europe. Paul wondered especially if it had not been a mistake to split up Austria-Hungary into little pseudo-powers. Without even such a friend as Austria-Hungary, Germany's enemies were now regrouping on all sides, and great danger lay ahead. He hoped that "we old ones may be spared experiencing that."

Equally disturbing was any reminder of his political exclusion. At one wedding party, the hostess boldly played what Paul called the unsurpassable march by Mendelssohn. The composer's monument had just been torn down in Leipzig where it had stood in front of the Gewandhaus concert hall. The city's mayor, Carl Goerdeler, had given instructions against the demolition and resigned in protest when it was carried out anyway. (Goerdeler soon became one of the leaders in plots against Hitler, was the designated chancellor, and in 1944 was arrested and executed.)

Still Carrying the Banner

At times, Paul attended operations and gave advice, noting that surgeons and assistants nowadays addressed each other with the familiar *Du*, something he had never tolerated. He relished the expressions of joy in the eyes of patients who learned that he would be there during an operation, even if not wielding the cutting instruments himself. The last words of one patient before the anesthetic took effect were, "How can I ever thank you?" Paul thought that such words compelled him to keep going (February 22, 1938).

But publishing was different from healing. In 1933, he had reconstituted a malfunctioning, severely damaged uterus by repositioning and reshaping a fallopian tube so that menstruation resumed. Medical historians have written that this operative procedure and its results underscored Paul Ferdinand's pre-eminent capability for reconstituting female genitalia.[8] Four years after this vaginal operation, the patient became pregnant and delivered a 2,500 gram (5 pound 8 ounce) boy on June 12, 1937, at the Getrauden Hospital. The baby was baptized Dieter Paul. Paul wrote an article about the procedure,[9] and to his diary he confided on September 16: "I invited a human egg to settle in the transplanted tube, which it did, growing into a living offspring in a previously ravaged womb.... I still carry the banner."

The report, "Geburt nach vaginaler Verpflanzung der Tube zur Wiederherstellung des Cavum uteri" (Birth after Vaginal Transplantation of the Tube to Reconstruct the Uterus), was accepted as the lead article by Walter Stoeckel in the *Zentralblatt für Gynäkologie*, dated December 18, 1937, although publishing such ipso facto "Jewish science" was now a criminal act.

What was the Nazi rationale against "Jewish science"? As summarized in the *Preussische Zeitung* of the time: "For a Jew, science is not a task, not a duty, nothing to do with creativity. For a Jew, science is business. But for the Jews, science is also a means for destroying the culture of their hosts.... Science should be administered by German men in a German way. If Jews want to do science, they should do Jewish science and move to Jerusalem.... But they should spare us."[10] Paul, aware of all that, wrote in his diary: "The *Zentralblatt*, Nr. 50, will present my work as the lead article. I feel as if a masterpiece has been recognized. All respect is due to Stoeckel, who dares to print it. Now I may calmly bid farewell. This operation and this moment ... will not be forgotten in the history of gynecology" (September 16, 1937).

In the newspapers in February 1938, Paul read that the Directory of German Gynecologists would no longer list "non-Aryans." Stoeckel had signed the announcement. In his diary Paul wrote: "My name does not have to be there. It appears in the history of gynecology" (February 26, 1938). A few days later Stoeckel returned to Paul an article submitted by Erwin about fetal electrocardiograms. He praised it but said henceforth he had to exclude work by "non-Aryans." Even Stoeckel's courage had its limits. Paul wrote Erwin to publish in free Switzerland, and Erwin did so.

During the 1930s, Walter Stoeckel (1871–1961) was neither a Nazi nor an active opponent of Nazism, although he allowed the Jewish scholar, Robert Meyer, to work in his clinic until he emigrated in 1939. Stoeckel edited the *Zentralblatt für Gynäkologie* for no less than forty-eight years. In publishing Paul Strassmann's last article, Stoeckel went against the prohibition of publishing works by Jews perhaps for the last time.

A 1949 issue of the *Zentralblatt* was devoted to gynecologists who had died in the recent past. Of Paul Strassmann, Stoeckel wrote: "He was an excellent clinician and surgeon, whose handsome private clinic in the Schumannstrasse attained great importance. He was an enthusiastic exponent of vaginal surgery.... His scientific originality and the joy in his work were expressed in a long series of publications that will assure him a permanent place in the history of our specialty.... His versatility and lively interest in all the arts, as well as his helpful amiability, earned him the sympathy of his colleagues and the adoration of a great clientele, who will cherish his memory."[11]

Surprises

On the first anniversary of the clinic's closing, two former nurses of the Schumannstrasse invited Paul and Hedwig to lunch at a new restaurant, Alois, in their apartment building at the Wittenberg Platz. The owner was Adolf Hitler's older half-brother, Alois Hitler, Jr., who had worked as a waiter in Dublin and who had unsuccessfully operated a restaurant and a boarding house in Liverpool. Paul found it "a modest, clean, inconspicuous place. Good sandwich for 1.70 marks.... The waiter seemed to detect us as being somehow prominent. As we left, he asked, 'Don't you think we have quite a decent clientele here?' [Nicht wahr, es ist doch ein gutes Publikum hier?] Was he Alois himself?" (November 11, 1937).

On March 14, 1938, Paul returned to Schumannstrasse 18 to retrieve needles of radium that he had lent to the new occupants. A sign above the clinic now read, "Universitätsklinik für Geschwulstkrankheiten" (oncology), but the Aesculap-like "PS" was still carved above the entrance. Paul wondered, could he have attained more? Probably not. The entrance looked odd without the sculptures of Hellmuth and Gerhart Hauptmann facing one another, yet that was expected. But why did they have to clear the courtyard of all trees and shrubbery? Why was all woodwork now painted a glaring white? He was taken to a waiting room that had once been his private study. Over a sofa had once hung the large Pfannschmidt painting showing Jesus pleading ardently with a skeptical Nicodemus staring grimly ahead. In its place now hung a portrait of Adolf Hitler. The radium was returned, and Paul was shown large new X-ray installations. Fräulein Dürselen, the photographer-technician who had worked for the Strassmann Clinic for fourteen years, was still employed there. Paul asked if the laboratory functioned well. He could not bear to go in.

On May 1, 1938, Paul read about folk festivals organized all over the country and wrote: "On such holidays I feel like a beaten dog that runs after his master all the more! If I did not have Goethe at hand! And my wife!" In general he thought: "This diary is not worth much. My ultimate thoughts and many … events cannot be expressed in writing" (May 12, 1938).

Unable to resolve his own conflicted feelings, Paul wrote:

> Among the reasons that keep us two here, resisting all temptations to emigrate, is that it would be unbearable for us in Switzerland or the United States to hear one word against Germany. I come from this land, and we have lived for it. Must it be, we shall die here, but we shall honor it forever. (May 15, 1938)

> New times are asserting themselves and definitely make errors. These have to be recognized and corrected, while good aims are faced and promoted. Only optimism is fertile. Psychological changes in the public have to be watched, however, especially since these have an effect abroad. (May 18, 1938)

Ever since March 1937, Paul had spasms in his abdomen that grew worse as 1938 came along, and he wondered if it was angina pectoris. The attacks were on the left side and involved neither shortness of breath nor digestive problems. Sometimes he had difficulty moving about, and to sleep he had to resort to codeine. He did not ask anyone to examine him.

Switzerland for the Last Time

In the months of July and August 1938, Paul and Hedwig saw their Gutzwiller grandchildren in Switzerland again, as well as their daughter Gisela and her husband Max. They were once more to be joined by Antonie. Paul decided not to take his diary on the Swiss trip and wrote a final entry:

> July 27, 1938, Wednesday. Sultry and hot. Hedwig labors at packing, and I am allowed to participate. There is almost no way to be in the garden, except that we take our meals on the flagstone terrace.… A thousand things have to be arranged; dozens of small and big bills have to be paid. Fortunately, one can do that with checks. From Erwin and Antonie, affectionate letters.… How difficult it is for the aged to give up their home, growing nervous about traveling! We shall remain in our homeland, loyal, as long as we breathe.

After a joyous reunion with the Gutzwillers at the railway station in Fribourg came a drive to the new house and a detailed tour of inspection. The next Sunday, on August 2, the whole family went on an excursion by bus to Gruyères, the fortified village thirty kilometers south of Fribourg, a region world-famous for pungent cheese.

One night the spasms came and grew worse, and Paul fell to the floor in agony. Local doctors were called, as well as the distinguished Dr. Otto Gsell from Basel. It was the pancreas, but with medicines and a special diet, it settled down. The doctors said the worst was over. So Paul Ferdinand and Hedwig left Fribourg with Antonie for nearby Gstaad and checked into the Grand Hotel Bellevue. As in the previous year at Locarno, Antonie had to leave for negotiations about international aviation patent licensing in Zurich. The next days were described by Paul in letters to Erwin and Antonie.

> To Erwin and family in Houston, August 9, 1938:
> As of September 30, all Jewish doctors [in Germany] will lose their licenses. They may not even work as health practitioners. "Worthy ones" who are combat veterans may treat Jewish patients as an exception. For me it's a blow, insofar as I still earned 7,000 marks [$94,000 in year 2000 dollars] in 1937. Half of it went for the secretary and expenses. I fear for our return and all the misery among Jewish colleagues, where many are worse off than we are. Details are not reported to me here.
>
> You will also have read that all [Jewish] street names, including those of "first-degree half-breeds" will vanish. Ours prevailed half a century in honor. All this burdens our thoughts, no matter how much Antonie tries to keep up our spirits.
>
> Naturally, we have discussed all inheritance possibilities thoroughly. No differences in opinion arose between Muttchen and me. It would be an injustice to burden any child with a moribund patriarch. I suffer much from "spasms," which spread from the scar of my gall bladder operation to the peritoneum. That ties me to our old home, which will also remain most convenient for Muttchen.... We did not set this wagon of history rolling over us in motion, and we cannot stop it. We shall try carefully to step aside.
>
> Now let us strike a more cheerful note. Gstaad is exactly the right place for us.... Several valleys come together here, and we old ones wander among them for three, four, or five hours, since I have to walk slowly. Our muscles are in good shape and I sleep well. Abdominally, I am the troublemaker.
>
> That we could once again visit this beautiful free country is a gift of Heaven. May 1939 grant us another visit! If you were still in Rochester, I would go there and let my intestines and gall bladder be diagnosed. But we know that the best illnesses cannot be figured out, so they go away nicely all by themselves.... In support of that, a thunderclap has just crashed above the Oldenhorn. I cannot imagine a better omen than that, so I will seal my letter with it.

The last letter, dated August 13, 1938, was sent to Antonie in Zurich. It was written on the rainy day after she had last seen him, standing in his bathrobe at the hotel entrance, waving as the taxi rolled away. Hedwig had trouble persuading him to come in from the wet steps. He wrote:

> Who will ever restore those days to us? It feels quiet and deserted here. But I know you are near, little raindrop, you, who will prevail as the winner and deal the last blow!
>
> It is raining and I am on a diet: that suffices. Mother and I played a desperation game of Ping-Pong. Peasant boys and girls will sing here this evening. News has come from Berlin, Nauheim, and Princess Hermine in Holland, who is very satisfied with the worthy one [the former Kaiser, her husband]....
>
> We won't stretch out our stay here much longer. Such old people should:
> 1. Not be born.
> 2. Remain at home unless they are with their children....
> Sneaking through the eighth decade, looking dashing but only on the outside,
>
> your Father

Two nights later, on August 15, Paul died. His last letter to Texas arrived days after the fateful telegram. I remember my mother, in a slip because of the heat, telling me tearfully at the top of the stairs, "Päpchen has died." His letter seemed strange when it came the following week, as if written by a ghost.

Post-mortem

Gisela sent Hellmy and Martin off to Appenzell and the Trogen School as scheduled without telling them the news. She then accompanied Max to Gstaad. Dr. Otto Gsell and another physician diagnosed pancreatitis as the cause of death (perhaps involving displaced gallstones, which were the cause of an operation in 1919). To cope with severe pain, Paul had occasionally injected himself with morphine. Hedwig, however, believed that he had suffered a heart attack. An appropriate certificate of death by natural causes was issued, and with that the remains could be taken to Berlin. Paul would never have committed suicide, as some people later assumed, since he was making travel plans to America for 1939, as his letters show, and especially not in a hotel, leaving his beloved Hedwig in chaos. Among the many tributes to her in his diary was this one written four days before leaving Berlin: "My good Hedwig, who can always find the right encouraging word for me. She is the light of my life." Gisela and Max accompanied Hedwig to Berlin on her sad journey.[12]

On August 25, 1938, Paul's remains were buried in the St. Andreas Church Cemetery on the Lindenstrasse at Wannsee after brief ceremonies conducted by Pastor Paul Anton in the Dahlem house, at the church across the street, and at the gravesite. Of the many letters of condolence that Hedwig received, I shall quote only one, written by Dr. William J. Mayo of Rochester, Minnesota: "Dr. Strassmann was a fine human being, a great surgeon and teacher, a loyal friend. Dr. Charlie [Charles H. Mayo] and I will never forget his inexhaustible friendliness toward us during our early visits to Germany. His politeness and the great esteem he gained in his profession and scientific work were an inspiration to us in our professional career" (August 30, 1938).[13]

To Switzerland with No Return

Hedwig, Gisela, and Max stayed in Berlin until September 10, long enough to make decisions about closing the house and executing the will. Käthe Wens, my other grandmother, was in Germany for the year and offered to go to Berlin later for the actual closing work. By returning to Fribourg right away, Hedwig avoided getting a "J" for *Jüdin* (Jewess) stamped in her passport, as decreed on October 5.

The Berlin police now wrote to Hedwig in Fribourg, Switzerland, and charged her with having made an illegal trip abroad. They demanded that she return to Berlin at once and report. They planned to revoke her passport. Hedwig replied on October 7, 1938: "Since there is now an obvious intention to deprive me of my passport, I prefer not to return to Berlin. My three children all live abroad, and being a nearly seventy-year-old woman, I cannot face new difficulties alone. I therefore ask you to note cancellation of any appointment."

Legacies

Hedwig renounced any inheritance for herself to facilitate transfers to her two daughters, who were citizens of Switzerland and the United States. Eventually, when he became an American citizen, Erwin was to get his financial third. Hedwig had a major operation in the fall of 1938 but applied for a visa to enter the United States to live with Antonie in November 1938. In the meantime, children classified as Jews were excluded from German schools, "non-Aryan" attorneys suffered further restrictions, and the murderous *Kristallnacht* of November 9–10 was carried out. Applications for emigration rose by many thousands, causing delays in processing. Hedwig could not sail until a year after that Swiss vacation, arriving in New York on August 17, 1939, two weeks before the invasion of Poland.

Six years later, on October 17, 1944, when Germany was itself already invaded, Nazi officials at the Vermögensstelle Berlin (Berlin Property Office) were still trying to get a priority rating (*Bevorzugte Bearbeitung*) from the Gestapo to identify and to expropriate the "great fortune of the Jew, Paul Israel Strassmann." All men classified as Jewish had "Israel" as a middle name imposed on them. (File 0 5210-4327/44 read "legacy Paul Israel Strassmann.") Perhaps the Vermögensstelle officials only wanted to look busy and shirk combat, or else they really were that fanatical.

Chapter 12

Beginning Again in Minnesota: Erwin and Family

When Erwin awoke in his cabin at 6:30 AM on Thursday, March 19, 1936, the SS *Manhattan* was sailing through the Verrazano Straits and soon passed the Statue of Liberty. Immigration officials had come aboard, and after breakfast they examined everyone's passports and documents. Tugboats pulled and nudged the liner against the Hudson River dock by 9:00 AM. From the railing Erwin saw the crowd below, and, yes, there was Antonie!

A New York Welcome

"Tag, du alter Schweinehund! [Greetings, you old bastard!]" were Antonie's first words as Erwin came off the gangplank. They hugged. Two days later, Erwin would recall it all in a letter:

> Now I have been forty-eight hours in New York and am collecting my thoughts. At first everything kept swinging like the ship, and things were hectic and overwhelming as always upon arriving in this country, especially this city. I mainly feel a vast gratitude. Here, as well as over there, things have been prepared for me in such loving detail that I merely let them roll over me.... Antonie is full of pep, looks splendid, and is unimaginably touching in her devotion.... She brought me to this Barbizon Plaza Hotel, two minutes distant from hers. My room with bath is on the eleventh floor. Breakfast is shoved through a flap in the door (coffee in a thermos, two rolls, etc.). We went right on to lunch with the Schmitz's—quite merry. Afterward, a two-hour nap until 5:30 PM. A fabulous dinner with Mrs. Manville [the asbestos heiress] at the Savoy Plaza called for a tuxedo. Then came a drawing room comedy on Broadway, and I understood almost all of it.
>
> Finally, we danced and had champagne at the new Waldorf Astoria. A bit worn out from the whirl, at 2:30 AM I sank into my pillows.
>
> So that's New York—America—life. Not a penny in my pocket, no job, an absolutely uncertain and insecure future, but elegantly dressed I go to one amusement after another ... best hotels, wines, dinners, and theatre with millionaires chomping real Havana cigars, chauffeured off in their Rolls Royces....
>
> The second day was one of sorting things out and talking them over with Antonie. A friend of hers invited us for lunch in a Park Avenue restaurant. Then she drove me all over

Manhattan in her car, across one of those large bridges to Brooklyn and along the ocean to a lawyer to discuss basic formalities. Back in the skyscrapered city and Park Avenue, the Schmitz's served a superb dinner and played a few rounds of cards [Skat] with us, using all those Schumannstrasse expressions. It was most reassuring, something familiar after days aboard ship and those New York excitements.... Everyone is encouraging and says my English is good enough. Antonie was amazed at my progress.

Killjoys don't exist here; everyone is buoyant, optimistic, and confident, especially about things concerning me. I am therefore in good spirits because I have every reason for it. Breathing the fresh air of freedom prevents all depression. The big jump has been made. With that, the crucial emotional hurdle is overcome. Now ordinary, matter-of-fact problems can be solved easily. What spurs me on is the feeling of laying the groundwork for you and the children. I am happy to have made it this far. Seen from here, the decision looks one hundred times as good.

Meanwhile, Ilse wondered in a letter: "I would give so much to be with you just for a very small moment, just to see the expression in your eyes. Are you as captivated by life there as you were seven years ago?... I still feel that any moment you might enter through that door and liven things up in your joyous manner. I truly cannot tell you how weirdly quiet things have become. It is unspeakably hard, what they are doing to us. I am afraid of the strange new land and unknown language, the immense distance, and need much courage ... but in no case do I wish to remain here under these conditions" (March 22, 1936).

Erwin's first letter was forwarded to her during Easter vacation, and on April 3, Ilse wrote from Diepholz (near Bremen), the village of her maternal ancestors, the grain-trading Schwarzes: "Since yesterday I have your first letter from over there with all those powerful impressions. Confidence and a great sigh of relief speak in every line, and that makes me happy. Only now can you truly feel what monstrous pressure has burdened us, even as I still feel it, living among people without worries and with no inkling of all we have had to go through." This letter was opened by German authorities on the pretext of looking for illegal money transfers.

In late April, Erwin attended meetings of the New York Medical Association at which fifteen hundred doctors met in general and specialized sessions. He was happily bemused at the way "Jews served as chairmen, speakers, and discussants—each judged according to his personal quality," with stereotypes rejected. At these meetings, however, someone announced that 186 German physicians had already been licensed and that an equal number were waiting to pass their language examinations. The association resolved that no more licenses be granted to foreigners who had not passed the New York Medical Board Examinations. "For me, it's all the same," wrote Erwin on April 28, "since I had planned to take the examination in any case." A few days later he wrote: "I'm still amazed about this country. On the one hand, there are ingenious, practical simplifications and sober matter-of-factness; on the other, you find unshakable decency, consideration, modesty, and courtesy. Inside and out, a high standard has been attained, and the atmosphere is as in the mountains—clear, cool, and healthy."

There were short trips to Syracuse, Philadelphia, and Baltimore, but mainly Erwin stayed in New York City until June 9. In the daytime he studied English, heard advice from German-American physicians, and worked on legal matters. In the evenings he was out on the town with Antonie, who even bought him a top hat. She thought he could not appear without one at a Sunday dinner with Mrs. Manville and later at an ice show featuring Sonia Henie, the Olympic star. Some nights ended at a club or revue in Harlem.

Antonie was back in Berlin in mid-April, and she described Erwin's every day in detail. Ilse wrote that she greedily hung on every word, especially all the confirmations of his success and well-being. Days later they went to the opera (*Così fan tutte*). Looking ahead, Ilse invited Antonie for tea together with Dr. Clara Duncan, who was visiting the Strassmann Clinic from Houston, Texas, and would eventually become Erwin's office partner in private practice. Ilse wrote that Antonie was already raving about Texas and showed photographs of the state. She gave Ilse a set of records to help her learn English. Ilse added: "I believe Antonie is happily anticipating the moment of her return [to America]."

Ilse was amazed at Antonie's style with her parents. When playing Skat, Antonie used the standard vulgar exclamations for that card game, shocking Päpchen but amusing Hedwig. Ilse wrote: "Antonie tells Päpchen her views with stunning openness—I almost said callousness. There's no sentimentality in her, a trait that we'll have to copy" (April 18, 1936).

Another Welcome: Rochester, Minnesota

After brief stopovers in Cleveland and Chicago, Erwin arrived by train in Rochester, Minnesota, on June 14, 1936. He sent a telegram to Berlin at once ("HOORAY. HEARTILY WELCOMED AT MAYO CLINIC") and followed it with a detailed letter a week later.

> My first impression of Rochester was beyond all expectations. To tell the main thing first, on July 1, I will be brought into the regular clinical routine. Dr. Wilson told me to take eight to ten days to see everything without pressure and then express my wishes. I told everyone in charge of anything, especially Dr. Will Mayo, that I wanted to start from scratch as the most junior fellow. Such an opportunity is obviously a thousand times better than being a "distinguished visitor." I shall therefore begin with a quarter of a year in the gynecological diagnostic department. Dr. Braasch has already invited me to spend another quarter in the urological department. Soon afterward comes the operating room. This is the best path with unimagined possibilities, not least the chance for training and learning the procedures of an institution that is unique in the world. Imagine, the day I came, more than seven hundred new patients were admitted and more than one hundred operations were performed, including twelve major gynecological ones.
>
> What makes me happiest is the unsurpassable personal welcome I have received. I had not written young Mayo the time of my arrival on purpose, but within ten minutes he arrived in the hotel room that he had reserved for me and stayed with me all day. He took me to all the leading people, beginning with his father, Charles Mayo, and Dr. Wilson. The day ended at his farm with dinner, rowboating, etc. The next days were similar. Among hundreds of doctors, I have had a special start ... luncheons, evening picnics, etc. Touching! I retaliated with an oil painting. At a Rotary Club luncheon attended by the leading physicians, young Mayo gave me a laudatory introduction and without asking me said he hoped they would soon have the pleasure of a lecture from me. Afterward, we drove to Dr. Wilson's house to inspect his outstanding arms collection. In an engaging manner he showed me his souvenirs of the war.
>
> But get ready for the big bang. Of the two brothers, Dr. Will Mayo is older but is unbelievably fresher. (Dr. Charles, with whom I spoke briefly, has aged markedly after a stroke.) On Thursday, I finally spoke to Will Mayo formally, and, as I said, he ... seemed relieved that I did not insist on operating. "You can stay one, two, or three years, and in the meantime we'll find something for you. You will learn on your own what development is best for you and what you prefer." He agreed that wife and children should not remain separated from me too long....
>
> Will Mayo invited me for a Saturday lunch, eaten with organ music in the background. Who can describe my joy when he asked me, if I had nothing better to do, would I spend three days with them on the Mississippi? I bounced to the ceiling! The yacht is 120 feet long,

has 500 HP motors, 3 decks, and rooms and baths for 12 people. An idyllic life. I painted two watercolors and dedicated them to Mrs. Mayo. Will was full of fun and sympathy. I talked about my affairs only if people asked. I felt relaxed and cheerful inside and out, and I mention this to show you how well things are turning out and how grateful we have to be.

Good Lord, things could not be better or go faster. I have even played my violin. At my boarding house [Nachreiner's], obtained by young Mayo, lives a young Englishman [Dr. Kenneth Latter, later a British professor] who plays piano. Be glad and confident that my boldest dreams have been surpassed.... My chief is Dr. Murray, a well-known gynecologist, and he had a long talk with me. I assured him that I would not posture as an experienced expert but would subordinate myself entirely, a role that should be easy for me after years with Father. Result: he invited me to his cottage, a weekend house in a forest above a lake. He had invited all the physicians and nurses of his department—forty people. The picnic went smoothly with rural simplicity. One sat around a big fire, ate cold cuts from paper plates, sang songs, and rowed on the lake.

Here is an ideal landscape for you and the children. Rochester is a garden town with less than twenty thousand inhabitants, much smaller and more rural than Nauheim. All houses are in gardens. The landscape is picturesque, North German. A bit hilly. I wish you were already here!!

Further good news has just arrived. I have received my license for the State of New York. Isn't that marvelous? I'm overjoyed. Will Mayo thinks that makes a Minnesota license unnecessary. I could give each of you a smooch, one after the other.... Last year we celebrated my fortieth birthday [in the Wens hunting cabin of Hubertus in Hessen]. Then came crises and recovery, the year of decision.... The days on Dr. Mayo's boat reminded me of the Gebhardts [Berlin sailing and skiing friends]. The evening silence on the water and the morning sun! I enjoyed it here with a much freer heart. Too bad I had to give the watercolors away, you'll say. But I have to use all possible means here, and you'll get to see them anyway. Besides, they weren't so hot. Funny, how much I dream of you, always dear tales of you and the children.... Drink a punch of wild strawberries on my birthday. Be happy, since I am! Let the waves of wistful longing roll by, but don't let them swamp you. Truly, there is no reason for that. Don't be afraid of America! You will breathe a sigh of relief and soon be happy here.

To this letter Ilse replied on July 7, 1936, that she had never before received a letter filled with such happiness and bliss: "It's incredible how forthcoming and welcoming they are. But not without reason. You tried hard, are a total fellow, and *my* darling. There's a hint of fate in this development. What if you had not cultivated these American contacts in Germany? How often was I annoyed at once again having to invite Americans. Now I know how important and good it was. If I think of my future, I sometimes fear and tremble. Still I know that I can make the transition. You just have to be patient with me, since I move at a slower pace." Ilse asked for photographs and postcards of Rochester. She was puzzled by his report that no fences separated houses. "We can't imagine gardens without fences. Can anyone walk on the property of others?" (July 23, 1936).

A Special Fellow

In Rochester, Minnesota, about one in fifty persons was a physician, and some children were said never to have met a man called "mister." (Female doctors were rare.) About 2 percent of all physicians who had trained as residents in the United States were once at the Mayo Clinic. These trainees made up about 60 percent of Rochester doctors. Senior physicians were extremely well-paid and lived in a slightly elevated part of town called "Pill Hill."

They were all on salary and did not have to rent office space, pay nurses and secretaries, keep personal files, and fill out forms. Although the clinic's reputation was based on surgery, its example of an effective group practice might have been equally important. As a symbol of Mayo solidarity, for all their lives the famous brothers had a joint bank account with checks printed "Drs. Mayo."

Dr. Charles H. Mayo used some of his growing fortune to develop a 4,300-acre estate, called "Mayowood." The Zumbro River, which flowed through the property, was dammed to create a lake with several islands connected to one another by means of hanging bridges or Japanese arches. The grounds included a hydroelectric plant, greenhouses, boats, and bathing houses with solar heating. Several family members had houses on the estate.

In his autobiography, young Charles ("Chuck") Mayo wrote:

> Some doctors worry that group practice may mean a loss of autonomy for them, but I have found that the opposite is true. Doctors are free to attend medical conventions and make clinical trips, knowing that their salaries will continue to be paid.[1]

> The Mayo Clinic in those grim depression years had lean times, but was in no serious difficulty.... [It] was attracting a number of doctors from Europe, who had decided their careers would benefit by Mayo training. A number of them became good friends of mine, spending their Saturday nights and Sundays with us at Mayowood, and later keeping in touch even during the war years when communication was difficult. One such was Erwin Strassmann, who came from Berlin and after a time in Rochester became a citizen. His father, a renowned gynecological surgeon, had his own hospital in Berlin and was a close friend of Father and Uncle Will.[2]

In 1935, Chuck Mayo, accompanied by his wife Alice and by Jim Priestley (a Rochester doctor) and his wife Klea, had made a trip to Italy, France, Britain, Austria, and Germany. They happened to see Adolf Hitler in a Munich museum and "were shocked by the atmosphere of cruelty around him":

> Jim and I were shocked too at the doctors we were meeting. Most of them seemed sympathetic to the Nazi movement, and even saluted one another with a hard-edged "Heil Hitler!" None of us knew much about what was happening, but we took an instinctive aversion to the government. Its ruthlessness showed, we felt, in the attitude of doctors toward their patients. There was an absence of any humaneness or concern, and a disposition to treat patients as objects.
>
> ... Matters in the German capital were the most military and frightening of our entire trip; even patients rose from their beds and stood attention to return the "Heil Hitler" salute of doctors and nurses.... I wasn't surprised after [World War II] at reports that German doctors had performed experimental operations on helpless prisoners; it fit with the callousness that I had observed in 1935.
>
> I didn't always take a serious view of the gathering menace of the German army, I suppose, because on another occasion I couldn't resist goose-stepping along behind a German army band in a parade that went by our hotel. The Germans really can parade and I had a fine time joining in for a few hundred yards, but Alice didn't speak to me for the rest of the day.[3]

In 1936, a great tragedy befell the Mayo family, and having ever optimistic, buoyant Erwin around was good for Chuck Mayo. On November 9, 1936, his younger brother Joe, mischievous, a heaver drinker, and also a physician, was killed together with his dog when a train hit his car after a duck-hunting excursion in Wisconsin. Joe had been driving along the tracks. Chuck later recalled: "I lost the only person who really knew what I am and what I faced. I was left alone with the whole weight of being a Mayo successor. Until then, it had been easier to keep up my courage because Joe's irreverence cut through my gloomy self-consciousness and made me chuckle. With him gone, I felt utterly lonely and vulnerable."[4]

Erwin wrote about the incident to Ilse. Earlier he had sent photos of Joe cavorting for the camera during a summer swim. He remembered Joe as straightforward, modest, and popular, not a dedicated physician, but one who preferred his farm, riding, fishing, and hunting—a sporty type. "We understood each other on that level," remarked Erwin. Now all Rochester was grieving. Erwin paid his respects to the parents and Joe's young widow at Mayowood and found them "models of courage and dignity. Thus, no family is ever spared."

That same month, Chuck told Erwin that he would do whatever he could to keep him in Rochester. The two of them co-authored "Fertility and Sterility after Extra-Uterine Pregnancy," which appeared in *Surgery, Gynecology and Obstetrics* in July 1938.[5] Erwin also worked with the physicians Robert Mussey, James Masson, and Virgil Counseller. During his nearly two years at the Mayo Clinic, Erwin gave four lectures to the staff and published eight papers. After leaving the clinic, he wrote another twenty-seven papers for a life-time total of seventy-six.

From June 1936 until April 1938, Erwin was a special fellow in obstetrics and gynecology at the clinic with a fellowship that paid $70 and later $75 monthly during the first year and $85 during the second year. These amounts were supplemented by the Carl Schurz Foundation, including a personal loan from Ferdinand Thun, president of the foundation. Antonie added $125 monthly. Eventually, his debts approached $7,000 ($90,000 in year 2000 dollars).

Erwin wrote to his father in November that emigrating had been the only honorable course: "If I had to emigrate ten times, I would do it without ill will. I would do it to struggle for understanding with redoubled zeal, to plant what has been inherited from our forefathers ... to raise a little flag somewhere on Earth for you. Dawn must come again." He added: "That the clinic no longer functions makes it absolutely clear that one has to make it in the USA. These days are quite hard for me. After turning off the lights every evening, my thoughts wander to you, and every detail of the Luisenstrasse and the Schumannstrasse is pictured with love. Then I remind myself again why all this must proceed. Funny, how fast one forgets the bad of recent years and dwells on the good and personal" (November 15, 1936).

Christmas Eve 1936 reminded Erwin of his four December absences during World War I. "It wasn't too bad," he typed five days later. "I just hope that you also had sensible and unsentimental holidays. In that respect, I have already ... learned much from the Americans." After work on December 24, he and his English friend, Dr. Kenneth Latter, played billiards and drank a two-dollar bottle of Oppenheimer wine, expensive for those times. Later came a large party at Dr. Priestley's, and at midnight the two joined the young Mayos at an Episcopal service. The evening continued with other parties and concluded around 3:00 AM with oyster soup at Mayowood. "Thus, Christmas Eve was spent not in the usual way, but among nice people and with little time to feel sorry for myself. No German Christmas carols were heard, a good thing under the circumstances."

The afternoon of Christmas Day, Erwin was back at Mayowood and later wrote:

It is really touching the way that the old and young Drs. Charles Mayo are looking after me despite the death in their family. First I visited the young Mayos for an hour, and then we all went to a cold buffet at the senior Charles Mayo's, among a crowd of relatives. The Christmas tree stood where the coffin had been a few weeks ago. The blue electric candles made for an odd atmosphere. After the meal came serious, high-quality organ music.... Dr. Will Mayo, whom I revere especially ... asked me about everything and told me how superb the older staff members in my section have found my work. Lord knows, I don't want to brag, and it was actually not so great, but I know it pleases you when the top man has a good opinion.

Wife, Children, and Mother-in-Law

Like millions of other emigrants, Erwin had sought a secure footing and future in the new country before asking his wife and children to follow. Now that time had come. The thought of not emigrating and of not joining her husband seems never to have crossed Ilse's mind. A marriage was that kind of a bond. In her third letter, on April 3, 1936, she had written: "How intensely do I wish that you will find a clear road ahead with the single goal that we should soon be reunited. Without you, my life is nothing." The children belonged with their father, who had been heroic in the war, a responsible physician, and the sort of devoted, fun-loving parent that every family hoped for. In one letter, Ilse wrote that the children (myself and my older sister Renata and younger sister Angelica) were actually quite cheerful, except for sulking during dinner. "Their Mother has to do all the correcting, and there's no Dad to amuse them with nonsense."

Once informed about the forthcoming emigration, none of us children seemed apprehensive. Ilse was envious of that. Actually, we could not truly imagine emigrating. In September, Renate said, "When we visit Daddy in America, we're not going to return until he joins us. A second parting is too horrible." One day at age ten, I asked our mother who would govern after Hitler died, and Angelika, then six, answered me first without joking: "Hitler will have laid an egg to make a new one" (February 11, 1937).

We three did not like excursions with the grandparents because we were embarrassed to sing and recite poetry on hikes within earshot of strangers. Päpchen urged us to be more affectionate with his dachshund, Moki, but Mother thought Moki was a vile cur (September 18, 1936).

For the Easter vacations of 1937, Ilse and we children were joined in Nauheim by our English teacher, Fräulein Käte Friedländer, the sister-in-law of one of Ilse's friends from the Kassel finishing school, Luise (Ferber) Friedländer. Ilse described Käte as "a great joy ... she is fluent in English and French ... we'll speak only English. She is a charming, stimulating person, whom we all like. I expect much from all this." Born on March 31, 1891, Käte was murdered fifty-three years later at Auschwitz.[6]

The hardest part about emigrating for Ilse was the procedure itself: finding money, throwing out old letters, packing, and especially getting authorization for a visa from the American General Consulate in Berlin, which did not give clear instructions about procedures and forms. Sponsors had to use specific language promising exact amounts of monthly support, and statements of wealth needed to be notarized by bank officials. By 1937, affidavits from Antonie were not good enough because she had already given too many. Ten days before sailing on the SS *Bremen*, the issue of the visa was still uncertain, despite a supporting letter from Will Mayo stating Erwin's monthly income of $85 and urging approval. In her last letter, Ilse wrote to Erwin on August 2, 1937:

> Today in ten days our ship [the SS *Bremen*] should sail, and we have two cabins, one outside with four beds and another inside with three. [Ilse's mother, Käthe (Schwarze) Wens, and Ilse's long-time friend, Leni (Schoeller) Schmidt, were planning to come along.] How happy I could be in anticipation of the trip and our reunion if it were not for that nerve-racking

business with the visa. But today another flicker of light came … [the Brazilian ambassador] will call the general consul on our behalf and try to speed up that visa. I feel a weak beam of hope. Our entire separation was child's play compared with the exasperations of the last two months.

"Why did you do that?" General Consul Jenkins said angrily to Ilse, referring to pressure from the Brazilian ambassador. Ilse pretended she knew nothing about it. The Brazilian's wife was a close friend of Consul Jenkins's wife. The prime minister of Canada was a patient of Ilse's brother, Gerhard, and seeking his support was considered. Dr. William J. Mayo wrote to Jenkins on June 12: "I know Dr. Strassmann personally. He is a man of excellent reputation and character and is an authority in his special field of medical science and practice. If action is possible to facilitate and expedite the granting of a visa for Mrs. Strassmann and the children, it will be deeply appreciated."

Ilse's letters to Erwin during those last two months in Germany are full of transport, legal, and financial technicalities that had to be settled. On May 12, she wrote: "My hair has turned quite gray at the temples, so do me the favor and age along with me." On June 4, Erwin answered, not to worry, his hair was not only gray but partly white at the temples. Despite all the friendliness and hospitality in Rochester, a man could really confide only in his wife, and he missed her more than ever.

On June 10, Ilse wrote about a bit of luck—that "the representative of the furniture transport company has fallen head over heels in love with me (don't worry: *you are my little darling*), and he has taken on all sorts of hard tasks for me, be it dealing with the police or the customs. It's almost the way that you always find a patsy at the last minute to do your unpleasant things." Indeed, over the years quite a few patients and nurses had intense crushes on Erwin, but no scandal ever materialized.

Despite everything, Ilse had never doubted that in time the whole emigration to the United States would be allowed. "The consul just caused delays, asking for more and more affidavits of financial support and forcing us to go begging again and again," she told me decades later. Occasionally, some other country, such as Cuba, was mentioned but was never seriously considered an alternative.

Eight Months in Minnesota

To meet his family, Erwin left Rochester in an old Ford on the same date—August 12, 1937—that we sailed from Bremerhaven. He arrived in New York on August 17, the day before the SS *Bremen* docked. At 11:00 AM, the family celebrated a "*Wiedersehen* after one year and five months," said his diary. "Barbizon Plaza, Cocktails Rainbow Room, again to bed, St. Moritz, Broadway." Two days later, we crossed the Hudson on the Bear Mountain Bridge and stopped in the Catskills, an American version of the Taunus mountain range.

A week later, we arrived at Rochester, specifically, at Pollack's boarding house. It was a 1,400-mile trip (2,300 kilometers to us) on narrow roads at an average of 200 miles per day. Rochester was indeed a small medical garden town like Bad Nauheim, where Ilse had grown up. She was delighted at last to have a house and garden of her own after that fourth-floor apartment in Berlin, Luisenstrasse 47, in a part of town where streetcars screeched night and day and drunks bellowed after midnight. The two-story clapboard Rochester house was located at 1225 First Street, Southwest. It had a real American front porch with a climbable roof for boyhood adventures. One entered the living room more directly through the front door with no vestibule, a strange concept for Europeans. Even more exotic were the muggy August heat, all the insects, and the whirring of hummingbirds and evening cicadas in the backyard shrubbery. Then came an arctic winter.

"I was apprehensive, never enthusiastic, about emigrating," Mother told me in May 1978. "Dad never worried, but I did about paying back all we were borrowing from strangers. It was a terrible time. Yes, we were back together, but in such a foreign country. I don't like to reminisce about it. I leave that to you. For toothaches, all we could afford was aspirin. Despite uncertainties and hardships, however, there was never any thought of going back. We never considered it, since the Nazis seemed to be firmly entrenched."

My grade school was named after Abraham Lincoln, and my homeroom teacher, Mrs. Blomberg, had the name of the German minister of defense, a field marshal, although she was unaware of it. A boy named Bobby was designated as my guide for explaining homework and football. He would say, "Tackle der man mit der ball." Another boy had freckles, was named Dudley, and was Jewish. He could stay home during some novel holidays as a special, mysterious privilege that all others envied. Every morning we had to stand and say a pledge, but for months I had no idea what the word "allegiance" meant, so I was not sure if my pledge was valid. On the trip over, none of the American or English boys could understand anything I tried to say, and they themselves were unintelligible to me.

At Rochester, having our grandmother along was a great help. Ilse had been overjoyed when Erwin suggested bringing her. Throughout the past year, Käthe Wens had helped Ilse in Germany with housework, errands, and packing. She was only sixty-three years old and despite an unpredictable knee had the energy to walk to nearby grocery stores. For her, these buildings were miraculous shrines, not just because of the incredibly low price of butter, but also due to the sheer availability of oranges, lemons, pineapples, roast beef, and steak. That August and September, Erwin accompanied Käthe on the shopping trips to help with her English.

With dinner invitations from the Mayos and various staff doctors, reciprocating was socially necessary but financially difficult. What helped were two cases of Rhine and Moselle wine that Ilse had smuggled across the Atlantic. Packed inside several night tables, the wine was neither pilfered nor taxed. Also smuggled in was a handful of 20 mark gold coins with the head of Kaiser Wilhelm II. These were inside wax candles. No emergency arose to justify the risk of cashing them in when owning gold was illegal, so we still have them. I once asked my Mother to name the only crime she had ever committed. She had forgotten about the smuggled coins and replied, "Giving birth to you, right?"

In Ilse's Christmas letter, she wrote that it seemed strange not to pack up for the subway ride from Potsdamerplatz, Berlin, to Thielplatz, Dahlem—that she felt so close to Paul and Hedwig, she had to keep reminding herself how far the geographical distance actually was.

> Our life here is so cheerful and peaceful that I sometimes feel transposed to the time before the war. It is so unusual for us to get whatever we want, foodstuffs incredibly good and generous.... We spent a particularly nice evening at Charles Mayo's, a true house of culture. The senior Mrs. Mayo reminds me so much of you, dear Muttchen, so wise and generous. We shall be sad to leave this little town, where the children have also made good friends and where we feel at home among many former Germans.... But wherever we land, within our four walls, with our books and furniture, we'll create a bit of Germany.... The children came home with their second, improved report cards, and Angeli can skip a grade, which makes her less happy than us parents. She does not quickly get used to new children and teachers.... Let us hope for a happy and cheerful reunion together in the new year. (December 9, 1937)

That hope was not fulfilled.

While at Rochester, Erwin wrote a number of research papers with other staff members, such as Charles W. Mayo and Robert Mussey.[7] Eventually, in gratitude for their early support and continued friendship at the Mayo Clinic, on April 10, 1962, Erwin presented Chuck Mayo and the foundation's librarian, Thomas E. Keys, with a copy of a large, rare, and immensely valuable book that he had inherited from his father. This first edition of *De Humani Corporis Fabrica Libri Septem* (On the Structure of the Human Body, in Seven Books), by Andreas Vesalius (1514–1564), had been published in Basel, Switzerland, in 1543. It was one of 130 copies of about 500 with over 700 pages each that had survived for four centuries. The originals had more than 200 woodcuts, probably created by Jan Stephan Van Calcar and others of Titian's studio in Venice.[8] Dr. Mayo thanked Erwin, saying, "Very good. Now we have two of them." This event among others was recalled in 1996 in Berlin at a three-day Charité-Mayo conference with a paper on the Mayo-Strassmann family connection by Matthias David and Andreas Ebert.[9]

Charles W. Mayo retired in 1963 at the mandatory age of sixty-five, and he died five years later. In the year of Mayo's retirement, he was informed that his son, a third Charles Mayo, had been rejected as a Mayo Clinic staff physician. "It comes down to the name: so many people, particularly at Rochester, have glorified the name Mayo that quite a few people at the Clinic have a hostile reaction to it," wrote Chuck. The board of directors also "wanted to avoid having another strongly independent [and non-conformist] voice in the Clinic."[10] If there had been no wars and no Nazis, how would a fourth-generation Strassmann physician have fared in Berlin?

Chapter 13

On to Houston, Texas: City of the Future

In relocating his medical career from Berlin via Rochester to Houston, Erwin had a surprising amount of good luck While one hurdle followed another, compared with other immigrants, his luck stands out more. From 1933 through 1940, the number of physicians from all countries emigrating to the United States was 5,056. Of these, 3,215 or 63.6 percent came during 1938–1940, especially after the *Kristallnacht* pogrom, and 75.7 percent of the latecomers were Jewish. In 1935–1937, only 55.4 percent had been Jewish, and in 1933–1934, only 37.8 percent. These definitions followed stated religious preferences, not the racist notions of Nazis. During the decade, 72 percent of immigrant physicians came from Germany and Austria.

Foreigners Not Welcome

An influx of 5,000 doctors to compete with 180,000 already practicing in the United States may not seem threatening in retrospect, but the American Medical Association welcomed the newcomers only temporarily. When initial Nazi measures against Jewish doctors were reported in 1933, groups of American physicians passed resolutions of condemnation and proposed assistance in finding "scientific and professional opportunities in the United States."[1] As a result, 41 Jewish doctors arrived in 1933.

But when the Nuremberg Laws excluded one-sixth of German doctors from their profession and degraded them in other ways, the influx rose to hundreds per year. American doctors worried about their incomes, which were already lowered by the Depression. Soon, thirteen states required the immigrants to serve as interns in an accredited hospital before receiving a license to practice, and ten states made them regraduate from an American medical school. At least twenty states made it impossible for foreigners to set up practice at all. In addition, some county medical societies barred non-citizens from membership without waiting for state action. In 1939, twenty states required refugees to take licensing examinations, no matter how long they had practiced abroad, and by 1943, only Massachusetts and New York allowed non-citizens to take these examinations. This requirement assured a five-year delay for each applicant.

The journal *Medical Economics* published articles with titles such as "Don't License Foreigners!" (April 1937) and "Refugees Unlimited" (February 1939), painting the immigrants as incompetent and unscrupulous quacks who favored socialized medicine. It projected that another fifteen thousand doctors could be expected within five years, all helped by that evil triad—sentimental liberals, crusading labor leaders, and government bureaucrats.

Ninety thousand or half of American doctors were called for military service during World War II, creating the shortage that finally led to the absorption of the foreigners. Still, many American physicians resented that these foreigners seemed to be profiteering from the patriotism of those who had been drafted, in effect, "stealing" their patients. But aliens could not be commissioned as doctors in the armed services.

In analyzing all this, Kathleen M. Pearle has written: "In its treatment of the émigré physician, the organized medical community compiled a disgraceful record.... In addition to generalized hostility, the émigré physician—in New York and elsewhere—faced a powerful and well-organized medical lobby which was willing to use the courts, the legislature, the educational system, professional organizations and community institutions to exclude the potential competitor from medical practice ... [but] anti-Semitic slurs occurred rarely in the anti-émigré outpourings."[2]

As the end of Erwin's first year in Minnesota approached, he applied for a medical license and took the first of two required examinations. He passed with an average grade of 88.5 percent for six written parts and 90 percent for the orals. Then the law changed, and American citizenship became a prerequisite for a Minnesota medical license. He was not allowed to take the second examination. To Gisela and Max he wrote on May 8, 1937: "I have no alternative but to try a state that does not yet have that requirement. Probably it will be Texas, where the examination is in November, everything in one go."

Houston

In 1938, the city of Houston, Texas, with a population nearing four hundred thousand, had only eight or nine specialists in obstetrics and gynecology, some of whom were self-proclaimed and lacked national board certification. Most delivery of babies, and even surgery, was performed by general practitioners. Tall Dr. Allen Lamar McMurrey had studied in Vienna and had returned in 1926 with bow ties, a cane, and a goatee, but no certification. He worked well, did no research, and had movies made of himself operating. He had a tremendous practice but sent difficult cases to the Mayo Clinic. Altogether, there were some 400 physicians or one per 900 inhabitants. Before the emigration, Berlin had one per 650. Erwin visited Texas twice before moving there, in November 1936 and November 1937.

On November 28, 1936, Erwin had boarded a Pullman train for the 36-hour journey to Houston, taking two nights and a day. In a letter written four days later, he described the city as typically American, with a few skyscrapers twenty to thirty stories high "in a business district that looks like any other. It has 350,000 inhabitants and grows fast because of a new channel to the sea for exporting petroleum, wheat, and cotton. It is the fastest growing American city.... People live in single-family houses beyond the business district, everything from the elegant mansions of the oil magnates to modest one and two-story country houses and finally the shacks of Negroes." Although on the latitude of Cairo, Houston, Erwin thought, had "the climate of Milan, and Rochester that of Moscow. Great extremes in summer and winter. Houston is currently in the rainy season. The Gulf reduces the extremes. It's not much warmer than Rochester but more humid. Frost is rare. Nevertheless, vegetation is not at all tropical. By contrast, Galveston, 50 miles to the south is an island of palms and oleanders."

He had "a warm reunion" with Dr. Clara Duncan, aged fifty-nine, a physician who had recently studied in Berlin and had returned in August 1936. Clara Kocher Duncan had moved to Texas from her native Pennsylvania and had studied at the University of Texas

Medical School at Galveston, receiving her degree in 1919. Erwin saw Duncan's office in the Shell Building and the empty office next to hers, which was available for him. Dr. Duncan introduced him to other doctors, and in the evening he gave a lecture. "It went well and led to a lively discussion," he reported.

So after five last months in Rochester, Erwin and family drove thirteen hundred miles in four days to Houston in a large Pontiac, arriving on May 2, 1938. Erwin then worked for three years in partnership with Dr. Duncan. I have often said that my father's choosing Houston was a better economic decision than I (a professional economist) ever made, but in 1978, Mother told me, "Houston was not the best but the only choice." Erwin had to join an ongoing practice to learn the procedures, and that was not possible anywhere else where foreigners could get licenses.

In 1938, from May 15 to December 31, Erwin had twenty-six patients who paid about $50 each for a total of $1,290 (or $17,200 of 2000) for the calendar year. No more than three or four patients came per day. In 1927, his first year of private practice in Berlin eleven years earlier, he had earned only 2,718 marks, and in the second year his income had risen to 8,645 marks. He hoped for a similar rate of growth in Houston. But now in June, $42 were due for insurance, $27 for car payments, and $85 for rent. That left the family only $5 for expenses. To Antonie he wrote: "It looks gloomy. I will actually reach zero dollars. You can imagine what it does to my spirits.... I told one patient that she needed an operation, and she promptly went to another doctor, who said the opposite.... Of course, her pains have returned, and she might come back.... With writing and consultations with Duncan's patients, I'm busy all day long.... But to feel grateful, I just have to think of those poor slobs on the SS *St. Louis* who are being forced back to Germany" (June 8, 1939).

By now, even Texas excluded new refugees from medical practice. Altogether in 1939, Erwin had fifty-two new patients and collected $3,591 (or $48,200 of 2000). During the first half of 1940, another fifty-six new patients appeared, and Erwin now earned more than his 50 percent share, three-quarters of the total. His collections exceeded $500 monthly, just enough to cover professional and living expenses, but not enough to repay debts. Modest living and the expenses of the medical practice required collecting an annual income of $6,000 ($80,600 of year 2000 dollars). By late June 1940, he often had eleven patients daily and over sixty weekly. A year later he had twice as many, and four years later, in 1945, he saw as many patients per day as he had once per week—fifty. Basically, his practice doubled yearly.

During 1936–1938, Erwin borrowed a total of $6,855 ($92,000 of 2000). Half of it came from Antonie, and a fourth from Ferdinand Thun of the Carl Schurz Foundation. Among eight other lenders were Max Gutzwiller and Dr. Häfeli in Switzerland and a few American doctors, including C. W. Mayo. Mr. Oberlaender, the industrialist who had vainly asked Hitler to transmute Dr. Franz Groedel of Nauheim into an "Aryan," lent $125. All were repaid.

Last Letters to Paul Ferdinand

Erwin wrote three last letters to his father in June and July of 1938. In the first he expressed pride that his father had resolved to hold out in Berlin, no matter what. Still, they should visit their children in Switzerland and America as often as possible.

> Digging among old papers, I came across my wartime diary of 1917. Despite all the worries and dangers, how idyllic those times seem now. A furlough in Wannsee with violin lessons.... Americans (how carefree!) are focused on the forthcoming boxing match between Schmeling and Louis. Although the odds are against him, we hope the German will win. (June 19, 1938)

I spent a nice evening at the Houston Saengerbund 1893, a singing club of German-Americans where they speak only German. First, we sang in harmony (myself as bass), practicing Mendelssohn's "Wer hat dich, du schöner Wald" (Who Made You, Beautiful Forest). Then games of Skat at six tables. I won [but] twice had to buy a round of beer for all, according to their custom, because I had four Jacks. The Saengerbund incidentally has two principles: 1. No flag can be displayed but the American, and 2. No discriminating paragraphs against the admittance of new members exist or can be introduced.... I enjoyed the evening in familiar surroundings and could even meet a few former Berliners.

For a casual after-dinner party—ice cream and ice water—we invited a few colleagues and the youthful director, Mr. Chillman, of the local art museum, recommended by the Carl Schurz Foundation. The new local museum is a beautiful building, nicely situated, and has a bit of everything from Antiquity to the Renaissance to the Impressionists. Having an art school on the premises is what makes American museums so lively. Mr. Chillman was much impressed by our little Adrian van Ostade, Willy Herrmann's landscapes, the Biedermeier furniture, and, to a lesser degree, my own efforts.

Mother Wens is undergoing the chronic symptoms of departure anxiety. She will leave on July 20 and after Diepholz and Nauheim plans to visit you in Berlin at a convenient time for you. Ilse and the children are well. All of us are finding our bearings and are in every respect grateful and content. (July 10, 1938)

A Return to Sorrows: 1938–1939

Käthe Wens—Ilse's mother and "Granny" to my sisters and myself—stayed with us for twelve months in Rochester and Houston. She then returned to Germany on the SS *Europa* in August 1938 and came back on the SS *Bremen* in August 1939. I remember both her departure by car for New York with Bruno Beckmann from Minnesota, and a year later her docking at Galveston, Texas, on a misty September dawn. Käthe's plan was henceforth to spend alternate years with her daughter in Houston and her cardiologist son, Gerhard, in Bad Nauheim. She was sixty-four years old, and, except for a bum knee, her health and adventurous spirit were up to such travel. At Bremerhaven on August 2, 1938, she was met at the pier by her brother, Otto Schwarze, and her daughter-in-law, Gertrud Wens, each carrying a bouquet of flowers.

From Nauheim in the house that she and Ferdinand had built thirty years earlier, she wrote that words could not describe her feelings on seeing her son Gerhard, endearingly called "Tertilein." Tears of joy were shed with the old cook, Lisbeth, and most lively of all, the brown dachshund Rocco, nicknamed "Pockilein," kept jumping up to lick her hands. Käthe's first letter went on about all the friends and neighbors who dropped by and brought flowers. Everything was gleaming and was so familiar and so comfortable.

But already her second letter, written only ten days later on August 13, had a different tone: "Our dear homeland is beautiful, but one has to adjust *more* than I had expected.... Be glad and thankful how you have managed and that you made the right choice in time! More than once have I said that to myself in recent days! Above all, I'm thinking of Päp [Paul]." She now had a great longing to see the Strassmann parents in Berlin when they returned from Switzerland, perhaps to cheer them up with news from Houston.

That visit up was not to be. Paul Strassmann died from an attack of pancreatitis on August 15 in Gstaad. My grandmother Hedwig and her daughters sent a brief note to Bad Nauheim and a telegram to Houston: "DESPITE ENCOURAGING RECOVERY REPEATED ATTACKS CAME AND MEDICAL HELP WAS IN VAIN. HIS LAST THOUGHTS WERE OF HIS BELOVED SON. SADLY, MOTHER, SISTERS." The senior Strassmanns were visiting Gisela and her family while Antonie was in Switzerland, partly on business. I remember my confused emotions that steamy August day when the telegram came, and my Mother in tears explained the news. I was twelve, and this was the first death of anyone whom I knew well.

Erwin telegraphed back: "WE ARE WITH YOU IN DEEP SORROW. MUTTCHEN IS NOW ESSENTIAL FOR ALL OF US." Then he drafted a letter:

> Your telegram just came, beautifully worded but catching us unprepared. To be so far apart and forced to accept such devastating news in so few words! Without doubt, the ghastly decisions and cruel degradation of recent weeks brought this about. He had to face the end of his professional activity and was forced to bitter thoughts about his beloved home and Fatherland. He is a victim of the barbarians leading the government. Without pity I could witness the destruction of a nation that allows that. You will hear from us again.

Three days later, on August 19, a last letter from Paul arrived. That letter spoke of plans to visit the Mayo Clinic in 1939 for a diagnosis. From Nauheim on August 17, Käthe wrote:

> A great shock! I was deeply moved reading Muttchen's lines yesterday. Päpchen has found peace and has been spared hard new disappointments. Thinking of Muttchen, I live through all the unspeakably heavy hours with her.... A bitter challenge faces her, but she knows where her future home must be. I hope that Gisela will accompany her and console her upon entering the empty house. Muttchen will be strong knowing that her beloved Paul's vocation had been destroyed by the latest decrees. That was more than he could bear! It is good to know he is now at rest and in peace! His name will endure!

On August 21, 1938, Käthe wrote that a strenuous month had passed since leaving Houston for the 1,852-mile drive to New York, followed by the voyage on the *Europa*. "Returning to the house was going back to a dear old routine, but facing this nation and its mores is hard! People do not mind their own business. I bless the Providence that gave you a new homeland in time! And that is how I think of Päpchen, hoping it is also a consolation for you!"

The Pogrom

Käthe now learned in Bad Nauheim about all the new discriminations, including "Israel" and "Sara" being imposed as middle names, the letter "J" being stamped in passports, and so forth. Paul was spared knowing about this and about the *Kristallnacht* of November 9–10, 1938. Erwin wrote in his diary: "In Germany, anti-Semitic riots, burning of synagogues, and plundering of ten thousand stores and dwellings." Four days later, he noted that German Jews themselves were assessed a billion marks for repairing the damage. Roosevelt recalled the American ambassador the next day, and the diary reads: "Storm in USA against Jewish persecution in Germany," and on November 17: "56,000 Jews in concentration camps. Planned deportations to Africa, South America, etc."

The *Kristallnacht* was a pogrom that the Nazis had planned for some time and that fit in well as a response to the assassination of a German embassy official in Paris by Herschel Grynspan on November 7. The *Bad Nauheimer Zeitung* reported on November 11, 1938:

> As in many other places ... yesterday a wave of indignation swept the spa as a natural reaction to the treacherous murder in Paris. The dam of patience has broken under the pressure of Jewish incitement throughout the world with criminal results. Popular indignation is expressed in the wish that the last Jew must leave Germany. In Bad Nauheim, Jews have enjoyed hospitality and played a big role in important occupations ... and so

Bad Nauheim does not lack examples of Jewish greed and their drive to dominate.... The people's anger about the international machinations of Jewry and the new atrocity has found an understandable outlet.

This account was false, and many Nauheimers knew it. Destruction in Nauheim was no spontaneous wave of popular indignation but a carefully planned attack on Jews and their property. Indeed, the attack was postponed by a day to November 10 until after a delegation of French physicians had left town. Nauheim was concerned about its international image. According to postwar hearings on the matter, the attacks were planned at the Pfälzer Hof inn at a meeting of local Nazi leaders and a representative of the mayor. I know the place well. It is a short walk up the hill from the Wens house, a low-ceilinged establishment where Gerhard often lodged visitors. On November 10, those attending the meeting later went out and broke into stores and homes to destroy property and throw it into the street. Quickly, the population joined in. The director of the gymnasium gave axes to students so that they could smash furniture in the synagogue on the Karlstrasse, just around the corner from the house of my Wens grandparents, now Uncle Gerhard's. We had passed it daily. Unlike conflagrations at nearby Friedberg and Butzbach, the synagogue was not burned and no one was killed. Just smashed up.

Bremen and the Pogrom

Fearing censorship, my grandmother Wens mentioned the *Kristallnacht* only in general terms in her letters. At that time she was not in Bad Nauheim but in her native town of Diepholz. From Bremen she wrote on November 29, 1938: "I would a thousand times rather be with you, helping bake Christmas cookies, than here!... I picture your life vividly, how cozily we lived there [Houston] and in Rochester. I am entirely oriented toward all of you. Here one has experienced enough after those last disturbances—a chapter that is better not mentioned. I have heard nothing from Muttchen and hesitate to ask her for news. Her heart must weigh heavy in these times.... I feel like a visitor here who does not belong."

In Bremen, thirty Jewish stores and dwellings were ravaged, as well as two synagogues. The one in the Gartenstrasse was thoroughly burned out while fire brigades stood idly by to keep flames from spreading to neighboring buildings. Occupants of a Jewish old-age home were beaten at night and driven out into cold streets. At 8:00 AM, 160 Jewish men were assembled and marched several kilometers to the prison of Oslebshausen. The next day they were shipped by train to Oranienburg near Berlin and marched to the Sachsenhausen concentration camp. Meanwhile, five people were shot and killed in their bedrooms: the aged doctor, Arthur Goldberg, and his wife Martha; Heinrich Rosenblum, a grocer; Leopold Simonsohn, a skilled machinist; and Selma Zwienicki, whose husband ran a bicycle shop and barely escaped. None of these had been politically active or provocative. A historian recalled decades later: "Open protests against these criminal actions did not take place in November 1938, for the bulk of citizens were indifferent.... Only some merchants thought reactions abroad might negatively affect trade."[3]

Closing up Dahlem and Sailing Away

In April 1939, Käthe Wens agreed to be in charge of closing the Dahlem house of the senior Strassmanns; to arrange shipments of inherited goods to New York, Houston, and

Fribourg; to obtain a long series of legal permits; and to dispose of everything else. Four months later, on August 22, 1939, she sailed away on the SS *Bremen*, the same ocean liner on which we had left two years earlier. A year had passed since the death of Paul Strassmann, and Käthe had often thought of that as she packed. She spent the last days with her brother Otto and his wife Martha in Diepholz. Otto's only son, Rolf, aged thirty-three, worked for the Bremen branch of the Schwarze grain-trading firm and was a member of the SS in that city.

The SS *Bremen* was the only German liner allowed to reach its destination that week. All other ships were ordered to turn back with goods and passengers. On its return trip, the *Bremen* steamed home empty. On September 1, 1939, Hitler's armies invaded Poland, and two days later, Great Britain and France declared war. That very evening a U-boat, without warning, sank the British liner *Athenia*, which was steaming westwards across the Atlantic. Of 1,400 passengers, 112 drowned. At that moment, Käthe was circling Florida aboard the small SS *Seminole*.

Erwin wrote in his diary on September 1: "War! Hitler invades Poland in three places," and he sketched a map with arrows. Then he added, "Stalin remains neutral," and on September 3, "England and France in state of war with Germany."

At dawn on September 5, 1939, Käthe Wens arrived at Galveston on the SS *Seminole*. We were all at the dock, and there was much to tell.

More Bad News from Europe

Less than a year later, on June 21, 1940, Erwin wrote in his diary: "Hitler dictates armistice terms to France in Foch's railway car at Compiègne." That day, Ilse fell down the stairs but did not hurt herself seriously. Six weeks after the United States entered the war, on January 17, 1942, Erwin had to deliver the family's cameras, binoculars, and shortwave radio to the Harris County sheriff. The war delayed Erwin's American citizenship, since he was now classified as an "enemy alien." Like Japanese fruit farmers and Italian pizza cooks, the three German-Jewish physicians of Houston and their families, all "non-Aryans," were fingerprinted at the local post office. I remember that procedure: black ink sticky on each finger, photographs, signatures. Fortunately, none of my San Jacinto High School classmates saw that. We were forbidden to travel more than fifty miles without police authorization, except for the extra five miles to the Galveston beaches.

In those weeks of Axis triumphs, Erwin wrote in his diary entries such as "ghastly mood … dreary prospects for the future … uncertainty … everything is going to the dogs." I remember the heavy atmosphere around the dinner table in 1941–1942, the silence and my father's nervous fidgeting with his fingernails. The mischievous confidence was temporarily gone. Jewish or not, we were officially "enemy aliens," considered unworthy and looked on as possible secret plotters, working on behalf of Hitler, Mussolini, or Tojo.

But within a year, in the early afternoon of November 4, 1942, Erwin took his oath as an American citizen. He then made his rounds at Hermann Hospital with a friend, Dr. Ernst Bertner, Houston's leading political physician, who was in the process of organizing the Texas Medical Center. At home, Erwin received a star-spangled banner flag from Ilse. He telephoned his sister Antonie and his mother Hedwig in Peekskill, New York; his daughter Renata at Gulfpark College in Mississippi; and his fellow Houston physicians, Alfons Salinger and Franz Gruenbaum, who remained in the "enemy alien" category.

Texas Medicine

Air conditioning was still novel in the subtropical Houston of those days, and even the operating rooms of hospitals had no more than rotating ceiling fans pushing humid, ninety-degree air. One nurse had the task of wiping sweat off the surgeon's face. Drops that fell into opened abdomens had to be followed with a quick dab of ether. Some surgeons, like athletes, wore headbands with sponges.

In one case, Erwin saved a fifteen-year-old girl from the consequences of a self-inflicted abortion, an emergency treatment for which he expected to be paid only $25. In the preceding year, the same girl had already delivered a baby, and Erwin had arranged for its adoption.

"After a long time, I had to operate again yesterday," he wrote to Antonie on October 20, 1939, about a breast amputation. "With a local anesthetic I first removed the suspicious tumor, and its malignancy was rapidly established with a microscope. With a general anesthetic, everything then went perfectly. One assistant said, 'It looks as if you've done this operation at least a million times.' In accordance with Father's rule, I had that patient laughing ... that same evening." Her husband was an executive for a chain of Houston grocery stores, and Erwin hoped to collect $300, although not a word about money had so far been spoken.

In 1940, the American Society of Obstetricians, Gynecologists, and Abdominal Surgeons awarded Erwin its Foundation Prize for his paper, "The Theca Cone and Its Tropism toward the Ovarian Surface: A Typical Feature of Growing Human and Mammalian Follicles." Erwin wrote to Antonie that this prize solidified his status among his Houston colleagues. A local medical periodical called it "a well-deserved honor," and at a medical meeting, the chairman announced the event with pride. Erwin wrote to Antonie: "It is truly marvelous the way in this country even competitors will express their recognition."

The Houston hospitals then asked Erwin to organize a course for resident physicians so that they might qualify for board examinations in gynecology and obstetrics. Without such a course, the hospitals themselves would lack a certain accreditation. Erwin received an unlimited budget for microscopes, projectors, and equipment, but no salary for this work. He wrote to Antonie that the joy of it was its own reward.

The leading Houston obstetrician was Dr. Herman Johnson, a native of Vermont who had moved to Texas in 1920. He invited Erwin to drive with him to the October 1940 meetings of the Texas Association of Obstetricians and Gynecologists, and Erwin wrote to Antonie: "Thus, I seem to be catching on among my colleagues almost faster than among the population of patients. But that's the best way to get a solid foundation." Johnson and Erwin reminisced about World War I, where both had fought, on opposite sides, at Vimuy Ridge in France.[4]

In his memoirs, Johnson wrote: "I can claim to have been the first physician in Houston, or perhaps in Texas, to limit his practice to Obstetrics. But it should be recalled that there might be a difference between an obstetrical specialist and a doctor limiting his practice to this specialty."[5]

The Texas Medical Center

By 1940, one of Erwin's new friends, Dr. Ernst William Bertner, president of the Texas Medical Society, had already spent years trying to organize a major medical center in Houston. In 1913, at age twenty-four, Bertner had moved to Houston, where the leading banker, Jesse Jones, needed a house physician for his immense new Rice Hotel. The Bertners lived on the hotel's top floor from then on, except for one year Bertner spent studying advanced gynecology and obstetrics at Johns Hopkins University.[6] There he formulated his plans for building an even greater medical center in Texas. Erwin told me that Bertner was not a deep scientist, a man who read and wrote pioneering medical works; rather, he was a capable physician and a great politician. When the Texas legislature finally voted to spend half a million dollars for a cancer hospital, the M. D. Anderson Foundation matched the amount, and a 134-acre site was bought. The foundation then gave a million dollars to bring the Baylor Medical School to Houston from Dallas, and the Houston Chamber of Commerce supported that initiative with half a million dollars.[7] The foundation also promised another million for ten years of research.

Dr. Bertner became the president of the new Texas Medical Center, and Dr. Herman Johnson helped to organize the obstetrical-gynecological department of Baylor with Erwin on the faculty. Classes began in July 1943 in an old Sears Roebuck warehouse, but in 1947 they moved to the center's first structure, one equipped by donations from Mrs. H. Roy Cullen (wife of a philanthropic and lucky Texas oilman). In 1945, Erwin was promoted to full professor. Not only were half of American physicians overseas in the war, but Baylor's move from Dallas was made without many of the previous faculty. So Erwin was in demand.

Half a century later, in 2001, the Texas Medical Center reported on its Web site that it now served 5.1 million patients annually with its 61,000 employees in over a hundred buildings. More than $700 million was spent annually on research.

Unconditional Surrender

In Europe, the war ended on Tuesday, May 8, 1945. On April 21, Erwin had written in his diary: "Russians in Berlin—Pankow, Weissensee [where his Strassmann grandfather and great-grandfather, like others, lay strangely undisturbed in the great Jewish cemetery]." In early May, he recorded: "Last battles around Berlin.... Germany collapses.... Hitler and Goebbels dead." That Saturday, Erwin, the survivor, bought himself two elegant suits at Battelstein's clothing store, played nine holes of golf, and won four dollars playing poker with Ilse and friends.

Gradually, letters arrived from relatives, friends, and acquaintances, correspondence that at first was forbidden and had to be smuggled out by friendly GIs. I shall let one of these, dated October 14, 1946, stand for all the rest. It came from Käthe Wens's stepbrother and cousin, Walter Koch, the pathologist who had left Aschoff's institute in Freiburg and then, at age sixty-six, was a Wehrmacht physician in Berlin and living at Landauer Strasse 4 in the western Wilmersdorf area. Koch wrote:

> The time when Berlin was crushed was bad. The American and English air attacks never stopped, and during the last six weeks one was hardly outside but lived in the basement. Three times I personally had to extinguish fire in the roof.... I missed becoming a prisoner only because, with blocked transport in the last days of the war, I could not make it to the hospital. All the military in the hospital were imprisoned and mostly taken away. Many are still in Russia. In the night before the first Russians appeared, our street was under artillery fire from both sides, and I cared for the wounded until 4 in the morning. On the rose terraces in front of our house, the last German mortars were set up, and half their men were wounded or killed. Transporting the wounded was impossible, so I carried them into neighboring air raid shelters where people were cowering. One was used to everything. Not a window was unbroken in our apartment, and it's a wonder that we survived shrapnel sailing through our bedroom.

When the Russians came, they set up heavy artillery in front of our house and on the side, and a stream of soldiers came through our building. They broke all doors and made our home a wasteland with everything torn open and emptied. But we got off relatively well and did not lose much....

Tell [Ilse] that the whole Luisenstrasse is blocked off because its apartments are occupied by Russian families.... Despite all yearning, do *not* return to Germany until conditions here are somewhat more congenial. All I ask of you is a pair of stockings for Lotte [his wife].

Postwar Medicine

By the early 1950s, Erwin was considered one of the leading medical specialists in his field in Houston. From 1943 until 1965, he was clinical professor of obstetrics and gynecology at the Baylor University College of Medicine. When a portrait of Dr. Herman Johnson, painted by Roberto Fantuzzi, was presented to the college in January 1954, Erwin was selected to make the presentation. Johnson had changed from practicing medicine to full-time education in 1949 and now, aged seventy-one, was also retiring from teaching. Erwin recalled the 1949 ceremony and said, "Memories of you in the delivery rooms of the various hospitals will linger on. Moreover, we will not consider you as having deserted us, for ... we recognize that you will remain available to us for counsel and that your function of leadership will be greatly extended.... We are at your service just as we have been in the past." Afterward, kissed by nurses and doctors' wives, Johnson joked, "With many varieties of lipstick, some wet because of tears on my face, I looked like a badly mutilated person."[8]

Erwin organized an advanced research meeting on sterility in 1961 in Houston and was a guest speaker at various congresses of the International Association for Sterility and Fertility, including those held in New York (1953), Rome (1956), and Amsterdam (1959), among others. He retired in 1970 after thirty-two years in Houston. In forty-five years of medical practice, he once told me, knocking on wood, he had delivered over four thousand babies and had never lost a mother in childbirth.

Among his earliest patients in Houston were other immigrants from Germany. With one of these, Margaret Schoening Kaye, he delivered babies in 1942 and 1944 after she previously had suffered four miscarriages, two in Germany and two in the United States. In his autobiography, *Starting from Scratch*,[9] Walter Kaye, the children's father, wrote: "For all the past months Dr. Strassmann had been unbelievably caring and helpful ... he came by almost every day to cheer Margaret up and help her in any way he could. This was 'his' baby as much as ours.... For many years afterward ... whenever a patient of his would complain about having a miscarriage and be discouraged by it, he would point to the pictures of our children and tell the unhappy patient that Margaret had had four miscarriages before she had those two children."

Margaret, now over eighty but still fit enough to play tennis, told me in 1996: "He was very caring and really gave his whole life for his patients. When I was in the hospital, and, of course, fifty years ago, one spent much more time in there, I looked forward to his visits. Before he entered my room, I could hear him in the hallway as he cleared his throat [*er räusperte sich*]. He always had a flower in his buttonhole and looked dandy." Margaret was unaware that the flower usually came from the bouquet of a patient in another room.

The wife of a former classmate told me recently, "Your daddy was wonderful but not a man of many words. I remember being horrified and saying, 'Oh, no! Not a Caesarean!

I can't face that!' He said, 'It's very simple. Do you want to have this baby or not?' Then I had two more babies, both Caesarean. After the third, he said, 'All right, that was the last one!' We left it to him, and no further pregnancies took place."

I remember my father's offices in the Shell Building, the Medical Arts, and finally the Hermann Professional Building between Rice University and the Texas Medical Center. There were the library of medical books and the Biedermeier chairs in the waiting room, and on the walls were hung diplomas, awards, certificates, and photographs of Paul Ferdinand Strassmann, Ludwig Aschoff, the Mayo brothers, and dozens of presumably sterile women with their children, often twins, even triplets, some named "Erwin." Two examination rooms allowed one patient to be examined while another was being prepared. There was a smell of Mercurochrome and KY-jelly, and near Erwin's desk was a sizable statue of a monkey contemplating a human skull while sitting on a book inscribed "Darwin." V. I. Lenin had another cast of that statue.

Treating infertile or apparently sterile patients was Erwin's specialty. He would work for years with patients, making tests and trying procedures, anything that might help to cause ovulation, to remove obstructions, or to solve other problems. After years of effort, the patient was more likely to give up and look for an adoption than he was.

It is difficult to determine the percentage of pregnancies among his patients that were due to his treatment. If 80 percent of women are pregnant after a year of coitus without contraception, should the rest be considered problematic by definition? About half of them are likely to become pregnant during the second year, even without treatment. Much depends upon age and a variety of circumstances, so that no physician is likely to find himself treating a random sample of clearly designated infertile patients.

In Erwin's case, the vast majority of women did become pregnant and delivered healthy babies, so referrals came to him from the entire Southwest and Latin America. He began occasional lectures on the subject of sterility and fertility saying that it was "no field for the cynic or the half-hearted." The problems were difficult, but the rewards were gratifying, "working on the assembly line of life." He would go on to describe his first interview, in which he would ask about a patient's menstrual, sexual, medical, and even scholastic history—since he had to know the "whole person." Then would come an account of the first examination and some nine tests that he usually made. He did not believe that more than 10 percent of frustrated couples had impossible fertility problems. Often he closed his lectures with an explanation of "double uterus" operations.

In twenty years, from 1945 to 1964, Erwin had unified the "double uterus" of twenty-six patients with the "Strassmann procedure." A double uterus has two cavities instead of one, either because of a dividing septum or because the so-called mullerian ducts have not fused. Nine of Erwin's Houston patients with these conditions had primary infertility, and seventeen invariably had spontaneous miscarriages. After the corrective operation, twenty-one women became pregnant and in time delivered thirty children plus five miscarriages. Before the operation, there had been only one living child and fifty-three miscarriages. Reviewing the world literature, Erwin wrote that such congenital malformations occurred far more often than in one per seven thousand women, as was widely believed. "There is no operation for infertility that has similar results to offer." He deplored the omission of this operation from American gynecological textbooks, and mentioned that his father had developed it in 1907. He dedicated this, his seventy-sixth and last publication, "Fertility and Unification of Double Uterus," to his father, Paul Ferdinand Strassmann, on the anniversary of Paul's hundredth birthday.[10] The double uterus phenomenon is now mentioned in most texts.

Fun in the Promised Land

In Houston, Erwin, Ilse, Käthe, and children lived at 2310 Binz Avenue until 1955 and then at 3423 North MacGregor Way until 1971. Both were brick houses with four bedrooms, but the MacGregor house was air conditioned, had a large den, and had five rather than two bathrooms. With the familiar old Biedermeier furniture inside, plus the Oriental rugs and the Impressionist landscape paintings, the decor was Central European bourgeois. The Binz house stood in front of two pecan trees and had roses and crepe myrtle near the street. The MacGregor house sat among dozens of pine trees shading a circular driveway leading to a view of Brays Bayou beyond the road. Real estate agents thought "Braes" was a more elegant spelling, but we called it the "Mississippi" during hurricanes.

The only way to escape the heat during our first summer (in 1938) was a trip to the Galveston beaches or to the movies. We bought hardly any goods besides food, but the lifestyle was not austere. Even short family vacations were not affordable for four years. Then at last in 1941 came one long weekend in Teutonic New Braunfels near San Antonio and another to the state capital in Austin. A year later we were "enemy aliens" and forbidden to travel.

Erwin talked to his patients in a somewhat whimsical but nevertheless lordly manner that many women said they adored but that few would tolerate now. I am convinced that he would have adapted to new times as he did to a new country. But in the 1950s, patients who asked many questions and ventured their own diagnosis were told, "My dear, I didn't know you studied medicine! No? But then you were a nurse? No? Well, then I think it is amazing that you know so many medical words and terms!"

A few German refugee patients had taken a vow to speak only English from now on. Erwin told them, "My dear, I hate the Nazis as much as you do, but why should I make you suffer with my accent? And you me?"

One patient said about him, "he's crazy, but he knows his business." Her husband asked him if he knew American books like *The Last of the Mohicans,* and Erwin said, "Brother, all I have to do is look at you." With his chatty, raconteur manner, he was always behind schedule, but waiting patients claimed not to mind, provided that they, too, could leave with the latest joke or pun. They said that their husbands expected to hear them.

Thanking guests for coming to another commemorative dinner in his honor, he would usually be brief and say something like, "This gift warms our hearts, just as they've warmed the potatoes. And like our hearts, the potatoes are ready to serve. So thank you."

About his painting, he said that unfortunately most people considered him only a good painter for a doctor. Or a good doctor for a painter. In 1938, he won a bronze medal for a painting of a village stone bridge, which was exhibited in San Francisco. "Some day," he remarked, "I might even be good enough to cut off my ear." From vacations to New Mexico, Michigan, or the Black Forest, he usually returned with three or four new Impressionist oil landscapes. To visitors he said, "How about it, I promise you a picture. Then you have the joy of anticipation. After you get it, you'll be sore. Even the famous Mayo brothers could not escape my works of art. I painted a garden scene for Dr. Charlie and a boating scene for Dr. Will."

He recalled that one patient asked him, "Doctor, where did you ever get that cute accent?" He answered, "Tahiti, but why go there now, a place of bugs and worms? And Gaugin is already dead. But I'll tell you why. With great food, even Tahiti looks good. You can stand any landscape where the food is great, yes?" Actually he had been to New Zealand but never Tahiti.

Deep political discussions were not his style, and he once told me, "As a young man I also studied philosophy and struggled with a *Weltanschauung.* It was beyond me. After reading on and on, I could never recall anything afterward. Essentially, the truth is what we learned when we were young or what helps in business."

"Yes, Antonie is now Catholic," he said once. "But so far the Pope hasn't come to Peekskill."

While they were operating on one patient, an assisting resident physician commented that he had found the ideal house to buy, located near friends, but the down payment was too high.

"I give it to you," said Erwin.

"You're joking. I never heard of such a thing."

"No, take it," said Erwin. "No interest, no note, no deadline. I went into debt with friends here in 1936 and 1937. Now I'm in a position to help, and it wouldn't be right if I didn't."

My daughter Beverly has read the preceding pages and told me they were all right, even gave her a lump in her throat. But somehow the real comic Opi (German diminutive for "Grampa") does not come through. She remembers him when she was barely a teenager, a grandfather who was, in her words, an "incredible prankster with a great flair for mischief, a wonderful knack for jests, and a total ability to generate amusement with the right face." Erwin relished everyone's oddities but with elegant zest defused all strangeness. "Here's an ironic story from one pal to another" was his approach. "If I grin and whisper some mischief, how about a little smile from you?" His good-natured mockery suggested that all problems were minor, that the world was a pleasant, manageable place. Life was to be savored. As I finally left the room in which he died in October 1972, I turned back once more at the door. He gave me a thumbs-up sign.

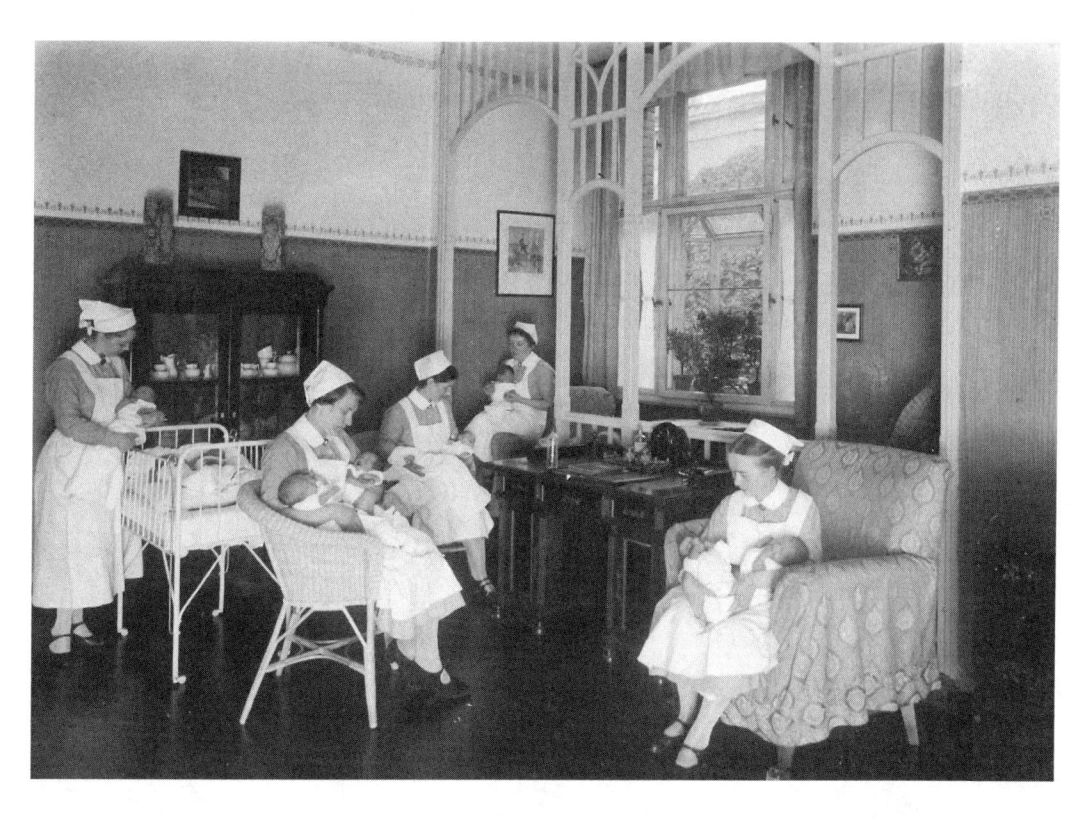

In the Strassmann Frauenklinik, 1912. On the right, Head Nurse Marianne Rudeloff.

Pastor Martin Niemöller.

Dr. Ferdinand Sauerbruch as painted by Max Liebermann.

Entrance to the Frauenklinik: On the left, a Fritz Klimsch bust of Gerhart Hauptmann, a good friend of the Strassmanns. On the right, the monument to Hellmuth Strassmann killed in World War I.

One of the two storks, Schlorchi and Bubi, who lived in the courtyard of the clinic to enlighten some young visitors about the origins of babies.

Hans and Eva Reis with the author in 1995. Hans was born in the clinic in 1926, and seventy years later, after German reunification, he helped the Strassmanns to regain ownership of the buildings.

Courtyard of the clinic with its sculpture, *Chained Woman*, by Reinhold Boeltzig, who had originally called it *The Sinner*.

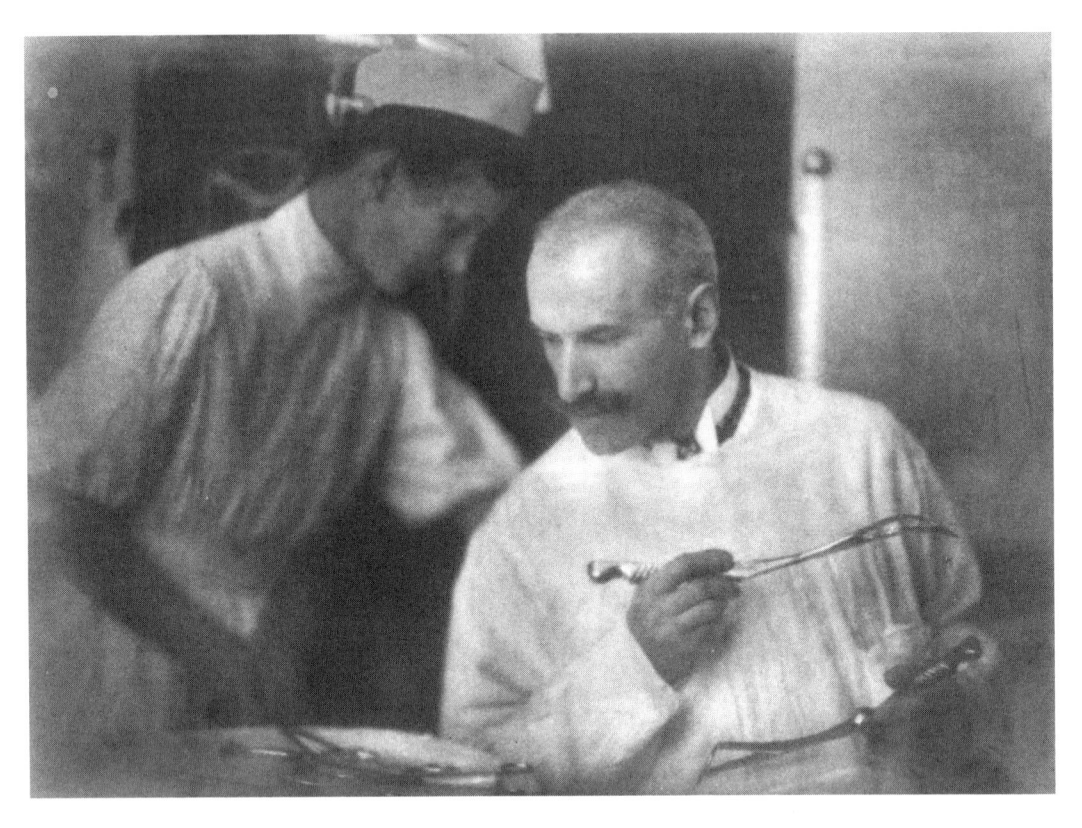

Paul Strassmann operating.

Postcard showing relief sculptures by Sandor Jaray along the Schumannstrasse façade of the clinic.

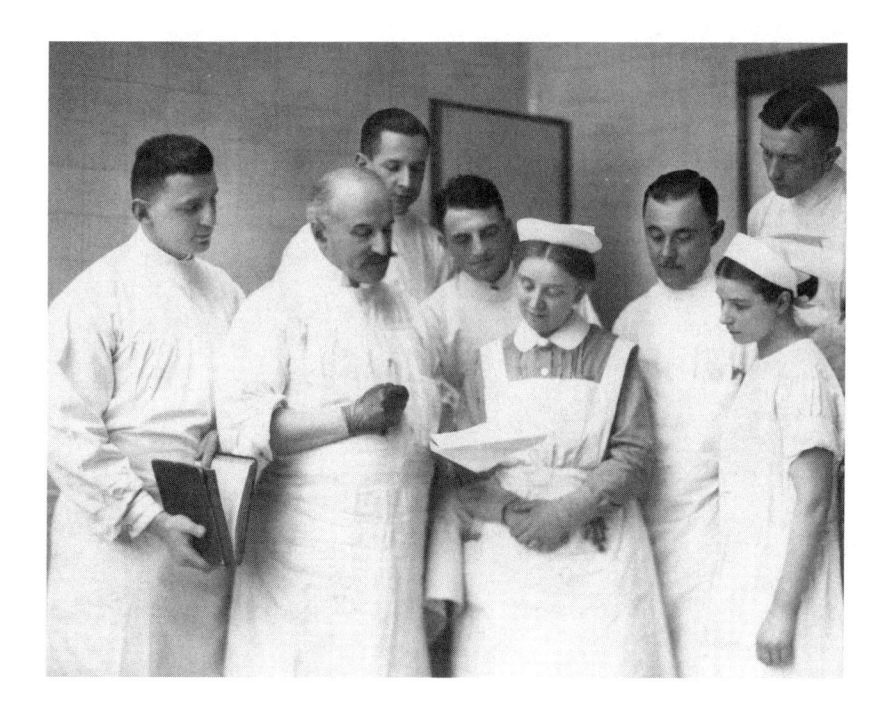

A photograph of 1926. From the left: Erwin and Paul Strassmann, Gerhart Zimmer, an unknown, Head Nurse Marianne Rudeloff, Martin Jung, and Nurse Amalie Mücke.

Paul Strassmann, 1935, in his study with his son Erwin.

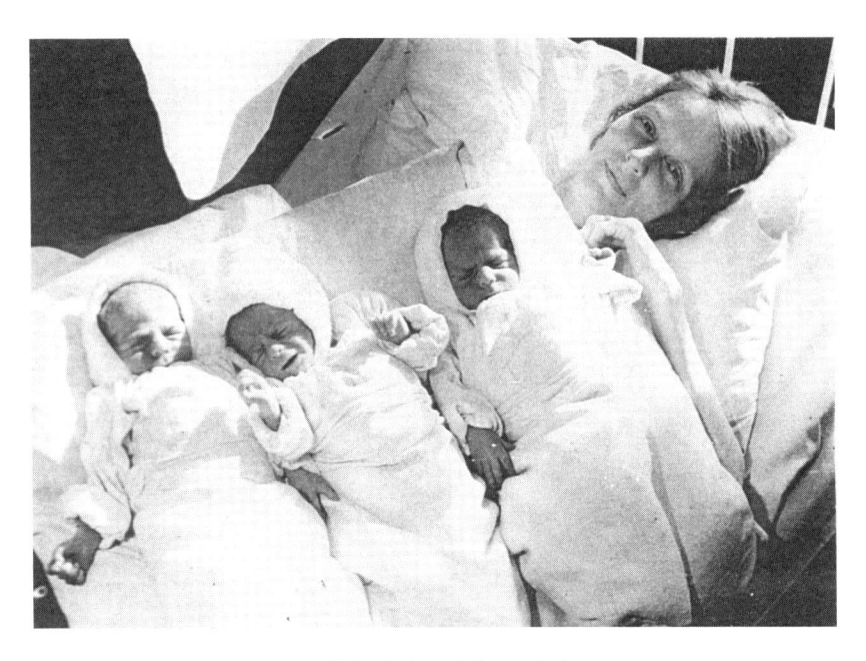

Gertrud Seidel with her triplets.

Document recording the birth of Baby 15,000 in the Strassmann Clinic.

Ilse Wens and her best friend, Leni Schöller, at Freiburg, Baden.

In the Siegesallee, Berlin, winter 1933. Erwin Strassmann, Ilse, and their children, Renate and Wolfgang.

Ilse and her parents, Käthe (née Schwarze) and Dr. Ferdinand Wens, around 1924.

Professor Ludwig Aschoff, director of the Institute of Pathology, Freiburg.

Charles W. Mayo, 1936.

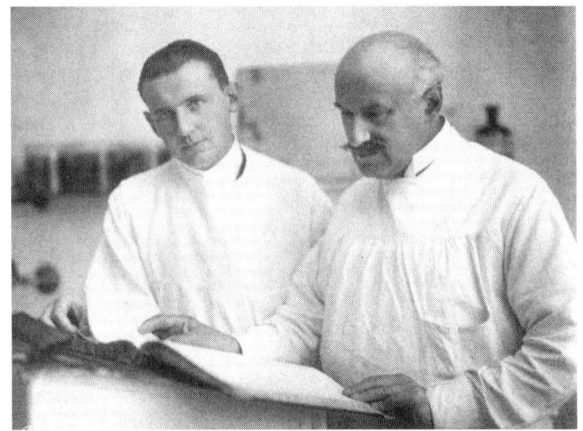

Erwin and Paul Strassmann, 1935.

In 1962 in gratitude for the Mayos' hospitality in 1936, Erwin gave them a copy of Andreas Vesalius's *De Humani Corporis Fabrica Libri Septem* of 1543. Here he looks at it with Charles W. Mayo.

Charles H. Mayo kissing Antonie at Mayowood, Rochester, July 1937.

Joe Mayo with Erwin on the Mayos' Mississippi yacht in the summer of 1936. That fall Joe died when a train hit his car.

Käthe Wens at a beach picnic in Galveston, Texas, with Dr. Clara Duncan, who was Erwin's office partner during 1938–1941.

A 1948 photograph showing Ilse, Erwin, and Ilse's mother, Käthe Wens. Standing are Erwin and Ilse's children: Angelica, Wolfgang Paul, and Renata.

Georg Strassmann with Priska Albert, Reinhold's hospital nurse and bride, near Obersdorf, Bavaria, September 1918.

During World War I, Reinhold Strassmann was wounded in his head and one lung. Aged 51, he was murdered in 1944 at Auschwitz.

The brothers Reinhold and Georg with their father, Fritz Strassmann, at Zehlendorf, 1938. To the right of the table is Putzi Esch, the housekeeper. On the far right is Georg's wife, Ilse. In the background is their son Fritz (Fred) Strassmann, who emigrated with them to the United States in October 1938.

Elisabeth (née Strassmann) and Ernst Keiner in Berlin, 1950.

Annemarie Keiner in front of Fritz Strassmann's Zehlendorf house, April 1939.

Georg, Fritz (Fred), and Ilse Strassmann in the summer of 1938. Fred was born in the Strassmann Clinic in 1929 and was adopted by Georg and Ilse.

Fred Strassmann and his sister Bettina in Frankfurt in 1996 when they met for the first time.

Ernst Strassmann, painted by G. Hennig about 1931.

Arnold Strassmann (1861–1940), Ernst's father, painted by G. Hennig in 1934. Arnold was a grandson of Chune Strassmann of Rawicz.

Ernst Strassmann in 1957 as director of BEWAG, Berlin's electric utility company.

The author's daughters. From the left: Joan, Diana, and Beverly, 1987.

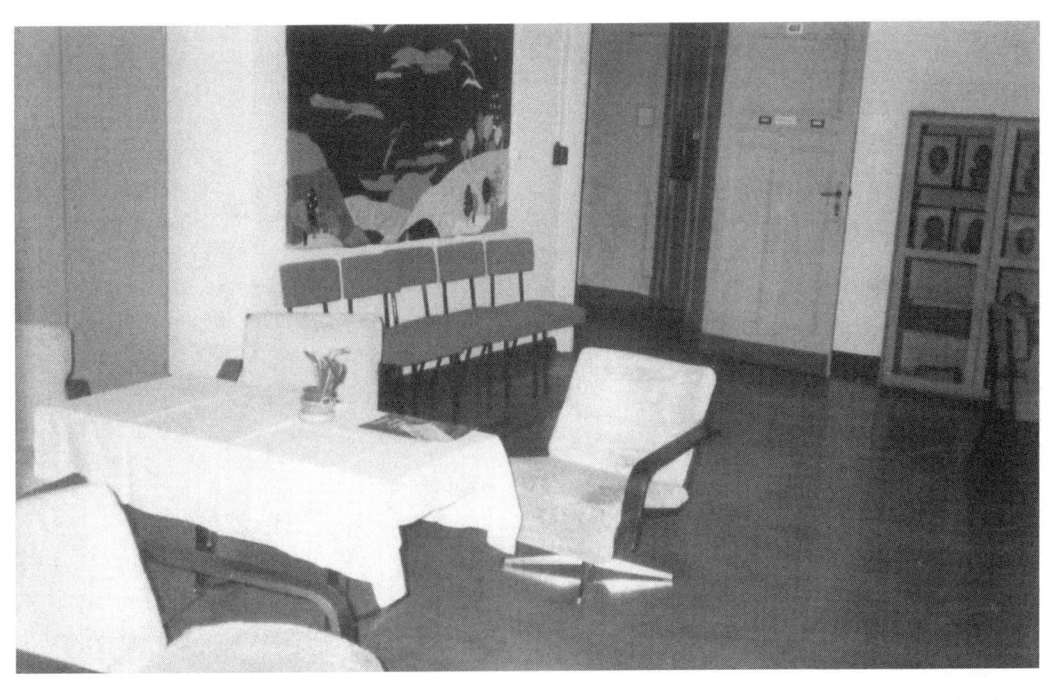

Paul Ferdinand's former study, a typical "Berlin room" that faced the courtyard, as it looked around 1990 after the fall of the Berlin Wall. The building was now a school for medical technicians. Adolf Hitler's picture had disappeared long ago.

The author on a German book tour in May 2006 with Hans Jürgen Fip, the Lord Mayor of Osnabrück, and Jutta Lange-Quassowski.

All that remains at the southern tip of historic Berlin's principal island, the Fischer Insel, is this ancient horse chestnut tree. Once it stood in front of Joseph Bender Levy's mansion, and the author's grandfather played here. Now the author's own grandchildren have done so, five generations later, as American tourists.

Chapter 14

Destination Auschwitz: Reinhold 1944

For the targets of persecution, staying in Nazi Germany meant hiding, concocting proof that you were not really Jewish-descended, committing suicide, or being abducted to concentration camps. The descendants of Schmuhl Molower Strassmann who stayed in Germany experienced one of those four fates. Elisabeth Strassmann Keiner and her daughter, Annemarie, hid in Hessian and Black Forest villages and survived. Richard and Marie Levy committed suicide in 1941. Reinhard survived at a branch of the Buchenwald concentration camp, while his brother, Ernst Karl Otto Strassmann, a judge, denied any Jewish ancestry and operated an underground resistance movement from 1933 until the Gestapo caught him in 1942. Helene Strassmann (Paul Ferdinand's sister) died at the Theresienstadt concentration camp, and Reinhold Strassmann (a son of the forensic pathologist, Fritz) died at Auschwitz. This chapter tells his story.

After being twice wounded in World War I, Reinhold married his Catholic nurse, Priska Albert, and became a poet and mathematician, solving actuarial problems for an insurance company. Already baptized but full of doubts, he finally became a devout evangelical Lutheran and declined to use his troubled marriage to avoid deportation in 1943. and as such declined to use his troubled marriage to avoid fatal deportation in 1943. Reinhold's closest friend, his brother Georg, had a different career and family, successful first in Breslau, then in Massachusetts.

Beginnings

Reinhold was born on January 24, 1893, in Berlin. His father was Fritz Strassmann (1858–1940), the first offspring of any of the five brothers from Rawicz and the leading developer of forensic medicine. Reinhold's mother was the former Rose Borchardt (1866–1934), whose soft almond eyes, wavy dark hair, and regular features he inherited. Georg (1890–1972), the oldest son, was blond but short and resembled Fritz. A third son, Werner, died at age eight in 1899 of misdiagnosed appendicitis and was buried at Friedrichsfelde. Photographs, poems, letters, and recollections of Georg and Reinhold Strassmann have come my way from cousins in the United States—Fred Strassmann of Belmont, Massachusetts and Elisabeth Strassmann Keiner (1899–1990) and her daughter, Annemarie Keiner Springer, both of Bloomington, Indiana.

Nothing unusual is known about Reinhold's childhood and adolescence, the years before he volunteered for the army in 1914 at twenty-one years of age. He adored his older brother Georg and loved poetry and mathematics, which he studied at the Technical

University in the Charlottenburg district of Berlin. The best of times for him were family vacations to Switzerland and Italy, and he enshrined memories of Neapolitan fishing boats and snowy Engadine pines in his poetry.

World War I put an end to studies and tourism but not to poetry. Photos show Reinhold at a family dinner on furlough in 1915, looking slim in his military tunic, or near a snowy front-line trench at Pinsk in 1916, chilled and wrapped in a great scarf and overcoat, hands deep in pockets. Poems written during the victorious years ring with the defiant patriotism of the era. Germans were not the only ones vulnerable to patriotic delusions and posturing that way ninety years ago.

> **Defiance**
> We defy fate! We never give in!
> Let our planet shatter first!
> If we collapse, don't ask us how!
> We defy fate, we never give in.
> In battle we die victoriously!

Reinhold, a machine gunner, was wounded twice in the war—in 1915 with a head wound affecting his hearing and again in 1918 when he lost a lung. Since the wounds also brought him his great love, the nurse, Priska Albert, he saw the national military debacle as a greater tragedy than his own wounds.

Doubly Wounded

Reinhold's head wound came in 1915 near Stryj, south of Lwow, in the Galician foothills of the Carpathians. He was on patrol and a grenade exploded nearby. Georg, who was serving in the same regiment as a physician, saw his brother carried into the dressing station. After some days in Stryj and a Breslau hospital, Reinhold was transferred to the Virchow Hospital of Berlin, where his uncle Moritz Borchardt was chief surgeon. With his Iron Cross, Reinhold convalesced in Berlin and again attended university lectures in philosophy and mathematics. By August 1917, however, he was ready for more combat and wrote to his brother: "Physically I am doing well and hope to be released from [the hospital] next week to proceed to an assembly base for reserve troops.... I think I can bear the strains out there and once more wear the steel helmet.... I also have special reasons for getting back there. First, it's necessary for any promotion, and second, there is no tranquility here.... Something special makes my efforts futile.... Something our parents know nothing about" (August 2, 1917).

Two weeks later, Reinhold wrote a twelve-page letter to Georg, still a front-line medical officer, to explain the new disturbance in his life. He felt rejected in love. He wanted to tell all but keep it in perspective:

> With the harsh times that you're going through out there, these small events can't be of great interest to you, so I don't know if I should tell you about experiences that moved me deeply, overwhelming me. Where will you be when this letter arrives?...
>
> I want to tell you about Nurse Priska [Albert]. It's been going on longer than you think, with the magic of her beauty making dreams of youth blossom. I liked her the first minute I saw her. That was November 16 [1916] in the ward for ear treatment. Things did not go any further then, but ... beginning in January she spent long hours next to my bed, late into the evening, and, although she had good medical reasons for it, I had never before known such devoted care.... When I awoke after the second operation in a strange ward and saw a different nurse at my bed, I was very depressed.... I did not see Priska again for a long time.

... Once she told me in the park that she had just one request from me, namely, to give her all photos of herself that I might have. When I asked her why, she said that after I left the hospital, they would all wander into my wastebasket, and she did not want that.... I asked her why she had such a bad opinion of me, she had no reason for that, she could see how serious I was. She said she did not think badly of me at all, but that was the way of the world, out of sight, out of mind, and I would be no different. With emotion she said that would be a great disappointment for her, like so many in life. Sometimes she was very affectionate with me, and every night we parted with such warmth and tenderness that I returned gratified to my room, feeling at peace.

I still can't grasp how everything then turned out so differently.... Avoiding her is all I can do for her now. I am not even bidding her farewell. Dear Georg, writing letters about such things is bad, but now you know how things have gone for me.

When Reinhold was finally back at the front in barbed-wire mud craters with artillery and machine guns rattling, he wrote more letters to Georg and sent more poems to Priska, such as the following:

Love Remembered
My beloved, do you ever recall
Those lovely days and how we laughed,
At endearments sweet and small
And the fear to lose it all.

Hopes and Gloom

During a losing battle in the last year of the war, shrapnel hit Reinhold again, and he lost a lung. In the same hospital he saw Priska again, needing her more desperately than ever, and she agreed to marry him. Photographs taken on a September furlough on an Alpine meadow in Bavaria show Priska as a tall girl with frizzy blond hair above a high forehead and a skeptical smile.

Georg announced late in 1921 that he too had wedding plans. Reinhold and Priska wrote a joint letter: "The time of your engagement is the most beautiful interlude of life with all its expectations and unfulfilled longing" (November 25, 1921). By now, Reinhold and Priska lived in Marburg, Hessen, where Reinhold completed his mathematical education at the university as fast as his health allowed. In the letter just quoted, he asked about plans for Christmas Eve and the holidays: "I would not ask about all that if I were in good shape, but since the state of my health is such that on occasion I could be a bother, I need to be fully informed. My questions are where you have to be, where the parents are, and what we should arrange."

In time, Reinhold recovered enough to pursue a career as mathematician for an insurance company in Berlin. He and Priska had no children but two miscarriages, and relations between them became strained by his gloomy moods, expressed in more poetry, such as the following.

In Despair
My God, why must my spirits droop?
Must my heart beat without fire?
You tore me from my playful group
Condemned me to retire
With those who walk the lonesome path.

Through entire lives they go
Quietly enclosed in gloom.
They miss every springtime sight,
All they sense is doom,
Without desire, with no delight.

Their tears flow in vain,
Their hearts: barren—lonely—cold.
They have no hope, not even doubt.
Their passionate yearnings remain untold,
As their desperate cries echo about.

One can imagine that Priska was not enchanted by these poems and the spirit that provoked them. Reinhold dedicated them to his brother in the 1920s.

Dedication
Save my poems in your heart,
Remember me with love.
Negation is how these poems start,
Negation is their end.
They sought eternal bliss in vain,
And on this earth found only pain.

Faith and Fear on the Ahrenshooper Zeile

Reinhold overcame this anguish by converting to intense evangelical Christianity. Lutheran instruction was a normal part of the curriculum of the Prussian schools that Reinhold had attended, but apart from observing Christian holidays, his parents had practiced no religion. The new zeal of his belief seemed strange, even fanatical, to everyone in the family. He could bring every conversation around to a religious point, quoting Jesus and explaining His message. Priska, although Catholic, could not abide it; and she was further discouraged by the two miscarriages and by strained relations with Rose, her mother-in-law, who found her *wesensfremd*, that is, different and alien in spirit. Priska left Berlin for a nursing job in Freiburg im Breisgau in Baden.

Around 1930, Reinhold's father, Fritz, had a stroke, and in 1934 his mother, Rose, died. The two had lived in a large villa on Ahrenshooper Zeile 35, an elegant street in the wooded Zehlendorf suburb of Berlin. Surrounded by ancient trees, the house was made of white stucco and brick and had handsome glass doors that led to a terrace above a pleasant lawn. To the right of the entrance were the quarters of Fritz and his housekeeper, Putzi Esch, who had served the family for years. Reinhold lived upstairs. The cook, Grete Gesellensetter, had a room in the attic.

A few years ago, I visited that shady street to look for the house and found the garden rather unkempt, with a moldy Ping-Pong table near a stack of rusty bicycles. But the house looked the same as in the photographs that Fred had sent me. One sees Fritz, Reinhold, Georg, and others having coffee and cake under sunlit foliage on the terrace with the great glass doors. In the faces looking at the camera, one sees no trace of the apprehension caused by current Nazi threats.

In the summer of 1935, Jews were assaulted by storm troopers in Berlin—on the Kurfürstendamm, in the Hansa residential district, and on the lakeside beaches of Wannsee. Laws promulgated at the Nuremberg party rally that September kept Christianity irrelevant to the identification of being Jewish. Three or four "Hebraic" grandparents made you Jewish, regardless of baptisms or faith, and Reinhold was henceforth a Jew, not a citizen who could vote or fly the flag. He was harassed with exclusion from theatres, cinemas, restaurants, and sports facilities, first at the discretion of their operators, later by law. He saw Jewish shops defaced with paint and park benches labeled "Forbidden to Jews." Landlords could evict Jewish tenants on any pretext.

At some point after 1935, Reinhold lost his job with the insurance company. After the *Kristallnacht* riots of November 9–10, 1938, all insurance companies were ordered to pay for the damage, and Jews were assessed a billion marks to compensate the companies. Henceforth, visits to theatres, museums, lecture halls, sports facilities and beaches were forbidden by law. All this has already been described in previous chapters.

Reinhold was now in charge of the household at the Ahrenshooper Zeile, and he allowed two other families to move in. One was beautiful cousin Marie Levy and her husband, Richard, a lawyer with a surprising Chaplin-Hitler mustache. Marie was the daughter of Fritz's sister Gertrud Fraenkel. The other family who moved in was Hildegard Hirschwald, her husband, Herbert, and their small sons, Walter and Rudolf. Hildegard was the daughter of Fritz's brother, Walter.

The Hirschwalds emigrated to England in August 1939, leaving their possessions behind. Herbert was of Jewish descent but a devout Christian, a lawyer, and a *Kammergericht* (appeals court) judge. A combat veteran, he had lost an arm in World War I. Abroad, Herbert changed his surname to "Hartwell" and studied theology at Oxford to become a non-conformist clergyman. His first ministry was to German prisoners of war on the Isle of Wight. Until then, Hildegard supported the family as a domestic for a wealthy English family. The couple rarely spoke German with their sons, and after the war, Herbert declined restoration of his appeals court chair in Bonn. Their son Walter (born in 1932) became a non-conformist minister like his father and is a classics teacher near Newcastle. When I telephoned him recently, all he could remember about life as a seven-year-old at the Ahrenshooper Zeile was the dog.

After the *Kristallnacht* pogrom in November 1938, two SS officers came with orders to arrest Fritz, aged eighty. The housekeeper led them to the room where the old man sat in his wheelchair, somewhat confused by another stroke, welcoming them. "Take him, if you think it's the right thing to do," said Putzi Esch. Embarrassed, the SS men left without Fritz.

By this time, Reinhold's brother, Georg, a forensic pathologist like Fritz, had emigrated to New York with his wife Ilse (Marwitz) and their adopted "Aryan" son, Friedrich (Fred) Werner, who has already been introduced in chapter 4. Reinhold's story contrasts starkly with the better luck of his older brother. My sources for Georg's life are Fred's recollections, letters, and two unpublished memoirs typed by Georg in German in 1964 and 1971, when he was seventy-four and eighty-one years old. The earlier diaries on which he based these memoirs are also helpful when legible.

Georg's Memoirs: The Early Years

Both memoirs necessarily begin with childhood and a survey of relatives, trips, and events, especially the great Christmas parties at grandmother Flora Levy Strassmann's home at the Lenné Strasse near the Tiergarten Park. After exchanging presents and feasting on lobster and caviar, all uncles and cousins turned with enthusiasm to the card game Skat.

Throughout his years at the Empress Augusta Gymnasium in the Charlottenburg district of Berlin, Georg was the shortest in stature and the highest in grades—*Primus*

Omnium. As such, he was selected to give patriotic orations on days such as September 2, celebrating the Prussian victory at Sedan in 1870 over Napoleon III. As a medical officer in World War I, Georg's patriotism and piety were undermined, however, when he found "the pastors of all armies praying narrowly for their own weapons' victory.... Still in times of military danger, I kept praying despite all doubts, although Father and his family were entirely unreligious." Georg and Ilse even asked Georg's former military pastor of the Thirty-Sixth Reserve Division to marry them in 1922.

Georg began his medical studies at the University of Berlin in 1908, and after interludes at Tübingen and Heidelberg in southwest Germany, he completed them in August 1913. His courses in gynecology and obstetrics were taught by none other than his father's first cousin, Paul Ferdinand Strassmann. Georg's doctoral dissertation dealt with the degeneration of the cells of killed rabbits and earned him magna cum laude honors. The following winter, 1913–1914, was spent as a "compulsory volunteer" with dragoons stationed in south Berlin. Georg had to jump horses across hurdles while carrying a heavy lance, rifle, and saber.

When war came months later in the summer of 1914, short Georg was issued a new gray-green uniform that was so ill-fitting, he was arrested at a railway station as a possible spy. Sent to Poland with his regiment, Georg and other German military physicians had to treat local civilians, among them many Jews. Later in Galicia, as told above, he was in the same regiment as his brother Reinhold. He helped dress Reinhold's wounds, caused by a grenade explosion, and he arranged transport to better hospitals, first at Stryj, then Breslau, and finally at the Virchow Hospital in Berlin, which was directed by his mother's brother, Moritz Borchardt.

During the last war year, 1918, Georg was assigned to agricultural production in eastern France, a less demanding activity that allowed him time to study forensic medical texts. As soon as the war ended, he began to practice his autopsy skills as a volunteer in the Institute for Legal Medicine directed by his father in Berlin. From there, Fritz arranged a position in Vienna for his son, one that led to a faculty appointment in Breslau three years later. During this period, 1920–1932, Georg produced ninety-five publications about different causes of death and achieved an international reputation.

Resolving to Emigrate

The first two years of Nazi power left Georg and Ilse uncertain about their prospects. Karl Reuter, the director of the Breslau Institute for Legal Medicine, dismissed Georg at once, partly catering to Nazi demands and partly to foster the career of his own son-in-law in the same field. With his status as a decorated combat veteran, however, Georg could still lecture at the university, and he raised his income by performing autopsies elsewhere. He even commissioned a Berlin architect to design a new house. But after the Nuremberg Laws were announced at the Nazi rally of 1935, Georg saw that his German professional career was over and that without emigration, he and Ilse might lose their adopted son, Friedrich. The new house had to be abandoned.

During three weeks in November 1937, Georg used a visitor's visa for travel to the northeastern United States to find American employment. He began with Karl Lehmann, professor of archeology at New York University and grandson of Wolfgang Strassmann of the Berlin City Council. Karl Lehmann was an expert on the Greek island of Samothrace and on its famous Winged Victory statue now in the Louvre. Next for Georg in New York came contact with Dr. Bernard Sacks, an innovative neurologist who was president of the Emergency Committee in Aid of Displaced Foreign Physicians. Especially helpful was

Dr. Thomas Gonzales, also of New York University and the medical examiner of Bellevue Hospital. Others were Paul Klemperer of Mount Sinai Hospital, Alfred Plant of Beth Israel Hospital, and Armand St. George and Abraham Flexner of the Rockefeller Institute, all famous and well-connected. Dinners and luncheons were given in Georg's honor, and he lectured at the New York Dental Academy and at Harvard University. Everywhere he saw collections of specimens and "wonderfully colored micro-photographs," but he concluded that only New York and Newark had "good medical examiner system[s]" for explaining deaths. Thomas Gonzales of NYU and George Baer, New York Mayor Fiorella LaGuardia's physician, were especially determined to find something for him, and soon Georg "had the definite impression that something was being done." For the return trip, he hopefully boarded the SS *Hamburg* on November 24. Also aboard were seventy-five mules.

Back in Germany, Georg and Ilse experienced the same agony and uncertainty as did all refugees in those years. New York University offered Georg an instructorship for one year in the Department of Legal Medicine at a yearly salary of two thousand dollars, insufficient for the US General Consulate in Berlin. After more correspondence and meetings, Karl Lehmann persuaded the university administration to extend the offer to two years. Even that remained insufficient, and the Emergency Committee in Aid of Displaced Foreign Physicians had to guarantee that four thousand dollars would be set aside for Georg. A further affidavit was nevertheless demanded, and a Swiss from Zurich, named Fleischmann, whom Georg had never met, was somehow recruited to give it. Finally, an Argentine cousin, Dietrich Borchardt, a banker who was a friend of the American consul in Hamburg, gave another affidavit and persuaded that consul to call his Berlin colleague to request favorable action. Medical examinations were the last step for getting visas.

Georg, Ilse, and Friedrich (aged nine) sailed from Cuxhaven nearly a year later on October 25, 1938, once again on the SS *Hamburg*. Friends, cousins, uncles, aunts, and other relatives saw them off at the railway stations of Breslau, Berlin, and Hamburg, but only Reinhold and a family maid, Gertrude Jahn, came all the way to Cuxhaven. As Georg wrote later: "Till the ship sailed at noon, Gertrude and Reinhold were standing on the pier. Only now did we realize that we could not go back again."

A New Beginning

In New York that November, Antonie, Karl Lehmann, and an old friend, Erich Hula, were again waiting at the pier. Antonie drove her cousins to a furnished apartment that she had rented and paid for at Waverly Place 146. At an annual rent of $720, however, its cost was too high for a family on an income of $2,000, so the Strassmanns moved again. Georg wrote: "Already on the next day [Saturday] I made my first visit to the institute or better to the Office of the Chief Medical Examiner in New York." Finally, in 1943 Georg was awarded a position at the Metropolitan State Hospital in Waltham, Massachusetts, and the family moved there. With far fewer autopsies to perform—two or three per month, instead of per day—Georg once again had time for research.

During his years under the Nazis, 1933–1937, Georg published only nine papers, and during his five-year transition period, almost none. After joining the Waltham hospital, his creative output resumed, and he published fifty-two works in twenty-seven years. Georg studied human corpses to explain death by drowning, bullet wounds, blunt force, hanging, strangulation, poison gas, electric shock, fire, alcohol abuse, poisoning, abortion, venereal disease, epileptic seizures, embolisms, ulcers, aortic occlusion, and boxing. These were generally analyzed in the context of legal issues and procedures, such as blood typing, determination of paternity, and the judgment of criminal acts committed by patients with senile dementia. Altogether, Georg wrote 167 publications. In the late 1950s, he resumed publishing in German, traveled to meetings there, and received a Federal Order of Merit (*Bundesverdienstkreuz*) from President Lübke.

Georg's memoirs were dedicated to the memory of his brother Reinhold, about whom he actually said very little. But what he did say was invariably admiring and affectionate. Reinhold, he said, was a good soldier, a brilliant mathematician, and a saint at Theresienstadt. If the marriage with Priska did not work out, it was surely the fault of both, a view suiting his mother's impression that Priska did not quite fit into the Berlin scene. Yet the Strassmann house in Massachusetts had no picture of Reinhold on display, and Friedrich (Fred) and Annemarie Keiner Springer tell me that Reinhold was not discussed for years at a time.

Letters Abroad

I have a few of the letters that Reinhold wrote to Georg during 1939–1941. On March 4, 1939, he said:

> When I think one worry has been resolved, a new one crowds in. Father notices little of this, so he's doing relatively well. It is a great consolation to me that Herbert and Hildegard are here. I chat an hour with Hildegard on the balcony every morning … and Herbert often gives me most valued and calm advice. The children have won the affection of all, and so I think everything will in time go smoothly.
>
> … Naturally, everything American now interests Father.… With Herbert and Hildegard I took a beautiful evening walk one day and quoted to them [Schiller's], "Everywhere the world is perfect until humans enter with their agony."[1] Hildegard said that Uncle Walter [her father] had often quoted that.

In a letter of April 1939, Reinhold repeated that father Fritz knew nothing of the perhaps transitory cares that affected them all. The only cares that Reinhold could discuss outright in censored letters were about his own health. His heart, eyes, digestion, and respiratory system all gave him problems; he thought it was "tactful" of these organs to wait their turns in assaulting him. He wore an early type of contact lens but could bear it for only an hour and a half, too short for a round trip to the city center. With his reading glasses, he could recognize street signs only if he covered everything except a vertical slit. They were not good enough for recognizing faces. At other times, heart and abdominal pains exhausted him. He regretted that he was too worn out after an Easter church service of seventy-five minutes to stay for Holy Communion. Nevertheless, the sermon had been splendid. If a church was too crowded, he could last for only half an hour. He thought one could hardly expect that worries would leave him unaffected (April 23, 1939).

Fritz died on January 30, 1940, five months after the war had begun. Reinhold wrote to Georg and Ilse the same day:

> Our dear Father has just fallen asleep and drifted on to a better world. His transition started on the 8th of January and you have therefore received no more letters from me. On the first day, he could no longer use his right hand; two days later his right arm was paralyzed, and even his leg could barely move. Mentally, father was as always on top of things. On the 19th of January his heart grew weaker until he received an injection. From that day on we also had a night nurse.… As long as Father wanted to be read to, Marie [Levy] read to him about Lagerlöf's wild geese.… Your last letter was a great joy for him. We can console ourselves that to the end we did everything to ease his burden. Once he said to me that I

had done all that a son could do for his father. Still, I asked if he had any wish, and he said, yes, but it was one that I could not fulfill. It was his release from this world.... I hoped that our Father in Heaven would surround him with His angels. (January 30, 1940)

In a letter to Georg, Reinhold listed the fifteen people who came to the burial at the large Stahnsdorf forest cemetery on an icy February 3. He wrote that all of them, as well as others who had sent wreaths, had thought of the son in America and his family. The letter continued: "At the end he looked so peaceful and relieved, it almost seemed as if a smile from eternity had transfigured his face.... Let us grant this rest to our dear Father, who is now reunited with Mother, a rest that he earned with his long and varied life, filled with great wisdom, deep love, goodness, and patience" (February 9, 1940).

When Fritz died, all of his property was inherited by Reinhold since brother Georg and his family had emigrated to the United States, and there was no way to transfer funds abroad. Frau Esch and the cook, Grete Gesellensetter, had to be dismissed, but Reinhold kept paying them monthly with funds released with difficulty from blocked accounts. Soon, all Jewish assets, including silverware, were confiscated in accordance with decrees designating Jews, like Communists, as "enemies of the people and the state."[2] Cousin Annemarie and her mother Elisabeth Keiner visited the Ahrenshooper Zeile about every two weeks, and Reinhold recorded those occasions with joy. Annemarie remembers how one day, before its confiscation, Reinhold had spread the family silver out on the dining room table. There were dozens of place settings, including fish forks, decanters, and silver goblets. With a touch of irony, he told her that this was his humble contribution to the war effort. But he had no choice.

Welcome to Work

The enlistment of Germans in the armed forces created a shortage of workers, and some officials saw that forty thousand Jews of working age in Berlin, dismissed from previous employment, could make a contribution. Employment in the post office for the 1940 Christmas rush was rejected by the Gestapo, which favored hard labor, cleaning streets, collecting garbage, digging graves, and working on construction. Reinhold, with all his ailments, was among those drafted for these tasks. He asked Putzi Esch to sew the required yellow Stars of David on his coats. Berlin's shortage of workers was even great enough to have some Jews brought in from other German cities. In July 1941, the number of forced Jewish laborers in Berlin was estimated at twenty-seven thousand.[3]

Throughout this time, Reinhold's correspondence with Georg and Ilse in New York continued. Despite war with France and England and the invasions of Denmark, Norway, Belgium, and the Netherlands, mail could reach the United States by way of Switzerland and Portugal and, including censorship, took six weeks. Nothing ideological or political appears in any letter, or anything more controversial than religious sentiments. The house was valued at 80,300 marks and involved taxes and mortgage payments that Reinhold reported from time to time. He was concerned about Georg's professional career abroad and took a special interest in his nephew Friedrich's progress, adjustment to schools, physical growth, even Easter egg hunts and birthday parties.

In March 1941, Reinhold wrote to Georg and Ilse to expect a reunion that very year with Marie Marwitz, Ilse's mother, as well as with Uncle Julius Levy and Richard and Marie Levy. Affidavits and papers were being processed. As for himself, he was still studying languages, so "let us keep this hope in our hearts and leave things in the hands of our Lord in Heaven, who will lead us in paths that are best for us, giving us reasons for gratitude every morning." But these hopes were futile. The further emigration of Jews was forbidden in September 1941. One day Reinhold heard that Richard and Marie Levy had checked into a friend's clinic and committed suicide there.

Later in 1941, most Jews were evicted from their homes and resettled in barracks. The pretext was that thereby space became available to true German families who had been bombed out. In August 1940, British bomb attacks on Berlin had begun. They were intensified during 1941, but let up in 1942. Jewish furniture was now commandeered by the government and sold to furniture stores. Jewish pets, like Reinhold's dog, were forbidden, confiscated, and killed. The posh Western districts, including Dahlem and Zehlendorf, were "cleansed" of Jews, as was the Tiergarten area in the center.

In all this torment, Reinhold turned ever more to religion. He prayed, read religious books, heard sermons, took Holy Communion, and went to the cemeteries at Stahnsdorf and Friedrichsfelde. His favorite books were the Bible, hymnals, and two books by Otto Riethmüller, *Der König aller Gewalten* (The King of All Powers) and *Des Todes Tod* (The Death of Death). Apart from those, he read a book about Napoleon and tried to translate Hans Christian Andersen's fairy tales. In letters he relived church ceremonies. After a Sunday service before Christmas 1940, he felt as deeply moved as if he had never before heard the story of Bethlehem. The ceremony had shown the agonizing desperation of mankind crying, "O Redeemer, reveal to us the heavens!" Then a great light banished the darkness and overwhelmed shepherds and kings with joy. "They saw the newborn Savior!" Reinhold wrote that he often thought with gratitude about all the undeserved blessings and mercies that he had received from his Heavenly Father and cited Psalm 116: "Gracious is the Lord and righteous; yea, our God is merciful.… What shall I render unto the Lord for all his benefits toward me?"

The last letter to Georg that Reinhold wrote from his own house was dated September 12, 1941, before the Levys' suicides took place. Reinhold was happy to hear that a vacation to Rhode Island had at last been affordable. He relished a reference to Goethe's metaphorical observation that "stepping on curd may spread but not strengthen it." As for himself, he wrote:

> I lay in the garden happy with yellow and multicolored flowers, green foliage was all around, and above a blue and radiant September sky filled my heart with gratitude to our Creator.… I have been in church often, last Sunday a beautiful Holy Communion. I also prayed a long time at the grave of our parents. Wind blew in the treetops and I sensed the eternal peace of God.… "Jesus Christ is the true God and eternal Life." … Many thousands of good wishes and heartfelt greetings from one who thinks of you daily with love,
>
> Reinhold

Deportation

On January 20, 1942, the "Final Solution," Hitler's plan for the total extermination of Jews, was worked out by Adolf Eichmann, Reinhard Heydrich, the Gestapo chief Heinrich Müller, and a dozen others, not far from the Ahrenshooper Zeile at a meeting in a Wannsee mansion. By the following June, Reinhold's name (since 1938, Reinhold "Israel" Strassmann) was on the list to be transported to the concentration camp at Theresienstadt. This camp was designated for Jews with status, possible connections abroad, or war decorations.

A non-Jewish friend of Reinhold was Ernst Keiner, the gymnasium Latin teacher married to Reinhold's cousin Elisabeth, the daughter of his uncle, Walter Strassmann. Ernst sent a telegram to Priska, now living in Freiburg, Baden, that Reinhold was in trouble and needed her. Priska took the next train to Berlin and protested to the authorities that her husband had suffered a head wound and lost a lung in combat in 1915 and 1918 and should not be deported. As his "Aryan" wife, she requested his release. She was effective, and he was not among the twenty-four thousand sent off. So Reinhold stayed in Berlin, but he had to move into a room with his cousin, Konrad Fraenkel (a physician who survived the war and lived to 1957). In the Bayerische Viertel district, bomb-damaged buildings were reserved for Jews, making up a regular ghetto. The remaining thirty-five thousand Jews had to continue with hard labor.

Reinhold's marriage was not restored, however, and Priska returned to Freiburg. An Italian relative, Camilla Faitini, wrote to Reinhold's sister-in-law, Ilse Strassmann, after the war that she had seen Reinhold in Berlin in 1942: "He lived with [Konrad Fraenkel] at Bayrischer Platz. He came often to me. He worked very hard on houses damaged by bombardments. But he never lost his will to live. It was astonishing how he managed to work so hard. One day he was brought away and lived for three weeks in a camp, but then he became free again, because he was not divorced from his wife" (January 11, 1946).

In 1943, Reinhold's name was again on the list for deportation to Theresienstadt on the eleventh transport. This time, having a mixed marriage was of no avail. Goebbels had set himself the target of making Berlin totally *judenfrei* (free of Jews) by the end of March. It is doubtful that Priska could have helped again, but Ernst Keiner said after the war that Reinhold had no longer wanted her help. At fifty years old, he was ready to be part of the exodus. Camilla Faitini, however, thought Priska now refused to intervene because Reinhold no longer wanted to live with her. Camilla's opinion seems puzzling since Priska and Reinhold had already lived separately for years, apparently at her initiative.

The deportation trains left from the Grunewald station a few kilometers across the park from Zehlendorf. About a thousand people were crammed into each train that left for Auschwitz or Theresienstadt, and many trains were needed. Taking Jews to death camps lost no wartime priority.

Theresienstadt

Before its transformation into a concentration camp in 1941, Theresienstadt was a town of 3,700 people, including ten Jewish families. The Austrian emperor, Joseph II, had founded this garrison town in 1780 and named it for his mother, Empress Maria Therese. Behind ramparts, sixteen streets made a grid of thirty housing blocks around a market square.

The Reichssicherheitsamt (security branch) of the SS supervised the camp, using Czechs as guards, but left much of its internal administration—the allocation of work, food, housing, health facilities, and even the designation of deportees—to the Jewish council of elders. As Theresienstadt reached its greatest population of 53,000 in 1942, deportations to the ghettos of Riga, Warsaw, Lodz, Minsk, and Bialystok, or directly to the extermination camps of Treblinka, Madjanek, and Auschwitz, began to take place. Altogether, 88,000 people were deported, while 33,000 died of starvation and epidemics. A crematorium south of town burned almost 200 corpses daily.

About 90,000 of the prisoners came from Czechoslovakia and Austria, and 42,000 came from Germany. Many were prominent, old, or had "special merit" such as World War I military decorations. They were allowed to send out one letter per month. Those who had come with musical instruments and books organized lectures, theatre performances, cabarets, concerts, operas, classes for children, and clandestine religious observances. Of 141,000 people sent to Theresienstadt, only 19,000 survived, including perhaps 1,000 from Berlin.

One of these survivors, Susanne Fraenkel, the wife of another physician related to the Strassmanns, reported to Ernst Keiner that she had seen Reinhold Strassmann, a good Samaritan, give his overcoat and other winter clothing to shivering fellow prisoners. She also stated that Reinhold was sent to Auschwitz in October 1944. Reinhold's aunt, Helene Keiler (née Strassmann), was shipped to Theresienstadt as a seventy-year-old deaf-mute. Her date of death is given as November 19, 1942. For Reinhold, the records merely say, "verschollen—Auschwitz" (disappeared—Auschwitz). The official register of Nazi victims lists Reinhold among seven other Strassmanns (none of them relatives, and only one other from Berlin, Meta Strassmann, née Kraft).[4]

So we know little of Reinhold's last weeks. By July 1944, he had been in a Theresienstadt hospital for a "long time," according to a letter from Gertrud Zuelzer, a friend of his sister-in-law Ilse, who saved that letter all her life. It is not clear to whom the letter was addressed, perhaps to Ilse's sister, another Gertrud, but it mentions the good luck of another friend who had been transferred to the hospital too late to join "the last train transporting people to Poland."

By the summer of 1944, Reinhold surely knew that German armies had again been defeated by the Americans, British, and French in North Africa, Italy, and France and had surrendered to the Russians at Stalingrad. The Fatherland was losing again, and defeat would surely end this barbarism against Jews, Gypsies, and others. All those poems he had once written in dread of death and extinction, the absence of beauty, and pointless injustice were now reality. Reinhold was deported from Theresienstadt to Auschwitz on October 23, 1944.[5]

In the end, Reinhold was one of dozens transported in a sealed freight car, one of hundreds marching from a barracks and stripped naked in a concrete room waiting for Zyklon-B hydrocyanide, one of thousands incinerated that week, and one of millions who in the 1940s were industrially butchered. In 1933, he was probably counted among the 161,000 Jews of Berlin. Twelve years later, he was not among the mere 6,000 who had survived in the city.

Legacies

After 1945, assets taken from murdered Jews were slowly identified and restored to surviving heirs according to elaborate procedures. Reinhold had left everything to Priska, a decision that his brother Georg in Belmont, Massachusetts, questioned. But Ernst Keiner insisted that the inheritance should go to her, and he prevailed.

A letter from Priska to Ernst, dated November 3, 1949, reads:

> Today I approach you with an urgent plea. For straightening out various family affairs, I *urgently* need *official* documents about Reinhold's death. Some time ago you were going to send me a death certificate, but I never received one.… Without too much trouble could you also request a wedding certificate from the appropriate office, or send me their address so I can do so? Many requests at once, but I don't know whom to turn to otherwise since I need these documents so fast and urgently. I hope that I am not causing too much work and that I can some day return the favor.…
>
> Priska Strassmann

Georg did not hear from Priska, his sister-in-law, for another five years until she replied to a letter of his. She mentioned that too much work had drained her of energy, "especially since so many, many years of silence have separated us." She was grateful that he called her attention to possibilities for indemnification as Reinhold's widow. She had already applied, but the authorities had been unresponsive, perhaps deliberately. She was happy to hear that Georg and Ilse were planning a vacation and hoped for good weather. In Germany it had been rainy summer, fall, and winter. "Since we live on hope, one must never become discouraged too soon, however." She also hoped that Georg was happy with his work, but she had no idea what it was and if it resembled research at German universities (December 1, 1954).

Georg answered that letter and described his life and work. Priska answered with further apologies for another delay:

> I was pleased that you and Ilse have a small house but your work seems to be organized according to quite different principles as might be the case here. I hope that you will get used to it and will find joy and satisfaction.
>
> What should I tell you of myself? There is so much to say. After my mother some years ago, shortly before the collapse, became very ill, I came here to care for her. Sadly, we then had to lose her with her strength gone, and all our means and efforts too pitiful to help her. So I remained here and continued the household. I took some part-time work, but now I cannot do it anymore, serving two masters, much as I want to, being older and used up by the hard times and all the misery. Pecuniarily I am not doing splendidly, of course.... Since I live modestly with few demands, the amounts cover my needs. Herr Keiner long ago wrote to me that the pension will surely be raised, but that means waiting, and when it finally comes I will accept it gratefully. (April 11, 1955)

In reply, Georg sent Priska some money, and she answered that pleading for sympathy and begging had not been her aim at all. She did not want to be a burden to anyone. That year she also wrote letters thanking Ernst Keiner for pursuing her restitution claims. Priska thus kept working as a nurse in Freiburg, never married again, and lived to her eighties. All that Georg retained from his younger, taller brother were a few letters, some photographs, those poems, a claim on the Zehlendorf house, and memories.

Fred Strassmann has related to me that his parents, Georg and Ilse, once told him about Reinhold's death without any details and never talked about him again. They believed that an account might be unsettling to someone who showed little interest in the past. Fred had last seen Reinhold when he was nine years old and could remember only that his uncle was rather gruff with children, saying no more than "Tag, Junge" (Greetings, boy). But perhaps, thinks Fred, he himself had been an unfriendly kid. Only in the 1990s did he discover the letters, photos, and poems used in this chapter.

My cousin, Annemarie, last saw Reinhold in Berlin when she was already in her mid-teens, and she remembers the way he brought religion into every conversation. Annemarie and her mother, Elisabeth (Strassmann) Keiner, survived the last years of the war hiding in villages while Ernst kept teaching Latin at the Eckener Gymnasium at Mariendorf in suburban Berlin. "Reinhold was a little strange," Annemarie told me recently. "But a sweet guy."

Chapter 15

Leading a Liberal Resistance Group: Ernst Karl Otto

This chapter is about Ernst Karl Otto Strassmann, the resistance leader who survived two years and eight months in Gestapo and police custody, playing Nazi factions off against one another with charming impudence, conniving to have his deportation orders destroyed, and claiming that Jewish doctor Arnold Strassmann was not his biological father. Ernst Karl Otto (1897–1958) was descended from Schmuhl Molower Strassmann via Heiman's brother Chune, and Chune's third son, Ephraim or Eduard, and that man's son, Arnold. Ephraim, although the least educated, was the most successful merchant of Chune's three sons, according to Heinrich's memoirs. He settled in Raschkow (Raszkow) some sixty kilometers east of Rawitsch. Ephraim's son Arnold (1861–1940) portrayed his father as "a most correct tradesman … a free thinker, skeptical about all religious rituals, but tolerant of divergent philosophies." Ephraim served on the town council in charge of welfare for the poor.[1]

Arnold was a physician (*Sanitätsrat*) and opened a sanitarium at Falkenhagen near Seegefeld, west of Berlin. Ephraim's other son, Hugo, became a lawyer (*Justizrat*) and settled in Berlin. Both were in contact with their cousins descended from Heiman Strassmann. For example, Hugo joined Fritz Strassmann (son of Samuel) in setting up a bowling alley near the Oranienburg Gate. Fritz recommended Arnold's *Allerlei Ostmärkisches* (East Mark Medley of Stories, 1932) as a worthwhile book to his sons, Georg and Reinhold. In his diary, Paul Ferdinand Strassmann occasionally mentioned Arnold as a visitor.

Two Weddings

In 1899, when Arnold was thirty-eight, he married one of his patients, Emilie Ottilie Backhausen. Two years earlier she had married Alfred Hübner, an accountant, with Arnold serving as a witness at that wedding on July 20, 1897. But Hübner abandoned his wife within months, and the two were divorced in 1898. Arnold married Emilie the following year and claimed Ernst Karl Otto, born November 27, 1897, as his biological son. That action was more than a mere adoption; it was a legal change based on a humane prevarication. Writing about himself in the third person, Arnold described his feelings: "This deception inspired in [himself] the highest bliss, a joy in the child that was not his child, but that had become and remained his child, a grateful, loving child. Was he not happier, more enviable than the natural father, who had abandoned him and must remain far away? Was not this the consummation of an eternal justice?"² In 1900, another son, Reinhard, was born. Both boys were brought up as Protestants, although Arnold himself remained inactively Jewish. Emilie Ottilie died in 1920, aged forty-five, when her sons were twenty and twenty-two years old.

Both of Arnold's sons became lawyers. Reinhard (1900–1971) was a patent attorney until September 1933, when, as half-Jewish, he was disbarred from practicing. Arnold then bought him an iron foundry at Schöppenstedt near Braunschweig that he directed until, as a *Mischling* (a person of mixed heritage), he was arrested in November 1944 and became a forced laborer at Blankenburg in the Harz Mountains. The mineral dust and brutality of Blankenburg, a branch of the Buchenwald concentration camp, damaged his health. So after the war, lacking the energy to rebuild it, he sold the foundry and resumed work as a patent attorney as soon as Germany once again had a patent office in 1954. The family moved to Stuttgart in 1959.

Reinhard had married Hildegard Tolzmann (1904–1996) in 1928, and they had four children by 1946: Wolfgang, Gisela, Reinhard Jr., and Monika. Of these, Gisela wrote to me a few years ago that in the 1930s, Nazis had pressured her mother to divorce Reinhard:

> But she didn't want that and thus came to feel the contempt of people [in Schöppenstedt] insofar as they called her "Frau Levi," and I had to suffer at school, continually beaten by the teacher.... What such a war means for a child none can fathom who has not experienced it.... Then American troops came as [part of the Allied] occupation, and ... it took a Jewish officer of German origin to keep us from being evicted from our house.... After I completed my study of foreign languages, I went to Spain [and] ... stayed there seventeen years....
> The brothers Ernst and Reinhard had little in common.... At the very funeral of Ernst Strassmann in 1958, people were amazed that Ernst Strassmann had a brother.... I saw my Uncle Ernst only rarely, even though he was my godfather. (July 14, 2001)

To tell the story of the resistance hero, Ernst Karl Otto Strassmann, we now go back to 1914. Ernst went to the same Friedrichs Gymnasium in central Berlin as the other Strassmanns, but before concluding his studies with an Abitur examination, he patriotically volunteered for the army in October 1914, a month before his seventeenth birthday. He served on the eastern front for two years until he was shot in the abdomen, his fourth wound. While recovering, he resumed his studies in Berlin during 1916–1917; then as a lieutenant he was back in Flanders. In November 1918, he was elected to one of the soldiers' councils managing the retreat. During 1919–1923, he studied law at the universities of Berlin and Breslau, took examinations, and held legal apprenticeships near Hamburg. He became a junior judge (*Hilfsrichter*) at various Berlin courts in 1926 and a regular judge (*Amtsgerichtsrat und Landsgerichtsrat*) in 1930. In official files, his performance was evaluated as follows: "Strassmann is a competent, well-informed judge who ... is praiseworthy in every respect. He reasons clearly. His thorough knowledge and pleasant working style and his cheerful, natural temperament make him an agreeable colleague. His performance is far above average.... The refreshing and agreeable young judge is a healthy and flawless guide" (October 30, 1930).

In July 1927, Ernst married Hella Prestin (1897–1931) from Wismar, whom he had met in Hamburg. When Hella fell ill due to a kidney ailment, her younger sister, Resi Prestin (1910–1981), came to help. After Hella's death in August 1931, Resi stayed to become Ernst's companion and comrade. He married her in 1947 when Resi was still in her thirties and he close to fifty. They had no children. Sharing an interest in art, they assembled an impressive collection of paintings, including works by Edouard Manet, Auguste Renoir,

Arthur Degner, Max Kaus, Ernst Kirchner, Max Liebermann, Adolf Menzel, Emil Nolde, and Max Pechstein, as well as six paintings by Lesser Ury. Five works in the collection were donated to the National Art Gallery in Berlin, and the others were sold to support the Ernst Strassmann Foundation that Resi set up after his death.

Secrets Emerge

In the spring of 1933, Ernst had to state his racial descent, as did all Germans, especially government officials. Now Arnold finally told his son that he was not Ernst's biological father. So Ernst filled out the usual questionnaire on May 17, 1933, stating that "despite careful research, I know of no circumstances that could deny my Aryan descent, since neither my parents nor my grandparents at any time belonged to the Jewish religion."

A year after the Nuremberg Laws were proclaimed, on September 25, 1936, Arnold had to repeat the point in writing: "After the divorce from Hübner, when Mother and I were about to marry, she expressed the understandable wish to blot out even the least connection with Hübner, especially in your interest. To fulfill her wish and to bind you, whom I already loved as my own child, closely and permanently to me, I not only gave you my name but also legally declared you to be my [biological] child.... If after decades I reveal this to you, it is only because of the regulations about ancestry that are now in effect."[3]

Later in 1936, the issue came up again, and Ernst's superior in the court dismissed his earlier affiliations with the Democratic Party in the 1920s as a "recognized error" and stated that [Ernst] "is now successfully making his extraordinary zeal useful for the new Reich, so that his complete integration into the new Reich can hardly be in doubt" (December 1, 1936). Two years later, however, the court's vice president, who was hostile to Ernst, uncovered Arnold's legal claim of 1900 that he was Ernst's biological father. On October 4, 1938, Ernst was now accused of having "seriously compromised his duty by not honestly informing his superiors" of his mixed ancestry. These attacks and the defensive measures of Ernst's friends caused him high tension and physiological symptoms. Ernst took a ten-week leave of absence in the winter of 1939 on medical grounds. Arnold's letter of September 1936 was now used to prevent his removal from the bench. Ernst formally denounced Arnold as his biological father, and blood tests were ordered, which proved inconclusive. On January 16, 1940, the judge in the case decided in Ernst's favor and decreed that after a German victory in the war, Ernst would have to change his name to Hübner. Seventy-eight-year-old Arnold, who was bedridden after an accident, died the next day. Arnold understood Ernst's dilemmas and left three-fifths of the inheritance to him and only two-fifths to Reinhard.

Conspiring for a Democratic Society

In 1919, as a student, Ernst helped found the youth organization of the Deutsche Demokratische Partei (DDP). Jews were prominent in the DDP because it was the successor to the pre-war Liberals and Progressives. Around 90 percent of Jews had supported these two parties. Men such as Hugo Preuss, drafter of the Weimar constitution, Foreign Minister Walter Rathenau, and Theodor Wolff, editor of the *Berliner Tageblatt* newspaper, belonged to the DDP. In 1921, Ernst became chairman of the Brandenburg unit of its youth organization, the DDP-Jugendverband, and a member of its national board. While an apprentice attorney (*Referendar*) at Altona near Hamburg, Ernst worked closely with Hans

Robinsohn in 1924 to found the Klub vom 3. Oktober (Club of October 3), whose mission was to fight against persistent anti-liberal, anti-republican, monarchist authoritarianism in Germany. Robinsohn (1897–1981) was a lawyer, an economist, and the son of a family that operated fashionable Hamburg clothing stores. Ernst became secretary and editor of the Club of October 3. With the economic depression of 1930 and due to consequent ideological polarization, the DDP eventually faded away. One of its former delegates, Heinrich Landahl, even voted to empower the Nazis dictatorially in March 1933 with the law called the *Ermächtigungsgesetz*. As a response, Strassmann, Robinsohn, and Oskar Stark (a journalist) in May 1933 founded a secret anti-Nazi organization, informally designated by Strassmann as a *Widerstandsgruppe*, a resistance group. They began with about twenty members and eventually numbered some three hundred in cells in seventeen cities, with associates in thirty-eight others. The conspiracy is described in Horst Sassin's scholarly *Liberale im Widerstand: Die Robinsohn-Strassmann-Gruppe, 1934–1942*. Sassin worked on a definitive and detailed 546-page study for over a decade, examining all sources and interviewing survivors. The word *Liberale* as a designation, however, has overtones in German that seem politically more conservative than the actual views of Strassmann, Robinsohn, Thomas Dehler, and other group leaders.

Opposing Hitler was harder for left-wing republicans than for more authoritarian groups such as Communists, Catholics, and the military. Unlike the Communists, they had no party structure that could go underground and count on foreign support. The Catholic Church and the army could bargain with the regime but retained independent organizational structures for holding back full support and for starting plots. Social-democratic trade unions, like the transport workers, also had their international affiliates. Nevertheless, the Nazis worried about the liberals' failure to give Hitler salutes and their passive refusal to join the Nazi movement. A 1936 report of the Security Service (SD) of the SS noted: "The significance of liberalism is not in any formal organization but in the posturing of individual carriers of traditional liberal thought."[4] Nevertheless, the prevailing view in postwar decades has been that only people with an illiberal code of thought and behavior like Communists, Catholics, and Prussian soldiers had the nerve to plot an overthrow. Those liberals who schemed with Robinsohn and Strassmann, however, were less concerned with steps to end National Socialism's regime than with organizing what would come afterward.

In February 1948, Ernst Strassmann wrote a two-and-a-half page, single-spaced account about his *Widerstandsgruppe*—its origin, membership, and fate.[5] Here I shall translate and quote its main points:

> The core of the *Widerstandsgruppe* that Dr. Hans Robinsohn and I founded on Whitsunday 1933 were the younger politicians who had come together in 1925 as the "Hamburg Club of October 3." ... This club, which in republican times already had members from all parts of Germany, consisted of younger and active elements from all decidedly republican and progressive parties of those times.... Some fifty members had intellectual and tactical influence on the Center Party, the Christian trade unions, the Social Democratic Party, the free trade unions, as well as the left wing of the German Democratic Party, to which I as chairman, as well as Heinrich Landahl from Hamburg and Dr. Robinsohn, belonged....
>
> The resistance group began by collecting, sorting, and transmitting political material of all types against National Socialism.... After the emigration of Dr. Robinsohn, I, as sole director of the group, in the years 1938 and 1939 saw that the time had come to join other resistance groups and to make contacts abroad.... Because of my personal connection with Dr. Fritz Elsas, the former Berlin mayor later murdered by the National Socialists, I became close to the Goerdeler group, on the one hand, and on the other, with opposition circles in

the Wehrmacht's Abwehr [army counterintelligence unit] led by von Dohnanyi.... Because the resistance group had members from many political camps, it could be important in linking all fundamental and tactical plans of the German resistance movement.... In each of the small subdivisions of our membership, only one person knew of and maintained the connection with me. News was necessarily transmitted to these units only by especially trustworthy colleagues who could travel appropriately....

Aside from its tactical job of being the link between the military and the political opposition, the group was active in bringing splinters of opposition together and in developing opposition units among workers in the armaments industry.... In the event of a political coup, we were ready to take over the electrical power system of Berlin; and we were ready in the armaments industry of Berlin to accomplish important opposing tasks, as we also were in many other German locations, such as Breslau, Stettin, Hamburg, and Munich.

Very early on, the group had its own political program for the first years after the revolutionary downfall of National Socialism. It consisted of detailed proposals for reorganizing political and economic life with principles for the varied composition of the opposition.

Unlike other resistance groups, the Robinsohn-Strassmann *Widerstandsgruppe* kept no paper files or records of telephone lists, schedules, or resolutions, and they communicated via courier, usually unmarried members. Ernst sometimes traveled about under the guise of his hunting and fishing hobbies. His fortieth birthday party was one of the few occasions when some of the leaders had a pretext for meeting one another in the open. As the chances for a coup rose with the Sudeten tensions of the summer of 1938, thirty-five members held a singular meeting in Potsdam. Their aim was to set up a practical, pluralist, and democratic system once a coup led by the army had been achieved. They feared that another autocratic system might follow the Nazis and believed that only a free-market democracy was inherently fair and self-correcting. They fought the cliché that communism was the only alternative to right-wing dictatorship.

The conspirators had a list of measures that a post-Hitler government should enact at once—equal rights for all, an independent judiciary, restitution of property, compensation for injustice, etc. They thought that basing such measures on Christian theology was a step backwards and were appalled by Carl Goerdeler's view that Jews were indeed an alien race who nevertheless should be treated decently. Goerdeler, the conservative mayor of Leipzig from 1930 to 1937, was the leading non-military conspirator against Hitler and the designated post-coup chancellor. The Robinsohn-Strassmann group sought the complete, tolerant reintegration of Jews in society and saw anti-Semitism as "symptomatic of the attitude of the [Nazi] regime toward democracy and liberalism as a whole ... [its] rejection of equality before the law and of humane values."[6] According to Robinsohn in mid-1933: "In fact, the entire [Nazi] restructuring of Germany goes less against socialism than against liberalism. In restricting personal freedom, in opposing parliaments, in economic corporatism, German fascist ideas converge with socialist views."[7]

Robinsohn and Strassmann rejected as naive the wish of some Nazi sympathizers to replace politicians with experts, as if these were good at forestalling and resolving conflicts. It was a losing way of playing into Hitler's hand. As a result, the country no longer had a government of laws (a *Rechtsstaat*). Re-establishing the rule of law was Ernst's overriding priority. In meetings with Brigadier General Hans Oster and Admiral Wilhelm Canaris, both leading military conspirators, Ernst sought as early as 1937 to show them that deposing Hitler was needed to prevent war and that it would be only the beginning of reform. The restoration of legal rights and procedures had to follow at once.[8]

A number of conspirators helped Strassmann to make contacts with other resistance groups among the military (General Ludwig Beck, Brigadier Hans Oster, and Admiral

Wilhelm Canaris), the socialists, the trade unions, the Catholic Church and the Confessing Church, the Kreisau Circle (Kreisauer Kreis, a resistance group made up primarily of aristocrats and gentry), even monarchists, and eventually the French *résistance*.[9] Of these, the military were the most important. Organizing the *Widerstandsgruppe* of former Club of October 3 members and others was completed by 1937, including its choice of leaving violence to others. In the 1937 words of Robinsohn: "Heroic gestures of opposition are now pointless. The fighting courage that such deeds call for had a place before 1933. Open battles were justified then, but by contrast now the prerequisite for all opposition is rigorous avoidance of all grandstanding. Meanwhile, all groups should agree on a basic agenda and be 'islands of integrity in the slimy morass of the Third Reich' [Charakterinseln im Schlammsee des Dritten Reiches]."[10]

After the expected collapse of the dictatorship, a military administration with the participation of the *Widerstandsgruppe* would take over until civilian ministries could be organized with reliable Robinsohn-Strassmann group members in the leading posts. Staffing the administration of provinces, cities, and communities would follow in a second stage. Democratic governance had to be ingrained slowly, step by step, beginning with participatory, politicized decision-making at the local level, the lack of which had allowed the sabotaging of the Weimar system by reactionary and authoritarian men. Such men could not again be allowed to have free rein in the early years of liberal democracy. Freedom called for an education in stages so that people would experience its value and learn to protect it. The appearance of contesting democratic parties would be a sure sign of a healthy new social and legal system.

Waiting for "Day Two"

The forty leaders of the *Widerstandsgruppe* in the mid-1930s were almost entirely middle class. Twelve lawyers, six other independent professionals, nine managerial employees, four teachers, eight public officials dismissed in 1933, and only one blue-collar worker made up the group. Most had belonged to the DDP before 1930, and a few were Freemasons. About 7 percent of the members of the Robinsohn-Strassmann resistance group had Jewish affiliations, although they were assimilated. Some were married to Jews, while others were converted and married to Christians. For example, the former mayor of Berlin, Fritz Elsas, who had been baptized as a child, was descended from Jewish textile entrepreneurs in Stuttgart. He was the group's contact with Carl Goerdeler. Both were killed after the 1944 assassination attempt on Hitler. As the repression grew worse, two Jewish professors in the group from the University of Halle, Ernst Grünfeld and Max Fleischmann, committed suicide. Several others emigrated. Among these were Robert Kauffmann of the Berlin electrical utility, BEWAG, and Hans Robinsohn himself. Kauffmann went to England and Robinsohn to Denmark after the 1938 *Kristallnacht*. Robinsohn was part of the famous overnight exodus to Sweden in October 1943.

Such emigration allowed the group to make contacts abroad in Britain, Denmark, Sweden, Switzerland, and the United States. Since the Strassmann group was not directly plotting an overthrow of the Nazi government, however, the British Secret Service gave no financial support. In Denmark under German occupation, Robinsohn continued to draft lengthy and detailed plans for reorganizing the government—its legal system, economy, finance, and foreign policy. He went into details such as recommending that it would be "absolutely necessary to forbid uniforms," apart from the military and the police. The bad habit of uniforms contradicted the spirit of a democratic civil society. After taking the main role in deposing the Nazis, the army had to be "republicanized" as a militia run by civilians. Nor should there be economic protectionism or inflationary disguising of government spending or price controls. No economic or social group should be left out. Reconciliation with France and Poland had to be at the heart of foreign policy.

As early as 1941, Strassmann told trusted friends that after the war, Hitler and his accomplices should be tried in an ordinary criminal court for murder, not by some special procedure. They did not deserve any treatment that might let them appear to be martyrs.[11]

Only the military could strike the first blow. The generals were indeed conspiring because they did not like the Nazis' demagogic ravings and were pessimistic about the army's prospects in any rash and untimely war. During 1938–1940, the Robinsohn-Strassmann group was ready to enact nationwide reorganization, as outlined above, following any military coup. But Hitler outmaneuvered the generals by gaining a berserk popularity among Germans. By 1941, the *Widerstandsgruppe* leaders concluded that, rather than a coup, only devastating military defeat would ripen the government for collapse. After the Soviet Union and the United States came into the war, that time seemed closer, but in the meantime the republican cells communicated only cautiously with one another, and recruitment of new members faded altogether after Strassmann's arrest. In a deposition of March 1, 1948, Thomas Dehler concluded: "The activity of the resistance group continued after Strassmann's arrest but suffered from lack of central coordination." The strategy was mainly to wait for "day two" after the military collapse.[12]

Caught by the Gestapo

Ernst Strassmann, who served as a judge of civil law in Berlin throughout these years, had long been considered a suspect by the Gestapo, especially after his trips to Copenhagen and London in early 1939. There he had met Nazi opponents in exile and British leaders, such as Harold Nicolson and Robert Vansittart, who were close to Churchill and the British Secret Service. Vansittart was also the chief diplomatic adviser on Germany for the British foreign secretary. Colonel Claude Dansey (1876–1947), a leader of the British Secret Intelligence Service, apparently "knew Strassmann before when he made a good impression … [and reported that] the true spokesman of this wing group is possibly Strassman [sic], who was a colleague of *Leper* [code name for Carl Goerdeler]."[13]

Strassmann planned a trip to Stockholm in the summer of 1942 to contact the British again, but he was arrested on August 19. That morning, at 11:30 AM, Gestapo agents barged into the small hotel at Dömitz on the Elbe where Ernst was on vacation with Resi Prestin. The agents drove him to Berlin and put him in solitary confinement at the Gestapo headquarters at the Prinz Albrecht Strasse. Treatment by the police there consisted of interrogation, thin soup, and two daily slices of bread. Meanwhile, Resi burned a few documents in their Berlin apartment at Sybelstrasse 68, Charlottenburg, and warned friends. None were arrested at this time.

Strassmann had been denounced at Aschaffenburg by someone identified as Theodor N., a young businessman, aged twenty-four, who had made skeptical remarks about Nazi prospects and was now safeguarding himself and his father's factory by being an informer. Specifically, Theodor N. reported that Strassmann had been recruiting a soldier, Fritz Koch, as a courier to the army fighting in Russia. The Gestapo asked both Theodor N. and Koch about names, goals, and tactics before confronting Ernst. Records of the interrogations show that Fritz and Theodor described Ernst as a man of disloyal doubts but not an active plotter. They said that Ernst lacked enthusiasm for National

Socialism, thought Germany would lose the war, and believed that mass executions in the east would make the Allies implacable toward Germans after the war. They declared it was shocking that Ernst had even criticized the Führer's sense of justice. The Gestapo arrest order summarized the case against Ernst: "According to police determination, his behavior endangers the people and the state by integrating in a hostile way political information that his former political friends have provided for a long time, making us highly suspicious that the organization he has established will be misused for high-treasonable aims."[14]

Weeks of Interrogation

After some days at Gestapo headquarters in the Prinz Albrecht Strasse, Ernst was moved to the Polizeipräsidium jail at the Alexanderplatz. There, Felix Bartoll, a Gestapo *Kriminalkommissar*, interrogated Ernst for weeks, beginning in May 1943. Ernst later described him as "a youthful fanatic with a good family background who succumbed to occasional surges of decency. This type was impressed by anyone not flinching, not taking his own case too seriously, and keeping a sense of humor while in danger."[15] The notorious judge, Generalrichter Dr. Manfred Roeder, also interrogated Ernst and sent reports to Walter Huppenkothen, the manager (*Amtsleiter*) of the Reichssicherheitshauptamt, the principal office for national security.

As a former judge with interrogating experience, Ernst knew when to concede the obvious lightheartedly and when to seem uninformed. His group for years had pondered ways of dealing with interrogations. He reminded Bartoll that the Nazi Party had said that the collapse of National Socialism meant chaos, so why was it unreasonable to think of ways of organizing Germany in that case? Someone had to. Ernst told interrogators that his activities were just an information service for the army. When the Gestapo sought to verify this claim, the Army High Command (OKH), specifically, Baron Karl Ludwig von und zu Guttenberg, supported Ernst's claim. Actually, Guttenberg—like Hans Oster and Hans von Dohnanyi—was a member of the resistance circle in military intelligence and was killed after the Stauffenberg assassination attempt in 1944.

Long before that, Ernst's case became part of a jurisdictional conflict between the Gestapo-SS security agency of Reinhard Heydrich, the Sicherheitsdienst, and that of the military Abwehr under Admiral Wilhelm Canaris, an anti-Hitler plotter. For years, Strassmann had helped to recruit trustworthy conspirators for these plotters. Gestapo officials believed that through Strassmann they could learn more about Abwehr machinations. When they gave up on that, Ernst should normally have been shot, but Felix Bartoll forestalled that by ceasing to report on the case and letting files disappear. Suspected associates of Ernst were protected by their Abwehr contacts. His case remained inconclusively "under investigation."

A Forgotten Prisoner

Higher police officials and the Gestapo appeared to have forgotten about Ernst, while the ordinary police, elderly stolid fellows, had to incarcerate him as long as his name was on the roster of pending cases. His disappearance could spell trouble. But they liked him. They let Resi visit often and bring him French books, tomatoes, and even a fur jacket. Of course, she also whispered the news to him. She passed on his demand that nothing be done on his behalf since that could only result in his execution.[16] But friends did send food, including butter, and Ernst was allowed to cook his own meals. Solitary confinement ended when Ernst, with his engaging personality, had gained the trust of his jailers. At first, he was in charge of storing the property of other inmates, but as an experienced judge, he soon became a general adviser, with keys for all cells and even to the outside gate. Nominally accompanied by an old watchman, he could shop in nearby streets and visit his barber. As an interpreter, he also had jurisdiction over conscripted French workers, who considered this a stroke of good luck. At times, the inspector and the prison physician played cards with him.

During the night of November 22, 1943, the Alexanderplatz district, including police headquarters and the jail, were bombed by air. Nearby, the railway station and warehouses burned down. A friend of Strassmann, Wolfgang Stoecker, a decorated military officer, found a female employee of the police station living in Strassmann's apartment at his suggestion because her own home had been destroyed. She described the night of the bombing: "There were more than forty dead and severely wounded. When the first bombs hit, killing and wounding people, Strassmann called out, 'Everyone follow my orders!' and he took over. All the police obeyed him. He advised foreign workers not to flee in the confusion because they would surely be shot when caught. Their help now would count in their favor. His decisive action was so successful ... that police officials proposed to award him the War Service Cross [*Kriegsverdienstkreuz*], Second Class!"[17]

Stoecker's report continues with an attempt to visit Ernst with a book and some Ukrainian sausage to show that his friends remembered him. The female employee arranged for a meeting of Stoecker with the prison director, and Stoecker remembered the following:

The police lieutenant colonel was very friendly but not without suspicion. He told me that Strassmann indeed played a special role in the prison that other prisoners normally could never play. But he did not feel empowered to let him speak to outsiders unless I obtained permission from a Gestapo office on the fifth floor.... There, the employee in civilian clothes proved to be a very helpful person. He looked among folders ... and finally reported that he simply could not understand what might be happening with this case since the main files had been sent off one and a half years ago. He regretted that the accused had to linger under arrest for so long without being processed.... I told him that Strassmann's closest relative, his sister-in-law [Resi Prestin], was in a sanitarium and that I had to take care of her. I wanted to tell Strassmann about her. That persuaded him, and he recorded the reason for my visit as "family affairs."

... I then saw Strassmann in a corner of the lieutenant colonel's quarters on a sofa, where we could whisper privately. When I gave him the book, Strassmann told me that he had no time for reading. He had infinitely too much to do! We talked about half an hour. I told him as much as I knew about our circle of friends. He begged me again not to undertake anything in his case, which must not be touched. I whispered to him that *Reichsgerichtrat* [Hans von] Dohnanyi had been arrested, and we had information that he had been a contact. Strassmann confirmed it.

Besides that, Strassmann looked very pale but not at all sickly or weakened, rather a strong, normal impression.... It was extraordinary that a prisoner under investigation should remain a long time in the jail of the *Polizeipräsidium* without anything happening in his case.... I still did not believe that he would survive, but at least I was encouraged to think he had a good chance.

... When I returned from being a Russian prisoner of war in late 1949, Strassmann told me the amazing story of the [Gestapo] commissar [Felix Bartoll] who interrogated him.... I still can't grasp how it was possible, but he gave that man's son instruction in Latin and helped him with his homework. This commissar then somehow let Strassmann's file disappear in some inexplicable fashion."[18]

A Failed Revolt

Because Ernst Strassmann had been arrested as early as 1942, he was not directly implicated in the plot against Hitler that led to the July 20, 1944, assassination attempt. But the SS general, Ernst Kaltenbrunner (1903–1946), who had taken over the SS Sicherheitsdienst after the assassination of Reinhard Heydrich and who was in charge of vengeance, had his suspicions. On September 15, 1944, he wrote to Hitler: "Further connections of the [Kreisau Circle] consisted of the lawyer GERSDORFF and the *Landgerichtsdirektor* STRASSMANN, of whom LUKASCHEK as well as Count MOLTKE knew that they were working for the Abwehr."[19]

Gestapo records show that seven thousand people were arrested as implicated by the conspiracy, and about five thousand were tortured and killed. At first, Hitler believed that only "a very small clique of ambitious, irresponsible and at the same time senseless and stupid officers" had attempted a coup. They and all their families were to be punished. But soon the SS and the Gestapo reported what they had long suspected—that the conspiracy was quite large and had detailed plans to make Carl Goerdeler chancellor and Field Marshal Erwin von Witzleben head of the army. As early as 1938, the conspirators had doubts about harassing Jews and going to war.

Hitler raged against "this riff-raff from a dead past": "This time I'll fix them. There will be no honorable bullet for … these criminals; they'll hang like common traitors!… The courts will act with lightning speed. The sentences will be carried out within two hours! They must hang at once, without any show of mercy! And the most important thing is that they're given no time for any long speeches.… I want them to be hanged, strung up like butchered cattle."[20] Torture included medieval racks, spikes screwed into fingertips, and a piano wire noose causing a slow death by strangulation. Movies of these proceedings were sent to Hitler at his Supreme Command Headquarters (known as the "Wolf's Lair") in East Prussia.

Investigations, mock trials, and executions continued for months as Anglo-American armies rolled in from the west and the Soviets from the east. When Berlin courts and jails were damaged by bombs, Hitler directed that conspiracy prisoners should be sent first to Buchenwald and then to Flossenbürg in the Palatinate as trials continued. Near the end, in April 1945, he ordered the SS to execute the last suspected conspirators. Men like Admiral Wilhelm Canaris, General Hans Oster, deputy head of the Abwehr, and Dietrich Bonhoeffer, a founding member of the Confessing Church, were thus killed in the last month of the war. On April 23, the SS took charge of the prison in the Lehrterstrasse in Berlin, telling the prisoners that they would be released after a midnight transfer to Gestapo headquarters at the Prinz Albrecht Strasse. Outside in the rain, each was shot in the neck. In the confusion of it all, with chaotic bombing, artillery fire, and Russians marching into the city, Strassmann remained forgotten at the Alexanderplatz.

In the winter months of 1945, Ernst had made himself a cave-like shelter under piles of heating coal in the spacious Alexanderplatz police basement. As the Russians approached, lists were drawn up by the Gestapo for transporting prisoners to executions. Ernst himself or the friendly lieutenant colonel removed the name "Strassmann" again and again. Soon the battle raged in central Berlin, and the police vanished. Ernst hid in his shelter of coal for five days with a food supply stashed away that he had saved from his own rations. On April 21, nine days before Hitler shot himself, Ernst walked away from the jail with signed and stamped discharge papers that a friendly jailer had made for him. Russian artillery and mortar shells burst further away, and machine guns rattled amid smoking ruins. Ernst hid with friends until the shooting ended in Berlin on May 2. Nazi Germany surrendered unconditionally on May 8.[21]

Postwar Recognition

In early June 1945, within a month of the Nazis' surrender, Allied occupation authorities made Ernst a commissioner for administering Berlin and chief director of BEWAG (Berliner Elektrizitätswerke, a.g.), the city's electric utility company, where he had contacts among fellow conspirators, the friends of Robert Kauffmann. Two years later, now married to Resi, and as a Social Democrat and member of the Europa Union, he was appointed deputy chairman for the economic administration of the newly joined British and American occupation zones of West Germany. The Soviet administration of Berlin sought to remove Ernst from BEWAG during the blockade and airlift in 1948, but the Western Allies insisted on his continued service. Soon he was on the board of other political, industrial, and financial organizations. He was sought as a Berlin senator by Mayor Ernst Reuter (1889–1953) and was actively considered as the mayor's successor for West Berlin. It suited his ambitions, but he had to face that his health had suffered too much in captivity to allow that. So Willy Brandt became the next mayor. After a reunion with Hans Robinsohn in 1954, Ernst refounded the Club of October 3 to fight obstinate authoritarian tendencies and the rise of former Nazis in the country's administration. But the new Cold War with the Soviet Union changed German priorities again.

Among members of the *Widerstandsgruppe*, Ernst's career was not the only impressive one after the war. Most were now Social Democrats, not Free Democrats, as one might have expected. The FDP was too conservative for them, although Thomas Dehler of Bamberg did lead this party in Bavaria and became minister of justice in Munich and vice president of the Bundestag in Bonn. At the same time, ex-member Friedrich Wilhelm von Prittwitz led the Christian Social Union in the Bavarian Landtag. Among Social Democrats, Walter Dudek was senator for finance in Hamburg and a member of the Bundesrat in Bonn. Erich Dahnel was permanent secretary (*Staatssekretär*) in the Ministry of the Interior in Lower Saxony. Horst Sassin has outlined the postwar careers of these and twenty-six other leading members of the group.[22]

In 1948, Ernst wrote the previously quoted deposition and concluded: "The *Widerstandsgruppe*, like all other opposition, could not accomplish the great task that it aimed for. But it did its part in the plot of July 20, 1944, the revolt against Hitler, showing the world that spirited opposition existed and giving Germans a model for the way freedom-loving citizens should deal with a dictatorship."[23]

Unlike most Strassmanns, Ernst still saw the country as a place with a future for men with practical ideals, tolerant humor, and courage. Where did he get the stamina to conspire for that future in such danger? No doubt from his father, Arnold, the warm-hearted Jewish physician who married Emilie Ottilie Backhausen. Arnold, in turn, had the values of his father, that freethinker from Rawicz and Raszkow, Ephraim Strassmann, son of Chune. Any name matters no more than a bit of yarn, threading diverse persons and decades together in the quilt of history.

Epilogue: Looking Back

Schmuhl Molower invented the name "Strassmann" and had an optimistic vision, as shown by the sculpture of Promised Land scouts above the door of his Rawicz house. He was a merchant on roads and streets leading somewhere to the east, to Mohilew around 1790, and he thought of himself as a "street man." Whatever Schmuhl's vision was, the Napoleonic wars put an end to it. His sons Heiman and Chune and their wives encouraged their children to leave Rawicz and seek blessings westward in Prussian Berlin. Would they have done so had they foreseen its chaotic destiny marked by further wars and devastating defeats? Five sons and one daughter of Heiman and three sons of Chune did succeed in the newborn German empire. The third generation, born like the empire itself around 1870, did as well but lived to experience turmoil, rejection, and persecution. In old age, they lost their legal rights, their professional standing, their wealth, their homes, and even their lives in suicidal despair or in industrial murder camps like Auschwitz.

In telling the story of one family over two centuries, this book has found recurring themes in medical advances, politics, and persecution. For young Jews living two hundred years ago, the study of medicine was the best opportunity to leave stagnant settings like Rawicz for thriving German towns, especially Berlin. But promoting better health came to be seen as more than treating patients individually. Epidemics had to be fought with public action for clean water supplies, comprehensive sewerage systems, meat inspection, and other measures, hence with politics. Wolfgang and Ferdinand Strassmann were leaders in these battles. Later, in the field of legal medicine, no physician did more to establish forensic pathology than Fritz Strassmann. These three received distinctions such as being named an Honorary Citizen and having a street or a building named after themselves.

In Prussia's series of wars, Strassmanns became commissioned officers and saw combat, but their children were later persecuted because of a pseudo-medical theory that identified "Jewish blood" as a cancer contaminating the German race. More than members of any other occupational group, "Aryan" doctors joined the Nazi Party, and some developed mass extermination methods for killing handicapped children, Gypsies, homosexuals, and Jews.

The life stories told here include some about non-physicians, such as the lawyers Max Gutzwiller and Ernst Strassmann, both of whom opposed National Socialism, openly in one case and surreptitiously in another. There is also Antonie, a performing artist, an adventurous flier, and an international businesswoman who helped many friends to emigrate. She was placed on a Gestapo hit list, even though her patent negotiations may have helped Germany more than America.

Some descendants of Schmuhl Molower Strassmann survived the Nazi regime and its wars, mostly by moving away. Few returned to Germany to see what remained. I am one of those returnees, and I even traveled to Rawicz itself, as I will tell.

Eventual Recognition

One who never planned to emigrate but nevertheless died while away on a summer visit to Switzerland was Paul Ferdinand (1866–1938). At least his body returned home in a coffin. At Antonie's house, Hemlock Hague, on a wooded hill near Peekskill, New York, Grandmother Hedwig Strassmann, told me in the summer of 1949 that Grandfather had always been politically moderate. To her, that meant rather conservative.

> Grandfather even wondered if the family, with its anti-Bismarck feelings, had not overshot the goal. For me, however, Bismarck ruined the German people with militarism and force. Although one could not agree with them, Wilhelm II and Bismarck were human beings. Nazis, however, were criminals. Grandfather could not imagine what evils lay ahead. I resent how they robbed him of his German identity. They changed him from a joyful to a sad man. Gerhart Hauptmann wrote to him in 1936, "God is my witness: I know of no better German than you!" But the Germans with their famous courage proved themselves extreme cowards. With different ancestors and no reason to emigrate, who knows how we would have behaved? Differently, no doubt. But that cowardly? Never.

Upon the request of the Berlin Society for Obstetrics and Gynecology, the Senate of West Berlin in 1984 declared Paul Ferdinand Strassmann's grave in Wannsee to be in the Honored category. Also located on the Strassmann plot are the granite monument to Hellmuth in uniform and a memorial stone for Antonie.

After the war, the Strassmann Clinic building became the East Berlin university school for medical occupations, such as nurses, dietitians, radiologists, and physical therapists. It was named the Jenny Marx Schule für Medizinalfachberufe (Jenny Marx School for Specialized Medical Occupations) after the long-suffering wife of Karl Marx, who had once lived around the corner in the Luisenstrasse. When the Berlin Wall fell and Germany was reunified, Nazi- and Communist-confiscated property was restored to former owners or their heirs. In June 1992, I therefore visited the buildings together with my Swiss cousins, Ruth Sutermeister and Hellmy Gutzwiller, and with our close friend and attorney, Dr. Hans Reis, born a few months before me in 1926 in the Strassmann Clinic. We had not been inside in half a century. We were accompanied by an ultra-dignified white-haired real estate agent and by a flamboyant jewelry-wearing developer from Osnabrück. Both men seemed like characters from a Balzac novel, and we never saw either of them again.

We took the familiar stairs to the first-floor corridor and entered a room painted beige and pastel green like all others. Gone were the carpets, heavy curtains, ornate wallpaper, mahogany and leather furniture, dark paintings, books upon books, and clutters of memorabilia. An official talked about the heritage of this building and said that what Japanese speculators wanted to do with Berlin real estate was outrageous, and we should all remember that. The developer from Osnabrück whispered in my ear that never in his life had he heard anything so imbecilic (*blöde*).

During a tour of the premises, the Osnabrück developer stayed next to me and said that all radiators, plumbing, light fixtures, appliances, windows, and doors would have to be radically removed, even if some were in fair condition, because they were no longer of standard sizes. But the raw structure could be salvaged and had to be, since it was under historical protection. It might be worth some money. I half-listened as we went through the old dining room where great festive dinners had once been celebrated, where the Strassmann stained-glass window with the men bearing grapes from the Promised Land had once glittered. Stains among the rafters at one place indicated a faulty joining of roof slopes, perhaps during the 1914 war when Grandfather had donated the original copper roof to the war effort. The Osnabrück developer pointed out such flaws and made calculations of rents per square meter and costs per cubic meter.

Many rooms had a quality never previously found at Schumannstrasse 18: shabbiness. I saw cluttered bulletin boards and graffiti, with jokes about tension between East and West Germans, *Ossis, Wessis*, and even Prussians. A pastel room that once had been my grandfather's consulting room now had a soft-drink dispensing machine. A modest room in one upper story was the former delivery room, with a floor of hexagonal tiles designed for drainage of water and blood. Hans, Fred, my sisters, and I, as well as fifteen thousand other babies were born in this very room.

On some anniversaries of Paul Ferdinand's birth or death, tributes are spoken and published nowadays, and delegations of physicians formally pass by the historically protected Schumannstrasse 18, redeveloped as administrative offices, but still under landmark protection. On May 6, 1998, I accompanied a group and heard Professor G. Dellas, the organizer, praise a few of Grandfather's innovations and deplore that, apart from Ferdinand Sauerbruch, no one had stood up for him in 1936. Five months later, I heard Dr. Matthias David of the Charité give a lecture, using slides, in honor of Paul Strassmann. With respect to Paul's successful adaptation of a fallopian tube for a dysfunctional uterus in the mid-1930s, he said, "This operation and its result [a baby] showed how Strassmann's ability in female genital surgery towered above others."[1]

Shortly afterwards, the buildings of the former clinic were returned to the Strassmann heirs. In September 2003, the historical authorities of reunited Berlin designated Schumannstrasse 18 as the Strassmann Haus and had a bronze memorial plaque, 50 by 70 centimeters, affixed below Sandor Jaray's relief sculpture of a mother and her nursing baby. Noting Paul's achievements in medicine and the arts, the plaque gives his birth and death dates, as well as the building's date of construction. About Paul, the text states that "because of his Jewish descent, he was robbed of his academic credentials in 1935 and was forced by National Socialists to close and sell the clinic in 1936."

No Plans to Return

Like many exiles, Antonie never had plans to revisit Germany. As early as June 11, 1946, the airplane manufacturer, Ernst Heinkel, wrote to her: "Your friends urgently hope that you'll come to Germany for a few months.... In your letter I discern a certain bitterness toward your former country." Antonie did not answer until December 19, and in capital letters she told him about the attempt in 1938 to abduct her, which had possibly been instigated by a frustrated rival pilot, Thea Rasche, who denounced Antonie. "HAD THEY NOT GOOFED, I'D NO LONGER EXIST! BUT BITTER—NOT PERSONALLY!" In a later letter she elaborated:

> With respect to coming over there, dear Ernst, I have neither the intention nor any reason to do so, and, what is the main point, no longing for Germany or Europe. As much as I'd like to see this or that dear friend, I have no urge to see the grim destruction that Hitler and his buddies have wreaked in Germany and Europe within people and their culture as much as externally among buildings....

I finished with Europe when I came here. What roots I might have retained from the past were shattered by the Nazis—with the agreement of the entire population—and befouled. I disown all that....

Please let me know if you and your family need anything and *what*.

Hugo Eckener, the celebrated Zeppelin captain and director of the Zeppelin factory, also wrote Antonie a year after the German capitulation. In her reply of July 22, 1946, she reminisced with joy and summed up her years since then:

My dear, dear Dr. Eckener:
I cannot express the incredible deep joy your beautiful letter brought me. It speaks for your total personality—unchanged despite all. How infinitely difficult these last years must have been especially for you, who saw the entire catastrophe coming—and you still see the future far more clearly than others. The fate of Cassandra has never been enviable....

How often I have quoted you here playing Skat—my Mother reminds me not to keep that from you in this letter—a bit silly, but maybe a dear proof of how you have lived with us all these years.... You once asked if I had a humanistic education—because that shapes one's thinking throughout life!...

That swine [Hitler] and his comrades could not rob us of all [those memories]—and those of us whom he threw out (and who survived) are best off....

The first bits of news are coming from abroad. Mother is happy that Father's clinic astonishingly survived unharmed. It was his life's work, and he survives in that even if the Nazis more or less stole it from him in 1936.

Three years later, Antonie told the Hearst *American Weekly* magazine, dated April 24, 1949: "Europe is a worn-out civilization, trying to hang on to what it has. The United States holds the key to the future." But two years later, on August 14, 1951, Antonie wrote to Ernst Heinkel that she might come after all: "Ernst—next summer it will have been twenty years—the excitement of Warnemünde—the Do-X flight—what fun we had at your hospitable place! And the bonds of friendship have endured through dark and stormy years!" Regrettably, Antonie died five months later. Over fifty years later, in the summer of 2004, an exhibit in Friedrichshafen, "The Sisters of Icarus—Flying Women," featured the aerial exploits of Antonie among others.

A Reconciliation

On April 10, 1965, my father, Erwin Strassmann, received the Great Service Cross (*Grosses Verdienstkreuz*) of the Federal Republic of Germany. The medal and a document signed by President Heinrich Lübke recognized Erwin's help in re-establishing good German-American relations after World War II.

No longer "enemy aliens" but now US citizens, in 1945 Erwin and his family were allowed to travel again within the United States. They first sought mountains and chilly non-Texas air in Cuernavaca, Mexico, Taos, New Mexico, and Estes Park, Colorado. For six postwar years, Europe seemed too poor and shattered to visit. During the first trip back, on July 20, 1951, Erwin wrote to me in Washington from Wengen in the Bernese Oberland: "Our trip is most delightful. We expected Paris and Switzerland to be the highlights. As it turned out, Germany, with all the *Wiedersehen* and celebrations, outshone them all. The human angle proved to beat scenery, luxury, and history all along the line. You have no idea how these people outdid themselves to make us feel good. We'll tell you all about it in Peekskill [at a forthcoming reunion with Antonie]."

Epilogue: Looking Back

That year, German cities were still fields littered with bombed rubble, but the countryside, with its half-timbered villages, were a summer garden. Near Bad Nauheim, at the village of Ziegenberg, they hiked with Ilse's brother Gerhard past the detonated ruins of the Adlerhorst (Eagle's Eyrie), Hitler's western headquarters for the Battle of France. Golf courses were still reserved for British and American officers. Acquaintances in a few places were single mothers with children fathered by Americans. For everyone, the politics of the past was a topic to be avoided.

Several people asked about emigrating to America, and everyone reminisced. It had been fifteen years. In Berlin, Erwin and Ilse saw former staff of the Strassmann Clinic—doctors, nurses, secretaries, and maids. Some old friends and former personnel of the clinic marveled at Erwin's current resemblance to his own father, who had reached fifty-six in 1922. Among others, Paul Meyer, a former chief of staff at the clinic in the early 1920s, made that observation. The city was in ruins, but a surprising number of friends had somehow survived. At the Kurfürstendamm, Kempinski's was again serving twelve types of lobster.

One of Ilse's Bremen first cousins, Rolf Schwarze (1906–1977), seemed especially agreeable. Ilse remembered that in August 1937, when she and the children left for America, Rolf, aged thirty-one and an ambitious young SS man, had not bid her farewell. He was busy organizing a festival for over a hundred thousand participants, a *Gebietsaufmarsch* of the Hitler Youth with fighting games, the Nordsee-Kampfspiele, to be staged in the Weserstadion stadium. Military bands had to rehearse, and streets had to be decorated with garlands and a myriad of swastikas. After a parade, two thousand new flags were to be consecrated to Adolf Hitler. At age twenty-four, Rolf had joined the Nazi Party in August 1930, believing its apparently egalitarian doctrines. In May 1933, after Hitler had taken power, Rolf shifted to its most aggressive branch, the SS.

Rolf ignored the fate of his cousin Ilse and her family, which cannot be said of others in the Schwarze family. As late as October 27, 1940, Rolf's father, Otto (1873–1942), wrote to Ilse by airmail via Portugal a letter that was opened by army censors: "The next generation is more or less involved in the war. One keeps asking oneself, was that necessary, how could it have been avoided?.... I especially enjoyed Erwin's letter, and I congratulate him warmly for his great success.... He will put up with disagreeable occurrences easily, knowing that everywhere his judgment will be respected and listened to. We were all convinced that he would eventually make his way ... but none dared to hope for such speed." The following two pages or so about Rolf represent him as one of countless millions of Germans who collaborated readily with the Nazi regime. A book like this would be incomplete without one.

During the war, Rolf was not in the military because he had lost an eye as a child from an air rifle shot, when playing soldiers. While two other cousins, Karl Theodor and Helmuth, were off in combat, Rolf managed the family grain trading business. With the Atlantic blockaded, he shifted the source of grain imports to the (temporarily) allied Soviet Union, to the subordinated parts of Poland, and to Hungary, not only for the Schwarze firm, but for all Germany as the chief official in charge of requisitioning grain via the Reichsnährstand für Getreide (National Grain Agency) in the Ministerium für Ernährung und Landwirtschaft (Ministry of Nutrition and Agriculture). To support the German army later in Russia, so much grain had to be confiscated that, according to an official planning document, "without doubt, millions will starve to death."[2]

Files of the official German archives, the Bundesarchiv, show that membership in the SS was not central to Rolf's ambitions: he never advanced beyond the lowest rank, *SS Mann*. On March 1, 1944, a year before the war ended, he left the organization "auf eigenem Antrag aus beruflichen Gründen" (on his own initiative for occupational reasons),

SS records show. Rolf did not serve full-time, was never promoted, and earned no awards in the organization.

As combat ended in 1945, the Allies began a "denazification" program, removing Nazi symbols, monuments, street names, and laws in Germany, while excluding Nazis from public life and interning the leaders. Excluded from influential positions were to be all those who had held high positions before the surrender, as well as people in a variety of other categories, including all members of the SS, regardless of rank, in accordance with an Arrest Categories Handbook, a special edition of a Public Safety Manual of Procedures, first issued by the Allies in September 1944. The highest leaders and worst war criminals were in time tried and punished by the International Military Tribunal, while other adult Germans had to submit questionnaires and be put in five categories.

The most serious was Category I, the "guiltiest" (*Hauptschuldig*). People in Category II, the "burdened" (*Belastet*), were not direct torturers and murderers but leading organizers, opportunists, and profiteers (*Aktivisten, Nutzniesser*), also called "desk perpetrators." Some family members told me that they had expected Rolf to be in that category. Less serious were Categories III and IV, "minor offenders" (*Minderbelastete*) and "fellow travelers" (*Mitläufer*). The "exonerated" (*Entlastete*) were in Category V. Of the four hundred thousand in the Bremen region who filled out denazification questionnaires, so few were "guiltiest" or "burdened" that they made up less than a tenth of one percent. A mere nine were *Hauptschuldig* (guiltiest), and only 124 were *Belastet* (burdened). The name Rolf Schwarze was not among them.

Hiding in his Steinbeck hunting lodge, Rolf was one of an estimated one hundred thousand "submerged" Nazi fugitives who evaded the most menacing phases of denazification. According to Bremen police records, Rolf and his family were owners of a house requisitioned by Americans in 1945, but his mother-in-law, Friederike Minna Klepper, was allowed to keep a few rooms. Rolf's family did not have a Bremen address until June 8, 1949. During his years in hiding at the lodge, Rolf remained nominally the director (*Geschäftsführer*) of the Schwarze firm, while a trusted employee, Herr Thiel, had power of attorney to sign contracts reorienting the grain and feed importing business back to its former transatlantic sources.

Years went by before the cousins, Karl Theodor and Helmuth, who were also at the July 1951 reunion with Erwin and Ilse, returned from prisoner-of-war camps to participate in the firm's management. Helmuth and his family of four were allotted only one room in a house with no bathroom on that floor. To British occupation zone investigators, Rolf claimed to be under American jurisdiction, but he never registered in Bremen during his secret visits to the port. He stayed in a room with his mother-in-law, sometimes sharing it with other men, clandestine workers like himself. Even in hiding, he still ran the Schwarze firm autocratically.

Eventually, Rolf was arrested, interrogated, and made to fill out the denazification questionnaire. He was imprisoned for a number of days, perhaps weeks, but by now anti-Nazi prosecution had lost its momentum. The German hearing boards (*Spruchkammern*) that were in charge of the denazification process no longer invoked the *Nutzniesser* (opportunist) charge to put anyone in Category II, *Belastet* (burdened). The boards now saw their task as rehabilitating the accused as quickly as possible. Thus, Rolf had no trouble dealing with the charges. He believed that his denouncer was someone in Steinbeck.

Nevertheless, in 1951 Rolf saw that his Nazi past had become a liability, and at the reunion, he asked Erwin's advice: "Germany now is an unsafe place. For the sake of the children, should Leni and I consider emigrating?" He was ambitious for his toddling, fourteen-month-old son, dressed up cute for the party. "Desert your country now? With what cause?" said Erwin. "Maybe not. Just a platonic idea," replied Rolf. In the 1950s, Rolf was again the country's leading feed and grain trader by volume and president of both the Bremen and the Federal Chambers of Grain and Feed Traders. Nevertheless, he was still not a member of the inner circle of Bremen's Hanseatic patrician elite, the *Haus Seefahrt*.

In 1974, the Schwarze firm went bankrupt, losing millions. What hurt was the failure of the Peruvian anchoveta catch and US concern for rising feed prices, which led to a partial American embargo on exports of soybeans and soymeal. World prices quintupled. The Schwarze firm had "sold short," meaning contracts were sold at about one-fourth of the market price. The bankruptcy court forced Rolf to give up his mansion in a private park, the dairy farm, the pigsties, and the Rennberg animal feed subsidiary, as well as warehouses, buildings, and office equipment. Nearly fifty people lost their jobs. Since Rolf's sisters, children, cousins, and other relatives were all partners with unlimited liability, in the Hanseatic tradition, they all lost much property and income. For Rolf, the bankruptcy was more humiliating than his Nazi past and ruined his health, so that he died within three years.

A Historian's Anguished Perspective

The historian Gerhard Strassmann Masur, a son of Paul Ferdinand's sister Frieda, did not return to Berlin for nearly twenty years, ten years after the Nazis' surrender. After twelve years in Colombia, he found a teaching position in 1947 at Sweet Briar College in Virginia and resumed contact with colleagues in Germany, especially with his mentor, Professor Friedrich Meinecke. In 1955 and 1956, Gerhard had his first invitations to lecture at the Free University in West Berlin and found students receptive to his views. At the same time, "the destruction of Berlin was so enormous, especially in the Communist sector, that nostalgia could not arise." The city resembled his hometown as little, he said, as Mexico City looked like the Tenochtitlan of Moctezuma. Nevertheless, he kept returning.

By 1959, his definitive biography, *Simon Bolivar* (originally published in 1948), had been published in German, and his next book, *Prophets of Yesterday* (1961), was in press. In the mid-1960s, he began *Imperial Berlin*, a major history of his hometown between 1870 and 1920. Masur's long-time friend, Wilmont Haacke, described the book as the attempt of a passionate Berliner to free himself from nostalgia for old times in the city. "Never before," wrote Haacke, "has the universality and urbanity of the old Berlin been portrayed with so much love and understanding."[3]

Gerhard's next-to-last publication was an edited version of his grandfather (my great-grandfather) Heinrich's memoirs of Rawicz and that emigration. In the introduction, Gerhard wrote:

> Today we know all too well that the experiment of German-Jewish symbiosis failed. Should one therefore say that the attempt to assimilate was misguided?... The process of assimilation has so far not been studied enough, nor has the reason for its ultimate failure. We have biographies of a few of the best-known Jewish men and women, Rahel Lewin, F. J. Stahl, Lassalle, Bleichröder, and others; but the great mass of Jewish men and women who were involved in the assimilation process have remained anonymous....
>
> The memoirs of Heinrich Strassmann may allow this complex development to be understood better. By 1871, his concluding year, ... the virus of anti-Semitism was no more than an undercurrent, if anything, and the Prussian state and society not only did not hinder the rise of Jewish citizens, but actually promoted and welcomed it. What caused

the change in direction toward full rejection of Jews by the German people remains an unexplored chapter of history.[4]

Although offered a permanent professorship at the Free University of Berlin and at Tübingen, Gerhard limited himself to sporadic contracts, feeling that "I could not live in a country where people cannot face themselves without lying.... The moat of blood surrounding Germany since 1933 was too broad and too deep to jump across, and it would also be the peak of ingratitude to slough off American generosity and help as if it were a snakeskin." At the end of his autobiography, he wrote that he had nowhere felt part of a community, that his fate was the "inability to use the word, 'we,' not in Germany, not in Colombia, not even in America."[5] With irony, he closed his last lecture on German character at Braunschweig on October 5, 1974, as a historical problem, saying, "So, let's let it go at that, noting oddities in German history, and let us leave it to the prophets to proclaim that whatever happened had to happen the way it happened."[6]

A Brother Remembered

In August 1936, seventeen years after emigrating, Georg and Ilse traveled back to Berlin. They had emigrated because teaching at Breslau University and practicing legal medicine were forbidden to Georg in 1935 and because they feared that their adopted and inalterably "Aryan" son, Friedrich, might be taken from them. As told in chapter 14, Georg began work as a pathologist at the Bellevue Hospital in Manhattan and had a faculty appointment in the Department of Forensic Medicine of New York University in November 1938. After five years, he transferred to the Metropolitan State Hospital in Waltham, Massachusetts. Not until the mid-1950s did Georg and Ilse feel like revisiting Berlin.

In an account of his trip, Georg wrote:

> In the evening we were together with my cousin, Dr. Konrad Fraenkel, who is living in an apartment house in Wilmersdorf. There are still many buildings destroyed in the neighborhood, and the empty windows make a desperate impression.... To see him, who had survived the Nazi time, again was very moving for me. We were both moved very much, especially since he told me so much about the last months when he lived together in a bombed-out and destroyed apartment with my brother before Reinhold was taken away by the Nazis, first to Theresienstadt, and then to Auschwitz, where he perished with millions of other victims of the Nazi terror.

The next day, Georg met the widow of a close friend whose son had been killed at Stalingrad. Both encounters were so upsetting that they brought on acute intestinal symptoms, and a tour of Communist East Berlin had to be canceled. Georg felt better only after reaching Switzerland.

Georg later returned to Germany for lectures and for professional meetings on legal medicine. In 1966, he received a medal, the Federal Order of Merit (*Bundesverdienstkreuz, Erste Klasse*), from President Lübke "as an outstanding scholar [who] for decades has contributed to the worldwide reputation of German legal medicine." He became an honorary member of the German Society for Legal and Social Medicine (Deutsche Gesellschaft für gerichtliche und soziale Medizin). His father, Fritz, had founded that society in 1904, and a hundred years later its base at Berlin's Humboldt University and Free University was renamed the Fritz Strassmann Institut. Prizes in his honor are now awarded annually for major contributions in the field.

Discovering a Second Family

Time and again, Georg and Ilse asked their adopted son Friedrich, now a young adult known as "Fred," to join them on trips to Europe or to travel there on his own, but he always declined. Finally, in 1996, as a grandfather, Fred flew to Frankfurt to meet a sister and three brothers for the first time.

Fred's mother, Ilse Marwitz Strassmann, had long agonized about revealing his adoption. In August 1977, she drafted a letter that she kept secret for years. It read:

> Uncle Paul informed us that a child would be born in his clinic. The mother—whose name, by the way, was Ilse, too—was quite young and unmarried. Her father, a high German official of an old Silesian aristocratic family, insisted that the child be given in adoption into a good, cultured family.... We were happy and willing to adopt this child if it was a healthy one. Uncle Paul informed us about your birth, that you were a beautiful baby.
>
> The biological mother, who had lived under a false name in Berlin for the last months, stayed for three weeks in the clinic. She never saw her lovely baby. After she left, we went to Berlin to see you and fell right away deeply in love with you. You were the darling of the nurses. After barely three months, the adoption papers were accepted.... Your father and I brought you home to Breslau. It was an exhilarating experience and one of the most beautiful moments of our life.
>
> When you were three and a half years old, the Hitler regime came to power. You may have guessed about our background. Opa [Georg] and I are both in Hitler's terminology so-called "non-Aryans," while you are of course completely "Aryan." ... So you can imagine the agony we suffered until we were able to emigrate. If we would have told you during this time about the adoption, you might have spoken about it to other people in a childlike way. We had to keep it a secret as long as possible.
>
> ... So the years went by, and we almost had forgotten about the adoption.... When once in a while I thought about it and asked Opa if we should not tell you, he definitely refused that you should know. But now, at the end of my life, I feel an obligation that you should know about your background.... We have never met or talked with your biological family. It was their wish and a gentleman's agreement that we would never mention their names. Your biological father also belonged to an old German aristocratic family. I have almost forgotten their names.
>
> My beloved son, I hope you have read this in the right spirit with understanding and forgiveness. We were greatly blessed to have had you as our son, who was always loving, kind, and a great comfort and joy to us. We could not have asked for a better son. God bless you, my darling.... Your Mother

Not until April 25, 1981, did Ilse give that handwritten letter and a newer typed one to Fred, now fifty-two years old. She reminded him that if a new branch is grafted on to an old tree, the whole plant is called an apple or peach tree without analyzing the different branches. "So it is with families. You can be proud of both your families, but you are truly one of us. Don't insist on asking more because it is against the agreement and does not help in any way."

After reading the letter, according to Ilse, Fred went into her room, hugged her, and said affectionately, "Don't worry about anything. It doesn't matter. Everything is the same." Ilse wrote to a nephew the next day that she felt relieved, freed of doubts that had tortured her for years.

My grandfather, Paul Ferdinand Strassmann, was probably approached for help with the out-of-wedlock pregnancy by those Silesian nobles because of his friendship with the Schönaich-Carolath family, including the Kaiser's last wife, Hermine, who knew the young parents. So the pregnant girl lived in Berlin for three months under an assumed name, including three weeks in the Strassmann Clinic without ever seeing her baby. In Berlin's records of births, the mother's name is correctly indicated and that of a father is lacking. Indeed, Fred's parents were married in 1930 in proper military-aristocratic fashion, a year after secretly giving him up for adoption.

The father and one uncle were lawyers, while another uncle rose to be a celebrated colonel, who on March 21, 1943, tried to blow himself up together with Hitler, Göring, Himmler, and their entourage at the Berlin Armory (*Zeughaus*). In this well-known incident, the Führer unexpectedly cut short an inspection of captured Russian equipment, and the colonel had to rush to the toilets to defuse the plastic bombs in his overcoat. Fred's natural parents had four more children, full siblings of Fred, all still living in 1995, as was an aunt, his natural father's sister. In that year, Fred's son, Franz, began research into his ancestry because he sought German citizenship, in part to join the German baseball team for the 1996 Atlanta Olympic Games.

Fred not only resembled his father and brothers but also the resistance hero, as portrayed in the book of peerage, the *Genealogisches Handbuch der Freiherrlichen Häuser* (1994). On July 8, 1996, after meeting Franz, a newfound sister wrote to Fred: "At first I was speechless, but very soon the first 'shock' changed into a boundless gratitude that this wonder may have happened: the wonder that means that we had the chance to hear of your existence. The greatest wish we have is to become acquainted with you, although we can imagine that it might be an important decision for you whether you will meet us or not."

Two months later, Fred traveled to Frankfurt and all over Germany, meeting his aunt, his siblings, and their families. By now, all their houses displayed photographs of young Fred, among other family pictures, which Franz had supplied. At one dinner, the senior brother raised his glass in a toast: "Dear Fred! We welcome you to our family, which is also your family. We also greet Franz, who has earned great merit for doing the necessary research and making the first contacts. We belong to one family, although you carry the name Strassmann, which is well-known in Germany—and not just here.... These different names shall make no difference to the way our family belongs together. My sister and brothers hope to see you often in our homes. We raise our glasses to the well being of Fred and Franz Strassmann."

Fred wrote to me in December 1996, and I thank him for letting me quote from this and other letters: "It still feels strange to think that I have three brothers and a sister, after being an only child for such a long time. Their acceptance of me was very touching.... Still I feel lucky to have had Georg and Ilse as parents and to have grown up in America. I was lucky to have missed the whole Hitler Youth thing."

Since then, Fred has visited his relatives in Germany almost every summer, and they have visited him in New England. On a tour promoting the German version of this book, I had the pleasure of meeting ten of them myself in 2006.

Surviving to Rebuild: Ernst Karl Otto

Within Germany, Ernst Karl Otto Strassmann's return was the opposite of Rolf Schwarze's—not from Nazi elitist to fugitive, but from Nazi victim to manager of major public and private enterprises. Ernst's geographic return went from the Alexanderplatz jail cell back to his Wilmersdorf, Berlin, apartment. After two and a half years in Gestapo captivity, at age forty-eight, he stayed in the city to help restore Germany to civilization. He declined cabinet offers from the Soviet occupation zone authorities, but in 1945 he agreed to serve on Western economic commissions and boards, above all as director of economic planning of BEWAG, the electric power utility of Berlin. Mayor Reuter asked him to become a Berlin senator, but Ernst declined because of failing health. On his sixtieth birthday, on November 27, 1957, the newspaper, *Berliner Morgenpost*, reported:

> Electric power failures are still common in the Soviet zone, while every inhabitant of West Berlin takes flawless delivery of power for granted. That is not just a function of the German *Wirtschaftswunder*, but the work of BEWAG's leading men.... Its commercial director, Dr. jur. Ernst Strassmann, is sixty years old today.... Baptized with water from the Spree, he comes from an old Berlin family that has produced several representatives in science and public life.... Since 1945, he has proven at BEWAG that organized opposition to and imprisonment by the [Nazi] regime did not break his energy or cheerful sense of duty. His co-workers both feared and treasured his well-aimed comments in Berlin slang, like his critical "Dett soll sich wohl von alleene in' Teppich treten?" (Will that get mushed into the carpet by itself?) for anything neglected.

Ernst had held his own in many a fight but lost against cancer. He died three months after that sixtieth birthday, on March 11, 1958. At the funeral eulogies were read by Willy Brandt, the mayor of Berlin and later chancellor of Germany, by two BEWAG executives, and by his former co-conspirator, Hans Robinsohn, who said:

> In the nearly four decades of our close friendship, I have seen Ernst Strassmann in all conceivable moods—cheerful and relaxed, worried, angry, even furious. But I never saw him lose control, and I always admired that as a sign of his inner strength.... Since he was hard on himself, he shied away from no conflict when great and important things were at stake. His goal was to emerge from such conflicts clean and upright, and with his last breath he could still say that he had never been a fellow traveler, had never avoided trouble for the sake of comfort or cowardice, had never taken advantage, had never compromised his inner dignity.... He had a most rare, almost brilliant talent for friendship. That came from his humane understanding of others—no matter how different in personality—a warm heartfelt sympathy combined with critical realism.... His great, unshakable sense of humor was his bond to everyone.[7]

Wide recognition of Ernst's secret masterminding of the *Widerstandsgruppe* was slow in coming because the group had kept no records and left the initial overthrow to more authoritarian groups, especially the military, who failed to deliver. Ernst wanted to be ready on "Day Two" with a liberal plan of action. Horst Sassin's research has revived his reputation, and the activities of the Robinsohn-Strassmann group are now featured in books such as *the Encyclopedia of German Resistance to the Nazi Movement*.[8]

After Ernst's wife Resi died in 1981, an Ernst-Strassmann-Stiftung was set up within the Friedrich-Ebert-Stiftung, the foundation honoring the first president of the Weimar Republic, a Social Democrat. The Ernst-Strassmann-Stiftung has provided for scholarships in art, music, and social research that "would consolidate German constitutional democracy in view of the painful historical record." Its first social theme in 1982 centered on proposals for more appropriate memorials for the victims of National Socialism, but soon the focus shifted to fighting neo-Nazis and right-wing radicals. The foundation has been managed by Dr. Jutta Lange-Quassowski and Dr. Bernd-Peter Lange, the son of Ernst's long-time resistance friends, Hermann and Margarete Lange. In the twenty-five years of its existence, the foundation disbursed over two and a half million marks.

Repatriated Swiss but Still International

Another active opponent of the Nazis was Gisela Strassmann's husband, Max Gutzwiller. Emigrating in 1936 meant crossing the border to his native Switzerland. After 1945, Max occasionally traveled through Germany on trains to Holland, Belgium, and Scandinavia, but he rarely stopped in his wife's native country. In 1967, the University of Bonn invited Max to give an honorary lecture fifty years after he had completed his studies there. Heidelberg University paid him a pension and restitution. It celebrated his ninetieth birthday by naming the room where international private law is taught the Max Gutzwiller Saal. At its entrance is a commemorative plaque and a large photograph of Max, while inside a life-sized bronze bust sits on a bookcase. During the celebration, Neckar wine bottles with "In Honor of Max Gutzwiller" on the labels were used, and extra cases of this vintage were shipped to his new house in Muntelier, Switzerland. His name was also engraved on a plaque at the university entrance honoring the thirty-one Heidelberg scholars who were dismissed and persecuted by the Nazis.

Max had a distinguished postwar career in international law and won much recognition. For two decades, from 1949 to 1969, he was the editor of a Swiss law journal, *Zeitschrift für Schweizerisches Recht*, published in Basel. He chaired the Swiss delegation to international legal conferences and was himself elected president of the International Law Association when its convention was held in Lucerne.[9]

After my last visit to him in Muntelier in April 1981, I noted: "Max, aged 92, is alert, playful, but weakened. Wide range of topics—politics, culture, family, careers, travel." We sipped port in his room with the Gobelin tapestries, drank the Heidelberg wine labeled in his honor with dinner, and afterward walked a kilometer along the lake with his dachshund, Charlie. Max asked me to explain the continued importance of gold, if any, in international finance. In his last letter to me after his ninetieth birthday, he had written:

> I will try to answer your gracious and interesting letter, which I received with the greatest joy, in English. Vous êtes formidable, my dear! You are under way in Sri Lanka, Kenya, and Tunisia! That's wonderful indeed. And you drove around Greece for ten days with Joan and her husband! I read with the greatest interest the report of Joan about the wasp, *Polistes*. And Diana at Harvard will become a learned researcher in economics! Grandfather Paul said always that a special luck is with us all. I noticed with pleasure that the very nice Beverly received the master's degree in biological science and that she writes articles. You must be very happy with all this! Tell Betty my warmest feelings and have yourself all my thanks for your congratulations.
>
> Yours as ever, Uncle Max (September 29, 1979)

Three years later, my cousins told me that they had all gathered for a dinner in honor of Max's oldest son Hellmy's sixtieth birthday, September 28, 1982. One toast after another was ceremonially offered for the welfare of Hellmy, the archivist of the canton of Solothurn, Switzerland. Max, aged ninety-two, seemed in good form. When he stood up, glass in hand, everyone expected his usual clever turn of phrase in honor of both Hellmy and his wife Rosemarie.

"I hope you're happy, Hellmy, and will always be happy," Max began. "I hope no tragedies come your way." He paused. "The greatest tragedy of my life was losing Gisela, your mother. Nothing is sadder than losing a wife you're happy with." He stopped talking, and his eyes turned moist. He looked down, waited, but could not go on. "Forty years without Gisela have gone by," he said finally and sat down. He wept softly. Nobody had ever seen him that way before.

Epilogue: Looking Back

Separated, Then Reunited

More complicated as a departure from Berlin and then as a return was the trek of Elisabeth Strassmann Keiner and her teenage daughter, Annemarie. Both had hidden for years in the Hessian village of Werdorf and in the Black Forest. After the war, Annemarie worked for the denazification process until she emigrated to the United States in 1947, while Elisabeth returned to her husband, the classics teacher, Ernst Keiner, in Berlin. Ernst, as the new director, had addressed the Eckener Gymnasium students' parents in 1946:

> Our boys are to be educated as democrats for democracy.... The best support for that is the Nuremberg trials. The crimes that are brought to light there are warnings for the future of our youth. Never again shall such creatures stand at the peak in German lands. Never again shall such criminals govern our people, they, who brought us such misery and distress and made the whole world despise us.... I am an optimist. I know that you parents will support us teachers in this hard task. If school and home proceed hand in hand at this task, we must and will succeed. Then our youth will be admitted to the company of free nations and will some day say, "Thank God that our parents and teachers so educated us that we can live in happier times than they experienced."

Annemarie has told me that she never again felt comfortable in Germany, "but when I speak the language, I feel very good. It's crazy, but it's true. It's the language that keeps me connected, especially Berlin dialect."

After becoming a widow, Elisabeth, Annemarie's mother, traveled to the United States almost annually from Berlin and then made the move permanent with emigration in 1973. A lively woman, she willingly shared her fund of family stories, not all of them convincing. She did not mind my interrogation, explaining, "With whom else could I otherwise talk about all this?" She interrupted her most outrageous stories, saying, "Forgive me, I really had better not say this. What will you think of me?" Then came the details.

From Quintet to Clan

For me, it was amazing, a regular time warp, to meet Elisabeth and Annemarie, who remembered meeting one of the five original Rawicz brothers—Ferdinand, the Honorary Citizen. Annemarie was just five years old at the time, in 1929, but she says that the lanky old man, aged ninety-one, rising from his wheelchair, had made a stunning impression. It was the way he stood tall and welcomed visitors. Had he any inkling of the impending cataclysm in Germany? Could he imagine that within seven years the Strassmannstrasse would be renamed? Under Hitler, Wolfgang's street was called the Ermelerstrasse, but in 1945 it was the Strassmannstrasse again, and new street signs gave Wolfgang's position and dates (not quite accurately).

I first saw the Strassmannstrasse on a sunny afternoon when Communists still ruled there. A residential street five blocks long, in the eastern district of Friedrichshain, it was pleasant with young trees and an outdoor café. Later, I saw it flourishing under capitalism, with some twenty stores, pubs, and restaurants, including a Strassmann Bistrot. Its strapping owner, Reinhard Klamm, was astounded to meet an authentic Strassmann descendant. The pride of the street was still the old, five-story library built in Amsterdam style with a high gable patterned in white and red bricks like those of City Hall. In a *Rathaus* corridor a mile away, I later saw Ferdinand's portrait displayed among the other Honorary Citizens.

All five brothers from Rawicz had felt accepted and even honored in Berlin during the mid- and late nineteenth century. Their father, Heiman, had seemed content in 1878 when he wrote from Lissa in Posen: "For the evening of my life, my heart longs to see all of you together in Berlin."

The five brothers from Rawicz had thirteen children—six sons and seven daughters. These in turn had twenty-four children—ten girls and fourteen boys, born within a decade of the year 1900. The exact number of three later generations is uncertain because in patriarchal cultures, one easily loses track of cousins who are the daughters of daughters. All the while, assimilation crept on. The original five brothers married observant young Jewish women around 1860, but the next generation around 1890 married secularized Jews like themselves, some baptized, others not. About half of their children married regular Christians. My generation, the fourth, was born in Germany, mostly in the 1920s, and all of us emigrated, except for the "three-quarters Aryan" grandchildren of Arnold (via his son Reinhard and Hildegard Tolzmann) and some of Samuel's daughters' daughters' children, obscurely intermarried away from Berlin. None of us have otherwise married Germans or emigrants from Germany.

Rawicz Revisited

As far as I know, I am the only Strassmann who has ever returned all the way to Rawicz. In the summer of 1993, my long-time friends, Hans and Eva Reis, knowing I might begin this book, said we must visit the ancestral town of Rawicz. It would be my birthday present. So one Sunday in July, with church bells ringing, we drove north from Wroclaw (once Breslau) on narrow highway E-83 the thirty-five miles that had once taken Judith Guhrauer Strassmann all day to traverse by horse-drawn coach. The road was shaded by lindens and willows, rows and rows of them in a checkerboard landscape of green and yellow fields sprinkled with red poppies. On slight hills were the relics of windmills, perhaps survivors of the ninety-nine reported by Great-Grandfather Heinrich.

The sign for Rawicz came ahead of a spread of horse chestnut trees, a forest with bits of roof and a few spires showing through. We drove along a darkly shaded street to a small square, named Plac Wolnosci (Freedom), with a statue of General Thaddeus Kosciusku (George Washington's adviser and Polish freedom fighter in 1792–1793) at one end and at the other a larger Soviet-realist infantry man with a monstrous rifle. People were out on the neat streets for Sunday walks—parents with tykes in strollers, the limping aged, gesturing women, gangs of teenagers, everyone buying ice cream. No other stores were open. Houses, painted in various pastels, had geranium boxes on upstairs windows and red tile roofs like the city hall on the central square. Rawicz lacked that shoddy, run-down, demoralized look of Communist settlements in newly freed East Germany.

We walked about and found the town not very large. No street sign read Judengasse, as was to be expected. We looked for a two-story house with a store on each side of the entrance to pretend it might have been Schmuhl Molower's, provided it had space for a bas-relief of grape carriers above the door. At a corner café, Restauracja Polonia, we had beer in glass mugs and kashlik from thick plates on a red tablecloth. An American flag and a Coca-Cola sign were the only decoration. A tape played "La Paloma."

Later we found the school, austerely whitewashed, where the Prussian director, Herr Hippauf, although believed to be anti-Semitic, had boldly admitted young Wolfgang in 1827. We also found a mustard-colored church with a classic round tower and the date 1639. It was Count Przyna Przyjemsky's original Augustinian Protestant temple, now Catholic! Near the entrance hung an endearing but crude portrait of Karol Wojtyla, their very own Polish Pope, John Paul II. We went on to another high-spired red-brick church. In the covered entrance, a historical placard under glass mentioned Count Pryzna Przyjemsky, King Wladyslaw IV, and the date 1626. Perhaps this was a Catholic church that the Count had built for fugitives who came to his estate before he had a town charter for founding Rawicz. We thought of asking the priest. Rain came and briefly made the town dark and shiny.

An elderly church caretaker said that the priest was probably at Nr. 10 Buszy Street, where Walentyna Woderynska was celebrating her eightieth birthday. Dressed up with jewelry and a summery smock, Walentyna, feeling elated with her day, had a lively personality. Soon we met other animated Poles and stopped feeling like resented aliens. No priest was there. One woman had a cousin in Berlin and another a son in Toronto. Could we deliver messages to them? An older man had worked in a Düsseldorf shoe factory during the war and had no hard feelings about it. It was not all that bad. He was the chief interpreter. Everyone was related to the others somehow. Young women at the party, Walentyna's granddaughters, wore either very short skirts or tight blue jeans. A loud, friendly conversation ensued with people interrupting and talking at the same time. There was much translating into English and German but no information about where Jews had once lived in this town. Finally, everyone exchanged addresses.

Later we noticed an elevated park-like walk for pedestrians. It was the Promenade circling the town! Unmistakable! The level was high enough for having a city wall in rubbles underneath. The trees looked old enough by centuries. Petunias and roses grew in flowerbeds here and there. I had read Great-Grandfather Heinrich's memoirs again and remembered that he wrote: "The pride of Rawitsch was the Promenade set on the remains of demolished fortifications that had encircled the town.... Raised high, well-graded, and landscaped with trees and occasional flower beds, the Promenade allowed vistas of the town from all sides." Yes, so it was! And that explained why on our approach that morning Rawicz had seemed hidden inside a forest. As the sun glittered on wet leaves, a few Sunday strollers were back out with baby carriages or small leashed dogs. Could they be the direct descendants of Strassmann/Molower compatriots two hundred years ago?

Near its southern curve, the Promenade followed a high wall that enclosed a long, five-story cement building with rows of evenly spaced windows. What sort of factory could this be? No! The prison! Still there! Behind vertical and horizontal window bars were shirtless men, looking out, watching us. I remembered Great-Grandfather Heinrich hearing the screams of courtyard floggings and avoiding gruesome Head Warden Müller but not his beautiful daughters. I wondered what crimes each man might have committed and how long their sentences were. What atrocities had this prison seen when Nazis made Poznan the Warthegau and incorporated this province into the Reich? Was it part of the Holocaust system?

One of the prisoners shouted something through the bars. His arms were hanging out. Others were watching. Now all shouted the same thing. Was it "Mich foto!" (Photograph me!) or "Nix foto!" (No photographs!)? Which one? We pointed our cameras to click. The figures behind the bars disappeared into the darkness and never came back.

Over three million Jews had once lived in Poland. Now, only six thousand were left, apparently none in Rawicz. For centuries, the Jewish cemetery of Rawicz had been at the village of Sierakowo just outside of town. In the era of Bismarck, the community had reached its peak, and in 1889 they built a splendid synagogue with curious turrets and a large dome under a Star of David. Then emigration became rapid, especially under twenty years of Polish administration from 1919 to 1939. The Nazis removed the few Jews who were left and destroyed both the synagogue and the cemeteries, except for a gate with an inscription from the Book of Samuel in both Hebrew and German. Even that disappeared after 1960. At the time of our visit, all that remained was a small pile of broken tombstones.

My Return to Berlin, a City of Rubble

Four decades earlier, at age twenty-five, I had first returned to Germany. On May 6, 1952, I flew by Air France from Paris (where I was at the Sorbonne) to Berlin for a week's stay. The day before, an Air France plane, also going to Berlin, had been forced down over East Germany by Soviet fighter planes on the charge of violating air space. Big headlines. I thought it would not happen two days in a row, and it did not. During my first full day in Berlin, a friend's friend, the songwriter Helmut Gardens (composer of "Unter der Allee"), drove me around ruined districts and seemed to relish the vastness of the rubble. He emphasized again and again that these had all been five-story buildings. Some still had bits of wall with gaping windows holding a few shreds of glass, but others were mere piles of bricks with numbers painted on them. On one building, a diagonal series of bullet holes froze violence in time.

American sector, British sector, Soviet sector. Under gray skies, the Tiergarten Park was a prairie of low shrubbery and no trees. The zoo entrance, once so majestic and promising, now looked small and shabby. Rain drizzled, and traffic-directing policemen in their summer white uniforms ignored it—like Wehrmacht soldiers doing their duty. At the Schillerstrasse, we stopped and Gardens collected some musical papers from his publisher.

Eventually, we were at the Klopstockstrasse, and I tried to figure out which lot might once have been my Kritzinger grade school. The address, I remembered, was No. 27. No sign of that. My teacher, Johanna Franzkowski, had forbidden me to be left-handed. She gave me low grades in penmanship—my lowest. But I was allowed to have high grades in sketching using my left hand. My parents were on her side. Nothing remained now but weedy patches of grass and small piles of bricks.

We passed the Reichstag, still a ruined shell, its cupola gone. The Lehrter railway station remained in use, recognizable, the last elevated train station before the Soviet sector. We walked past the police, past others watching suspiciously, past places where rain dribbled through unrepaired places in the roof, to the end of the platform. From here, I looked across the river to the preserved red-brick Charité hospital buildings with pointed roofs and turrets, surviving haphazardly among trees in the Soviet sector. Invisible beyond must be Schumannstrasse 18, the Strassmann Clinic buildings, said to be intact, and Luisenstrasse 47, the place where I lived my first days until I was eleven years old. From that other side was the same view of trees and of mysterious red hospital turrets that we saw daily from our apartment windows and balcony, which we never thought about but were simply aware of. If I could go over there and wander about for an hour or two, I thought I would remember many things, scenes of rooms and people, certain voices, letting a panorama emerge. But Gardens and another man were talking inanities, asking questions, remembering that Professor Paul Strassmann was well spoken of and tried to keep up the new Dahlem house as much as his former clinic, especially the garden. I kept looking around, but with all the talking it was no use.

Later we saw the ruin of the Brandenburg Gate, shrunk to a third of its remembered size. It had no victory chariot on top but a giant red flag, solid red, no hammer and sickle. "You are now leaving the British sector," said a nearby sign. "You are now entering the democratic sector of Berlin," said another further east, "Prosperity, Happiness, Freedom, and Peace." Near the Soviet War Memorial in the Tiergarten, I stepped out to take a picture, and an east-licensed car stopped next to ours. A trench-coated man stepped out. Gardens called me into his car, and we sped off. "Never can tell," he said. "Others rush out from the bushes, usually at dusk, and one policeman can do nothing. Things don't happen as often as the newspapers say, but one can never tell. I don't want you on my conscience." The other car followed us for a while but then veered off. Helmut warned me not to come here alone. "Not a chance," I promised.

During that week in Berlin, I met family friends, distant relatives, acquaintances, and especially my old classmate and best friend from the Kritzinger School, Hans Reis. I spent the most time with him. At the time, he was a postgraduate legal assistant at law courts, preparing for the final qualifying hurdle for attorneys, the *Assessor Examen*. We visited historical curiosities, exchanged memories, and told jokes. He had saved all the letters and cards that I had sent from Minnesota and Texas, some with far-fetched claims. I thought he had the same ironic blinking smile as fifteen years earlier, the same half-serious petulant little arguments with his mother, the same long-winded fantastic theories for me, and a special fascination for history, geography, and coats of arms.

Hans was a *Mischling*, like me. In 1942, he was expelled from his gymnasium, as I would have been, and in October 1944, he was consigned to forced labor to transform a Hessian salt mine two thousand feet under ground into a factory for the Adlerwerke of Frankfurt. Fifteen hours of loading blasted rubble into carts were alternated with nine hours of rest, on a diet of bread and turnips, with brutal supervision. Hans's father survived in hiding, but his mother, a devout Catholic, was safe. She was, however, tainted by her artist brother, Johannes Molzahn, officially classified as "degenerate," who had emigrated to Seattle. Throughout those years, Hans had nightmares of being beaten on the street by plain storm troopers or overly decorated party chieftains (called "golden pheasants"). He wondered if a time would ever come without brown shirts, with no swastikas, no speeches, and no parades. It seemed hopeless. In 1952, Hans lived in the same Charlottenburg apartment that I had last seen in 1937, and more than fifty years later, he still lives there, now with his charming wife, Eva Maria (Korte).

Last Reminiscence

On Sunday, May 11, 1952, I was invited to dinner by the former head nurse (*Oberin*) of my grandfather's Frauenklinik, Marianne Rudeloff, a woman now in her seventies. Her apartment building was in the Wulffstrasse near the Botanical Garden in the Steglitz district. Here the rain had brought down a carpet of red-white horse chestnut blossoms. When I rang and knocked, no one answered. Finally, someone shouted from an upper window to just go in and look for the list of names on the stairs. I did, rang at the wrong apartment first, then at another, and finally a small, white-haired lady in black came to the door, ecstatic to see me and full of talk. Did I remember we had the identical July birthday? How I had grown. Unbelievable. How my parents had visited last summer, in 1951, and here were photos of that. I remembered her dark eyes, kind yet very intent. Her starched nurse's cap was missing, but her hair was still parted in the exact middle and pulled back toward a bun.

Head Nurse Rudeloff lived with another former Strassmann employee, Nurse Griebel. Together they tended a small garden nearby, proudly harvesting twenty pounds of strawberries and brewing a fruit wine. During the war, Nurse Rudeloff had sublet this apartment to others in order to live safely with a brother and nephews in Thuringia. The owner of this building had committed suicide before the Russians charged in. Upon returning,

Nurse Rudeloff had to share the apartment with a refugee couple who had a child and who stole some linen when they left. The apartment was still subdivided.

Mostly, *Oberin* Rudeloff reminisced about the Strassmann Clinic. "The years before 1914 were the best. Your grandfather did not concern himself with money. We just had to break even or reduce salaries. Later, people no longer had money, and we had to profit from little extra charges, say, for a glass of lemonade. During the first war, we had a goat, but no one knew how to milk her. Everyone took turns. Later we thought the animal was pregnant, but she was only fat, perhaps a tumor. One Sunday, on April 1, 1916, your grandfather ordered us to get her ready for a major operation. After we had her clinically prepared as best we could in the surgery, he came in and whispered, 'Ladies and gentlemen, Did you forget? April Fool!' We had a rare wartime laugh!"

"I remember when the news came of Hellmuth's death," she went on. "Hellmuth was a charming boy, a little shy. The news came by mail, not a telegram. The Professor crossed the courtyard, a broken man, to tell his wife. She bore up courageously."

"I worked for your grandfather for thirty-five years, half a lifetime, from 1901 to 1936," she said. "I learned so much about human nature but still have new things to learn. We heard that your grandfather died in Switzerland one evening after playing billiards. Two years earlier we had delivered his clinic intact to the Charité. I can still see how, for the last time, the old Professor stood there in the entrance. The taxi was already there. He looked at us in our tears but was calm. I remember he said something about everyone having some final luck and a last day. His flourish, yes, but not quite as always."

Notes

Preface

1. Horst Sassin, *Liberale im Widerstand: Die Robinsohn-Strassmann Gruppe, 1934–1942* (Hamburg: Hans Christians Verlag, 1993).

2. Jutta Lange-Quassowski, "Nachwort," in Gisela Lehrke, *Gedenkstätten für Opfer des Nationalsozialismus: Historisch-politische Bildung an Orten des Widerstands und der Verfolgung* (Frankfurt am Main: Campus Verlag, 1988).

3. Christoph Moß, *Briefe der Düsseldorfer Familie Glücksmann: Schicksal einer christlich-jüdischen Familie, 1939–1945* (Düsseldorf: Mahn- und Gedenkstätte Düsseldorf; Archiv der evangelische Kirche im Rheinland, 2000).

Introduction

1. Geoffrey Cocks, "Introduction," in *Medicine and Modernity: Public Health and Medical Care in Nineteenth- and Twentieth-Century Germany*, ed. Manfred Berg and Geoffrey Cocks (Washington, DC: German Historical Institute and Cambridge University Press, 1997), 6.

2. Jacob Toury, "Der Eintritt der Juden ins deutsche Bürgertum," in *Das Judentum in der Deutschen Umwelt, 1800–1850*, ed. Hans Liebeschütz and Arnold Paucker (Tübingen: Mohr Siebeck, 1977), 181.

3. Hans Pleschinski, ed., *Aus dem Briefwechsel, Voltaire—Friedrich der Grosse* (Zurich: Haffmans Verlag, 1992), 407, 409. My translation.

4. Ruth Gay, *The Jews of Germany: A Historical Portrait* (New Haven, CT: Yale University Press, 1992), 165.

5. Toury, "Der Eintritt der Juden," 180, 183.

6. Jacob Lestschinsky, *Das wirtschaftliche Schicksal des deutschen Judentums: Aufstieg, Wandlung, Krise, Ausblick* (Berlin: Energiadruck, 1932), 100, cited by John M. Efron, *Medicine and the German Jews: A History* (New Haven, CT: Yale University Press, 2001), 234.

7. Toury, "Der Eintritt der Juden," 183–184.

8. Efron, *Medicine and the German Jews*, 44, 62, 236; Wolfgang Benz, *Geschichte des Dritten Reiches* (Munich: C. H. Beck, 2000), 234–237.

9. Reinhard Rürup, "The European Revolution of 1848 and Jewish Emancipation," in *Revolution and Evolution: 1848 in German-Jewish History*, ed. Werner Mosse, Arnold Paucker, and Reinhard Rürup (Tübingen: Mohr Siebeck, 1981), 25–28; Rüdiger Hachtmann, "Berliner Juden und die Revolution von 1848," in *Jüdische Geschichte in Berlin: Essays und Studien*, ed. Reinhard Rürup (Berlin: Edition Hentricht, 1995), 53–84.

10. See chapter 2.

11. Arnold Bauer, *Rudolf Virchow* (Berlin: Stapp Verlag, 1982), 84, 105.

12. Johanna Bleker, "To Benefit the Poor and Advance Medical Science: Hospitals and Hospital Care in Germany 1820–1870," in Berg and Cocks, *Medicine and Modernity*, 26–27.

13. Bleker, "To Benefit the Poor," 20–25.

14. Günter Plum, "Wirtschaft und Erwerbsleben," in *Die Juden in Deutschland: 1933–1945. Leben unter nazionalsozialistischer Herrschaft*, ed. Wolfgang Benz (Munich: C. H. Beck, 1988), 282. According to

the census of June 1933, 5,557 Jews were physicians, or 11 percent out of 50,500. Forty-five percent practiced in Berlin, and 30 percent in other large Prussian cities.

15. Stephan Kolb, *Die Geschichte der Bad Nauheimer Juden* (Bad Nauheim: Magistrat der Stadt Bad Nauheim, 1987).

16. Andreas Ebert and Hans Karl Weitzel, eds., *Die Berliner Gesellschaft für Geburtshilfe und Gynäkologie, 1844–1994* (Berlin: Walter de Gruyter, 1994), 93–107; Efron, *Medicine and the German Jews*, 250.

17. Reinhard Rürup, *Deutschland im 19. Jahrhundert, 1815–1871* (Göttingen: Vandenhoeck & Ruprecht, 1984), 108.

18. Charles E. McClelland, "Modern German Doctors: A Failure of Professionalism?" in Berg and Cocks, *Medicine and Modernity*, 90.

19. Michael H. Kater, *Doctors under Hitler* (Chapel Hill: University of North Carolina Press, 1989), 13, 31, 37; Alfons Labisch, "From Traditional Individualism to Collective Professionalism," in Berg and Cocks, *Medicine and Modernity*, 85–86.

20. Kater, *Doctors under Hitler*, 54–57.

21. Ibid., 60, 69–70, 74, 116.

22. Fritz Lenz, *Outline of Human Genetics and Racial Hygiene* (n.p., 1927), quoted by John M. Efron, *Defenders of the Race: Jewish Doctors and Race Science in Fin-de-Siècle Europe* (New Haven, CT: Yale University Press, 1994), 19.

23. Robert N. Proctor, *The Nazi War on Cancer* (Princeton, NJ: Princeton University Press, 1999), 4, 29, 35, 47, 199, 287, 293, 300, 322.

24. Susan Bachrach, "Introduction," in *Deadly Medicine: Creating the Master Race*, ed. Dieter Kuntz and Susan Bachrach (Washington, DC: United States Holocaust Memorial Museum/North Carolina University Press, 2004).

25. Kater, *Doctors under Hitler*, 182, 197–198.

26. Benz, *Geschichte des Dritten Reiches*, 109.

27. Michael Burleigh, "Nazi 'Euthanasia' Programs," in Kuntz and Bachrach, *Deadly Medicine*, 132–153.

28. Benz, *Geschichte des Dritten Reiches*, 170–175, 219–227; Henry Friedlander, *The Origins of Nazi Genocide* (Charlotte: University of North Carolina Press, 1995), 58–59, 128–129; Robert J. Lifton, *The Nazi Doctors: Medical Killing and the Psychology of Genocide* (New York: Basic Books, 1986), 37, 91; *Trials of War Criminals before the Nuernberg Military Tribunals*, vols. 1 and 2 (Washington, DC: US Government Printing Office, 1949).

29. Kater, *Doctors under Hitler*, 12, 222.

30. Geoffrey Cocks, "The Old as New: The Nuremberg Doctors' Trial and Medicine in Modern Germany," in Berg and Cocks, *Medicine and Modernity*, 179.

31. Kater, *Doctors under Hitler*, 235, 237.

32. Ibid., 209, 221.

33. Ibid., 201.

34. Kathleen Pearle, "Preventive Medicine: The Refugee Physician and the New York Medical Community, 1933–1945" (University of Bremen: Working Papers on Blocked Alternatives in the Health Policy System, Nr. 11, n.d.); published as "Ärzteemigration nach 1933 in die USA: Der Fall New York," *Medizinhistorisches Journal* 19 (1984): 112–137.

35. W. Paul Strassmann, *Risk and Technological Innovation: American Manufacturing Methods in the Nineteenth Century* (Ithaca: Cornell University Press, 1959); reprinted by Greenwood Press in 1981. Six other books are not listed here.

Chapter 1

1. *Encyclopaedia Judaica* (Jerusalem: Keter Publishing House, 1972), 13:1586–1587.

2. Sophia Kemlein, *Die Posener Juden 1815–1848: Entwicklungsprozesse einer polnischen Judenheit unter preussischer Herrschaft* (Hamburg: Dölling und Galitz Verlag, 1997), 40, 58.

3. Heinrich Strassmann, "Erinnerungen aus meinem Leben: Niedergeschrieben für meine Kinder," 1904–1974; orig. draft typescript, 1899–1904, published as edited by Gerhard Masur in *Jahrbuch für die Geschichte Mittel- und Ostdeutschlands* 23 (1974): 229–230.

4. Strassmann, "Erinnerungen aus meinem Leben," 230.
5. Kemlein, *Die Posener Juden*, 42–43.
6. Strassmann, "Erinnerungen aus meinem Leben," 173.
7. Ibid., 174–175.
8. Ibid., 175.
9. Ibid., 174.
10. Ibid., 167–168.
11. Ibid., 166.
12. Ibid., 168–170.
13. Kemlein, *Die Posener Juden*, 78–84.
14. Strassmann, "Erinnerungen aus meinem Leben," 170.
15. Kemlein, *Die Posener Juden*, 84, 139.
16. Strassmann, "Erinnerungen aus meinem Leben," 176.
17. Ibid., 177.
18. Ibid., 178.
19. Kemlein, *Die Posener Juden*, 308–321.
20. Strassmann, "Erinnerungen aus meinem Leben," 179–180.
21. Ibid., 176.

Chapter 2

1. Rolf Winau, "Ärztliche Vereinigungen in Berlin im 19. Jahrhundert," in Ebert and Weitzel, *Die Berliner Gesellschaft für Geburtshilfe und Gynäkologie*, 6–7.
2. Heinrich Strassmann, "Erinnerungen aus meinem Leben," 190.
3. *Die Chronik Berlins*, ed. Bodo Harenberg (Dortmund: Chronik Verlag in der Harenberg Kommunikation Verlags- und Mediengesellschaft, 1986), 206.
4. Hajo Holborn, *A History of Modern Germany, 1840–1945* (Princeton, NJ: Princeton University Press, [1969] 1982), 53.
5. R. Gay, *The Jews of Germany*, 132.
6. Heinrich Strassmann, "Erinnerungen aus meinem Leben," 195.
7. J. G. Legge, *Rhyme and Revolution in Germany* (New York: New York University Press, 1917).
8. Heinrich Strassmann, "Erinnerungen aus meinem Leben," 195–196.
9. *Chronik Berlins*, 210.
10. Heinrich Strassmann, "Erinnerungen aus meinem Leben," 197.
11. Holborn, *A History of Modern Germany*, 115–117.
12. Heinrich Strassmann, "Erinnerungen aus meinem Leben," 215–216.
13. Gerhard Masur, *Imperial Berlin* (London: Routledge and Kegan Paul, 1971), 141.
14. Ibid., 140.
15. Holborn, *A History of Modern Germany*, 333.
16. Hans Herzfeld, "AllgemeineEntwicklung und Politische Geschichte," in *Berlin und die Provinz Brandenburg im 19. und 20. Jahrhundert*, ed. Hans Herzfeld (Berlin: Walter de Gruyter, 1968), 89.
17. Quoted in Bauer, *Rudolf Virchow*, 39.
18. Quoted in ibid., 105.
19. *Amtlicher stenographischer Bericht über die Sitzung der Stadtverordneten Versammlung*, January 14, 1875.
20. Ibid., January 4, 1877.
21. Ibid., January 3, 1878.
22. *Chronik Berlins*, 228–259, passim; Masur, *Imperial Berlin*, 53, 108–118; Ernst Hamberger, *Juden im öffentlichen Leben Deutschlands* (Tübingen: Schriftenreihe des Leo Baeck Instituts, 1968), 298, 328, 331, 545; Herzfeld, "AllgemeineEntwicklung und Politische Geschichte," 89–91; Reinhard Rürup, ed., *Jüdische Geschichte in Berlin: Bilder und Dokumente* (Berlin: Edition Hentrich, 1995a), 105, 129.
23. *Deutsche Illustrierte Zeitung*, December 1885, vol. 2, 20, 441.
24. Fritz Strassmann, "Aufzeichnungen über mein Leben: An meine Söhne Georg und Reinhold" (typescript, 1993).

25. Sten Nadolny, *Ullsteinroman* (Munich: Ullstein, 2003), 118–121, 126–128.
26. R. Gay, *The Jews of Germany*, 217–219.
27. Fritz Stern, *Gold and Iron: Bismarck, Bleichröder, and the Building of the German Empire* (New York: Alfred A. Knopf, 1977), 527.
28. Burkhard Asmus, *Berlin: Material zur Geschichte der Stadt* (Berlin: Gottfried Korff und Reinhard Rürup, 1987), 47.
29. Rürup, *Jüdische Geschichte in Berlin: Bilder und Dokumente*, 129.
30. Quoted by Walter Frank, *Hofprediger Stoecker und die christlichsoziale Bewegung* (Berlin: Reimar Hobbing, 1928), 105–106.
31. Quoted in Bauer, *Rudolf Virchow*, 75.
32. Frank, *Hofprediger Stoecker*, 107.
33. Quoted by Masur, *Imperial Berlin*, 109.
34. *Amtlicher stenographischer Bericht der Sitzung der Stadtverordneten-Versammlung*, December 8, 1885, 399–400.
35. *Deutsche Illustrierte Zeitung*, vol. 2, 20, 441
36. All translations are mine. For the originals, see W. Paul Strassmann, *Die Strassmanns* (Frankfurt am Main: Campus Verlag, 2006).
37. Werner Vogel, "Ferdinand Strassmann: Ein Leben im Dienste des Berliner Gesundheitswesens," *Zeitschrift für Ärztliche Fortbildung* 53, no. 8 (August 1964).
38. Gerhard Masur, *Das Ungewisse Herz: Berichte aus Berlin—über die Suche Nach dem Freien*, with an introduction by Wilmont Haacke (Holyoke, MA: Blenheim Publishing House, 1978), 12–13.

Chapter 3

1. Max Gutzwiller, *Das Büchlein mit dem Denkmal* (Freiburg im Uechtland: Paulus Druckerei, 1942), 31–32.
2. Nachum T. Gidal, *Die Juden in Deutschland von der Römerzeit bis zur Weimarer Republik* (Gütersloh: Bertelsmann Lexikon Verlag, 1988), 295.
3. Masur, *Das Ungewisse Herz*, 13–14.
4. After again inspecting the Weissensee Strassmann tombs in July 2006, I no longer believe (as stated in the earlier German version of this book) that these words refer to Louise Strassmann (née Levy), Ernst's own mother. She was buried at Weissensee. Professor Reinhard Rürup has suggested to me that the unintelligible word after "Mutter" could be "Stang" or "Streng," both possible last names. In that case, Ernst could be buried with "Mother Stang" or "Mother Streng," who could have been his mother-in-law, his wife Helene's mother, not an unusual reference. Professor Rürup has written to me that "one might well imagine that Helene had buried Ernst in the grave that had been intended for her parents" (letter dated February 16, 2007).
5. Masur, *Das Ungewisse Herz*, 15.
6. Ibid., 8–9.
7. My casual translation of a third of the lines. For the rest in German, see W. P. Strassmann, *Die Strassmanns*, 78.
8. Paul Strassmann, "Das Leben vor der Geburt," *Sammlung Klinischer Vorträge*, no. 353 (Leipzig: Breitkopf and Härtel, 1903), 967. Drs. Andreas Ebert and Matthias David brought this article to my attention.
9. Paul Strassmann, "Die operative Vereinigung eines doppelten Uterus," *Zentralblatt für Gynäkologie* 43 (1907): 1322–1335.
10. Paul Strassmann, "Neue Beobachtungen und Erweiterung der vereinigenden Operation bei Spaltuterus," *Zentralblatt für Gynäkologie* 50 (1926): 1051–1058.
11. Hedwig Strassmann, "Die beiderseitigen Familien, besonders unser Haus, in ihren Beziehungen zur nächsten Umwelt." Handwritten manuscript previously titled "The Strassmanns," written at Hemlock Hague, New York, 1941.

Chapter 4

1. Efron, *Medicine and the German Jews*, 239.
2. Ebert and Weitzel, *Die Berliner Gesellschaft für Geburtshilfe und Gynäkologie*, 141.
3. Myra Warhaftig, *Deutsche jüdische Architekten vor und nach 1933* (Berlin: Dietrich Reimer, 2006), 144–146.
4. K. Willam, commemorating the centenary of Paul's birth in 1966. K. Willam, "Paul Ferdinand Strassmann: Hundert Jahre," *Deutsches medizinisches Journal* 18 (1967): 244.
5. "Paul Strassmann zum 60.Geburtstage," *Monatsschrift für Geburtshülfe und Gynäkologie* 75, nos. 1–2 (1926).
6. Ibid., 1.
7. Gutzwiller, *Das Büchlein mit dem Denkmal*, 26–31.
8. The intricate pattern of rhymes cannot conveyed in translation, but the original poem can be found in W. P. Strassmann, *Die Strassmanns*, 93–94.
9. August Martin, "Schlusswort," *Monatsschrift für Geburtshülfe und Gynäkologie* 75, nos. 1–2 (1926): 188.
10. Viktoria Luise, Herzogin zu Braunschweig und Lüneburg, *The Kaiser's Daughter* (London: W. H. Allen, 1977), 161. Translated and edited by Robert Vacha from Viktoria Luise, Herzogin zu Braunschweig und Lüneburg, *Ein Leben als Tochter des Kaisers* (Göttingen: Göttinger Verlagsanstalt, 1965).
11. Helen Clapesattle, *The Doctors Mayo* (Minneapolis: University of Minnesota Press, 1941), 241, 294, 571–572, 681.
12. Paul Strassmann, *Aus der Medizin des Rinascimento: An der Hand des 'Leben von Benvenuto Cellini' nach der Übersetzung Goethes* (Leipzig: Georg Thieme, 1930).
13. Ibid., 54–55.
14. F. Strassmann, "Aufzeichnungen über mein Leben," 18–19.
15. Rolf Winau, "Die Familie Strassmann," in *Das neue Jahrtausend: Herausforderungen an die Rechtsmedizin. Festsymposium zum 60.Geburtstag von Volkmar Schneider*, ed. Markus A. Rothschild (Berlin: Institut für Rechtsmedizin, Freie Universität Berlin, 2000), 35.
16. Indo Wirth, Hansjürg Strauch, and Klaus Vendura, *Das Institut für Rechtsmedizin der Humboldt-Universität zu Berlin, 1833–2003* (Frankfurt am Main: Hänsel-Hohenhausen, 2003), 19. This publication draws heavily on ten research papers by Manfred Stürzbecher.
17. Wirth, Strauch, and Vendura, *Das Institut für Rechtsmedizin*, 34–41, 65.
18. Fritz Strassmann, *Lehrbuch der Gerichtlichen Medizin* (Stuttgart: Ferdinand Enke, 1895).
19. F. Strassmann, "Aufzeichnungen über mein Leben," 40.
20. Wirth, Strauch, and Vendura, *Das Institut für Rechtsmedizin*, 50.
21. Ibid., 51–53.
22. F. Strassmann, "Aufzeichnungen über mein Leben," 32.
23. "Zu Fritz Strassmanns 70.Geburtstag," *Ärztliche Sachverständigte Zeitung* 34 (1928): 272; cited in Wirth, Strauch, and Vendura, *Das Institut für Rechtsmedizin*, 84.
24. *Deutsche Medizinische Wochenschrift* (1928): 1428.
25. F. Strassmann, "Aufzeichnungen über mein Leben," 42–43.
26. Wirth, Strauch, and Vendura, *Das Institut für Rechtsmedizin*, 78–80.
27. F. Strassmann, "Aufzeichnungen über mein Leben," 55.
28. Wirth, Strauch, and Vendura, *Das Institut für Rechtsmedizin*, 86.

Chapter 5

1. Heinrich Strassmann, "Erinnerungen aus meinem Leben," 218.
2. Ibid., 208.
3. Ibid., 218–225.
4. *Chronik Berlins*, 279–280.
5. Letter by Hellmuth Strassmann, "Der Durchbruch bei Kakinowa," addressed to his Arminia *Burschenschaft* brothers and reprinted in the *Berliner Zeitung*, March 6, 1915. Another, dated July 24, 1915, is printed in Philipp Witkop, ed., *Kriegsbriefe gefallener Studenten* (Munich: Georg Müller, 1929), 253–255.

6. This telegram appeared in the journal, *Bund 5. Gardisten, die weissen Teufel*, Berlin, November 1936.
7. Letter by Erwin Strassmann, dated November 16, 1916, printed in Witkop, *Kriegsbriefe gefallener Studenten*, 255–257.
8. Wirth, Strauch, and Vendura, *Das Institut für Rechtsmedizin*, 134.

Chapter 6

1. Eduard von Winterstein, *Mein Leben und Meine Zeit: Ein Halbes Jahrhundert Deutscher Theatergeschichte* (Berlin: Osvald Arnold, 1947), vol. 2, 236.
2. Letter to Erwin, dated December 13, 1917.
3. Fred Hillenbrandt, *… ich soll dich grüssen von Berlin, 1922–1932* (Frankfurt: Ullstein, 1986), 125–127.
4. *Scherls Magazin*, October 1928.
5. Ernst Heinkel, *Stürmisches Leben* (Stuttgart: Mundus Verlag, 1953), 354.
6. *Der Tag*, November 22, 1929.
7. Heinkel, *Stürmisches Leben*, 355, 362.
8. William L. Shirer, *The Rise and Fall of the Third Reich: A History of Nazi Germany* (New York: Simon and Schuster, [1959] 1990), 781.
9. Heinkel, *Stürmisches Leben*, 451.
10. Leni Riefenstahl, *A Memoir* (New York: St. Martin's Press, [1987] 1992), 276–277.
11. "Selten traf ich eine Persönlichkeit, die so ganz lautlos für sich wirkte, als Mensch und Erscheinung rein und klar und ohne Narben und Scharte, von besonderem und auserlesenen Format." Hillenbrandt, *… ich soll dich grüssen von Berlin*, 127.
12. Jörg-Michael Hormann, *Flugschiff Do-X: Die Chronik* (Bielefeld: Delius Klasing Verlag, 2006), 119.
13. Ibid., 122.
14. Ibid., 123–130.
15. Ibid., 145, citing the *Dornier Post*, Nr. 3, May/June 1939, a Dornier in-house publication.
16. Jörg-Michael Hormann, *Ein Schiff fliegt in die Welt: 75 Jahre Dornier-Flugschiff, Do-X, D-1929* (Bonn: Deutsche Post AG, 2004), 112.
17. Shirer, *The Rise and Fall of the Third Reich*, 165.
18. Heinkel, *Stürmisches Leben*, 269.
19. ASAS (a Brazilian newspaper), September 9, 1932, 9. Citations provided by Professor Gertrud Pfister, Free University of Berlin, who is writing a book about Antonie as an athlete and a flier.
20. Quoted in *Diario de Pernambuco*, October 15, 1932.
21. Evelyn Zegenhagen, "'The Holy Desire to Serve the Poor and Tortured Fatherland': German Women Motor Pilots of the Inter-War Era and Their Political Mission," *German Studies Review* 30, no. 3 (2007): 579–596; Evelyn Zegenhagen, *"Schneidige deutsche Mädel" Fliegerinnen zwischen 1918 und 1945*, Deutsches Museum, Abhandlungen und Berichte, Neue Folge, Band 22 (Göttingen: Wallstein Verlag, 2007).

Chapter 7

1. Max Gutzwiller, *Das Büchlein mit dem Denkmal* (Freiburg im Üchtland: Paulus Druckerei, 1942).
2. Ibid., 54.
3. Ibid., 46.
4. Ibid., 48–49, 55.
5. Ibid., 59.
6. Ibid., 98.
7. Christian Jansen, *Professoren und Politik: Politisches Denken und Handeln der Heidelberger Hochschullehrer, 1914–1935* (Göttingen: Vandenhoeck & Ruprecht, 1992), 32.
8. Gutzwiller, *Das Büchlein mit dem Denkmal*, 101–106.
9. Ibid., 109.
10. Ibid., 99.

11. Norbert Giovannini, "Massnahmen und Grenzen nationalsozialistischer Studentenpolitik," in *Auch eine Geschichte der Universität Heidelberg*, ed. Karin Buselmeier, Dietrich Harth, and Christian Jansen (Mannheim: Edition Quadrat, 1985), 301.
12. Quoted by Jansen, *Professoren und Politik*, 33.
13. Birgit Vezina, *'Die Gleichschaltung' der Universität Heidelberg im Zuge der nationalsozialistischen Machtergreifung* (Heidelberg: Carl Winter Universitätsverlag, 1982), 75–77.
14. Ibid., 14; Arno Weckbecker, "Die Judenverfolgung in Heidelberg 1933–1945: Ein Überblick," in *Heidelberg unter dem Nationalsozialismus: Studien zu Verfolgung, Widerstand und Anpassung*, ed. Jörg Schadt and Michael Caroli (Heidelberg: C. F. Müller Juristischer Verlag, 1985), 282; Hermann Weisert, *Die Verfassung der Universität Heidelberg* (Heidelberg: Carl Winter Universitätsverlag, 1974), 109.
15. Max Gutzwiller, *Siebzig Jahre Jurisprudenz: Erinnerungen eines Neunzigjährigen* (Basel: Helbing & Lichtenhahn, [1978] 1989), 107, 112.
16. Jansen, *Professoren und Politik*, 235–236.
17. Ibid., 276–280.
18. Ibid., 296–297.
19. Gutzwiller, *Das Büchlein mit dem Denkmal*, 112–113.
20. Ibid., 113–114.
21. Jansen, *Professoren und Politik*, 247–248.
22. Quoted in ibid., 177.
23. Quoted by Vezina, *'Die Gleichschaltung' der Universität Heidelberg*, 29.
24. Gutzwiller, *Das Büchlein mit dem Denkmal*, 117, 132.
25. Ibid., 115–116.
26. Quoted in Vezina, *'Die Gleichschaltung' der Universität Heidelberg*, 109.
27. Gutzwiller, *Das Büchlein mit dem Denkmal*, 121–124; diary of Paul Ferdinand Strassmann, July 2, 1936.
28. Friedlander, *The Origins of Nazi Genocide*, 58–59, 128–129.
29. United States Holocaust Memorial Museum, *Historical Atlas of the Holocaust* (New York: Macmillan, 1996), 111–112.
30. Weckbecker, "Die Judenverfolgung in Heidelberg," 457–466.
31. For a century, dachshunds in five branches of the Strassmann family have been named Moki, as is one currently in Michigan.
32. Ibid., 133.
33. Gutzwiller, *Siebzig Jahre Jurisprudenz*, 151–152.
34. Gutzwiller, *Das Büchlein mit dem Denkmal*, 136.
35. Ibid., 159–160.

Chapter 8

1. Gabriel E. Alexander, "Die jüdische Bevölkerung Berlins in den ersten Jahrzehnten des 20. Jahrhunderts," in Rürup, *Jüdische Geschichte in Berlin: Essays und Studien*, 124; Wolf Gruner, "Die Reichshauptstadt und die Verfolgung der Berliner Juden, 1933–1945," in Rürup, *Jüdische Geschichte in Berlin: Essays und Studien*, 257.
2. Peter Schneck, "Die Gesellschaft für Geburtshilfe und Gynäkologie zu Berlin im Spiegel ihrer Verhandlungsberichte 1933 bis 1945," in Ebert and Weizel, *Die Berliner Gesellschaft für Geburtshilfe und Gynäkologie*, 179–192.
3. Alexander, "Die jüdische Bevölkerung Berlins," 119; Gruner, "Die Reichshauptstadt und die Verfolgung der Berliner Juden," 254–255; R. Gay, *The Jews of Germany*, 240–281.
4. Robert J. Lifton, *Ärzte im Dritten Reich* (Berlin: Ullstein, 1998), 54–57, 69 (originally published as *The Nazi Doctors: Medical Killing and the Psychology of Genocide* [New York: Basic Books, 1986]).
5. "Paul Strassmann zum 60. Geburtstage," *Monatsschrift für Geburtshülfe und Gynäkologie* 75, nos. 1–2 (1926) (a Festschrift with twenty-four contributions, a list of publications by Paul Ferdinand Strassmann, and an introduction by Paul Meyer)
6. Witkop, *Kriegsbriefe Gefallener Studenten*.
7. Kater, *Doctors under Hitler*, 199.

8. Wolfgang Genschorek, *Ferdinand Sauerbruch, ein Leben für die Chirurgie* (Leipzig: Hirzel/BSB Teubner, 1978).

9. Shirer, *The Rise and Fall of the Third Reich*, 251, 979, 1029; Lifton, *The Nazi Doctors*, 37, 91; Proctor, *The Nazi War on Cancer*, 4, 29, 35, 47, 199, 287, 293, 300, 322. At this time, Auler was at work on a book about fighting cancer (*Der Krebs und Seine Bekämpfung* [Berlin: Reichsdruckerei, 1937]), which appeared the following year. In it, he characterized cancer cells as revolutionary and National Socialism as inherently anti-carcinogenic: "It is fortunate for German cancer patients, and for anyone threatened by cancer, that the Third Reich has based itself on the maintenance of German health. The most important measures of the government … can all be regarded as prophylactic measures against cancer." Goebbels met with Auler and found his work "truly wonderful," so fascinating that, according to his diary, he even talked about it with Hitler in the pre-dawn hours of June 22, 1941, while waiting for Operation Barbarossa (the invasion of Russia) to start. Auler had become deputy director of the Cancer Institute of the Charité Hospital (around the corner from the Strassmann Frauenklinik in the Schumannstrasse) in September 1933 when the twelve other physicians in the institute were dismissed because of their Jewish ancestry. Among them was Ferdinand Blumenthal, who had led German cancer research as general secretary or vice chairman of the appropriate committees since 1919 and had been chief physician of the Charité's cancer center since 1906. Auler had worked with Blumenthal for years but now, due to his responsibility for cancer research and statistics, moved up in Nazi esteem, receiving extra funds for making ideological movies about cancer. Blumenthal fled to Austria, the Balkans, and Lithuania, and then disappeared in the Soviet Union after 1941. In 1935, Sauerbruch was put in charge of the Charité Cancer Institute, which would acquire the Strassmann premises in 1936. Soon after, however, cancer research activities were mainly centralized and shifted to a new institute, the Allgemeine Institut gegen die Geschwulstkrankheiten (General Institute against Tumorous Diseases) in the Virchow Krankenhaus, which had direct financial support from Hitler and was headed by Heinrich Cramer, a radiologist.

10. Kater, *Doctors under Hitler*, 138.

Chapter 9

1. Ludwig Aschoff, *Ludwig Aschoff: Ein Gelehrtenleben in Briefen an die Familie* (Freiburg im Breisgau: Hans Ferdinand Schulz, 1966), 215, 275–278.

2. Quoted in Kater, *Doctors under Hitler*, 122.

3. Erwin O. Strassmann, "The Theca Cone: The Pathmaker of Growing Human and Mammalian Follicles," *Proceedings of the World Congress on Fertility and Sterility* (Amsterdam, 1959), 135.

4. Erwin O. Strassmann, "The Theca Cone and Its Tropism toward the Ovarian Surface: A Typical Feature of Growing Human and Mammalian Follicles," 1940 Foundation Prize Thesis, *American Journal of Obstetrics and Gynecology* 41 (1941): 363–378.

5. Kolb, *Die Geschichte der Bad Nauheimer Juden*, 99.

6. Ibid., 204.

7. Andreas Ebert and Peter Schneck, "Ernst Bumm: Arzt und Lehrer mit Charisma," in Ebert and Weitzel, *Die Berliner Gesellschaft für Geburtshilfe und Gynäkologie*, 109–121.

8. Erwin O. Strassmann, "Das fetale Elektrokardiogramm," *Zentralblatt für Gynäkologie* 105 (1933): 332.

9. Clapesattle, *The Doctors Mayo*, 425, 442–446, 495, 513–515, 573–574.

Chapter 10

1. My principal source for these years are about seventy letters written especially during 1935–1937, mainly to Hedwig, Antonie's mother. Postcards, telegrams, newspaper clippings, and letters from other people were also examined. Antonie's letters deal with so many topics and personalities that presenting them chronologically would be confusing.

2. *New York Times*, December 11, 1933; November 23, 1939.

3. Leon G. Turrou, *Nazi Spies in America* (New York: Random House, 1939). Thirty years later he expanded this work in Leon G. Turrou, *The Nazi Spy Conspiracy in America* (Freeport: Books for Libraries Press, 1969). Additional material from FBI sources was used by William Breuer in *Hitler's Undercover War: The Nazi Espionage Invasion of the U.S.A.* (New York: St. Martin's Press, 1989).

4. Turrou, *Nazi Spies in America*, 294.

5. Evelyn Zegenhagen, "Vom Aufwind in den Sturzflug: Rollenbild, Chancen und Beschränkungen deutscher Sportfliegerinnen der Zwischenkriegszeit," in *Frau und Flug: Die Schwestern des Ikarus*, ed. Wolfgang Meighörner (Friedrichshafen: Zeppelinmuseum, 2004), 103, 108.

6. *Washington Post*, September 7, 1941.

7. In 1928, Joseph Roth described Schwannekes for the *Frankfurter Zeitung*, now translated by Michael Hoffmann: "The watering hole for Berlin artists and literary figures—where one can be sure to find at midnight all those who only hours before had sworn that they would never go there again, yes, that they hadn't set foot there for years—houses a class of established bohemian whose creditworthiness is beyond question.... He comes so as not to disturb the harmony—formed of fear and distrust of the nooks and corners—and to protect himself and his tablemates from the calumnies that are waiting on the lips of those at the next table.... I have reason to be irked by the design of Schwannekes: the long narrow interior, with square niches stitched along both sides, so that various groups of clients are kept separate from one another." Joseph Roth, "The Word at Schwannekes," *Frankfurter Zeitung*, June 2, 1928, and reprinted in Joseph Roth, *What I Saw: Reports from Berlin, 1920–1933* (New York: W.W. Norton, 1996), 141–145.

8. Eugene F. McDonald, *Youth Must Fly: Gliding and Soaring for America* (New York: Harper and Brothers, 1942), 45.

9. *New York Times*, April 30, 1977.

Chapter 11

1. Stephanie Barron, *"Degenerate Art": The Fate of the Avant-Garde in Nazi Germany* (Los Angeles: Los Angeles County Museum of Art; New York: Harry N. Abrams, 1991), 9.

2. Ian Kershaw, *Hitler, 1889–1936: Hubris* (New York: W.W. Norton, 1998), 567.

3. Proctor, *The Nazi War on Cancer*, 62.

4. Kater, *Doctors under Hitler*, 58, 289.

5. James Bentley, *Martin Niemöller, 1892–1984* (New York: Free Press/Macmillan, 1984), 42–43.

6. Ibid., 113, 120.

7. Ibid., 129.

8. Matthias David, Andreas Ebert, and Manfred Stürzenbecher, "Paul Ferdinand Strassmann, Vertreter einer Berliner Ärztedynastie," in Ebert and Weitzel, *Die Berliner Gesellschaft für Geburtshilfe und Gynäkologie*, 146–160.

9. Paul Strassmann, "Geburt nach vaginaler Verpflanzung der Tube zur Wiederherstellung des Cavum uteri," *Zentralblatt für Gynäkologie* 61, no. 50 (1937): 2893–2900.

10. Quoted in Genschorek, *Ferdinand Sauerbruch, ein Leben für die Chirurgie*, 152–153.

11. Walter Stoeckel, "Erinnerungen," *Zentralblatt für Gynäkologie* 71 (1949): n.p.

12. In a letter dated July 29, 2006, Dr. Manfred Stürzenbecher wrote that in the 1970s, he had explored the possibility of a suicide by Paul Strassmann. He had found that the Swiss authorities in August 1938 had officially stated that no reason existed for questioning that Paul's death was due to natural causes. Paul's remains could therefore be shipped to Berlin with appropriate documents called a *Leichenpass*. The cemetery administrators of the suburban district of Zehlendorf examined this *Leichenpass* and seeing the words "natural death" (*natürlicher Tod*) could admit the body for burial. Stürzenbecher found a record of the *Leichenpass*. If the remains had been shipped as ashes in an urn, a *Leichenpass* would have been unnecessary. We may therefore conclude that Paul's remains were buried that month in a coffin rather than as ashes in an urn (as my Swiss cousins had believed and told me). What matters is that these documents again contradict the idea that Paul Strassmann had committed suicide.

13. The second sentence here has already been quoted in chapter 4.

Chapter 12

1. Charles W. Mayo, *Mayo: The Story of My Family and My Career* (New York: Doubleday, 1968), 335–336.

2. Ibid., 148–149.

3. Ibid., 143–144.
4. Ibid., 113.
5. Charles W. Mayo and Erwin O. Strassmann, "Fertility and Sterility after Extra-Uterine Pregnancy," *Surgery, Gynecology, and Obstetrics* 67 (July 1938): 1–10.
6. Bundesarchiv, *Gedenkbuch: Opfer der Verfolgung der Juden in Deutschland, 1933–1945* (Koblenz: Bundesrepublik, 1986).
7. Robert D. Mussey and Erwin O. Strassmann, "Technique and Results of Routine Fetal Electrocardiography during Pregnancy," *American Journal of Obstetrics and Gynecology* 36 (December 1938): 1–12.
8. Quiana Johnson, "Anatomy of an Anatomy Text," *University of Chicago Magazine* (February 2001): 26–27.
9. Matthias David and Andreas Ebert, "Zur Erinnerung an Paul F. und Erwin O. Strassmann und ihre Beziehung zur Mayo-Klinik—medizinhistorische Anmerkungen," *Der Frauenarzt* 38 (July 1997).
10. Mayo, *Mayo: The Story of My Family and My Career*, 340.

Chapter 13

1. Kathleen Pearle, "Preventive Medicine: The Refugee Physician and the New York Medical Community, 1933–1945," Working Papers on Blocked Alternatives in the Health Policy System, Nr. 11 (N.d.: University of Bremen).
2. Ibid.
3. Herbert Schwarzwälder, *Geschichte der Freien Hansestadt Bremen*. Vol. 4: *Bremen in der NS-Zeit (1933–1945)* (Hamburg: Hans Christians Verlag, 1985), 314–319; see also Inge Marssolek and René Ott, *Bremen im Dritten Reich: Anpassung—Widerstand—Verfolgung* (Bremen: Carl Schünemann Verlag, 1986), 339–340.
4. Herman W. Johnson, *Reminiscences of a Male Midwife* (Houston: Texas Medical Center Library, 1955), 15–16.
5. Ibid., 32.
6. N. Don Macon, *Monroe Dunaway Anderson, His Legacy: A History of the Texas Medical Center* (Houston: Texas Medical Center Library, 1994), 82–88.
7. Ibid.
8. Johnson, *Reminiscences of a Male Midwife*, 45.
9. Walter R. Kaye, *Starting from Scratch: The Story of My Life* (Houston: n.p., 1992), 106–107.
10. Erwin O. Strassmann, "Fertility and Unification of Double Uterus," *Fertility and Sterility* (March–April 1966): 165–176.

Chapter 14

1. "Die Welt ist vollkommen überall, wo der Mensch nicht hinkommt mit seiner Qual," Friedrich Schiller, *Die Braut von Messina* (The Bride of Messina, 1803).
2. Law of May 26, 1933, as amended on May 29, 1941, *Deutscher Reichsanzeiger und Preussischer Staatsanzeiger*.
3. For details, see, for example, Gruner, "Die Reichshauptstadt und die Verfolgung der Berliner Juden," 229–266.
4. Bundesarchiv, *Gedenkbuch*.
5. Letter from Israel G. Jacobson, director of the American Joint Distribution Committee for Czechoslovakia, to Ernst Keiner, September 19, 1946.

Chapter 15

1. Arnold Strassmann, *Allerlei Ostmärkisches: Geschichten und Geschichtchen aus der verlorenen Heimat* (Leipzig: Engel, 1932), 28, 45, 97, 154.
2. Ibid., 206.
3. Quoted in Sassin, *Liberale im Widerstand*, 165. See also Horst Sassin, "Liberals of Jewish Background in the Anti-Nazi Resistance," *Leo Baeck Institute Year Book* 37 (1992): 381–396.

4. Horst Sassin, "Ernst Strassmann und der 20. Juli 1944: Anmerkungen zu Klemens von Klemperer und Joachim Scholtyseck," *Jahrbuch zur Liberalismus-Forschung* 13 (2001): 195–196, 197.

5. Ernst Strassmann, unpublished three-page deposition about the resistance group, dated February 19, 1948, and made available to me by Dr. Jutta Lange-Quassowski, head of the Ernst-Strassmann-Stiftung in the Friedrich-Ebert-Stiftung, Bonn.

6. Sassin, *Liberale im Widerstand*, 137, 390, quoting Robinsohn.

7. Ibid., 36.

8. Ibid., 51–55, 123.

9. Ibid., 382–390.

10. Ibid., 137.

11. Wolfgang Stoecker, "Dr. Ernst Strassmann (Wie ich ihn erlebte)," 2–3. This seventeen-page deposition, dated February 1986, was sent to the Ernst-Strassmann-Stiftung.

12. Document from the Archiv der Bayerischen Widerstandsbewegungen, Munich, Ludwigstrasse 15, March 1, 1948. Made available to me by Dr. Jutta Lange-Quassowski.

13. Sassin, "Ernst Strassmann und der 20. Juli 1944," 195–196, 197.

14. Gestapo report of October 6, 1942.

15. Quoted by Sassin, *Liberale im Widerstand*, 233.

16. Stoecker, "Dr. Ernst Strassmann (Wie ich ihn erlebte)," 4–5.

17. Ibid., 9–10.

18. Stoecker, "Dr. Ernst Strassmann (Wie ich ihn erlebte)," 10–14.

19. Sassin, *Liberale im Widerstand*, 242.

20. Quoted in Joachim Fest, *Plotting Hitler's Death: The Story of the German Resistance*, translated by Bruce Little (New York: Henry Holt, 1996), 292, 297. (Original German edition: *Staatsreich: Der lange Weg zum 20. Juli*. Berlin: Siedler Verlag, 1994.)

21. Stoecker, "Dr. Ernst Strassmann (Wie ich ihn erlebte)," 15–16.

22. Sassin, *Liberale im Widerstand*, 371–388.

23. Ernst Strassmann, unpublished three-page deposition, dated February 19, 1948.

Epilogue

1. David, Ebert, and Stürzbecher, "Paul Ferdinand Strassmann, Vertreter einer Berliner Ärztedynastie," 146–160.

2. Protocol quoted in Ulrich Herbert, "*Die Dynamik der Gewalt—der gescheiterte Versuch der nationalsozialistischen Krisenlösung*," in *Bürgerliche Gesellschaft in Deutschland*, ed. Lutz Niethammer (Frankfurt: Fischer Taschenbuch Verlag, 1990), 438. Schwarzwälder, *Geschichte der Freien Hansestadt Bremen*, 73, 153–154, 501, 630.

3. Wilmont Haacke, "Erinnerungen an Gerhard Masur," in Masur, *Das Ungewisse Herz*, vii–xxv.

4. Gerhard Masur, "Vorwort," in Heinrich Strassmann, "Erinnerungen aus meinem Leben," 161–163.

5. Masur, *Das Ungewisse Herz*, 313, 317.

6. Ibid., xxv.

7. Sassin, *Liberale im Widerstand*, 22–23.

8. Wolfgang Benz and Walter H. Pehle, eds., *Encyclopedia of German Resistance to the Nazi Movement* (New York: Continuum, 1997).

9. Gutzwiller, *Siebzig Jahre Jurisprudenz*.

Appendices: Family Trees

In a book about a family spanning two centuries, a glance at family trees may at times be helpful. Family Tree 1 concentrates on the descendants of Schmuhl's son, Heiman (1797–1881), and especially on those of Heiman's son, Heinrich (1834–1905). Since Heinrich was my great-grandfather, I have the most documentation about that family line. It includes my grandfather, Paul Ferdinand (1866–1938), and his siblings and my father, Erwin (1895–1972), and his siblings.

Heiman's third offspring, Samuel (1826–1879), had the shortest life span, fifty-three years, but with five children and fourteen grandchildren, his descendants need a separate chart, Family Tree 2. It includes Fritz (1858–1940) and Walter (1870–1937), some grandchildren who survived in hiding, others who emigrated, and one, Reinhold (1893–1944), who was killed at Auschwitz.

What I know about the line of Schmuhl Molower Strassmann's other son, Chune, is shown in Family Tree 3. His sons and grandsons were in contact with their Heiman-descended cousins and are occasionally mentioned in letters and memoirs. Most significant of them all is Ernst Karl Otto Strassmann (1897–1958), who organized and led a resistance movement against the Nazis from 1933 to 1942.

Family trees could proliferate into a forest, but with my wife, Elizabeth Marsh Fanck Strassmann, I dare to plant just one more such—Family Tree 4. It shows our three daughters, who use "Strassmann" as their last names, and their five children. All five grandchildren use "Strassmann" as a middle name except Patrick, who occasionally is "Patrick Smisek StrassmanN," with that capital "N" chosen by himself.

Appendices: Family Trees

Family Tree 1: Heinrich's Line

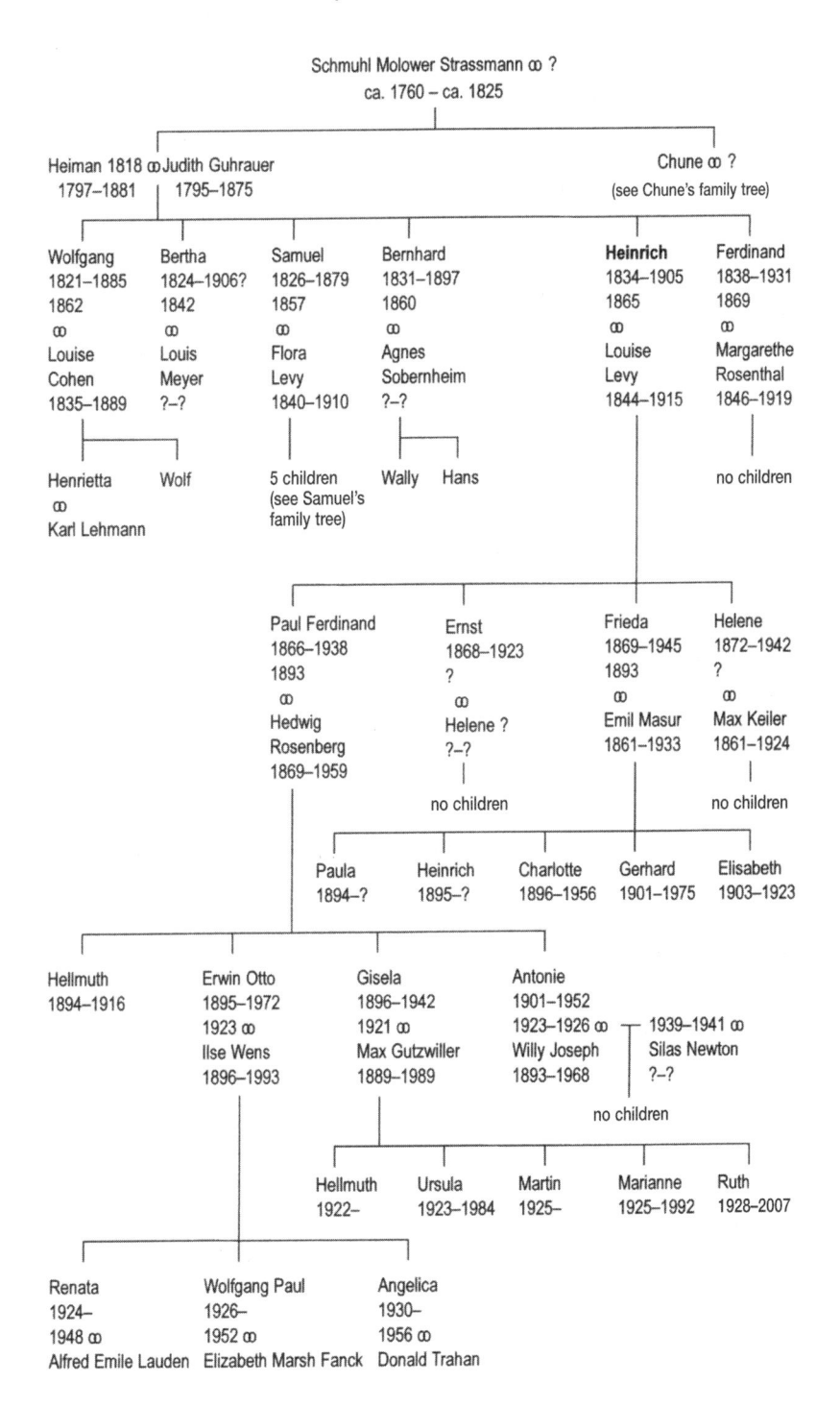

Schmuhl Molower Strassmann ∞ ?
ca. 1760 – ca. 1825

- Heiman 1818 ∞ Judith Guhrauer
  1797–1881   1795–1875

  - Wolfgang
    1821–1885
    1862
    ∞
    Louise
    Cohen
    1835–1889
    - Henrietta
      ∞
      Karl Lehmann
    - Wolf

  - Bertha
    1824–1906?
    1842
    ∞
    Louis
    Meyer
    ?–?

  - Samuel
    1826–1879
    1857
    ∞
    Flora
    Levy
    1840–1910
    - 5 children
      (see Samuel's
      family tree)

  - Bernhard
    1831–1897
    1860
    ∞
    Agnes
    Sobernheim
    ?–?
    - Wally
    - Hans

  - **Heinrich**
    1834–1905
    1865
    ∞
    Louise
    Levy
    1844–1915

  - Ferdinand
    1838–1931
    1869
    ∞
    Margarethe
    Rosenthal
    1846–1919
    - no children

- Chune ∞ ?
  (see Chune's family tree)

Children of Heinrich and Louise:

- Paul Ferdinand
  1866–1938
  1893
  ∞
  Hedwig
  Rosenberg
  1869–1959

- Ernst
  1868–1923
  ?
  ∞
  Helene ?
  ?–?
  - no children

- Frieda
  1869–1945
  1893
  ∞
  Emil Masur
  1861–1933

- Helene
  1872–1942
  ?
  ∞
  Max Keiler
  1861–1924
  - no children

Children of Paul Ferdinand / Frieda:

- Paula 1894–?
- Heinrich 1895–?
- Charlotte 1896–1956
- Gerhard 1901–1975
- Elisabeth 1903–1923

- Hellmuth
  1894–1916

- Erwin Otto
  1895–1972
  1923 ∞
  Ilse Wens
  1896–1993

- Gisela
  1896–1942
  1921 ∞
  Max Gutzwiller
  1889–1989

- Antonie
  1901–1952
  1923–1926 ∞   1939–1941 ∞
  Willy Joseph   Silas Newton
  1893–1968   ?–?
  no children

Children of Gisela / Max Gutzwiller:

- Hellmuth 1922–
- Ursula 1923–1984
- Martin 1925–
- Marianne 1925–1992
- Ruth 1928–2007

- Renata
  1924–
  1948 ∞
  Alfred Emile Lauden

- Wolfgang Paul
  1926–
  1952 ∞
  Elizabeth Marsh Fanck

- Angelica
  1930–
  1956 ∞
  Donald Trahan

– 243 –

Appendices: Family Trees

Family Tree 2: Samuel's Line

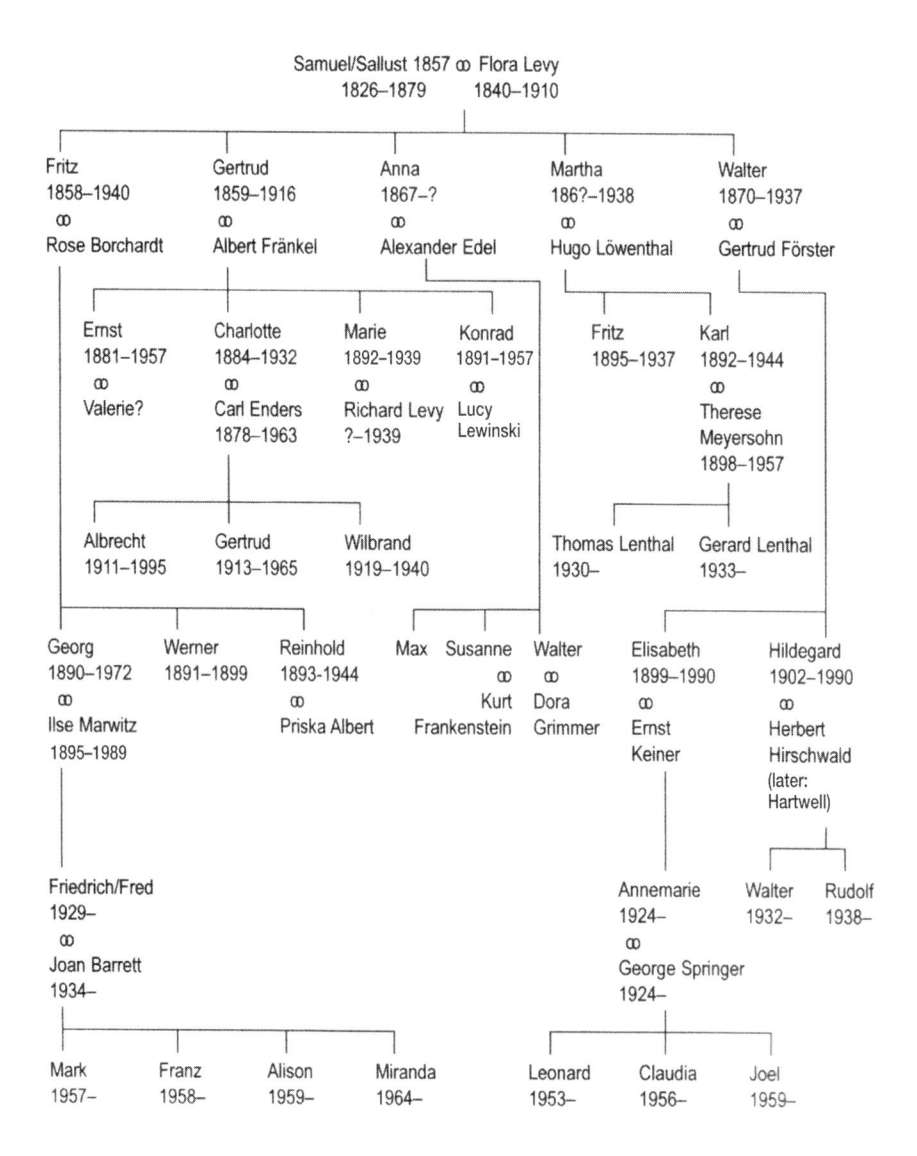

```
                    Samuel/Sallust 1857 ⚭ Flora Levy
                         1826–1879        1840–1910
    ┌───────────────┬──────────────┬──────────────┬──────────────┐
  Fritz          Gertrud         Anna          Martha          Walter
1858–1940      1859–1916       1867–?         186?–1938       1870–1937
   ⚭              ⚭              ⚭              ⚭              ⚭
Rose Borchardt  Albert Fränkel  Alexander Edel  Hugo Löwenthal  Gertrud Förster
```

Children of Gertrud & Albert Fränkel:
- Ernst 1881–1957 ⚭ Valerie?
- Charlotte 1884–1932 ⚭ Carl Enders 1878–1963
- Marie 1892–1939 ⚭ Richard Levy ?–1939
- Konrad 1891–1957 ⚭ Lucy Lewinski

Children of Martha & Hugo Löwenthal:
- Fritz 1895–1937
- Karl 1892–1944 ⚭ Therese Meyersohn 1898–1957

Children of Charlotte & Carl Enders:
- Albrecht 1911–1995
- Gertrud 1913–1965
- Wilbrand 1919–1940

Children of Karl & Therese:
- Thomas Lenthal 1930–
- Gerard Lenthal 1933–

Children of Fritz & Rose Borchardt:
- Georg 1890–1972 ⚭ Ilse Marwitz 1895–1989
- Werner 1891–1899
- Reinhold 1893–1944 ⚭ Priska Albert

Children of Anna & Alexander Edel:
- Max
- Susanne ⚭ Kurt Frankenstein
- Walter ⚭ Dora Grimmer

Children of Walter & Gertrud Förster:
- Elisabeth 1899–1990 ⚭ Ernst Keiner
- Hildegard 1902–1990 ⚭ Herbert Hirschwald (later: Hartwell)

Children of Georg & Ilse:
- Friedrich/Fred 1929– ⚭ Joan Barrett 1934–

Children of Elisabeth & Ernst Keiner:
- Annemarie 1924– ⚭ George Springer 1924–

Children of Hildegard & Herbert:
- Walter 1932–
- Rudolf 1938–

Children of Friedrich/Fred & Joan:
- Mark 1957–
- Franz 1958–
- Alison 1959–
- Miranda 1964–

Children of Annemarie & George Springer:
- Leonard 1953–
- Claudia 1956–
- Joel 1959–

Appendices: Family Trees

Family Tree 3: Chune's Line

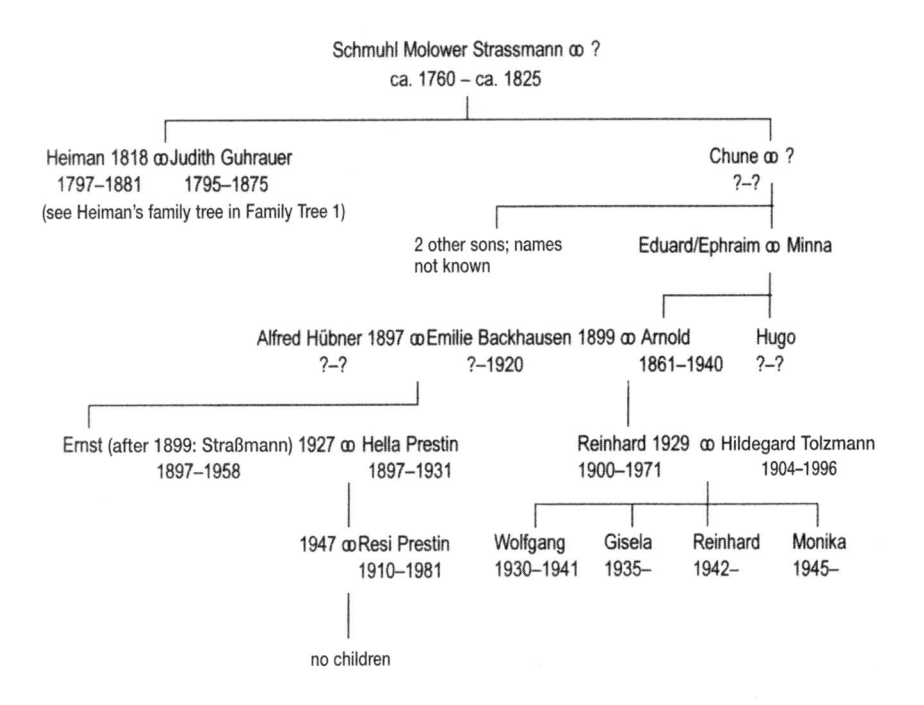

```
                    Schmuhl Molower Strassmann ∞ ?
                         ca. 1760 – ca. 1825
                                 |
        ┌────────────────────────┴────────────────────────┐
Heiman 1818 ∞ Judith Guhrauer                      Chune ∞ ?
1797–1881      1795–1875                             ?–?
(see Heiman's family tree in Family Tree 1)          |
                                        ┌────────────┴────────────┐
                                   2 other sons; names    Eduard/Ephraim ∞ Minna
                                      not known                      |
                                                          ┌──────────┴──────┐
                  Alfred Hübner 1897 ∞ Emilie Backhausen 1899 ∞ Arnold    Hugo
                         ?–?              ?–1920                1861–1940  ?–?
                                                                   |
        Ernst (after 1899: Straßmann) 1927 ∞ Hella Prestin    Reinhard 1929 ∞ Hildegard Tolzmann
                1897–1958                    1897–1931              1900–1971    1904–1996
                         |                                                |
                 1947 ∞ Resi Prestin                    ┌────────┬────────┼────────┐
                         1910–1981                   Wolfgang  Gisela  Reinhard  Monika
                         |                           1930–1941 1935–   1942–    1945–
                    no children
```

– 245 –

Appendices: Family Trees

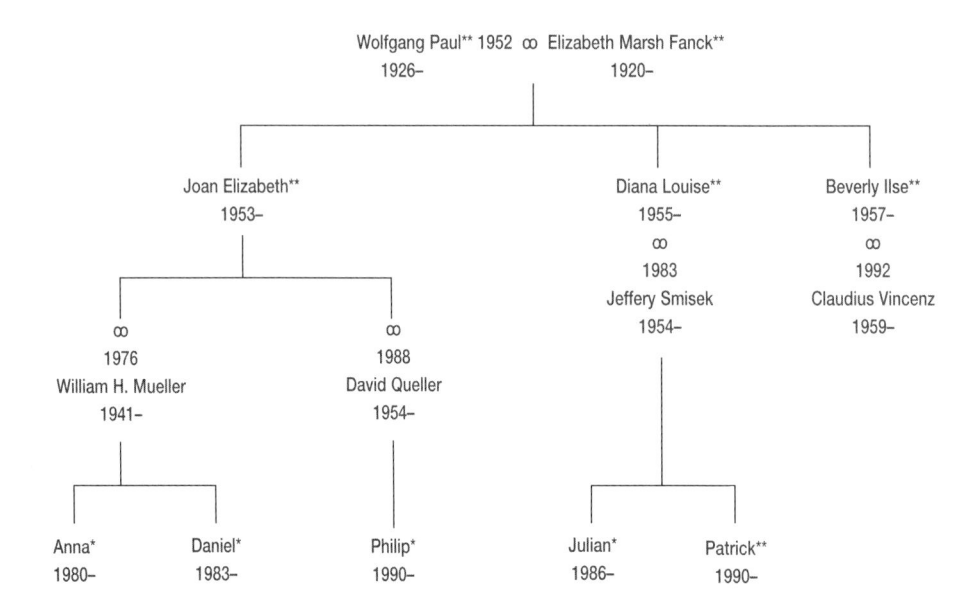

Family Tree 4: The Author's Line

```
Wolfgang Paul** 1952 ∞ Elizabeth Marsh Fanck**
      1926–                    1920–
                    |
    ┌───────────────┼────────────────┐
Joan Elizabeth**           Diana Louise**        Beverly Ilse**
    1953–                     1955–                  1957–
                                ∞                      ∞
                              1983                   1992
                         Jeffery Smisek        Claudius Vincenz
                              1954–                  1959–
      ∞            ∞
    1976         1988
William H. Mueller  David Queller
    1941–          1954–
    
  ┌─────┐          │                    ┌──────┐
Anna*  Daniel*   Philip*            Julian*  Patrick**
1980–  1983–     1990–              1986–    1990–
```

* Strassmann used as middle name.
** Strassmann used as last name.

All three daughters of the author and his wife, Elizabeth Marsh Strassmann, have kept up the family's dedication to science and retained the name "Strassmann." Joan is Chair of the Department of Ecology and Evolutionary Behavior at Rice University, Houston, Texas. She studies the genetics of social wasps and certain amoebae. Diana, now at the Center for the Study of Cultures, Rice University, analyzed airline deregulation for some years at Harvard University and then became the founding editor of *Feminist Economics*, ranked "the best new academic journal" in 1998. Beverly is Professor of Anthropology at the University of Michigan, Ann Arbor. She has spent over twenty years measuring and explaining the evolutionary significance of concealed ovulation, menstruation, and polygamy in several cultures, especially among the Dogon of Mali, West Africa. All three have won prizes for their work and are married.

Bibliography

Alexander, Gabriel E. "Die jüdische Bevölkerung Berlins in den ersten Jahrzehnten des 20. Jahrhunderts." In Rürup, *Jüdische Geschichte in Berlin: Essays und Studien*, 117–148.
Amtlicher stenographischer Bericht über die Sitzung der Stadtverordneten Versammlung, 1875, 1877, 1878, and other years.
Aschoff, Ludwig. *Ludwig Aschoff: Ein Gelehrtenleben in Briefen an die Familie*. Freiburg im Breisgau: Hans Ferdinand Schulz, 1966.
Asmus, Burkhard. *Berlin: Material zur Geschichte der Stadt*. Berlin: Gottfried Korff und Reinhard Rürup, 1987.
Augustine, Dolores L. "Die jüdische Wirtschaftselite im wilhelminischem Berlin: Ein jüdisches Patriziat?" In Rürup, *Jüdische Geschichte in Berlin: Essays und Studien*, 101–116.
Auler, Hans. *Der Krebs und Seine Bekämpfung*. Berlin: Reichsdruckerei, 1937.
Bachrach, Susan. "Introduction." In *Deadly Medicine: Creating the Master Race*, ed. Dieter Kuntz and Susan Bachrach, 1–13, Washington, DC: United States Holocaust Memorial Museum/North Carolina University Press, 2004.
Balfour, Michael. *The Kaiser and His Times*. New York: W.W. Norton, 1972.
Barron, Stephanie. *"Degenerate Art": The Fate of the Avant-Garde in Nazi Germany*. Los Angeles: Los Angeles County Museum of Art; New York: Harry N. Abrams, 1991.
Bauer, Arnold. *Rudolf Virchow*. Berlin: Stapp, 1982.
Beinhorn, Elly. *Ich fliege um die Welt*. Berlin: Ullstein, 1952.
Bentley, James. *Martin Niemöller, 1892–1984*. New York: Free Press/Macmillan, 1984.
Benz, Wolfgang. *Geschichte des Dritten Reiches*. Munich: C. H. Beck, 2000.
Benz, Wolfgang, and Walter H. Pehle, eds. *Encyclopedia of German Resistance to the Nazi Movement*. New York: Continuum, 1997.
Berg, Manfred, and Geoffrey Cocks, eds. *Medicine and Modernity: Public Health and Medical Care in Nineteenth- and Twentieth-Century Germany*. Washington, DC: German Historical Institute and Cambridge University Press, 1997.
Bericht über die Gemeinde-Verwaltung der Stadt Berlin in den Jahren 1889 bis 1895. 2 vols. Berlin: Carl Hemanns Verlag, 1898.
Bland, P. Brooke. "Paul Ferdinand Strassmann, M.D., L.L.D., 1866–1938." In *Transactions of the American Association of Obstetricians, Gynecologists, and Abdominal Surgeons*, vol. 52, for 1939. Minneapolis: Bruce Publishing, 1940.
Blasius, Dirk. "Zwischen Rechtsvertrauen und Rechtszerstörung." In *Zerbrochene Geschichte: Juden in Deutschland*, ed. Dirk Blasius and Dan Diner, 121–137. Frankfurt: Fischer Taschenbuch, 1991.
Bleker, Johanna. "To Benefit the Poor and Advance Medical Science: Hospitals and Hospital Care in Germany 1820–1870." In Berg and Cocks, *Medicine and Modernity*, 17–33.
Botting, Douglas. *Dr. Eckener's Dream Machine*. New York: Henry Holt, 2001.
Breuer, William. *Hitler's Undercover War: The Nazi Espionage Invasion of the U.S.A*. New York: St. Martin's Press, 1989.
Brunswick, Viktoria Luise, Duchess of. *The Kaiser's Daughter*. Englewoood Cliffs, NJ: Prentice-Hall, 1977.
Bruss, Regina. *Die Bremer Juden unter dem Nationalsozialismus*. Bremen: Selbstverlag des Staatsarchivs der Freien Hansestadt Bremen, 1983.
Bundesarchiv. *Gedenkbuch: Opfer der Verfolgung der Juden in Deutschland, 1933–1945*. Foreword by Richard von Weizsäcker. Koblenz: Bundesrepublik, 1986.
Burk, Heinrich. *Bad Nauheim in Alten Ansichten*. Zaltbommel, Netherlands: Europäische Bibliothek, 1986.

_____. *Dies ist meine Stadt: Bad Nauheimer Geschichten aus hundert Jahren*. Bad Nauheim: Buchhandlung am Park, 1995.

Burleigh, Michael. "Nazi 'Euthanasia' Programs." In Kuntz and Bachrach, *Deadly Medicine*, 127–153.

Buselmeier, Karin, Dietrich Harth, and Christian Jansen, eds. *Auch eine Geschichte der Universität Heidelberg*. Mannheim: Edition Quadrat, 1985.

Chronik Berlins, Die. Ed. Brodo Harenberg. Dortmund: Chronik Verlag in der Harenberg Kommunikation Verlags- und Mediengesellschaft, 1986.

Clapesattle, Helen. *The Doctors Mayo*. Minneapolis: University of Minnesota Press, 1941.

Cocks, Geoffrey. "Introduction." In Berg and Cocks, *Medicine and Modernity*.

_____. "The Old as New: The Nuremberg Doctors' Trial and Medicine in Modern Germany." In Berg and Cocks, *Medicine and Modernity*.

Cole, Wayne S. *Roosevelt and the Isolationists: 1932–45*. Lincoln: University of Nebraska Press, 1983.

David, Matthias, and Ebert, Andreas. "Alwin Mackenrodt, Forschung in der Privatklinik." In Ebert and Weitzel, *Die Berliner Gesellschaft für Geburtshilfe und Gynäkologie*, 122–133.

_____. "August Eduard Martin, Werden und Wirken eines deutschen Frauenarztes." In Ebert and Weitzel, *Die Berliner Gesellschaft für Geburtshilfe und Gynäkologie*, 76–92.

_____. "Zur Erinnerung an Paul F. und Erwin O. Strassmann und ihre Beziehung zur Mayo-Klinik—medizinhistorische Anmerkungen." *Der Frauenarzt* 38 (July 1997).

David, Matthias, Andreas Ebert, and Manfred Stürzbecher. "Paul Ferdinand Strassmann, Vertreter einer Berliner Ärztedynastie." In Ebert and Weitzel, *Die Berliner Gesellschaft für Geburtshilfe und Gynäkologie*, 146–160.

Davis, Norman. *A History of Poland*. 2 vols. New York: Columbia University Press, 1982.

De Sayon, Guillaume. *Zeppelin! Germany and the Airship, 1900–1939*. Baltimore: Johns Hopkins University Press, 2002.

Dick, Harold G., and Douglas H. Robinson. *The Golden Age of the Great Passenger Airships: Graf Zeppelin and Hindenburg*. Washington, DC: Smithsonian Books, 1985.

Dippel, John V. H. *Bound upon a Wheel of Fire: Why So Many German Jews Made the Tragic Decision to Remain in Nazi Germany*. New York: Basic Books, 1996.

Duggan, John, and Henry Cord Meyer. *Airships in International Affairs, 1890–1940*. New York: Palgrave, 2001.

Ebert, Andreas, and Wolfgang Pritze. "Adolf Gusserow, Ehrenpräsident der Gesellschaft." In Ebert and Weitzel, *Die Berliner Gesellschaft für Geburtshilfe und Gynäkologie*, 51–64.

_____. "Karl Franz der ungekrönte König der Berliner Gynäkologie." In Ebert and Weitzel, *Die Berliner Gesellschaft für Geburtshilfe und Gynäkologie*, 134–145.

Ebert, Andreas, and Peter Schneck. "Ernst Bumm: Arzt und Lehrer mit Charisma." In Ebert and Weitzel, *Die Berliner Gesellschaft für Geburtshilfe und Gynäkologie*, 109–121.

Ebert, Andreas, and Hans Karl Weitzel, eds. *Die Berliner Gesellschaft für Geburtshilfe und Gynäkologie, 1844–1994*. Berlin: Walter de Gruyter, 1994.

Eckener, Hugo. *Im Zeppelin über Länder und Meere*. Flensburg: Christian Wolff, 1949. Published as *My Zeppelins*. Trans. Douglas Robinson. London: Putnam, 1958.

Efron, John M. *Defenders of the Race: Jewish Doctors and Race Science in Fin-de-Siècle Europe*. New Haven, CT: Yale University Press, 1994.

_____. *Medicine and the German Jews: A History*. New Haven, CT: Yale University Press, 2001.

Encyclopaedia Judaica. Jerusalem: Keter Publishing House, 1972.

Esslin, Martin. "Modern Theatre: 1890–1920." In *The Oxford Illustrated History of Theatre*, ed. John Russell Brown, 341–379. Oxford: Oxford University Press, 1995.

Etzold, Alred, Joachim Fait, Peter Kirchner, and Heinz Knobloch. *Die jüdischen Friedhöfe in Berlin*. Berlin: Henschel, 1991.

Fest, Joachim. *Plotting Hitler's Death: The Story of the German Resistance*. Trans. Bruce Little. New York: Henry Holt, 1996. Original German edition: *Staatsreich: Der lange Weg zum 20. Juli*. Berlin: Siedler, 1994.

Fischer, Klaus P. *Nazi Germany: A New History*. New York: Continuum, 1996.

Fleischmann, Birgit. *Die Ehrenbürger Berlins*. Berlin: Haude & Spener, 1993.

Frank, Walter. *Hofprediger Stoecker und die christlichsoziale Bewegung*. Berlin: Reimar Hobbing, 1928.

Freie Universität Berlin. *Gedenkbuch Berlins der jüdischen Opfer des Nationalsozialismus*. Berlin: Edition Hentrich, 1995.

Friedlander, Henry. "From 'Euthanasia' to the 'Final Solution.'" In Kuntz and Bachrach, *Deadly Medicine*, 155–183.

_____. *The Origins of Nazi Genocide*. Charlotte: University of North Carolina Press, 1995.

Friedländer, Saul. *Nazi Germany and the Jews, 1933–1939*, Vol. 1: *The Years of Persecution*. New York: HarperCollins, 1997.

———. *Nazi Germany and the Jews, 1939–1945*, Vol. 2: *The Years of Extermination*. New York: HarperColllins, 2007.
Fromm, Bella. *Blood and Banquets: A Berlin Social Diary*. New York: Carol Publishing Group, 1990.
Fromm, Eberhard. *Die Ehrenbürger von Berlin*. Berlin: Kultur- und Verlagsgesellschaft des Luisenstädtischen Bildungsverein, 1993.
Gay, Peter. *Freud, Jews, and Other Germans: Masters and Victims in Modernist Culture*. New Haven, CT: Yale University Press, 1978.
———. *Weimar Culture: The Outsider as Insider*. New York: Harper and Row, 1968.
Gay, Ruth. *The Jews of Germany: A Historical Portrait*. New Haven, CT: Yale University Press, 1992.
Genschorek, Wolfgang. *Ferdinand Sauerbruch, ein Leben für die Chirurgie*. Leipzig: Hirzel/BSB Teubner, 1978.
Gidal, Nachum T. *Die Juden in Deutschland von der Römerzeit bis zur Weimarer Republik*. Gütersloh: Bertelsmann Lexikon Verlag, 1988.
Giovannini, Norbert. "Massnahmen und Grenzen nationalsozialistischer Studentenpolitik." In Buselmeier, Harth, and Jansen, *Auch eine Geschichte der Universität Heidelberg*.
Gruner, Wolf. "Die Reichshauptstadt und die Verfolgung der Berliner Juden, 1933–1945." In Rürup, *Jüdische Geschichte in Berlin: Essays und Studien*.
Gutzwiller, Max. *Das Büchlein der Einsichten: Eine Gabe zum 29. Dezember 1941*. N.p., 1941.
———. *Das Büchlein für Therese*. Zurich: Schulthess Polygraphyscher Verlag, 1973.
———. *Das Büchlein mit dem Denkmal*. Freiburg im Üchtland: Paulus Druckerei, 1942.
———. *Elemente der Rechtsidee: Ausgewählte Aufsätze und Reden*. Ed. Anton Heini. (Selected essays and lectures in honor of Max Gutzwiller's seventy-fifth birthday.) Basel: Helbing & Lichtenhahn, 1964.
———. *Geschichte des Internationalprivatrechtss: Von den Anfängen bis zu den grossen Privatrechtskodifikationen*. Basel: Helbing & Lichtenhahn, 1977.
———. *Siebzig Jahre Jurisprudenz: Erinnerungen eines Neunzigjährigen*. Basel: Helbing & Lichtenhahn, [1978] 1989.
———. *Das Quellenbüchlein*. Heidelberg: Richard Weissbach; Freiburg im Üchtland: Imprimerie Fragnière Frères, 1935.
Haacke, Wilmont. "Erinnerungen an Gerhard Masur." In Masur, *Das Ungewisse Herz*, vii–xxv.
Hachtmann, Rüdiger. "Berliner Juden und die Revolution von 1848." In Rürup, *Jüdische Geschichte in Berlin: Essays und Studien*, 53–84.
Hamberger, Ernst. *Juden im öffentlichen Leben Deutschlands*. Tübingen: Schriftenreihe des Leo Baeck Instituts, 1968.
Heinkel, Ernst. *Stürmisches Leben*. Stuttgart: Mundus Verlag, 1953.
Herbert, Ulrich. "Die Dynamik der Gewalt—der gescheiterte Versuch der nationalsozialistischen Krisenlösung." In *Bürgerliche Gesellschaft in Deutschland: Historische Einblicke, Fragen, Perspektiven*, ed. Lutz Niethammer, 413–511. Frankfurt am Main: Fischer Taschenbuch Verlag, 1990.
Hermand, Jost. *Kultur im Wiederaufbau: Die Bundesrepublik Deutschland, 1945–1965*. Munich: Nymphenburger Verlagshandlung, 1986.
Hermand, Jost, and Frank Trommler. *Die Kultur der Weimarer Republik*. Munich: Nymphenburger Verlagshandlung, 1978.
Herzfeld, Hans. "AllgemeineEntwicklung und Politische Geschichte." In *Berlin und die Provinz Brandenburg im 19. und 20. Jahrhundert*, ed. Hans Herzfeld. Berlin: Walter de Gruyter, 1968.
Hillenbrandt, Fred. *... ich soll dich grüssen von Berlin, 1922–1932*. Frankfurt: Ullstein, 1986.
Hoffmann, Herbert. *Im Gleichschritt in die Diktatur? Die nationalsozialistische 'Machtergreifung' in Heidelberg und Mannheim, 1930 bis 1935*. Frankfurt: Peter Lang, 1985.
Holborn, Hajo. *A History of Modern Germany, 1840–1945*. Princeton, NJ: Princeton University Press, [1969] 1982.
Holzapfel, Carl Maria, Käte Stocks, and Rudolf Stocks. *Frauen Fliegen*. Berlin: Deutsche Verlagsgesellschaft, 1931.
Homze, Edward L. *Arming the Luftwaffe: The Reich Air Ministry and the German Aircraft Industry, 1919–39*. Lincoln: University of Nebraska Press, 1976.
Hormann, Jörg-Michael. *Ein Schiff fliegt in die Welt: 75 Jahre Dornier-Flugschiff, Do-X, D-1929*. Bonn: Deutsche Post AG, 2004.
———. *Flugschiff Do-X: Die Chronik*. Bielefeld: Delius-Klasing, 2006.
Jansen, Christian. *Professoren und Politik: Politisches Denken und Handeln der Heidelberger Hochschullehrer, 1914–1935*. Göttingen: Vandenhoeck & Ruprecht, 1992.
Johnson, Eric A. *Nazi Terror: The Gestapo, Jews, and Ordinary Germans*. New York: Basic Books, 1999.
Johnson, Herman W. *Reminiscences of a Male Midwife*. Houston: Texas Medical Center Library, 1955.
Johnson, Quiana. "Anatomy of an Anatomy Text," *University of Chicago Magazine* (February 2001): 26–27.
Johnston, Marguerite. *Houston: The Unknown City, 1836–1946*. College Station: Texas A&M University Press, 1991.
Kampe, Norbert. "Von der 'Gründerkrise' zum 'Berliner Antisemitismus Streit': Die Entstehung des modernen Antisemitismus in Berlin 1875–1881." In Rürup, *Jüdische Geschichte in Berlin: Essays und Studien*, 85–100.

Kater, Michael H. *Doctors under Hitler*. Chapel Hill: University of North Carolina Press, 1989.
Kaye, Walter R. *Starting from Scratch: The Story of My Life*. Houston: n.p., 1992.
Kemlein, Sophia. *Die Posener Juden 1815–1848: Entwicklungsprozesse einer polnischen Judenheit unter preussischer Herrschaft*. Hamburg: Dölling und Galitz Verlag, 1997.
Kershaw, Ian. *Hitler, 1889–1936: Hubris*. New York: W.W. Norton, 1998.
Kogon, Eugen. *Der SS-Staat: Das System der Deutschen Konzentrationslager*. Munich: Wilhelm Heyne, 1974.
Kolb, Stephan. *Die Geschichte der Bad Nauheimer Juden*. Bad Nauheim: Magistrat der Stadt Bad Nauheim, 1987.
Kuntz, Dieter, and Susan Bachrach, eds. *Deadly Medicine: Creating the Master Race*. Washington, DC: United States Holocaust Memorial Museum/North Carolina University Press, 2004.
Labisch, Alfons. "From Traditional Individualism to Collective Professionalism." In Berg and Cocks, *Medicine and Modernity*.
Lange-Quassowski, Jutta. "Nachwort." In Gisela Lehrke, *Gedenkstätten für Opfer des Nationalsozialismus: Historisch-politische Bildung an Orten des Widerstands und der Verfolgung*. Frankfurt am Main: Campus Verlag, 1988.
Legge, J. G. *Rhyme and Revolution in Germany*. New York: New York University Press, 1917.
Lenz, Fritz. *Outline of Human Genetics and Racial Hygiene*. N.p., 1927.
Lestschinsky, Jacob. *Das wirtschaftliche Schicksal des deutschen Judentums: Aufstieg, Wandlung, Krise, Ausblick*. Berlin: Energiadruck, 1932.
Lifton, Robert J. *Ärzte im Dritten Reich*. Berlin: Ullstein, 1998. Originally published as *The Nazi Doctors: Medical Killing and the Psychology of Genocide*. New York: Basic Books, 1986.
———. *The Nazi Doctors: Medical Killing and the Psychology of Genocide*. New York: Basic Books, 1986.
Macon, N. Don. *Monroe Dunaway Anderson, His Legacy: A History of the Texas Medical Center*. Houston: Texas Medical Center, 1994.
Marssolek, Inge, and René Ott. *Bremen im Dritten Reich: Anpassung—Widerstand—Verfolgung*. Bremen: Carl Schünemann Verlag, 1986.
Martin, August. "Schlusswort." *Monatsschrift für Geburtshülfe und Gynäkologie* 75, nos. 1–2 (1926): 187–188.
Masur, Gerhard. *Imperial Berlin*. London: Routledge and Kegan Paul, 1971.
———. "Vorwort." In Heinrich Strassmann, "Erinnerungen aus meinem Leben," 161–163.
———. *Prophets of Yesterday: Studies in European Culture, 1890–1914*. New York: Macmillan, 1961.
———. *Das Ungewisse Herz: Berichte aus Berlin—über die Suche Nach dem Freien*. Introduction by Wilmont Haacke. Hoyoke, MA: Blenheim Publishing House, 1978. Written in 1973 and published posthumously.
Mayo, Charles W. *Mayo: The Story of My Family and My Career*. New York: Doubleday, 1968.
Mayo, Charles W., and Erwin O. Strassmann. "Fertility and Sterility after Extra-Uterine Pregnancy." *Surgery, Gynecology, and Obstetrics* 67 (July 1938): 1–10.
McClelland, Charles E. "Modern German Doctors: A Failure of Professionalism?" In Berg and Cocks, *Medicine and Modernity*.
McDonald, Eugene F., Jr. *Youth Must Fly: Gliding and Soaring for America*. New York: Harper and Brothers, 1942.
Meyer, Henry Cord. *Airshipmen, Businessmen, and Politics, 1890–1940*. Washington, DC: Smithsonian Books, 1991.
Moß, Christoph. *Briefe der Düsseldorfer Familie Glücksmann: Schicksal einer christlich-jüdischen Familie, 1939–1945*. Düsseldorf: Mahn- und Gedenkstätte Düsseldorf; Archiv der evangelische Kirche im Rheinland, 2000.
Mussey, Robert D., and Erwin O. Strassmann. "Technique and Results of Routine Fetal Electrocardiography during Pregnancy." *American Journal of Obstetrics and Gynecology* 36 (December 1938): 1–12.
Mussgnug, Dorothee. *Die Vertriebenen Heidelberger Dozenten*. Heidelberg: Karl Winter, 1988.
Nadolny, Sten. *Ullsteinroman*. Munich: Ullstein, 2003.
Niethammer, Lutz. *Die Mitläuferfabrik: Die Entnazifizierung am Beispiel Bayerns*. Berlin: J. H. W. Dietz, 1982. Originally published as *Entnazifizierung in Bayern*. Frankfurt am Main: S. Fischer, 1972.
"Paul Strassmann zum 60. Geburtstage." *Monatsschrift für Geburtshülfe und Gynäkologie* 75, nos. 1–2 (1926).
Pearle, Kathleen. "Preventive Medicine: The Refugee Physician and the New York Medical Community, 1933–1945." Working Papers on Blocked Alternatives in the Health Policy System, Nr. 11. Bremen: University of Bremen, n.d. Published as "Ärzteemigration nach 1933 in die USA: Der Fall New York," *Medizinhistorisches Journal* 19 (1984): 112–137.
Philipps, Cabell. *The 1940s: Decade of Triumph and Trouble*. New York: Macmillan, 1975.
Pleschinski, Hans, ed. *Aus dem Briefwechsel, Voltaire—Friedrich der Grosse*. Zurich: Haffmans Verlag, 1992.
Plum, Günter. "Wirtschaft und Erwerbsleben." In *Die Juden in Deutschland: 1933–1945. Leben unter nationalsozialistischer Herrschaft*, ed. Wolfgang Benz. Munich: C. H. Beck, 1988.
Proctor, Robert N. *The Nazi War on Cancer*. Princeton, NJ: Princeton University Press, 1999.
Rabel, Ernst. *The Conflict of Laws: A Comparative Study*. 4 vols. Ann Arbor: University of Michigan Law School, 1958.

Rae, John B. *Climb to Greatness: The American Aircraft Industry, 1920–1960*. Cambridge, MA: MIT Press, 1968.
Riefenstahl, Leni. *A Memoir*. New York: St. Martin's Press, [1987] 1992.
Roth, Joseph. *What I Saw: Reports from Berlin, 1920–1933*. New York: W.W. Norton, 1996.
Rürup, Reinhard. *Deutschland im 19. Jahrhundert, 1815–1871*. Göttingen: Vandenhoeck & Ruprecht, 1984.
_____. "The European Revolution of 1848 and Jewish Emancipation." In *Revolution and Evolution: 1848 in German-Jewish History*, ed. Werner Mosse, Arnold Paucker, and Reinhard Rürup. Tübingen: Mohr Siebeck, 1981.
_____, ed. *Jüdische Geschichte in Berlin: Bilder und Dokumente*. Berlin: Edition Hentrich, 1995.
_____, ed. *Jüdische Geschichte in Berlin: Essays und Studien*. Berlin: Edition Hentrich, 1995.
Sandler, Lucy Freeman, ed. *Essays in Memory of Karl Lehmann*. Foreword by Phyllis Pray Bober. New York: Institute of Fine Arts, New York University, 1964.
Sassin, Horst. "Ernst Strassmann und der 20. Juli 1944: Anmerkungen zu Klemens von Klemperer und Joachim Scholtyseck." *Jahrbuch zur Liberalismus-Forschung* 13 (2001): 193–199.
_____. *Liberale im Widerstand: Die Robinsohn-Strassmann-Gruppe, 1934–1942*. Hamburger Beiträge zur Sozial- und Zeitgeschichte, Forschungsstelle für die Geschichte des Nationalsozialismus in Hamburg, vol. 30. Hamburg: Hans Christians Verlag, 1993.
_____. "Liberals of Jewish Background in the Anti-Nazi Resistance." *Leo Baeck Institute Year Book* 37 (1992): 381–396.
Sauder, Gerhard. "Goebbels in Heidelberg." In Buselmeier, Harth, and Jansen, *Auch eine Geschichte der Universität Heidelberg*.
Sauerbruch, Ferdinand. *Das war mein Leben*. Bad Worishofen: Kindler und Schiermeyer, 1951.
Schadt, Jörg, and Michael Caroli. *Heidelberg unter dem Nationalsozialismus: Studien zu Verfolgung, Widerstand und Anpassung*. Heidelberg: C. F. Müller Juristischer Verlag, 1985.
Schmidt, Dietmar. *Martin Niemöller*. Trans. Lawrence Wilson. London: Oldham Press; New York: Doubleday, 1959.
Schneck, Peter. "Die Gesellschaft für Geburtshilfe und Gynäkologie zu Berlin im Spiegel ihrer Verhandlungsberichte 1933 bis 1945." In Ebert and Weitzel, *Die Berliner Gesellschaft für Geburtshilfe und Gynäkologie*, 179–192.
Schrader, Bärbel, and Jürgen Schebera. *Die 'Goldenen' Zwanziger Jahre: Kunst und Kultur der Weimarer Republik*. Vienna: Hermann Böhlaus, 1987.
Schwarzwälder, Herbert. *Geschichte der Freien Hansestadt Bremen*. Vol. 4: *Bremen in der NS-Zeit (1933–1945)*. Hamburg: Hans Christians Verlag, 1985.
Shirer, William L. *The Rise and Fall of the Third Reich: A History of Nazi Germany*. New York: Simon and Schuster, [1959] 1990.
Sieber, Emil. *Basler Trennungswirren und nationale Erneuerung im Meinungsstreit der Schweizer Presse, 1830–1833*. Basel and Stuttgart: Helbing & Lichtenhahn, 1964.
Simonson, G. R., ed. *The History of the American Aircraft Industry: An Anthology*. Cambridge, MA: MIT Press, 1968.
Sloan, Allan. *Three Plus One Equals Billions: The Bendix-Martin Marietta War*. New York: Arbor House, 1983.
Snyder, Louis. *Encyclopedia of the Third Reich*. New York: Paragon, [1976] 1989.
Solo, Roselyn. "André François-Poncet—Ambassador of France." PhD diss., Michigan State University, 1978.
Stahl, Friedrich. "Entwicklung und Verwendung der Luftschiffe und Fesselballone im Dienste des Feldheeres." In *Unsere Luftstreitkräfte, 1914–1918: Ein Denkmal deutschen Heldentums*, ed. Walter von Eberhardt, 67–78. Berlin: Vaterländischer Verlag C. A. Weller, 1930.
Stern, Fritz. *Gold and Iron: Bismarck, Bleichröder, and the Building of the German Empire*. New York: Alfred A. Knopf, 1977.
Stoeckel, Walter. "Erinnerungen." *Zentralblatt für Gynäkologie* 71 (1949): n.p.
Strassmann, Arnold. *Allerlei Ostmärkisches: Geschichten und Geschichtchen aus der verlorenen Heimat*. Leipzig: Engel, 1932.
Strassmann, Erwin O. "Fertility and Unification of Double Uterus." *Fertility and Sterility* (March–April 1966): 165–176.
_____. "Das fetale Elektrokardiogramm." *Zentralblatt für Gynäkologie* 105 (1933): 332.
_____. "The Theca Cone: The Pathmaker of Growing Human and Mammalian Follicles." *Proceedings of the World Congress on Fertility and Sterility*. Amsterdam, 1959.
_____. "The Theca Cone and Its Tropism toward the Ovarian Surface: A Typical Feature of Growing Human and Mammalian Follicles." 1940 Foundation Prize Paper. *American Journal of Obstetrics and Gynecology* 41 (1941): 363–378.
Strassmann, Fritz. "Aufzeichnungen über mein Leben: An meine Söhne Georg und Reinhold." Typescript, 1933.
_____. *Lehrbuch der Gerichtlichen Medizin*. Stuttgart: Ferdinand Enke, 1895.

Strassmann, Georg. "Fritz Strassmann (1858–1940)." *Die Medizinische* 35 (August 1958).

Strassmann, Hedwig. "Die beiderseitigen Familien, besonders unser Haus, in ihren Beziehungen zur nächsten Umwelt." Handwritten manuscript previously titled "The Strassmanns," written at Hemlock Hague, New York, 1941.

Strassmann, Heinrich. "Erinnerungen aus meinem Leben: Niedergeschrieben für meine Kinder," 1904–1974. Original draft typescript, 1899–1904, published as edited by Gerhard Masur in *Jahrbuch für die Geschichte Mittel- und Ostdeutschlands* 23 (1974): 161–230.

Strassmann, Paul Ferdinand. *Arznei-, diätsche, diagnostische und sozialhygienische Verordnungen für die gynäkologische-geburtshilfliche Praxis*. Leipzig: Georg Thieme, 1911, 1920, 1925, 1931.

_____. "Geburt nach vaginaler Verpflanzung der Tube zur Wiederherstellung des Cavum uteri." *Zentralblatt für Gynäkologie* 61, no. 50 (1937): 2893–2900.

_____. *Gesundheitspflege des Weibes*. Leipzig: Quelle & Meyer, 1912, 1915, 1918.

_____. "Das Leben vor der Geburt." Sammlung Klinischer Lectures, no. 353. Leipzig: Breitkopf and Härtel, 1903.

_____. *Zur Lehre von der mehrfachen Schwangerschaft*, Berlin: Inaugural Dissertation, Friedrich-Wilhelms Universität, 1889.

_____. *Aus der Medizin des Rinascimento: An der Hand des 'Leben von Benvenuto Cellini' nach der Übersetzung Goethes*. Leipzig: Georg Thieme, 1930.

_____. "Die operative Vereinigung eines doppelten Uterus." *Zentralblatt für Gynäkologie* 43 (1907): 1322–1335.

_____. "Neue Beobachtungen und Erweiterung der vereinigenden Operation bei Spaltuterus." *Zentralblatt für Gynäkologie* 50 (1926): 1051–1058.

Strassmann, W. Paul. *Die Strassmanns: Schicksale einer deutsch-jüdischen Familie über zwei Jahrhunderte*. Frankfurt am Main: Campus Verlag, 2006.

_____. *Risk and Technological Innovation: American Manufacturing Methods in the Nineteenth Century*. Ithaca: Cornell University Press, 1959; reprinted by Greenwood Press, 1981.

Tal, Uriel. *Christians and Jews in Germany: Religion, Politics and Ideology in the Second Reich, 1870–1914*. Ithaca, NY: Cornell University Press, 1975.

Thorwald, Jürgen. *The Dismissal: The Last Days of Ferdinand Sauerbruch, Surgeon*. Trans. Richard Winston and Clara Winston. London: Thames and Hudson, 1961.

Toury, Jacob. "Der Eintritt der Juden ins deutsche Bürgertum." In *Das Judentum in der Deutschen Umwelt, 1800–1850*, ed. Hans Liebeschütz and Arnold Paucker, 139–242. Tübingen: Mohr Siebeck, 1977.

Trials of War Criminals before the Nuernberg Military Tribunals. Vols. 1 and 2 Washington, DC: US Government Printing Office, 1949.

Turrou, Leon G. *Nazi Spies in America*. New York: Random House, 1939.

_____. *The Nazi Spy Conspiracy in America*. Freeport, NY: Books for Libraries Press, 1969.

United States Holocaust Memorial Museum. *Historical Atlas of the Holocaust*. New York: Macmillan, 1996.

Vezina, Birgit. *'Die Gleichschaltung' der Universität Heidelberg im Zuge der nationalsozialistischen Machtergreifung*. Heidelberg: Carl Winter Universitätsverlag, 1982.

Viktoria Luise, Herzogin zu Braunschweig und Lüneburg. *The Kaiser's Daughter*. London: W. H. Allen, 1977. Translated and edited by Robert Vacha from Viktoria Luise, Herzogin zu Braunschweig und Lüneburg, *Ein Leben als Tochter des Kaisers*. Göttingen: Göttinger Verlagsanstalt, 1965.

Vogel, Werner. "Ferdinand Strassmann: Ein Leben im Dienste des Berliner Gesundheitswesens." *Zeitschrift für Ärztliche Fortbildung* 53, no. 8 (August 1964).

Von Winterstein, Eduard. *Mein Leben und Meine Zeit: Ein Halbes Jahrhundert Deutscher Theatergeschichte*. Berlin: Osvald Arnold, 1947.

Wallenchinsky, David. *The Complete Book of the Olympics*. New York: Penguin Books, 1988.

Warhaftig, Myra. *Deutsche jüdische Architekten vor und nach 1933*. Berlin: Dietrich Reimer, 2006.

Weber, Marianne. *Lebenserinnerungen*. Bremen: Johs. Storm Verlag, 1948.

Weckbecker, Arno. "'Gleichschaltung' der Universität? Nationalsozialistische Verfolgung Heidelberger Hochschullehrer aus rassischen und politischen Gründen." In Buselmeier, Harth, and Jansen, *Auch eine Geschichte der Universität Heidelberg*.

_____. "Die Judenverfolgung in Heidelberg 1933–1945: Ein Überblick." In Schadt and Caroli, *Heidelberg unter dem Nationalsozialismus*.

Weisert, Hermann. *Geschichte der Universität Heidelberg: Kurzer Überblick 1386–1980*. Heidelberg: Carl Winter Universitätsverlag, 1983.

_____. *Die Verfassung der Universität Heidelberg*. Heidelberg: Carl Winter Universitätsverlag, 1974.

Willam, K. "Paul Ferdinand Strassmann: Hundert Jahre." *Deutsches medizinisches Journal* 18 (1967): 244.

Winau, Rolf. "Ärztliche Vereinigungen in Berlin im 19. Jahrhundert." In Ebert and Weitzel, *Die Berliner Gesellschaft für Geburtshilfe und Gynäkologie*.

———. "Die Familie Strassmann." In *Das neue Jahrtausend: Herausforderungen an die Rechtsmedizin. Festsymposium zum 60. Geburtstag von Volkmar Schneider*, ed. Markus A. Rothschild. Berlin: Institut für Rechtsmedizin, Freie Universität Berlin, 2000.

Winters, Peter Jochen. "Die Gemeinde der Toten: In Berlin zerfällt das Archiv des grössten jüdischen Friedhofs in Europa." *Frankfurter Allgemeine Zeitung*, March 31, 1992.

Wirth, Indo, Hansjürg Strauch, and Klaus Vendura. *Das Institut für Rechtsmedizin der Humboldt-Universität zu Berlin, 1833–2003*. Frankfurt am Main: Hänsel-Hohenhausen, 2003.

Witkop, Philipp, ed. *Kriegsbriefe Gefallener Studenten*. Munich: Georg Müller, 1929.

Zegenhagen, Evelyn. "Vom Aufwind in den Sturzflug: Rollenbild, Chancen und Beschränkungen deutscher Sportfliegerinnen der Zwischenkriegszeit." In *Frau und Flug: Die Schwestern des Ikarus,* ed. Wolfgang Meighörner, 86–109. Friedrichshafen: Zeppelinmuseum, 2004.

———. "'The Holy Desire to Serve the Poor and Tortured Fatherland': German Women Motor Pilots of the Inter-War Era and Their Political Mission." *German Studies Review* 30, no. 3 (2007): 579–596.

———. *"Schneidige deutsche Mädel" Fliegerinnen zwischen 1918 und 1945*. Deutsches Museum, Abhandlungen und Berichte, Neue Folge, Band 22. Göttingen: Wallstein Verlag, 2007.

Index

Aber, Eduard, 24, 25
Albert, Priska. *See* Strassmann, Priska
American physicians visiting Germany (esp. Strassmann Clinic), 2, 58, 109–110, 170
American Society of Obstetricians, Gynecologists, and Abdominal Surgeons, 112, 124, 183
anti-Semitism in Germany, xi, 4, 7, 10, 17, 62, 177, 180, 206, 219, 226
  anti-Semitic racial theories, 6–8, 114, 155, 161, 213
  anti-Semitic laws, 5, 7, 11, 43, 108–109, 110, 112, 113, 119, 120, 127, 163, 164, 203
  at Heidelberg University, 100–103
  in medical profession in the late nineteenth and early twentieth centuries, 47–48
  rise of, 4–5, 6, 22, 25–32, 219–220
  See also Glogau, Otto; Jews in Germany, persecution; Marr, Wilhelm; Nuremberg Laws; Stoecker, Adolph; Treitschke, Heinrich von
art in Germany, 9, 41, 45, 49, 52, 66, 74–77, 79–81, 153–154, 203–204, 229. *See also* Barlach, Ernst; Berlin, Deutsches Theater; Corinth, Lovis; "Degenerate Art"; Goethe, Johann Wolfgang von; Hauptmann, Gerhart; Kollwitz, Käthe; Mendelssohn-Bartholdy, Felix; Reinhardt, Max; theatre in Germany
Aschoff, Ludwig, and Aschoff's institute in Freiburg, 124, 125, 127, 184, 186
Augusta, German Empress, 31, 32
Auler, Hans, 7, 115, 123
Auschwitz (concentration camp), x, 10, 6, 35, 69, 103, 172, 189, 199, 200, 213, 220, 242
aviation in Germany
  commercial, 88–89
  development and international negotiations (1933–1939), 135–145
  military: balloons in World War I, 71–72; rise of the Luftwaffe in the mid-1930s, 83–84
  sport: 81–91; German sport aviation propaganda in the US, 84–87
  See also Do-X; Hindenburg airship; Junkers; Klemm, Hanns, Klemm airplane company; Koenig-Warthausen, Friedrich Wilhelm Freiherr von und zu; Siemens

Backhausen, Emilie Ottilie. *See* Strassmann, Emilie
Bad Nauheim (town in Hessen/Germany), 5, 110, 125–130, 163, 169, 172, 173, 178–181, 217
  Jewish physicians in, 5, 125–126
  Kristallnacht in, 180–181
Bamberger, Ludwig, 30
Barlach, Ernst, 154
Bartoll, Felix, 209, 210
Beck, Ludwig, 115, 206
Beinhorn, Elly, 83, 86, 141–143
Bekennende Kirche. *See* Confessing Church; Niemöller, Martin
Bergmann, Ernst von, 37, 43
Berlin, 1–3, 11, 17, 20, 21–34, 35, 37, 38, 42, 46–57, 59, 70, 89, 90, 94, 97, 105, 109, 117, 125, 129, 130, 137, 144, 147, 163, 164, 176–178, 184, 194, 199, 202–212, 213, 219, 225, 226, 228–230
  Brandenburg Gate, 1, 70, 228
  Charité, 5, 37, 38, 44, 47–49, 51, 114–116, 118–120, 123, 175, 215, 228, 230
  City Council, xiv, 21, 24–33, 46, 48, 49, 108, 154, 160, 194
  City Hall ("Rotes Rathaus"), 27, 32–34, 59, 225
  Dahlem (suburb of Berlin), 49, 56, 71, 105, 117, 121, 123, 143, 144, 151–162, 164, 174, 181, 198, 228
  Deutsches Theater, 45, 51, 66, 73–76, 120, 123. *See also* Reinhardt, Max
Fischerbrücke and Fischerinsel, 36, 145
Free University (Freie Universität), 219, 220
Friedrich-Wilhelm University of Berlin (Berlin University, University of Berlin, after 1945: Humboldt University), 4–5, 24, 25, 37, 45, 46, 51, 52, 59, 60, 63, 64, 68, 108, 109, 112, 113, 120, 127, 194, 214, 220
gymnasia: Friedrichsgymnasium 36, 53, 59, 66–68, 121, 203; Mommsen Gymnasium, 92, 97; Empress Augusta Gymnasium 193; Eckener Gymnasium 201, 225

Index

public works (1871–1914), 27–29, 33, 213
Reichstag (building and political assembly), 1, 24, 25, 27, 30, 32, 66, 67, 89–91, 228
Reichstag fire, 1, 11, 67, 136, 228
Rudolf Virchow medical complex (Virchow Klinik), 5, 48, 190, 194
Tiergarten, 25, 26, 67, 73, 89, 133, 193, 198, 228, 229
Unter den Linden, 1, 24, 2, 28, 42, 55, 66, 70, 127, 136
Weissensee (Jewish cemetery), 20, 43, 184
Zehlendorf (suburb of Berlin), 2, 117, 192, 198, 199, 201
Berlin Society for Obstetrics and Gynecology (Berliner Gesellschaft für Geburtshilfe und Gynäkologie), 38, 44, 45, 214
Bertner, Ernst William, 182–184
Bismarck, Otto von, 1, 2, 4–6, 24, 26–30, 32, 64, 66, 67, 151, 214, 227
Bleichröder, Gerson, 29, 219
Boeltzig, Reinhold, 49
Bonhoeffer, Dietrich, 211
Bonhoeffer, Karl, 115
Borchardt, Dietrich, 195
Borchardt, Gustav, 62
Borchardt, Moritz, 43, 190, 194
Borchardt, Rose. *See* Strassmann, Rose
Brandt, Karl, 8
Brandt, Willy, 212, 223
Brauchitsch, von, 138
Brazil, exploration by air, 90–91
Bremen, grain trade and Nazi affiliations, 181, 217–219
Breslau, 4, 5, 9, 15, 17, 21, 25, 42, 56, 57, 117, 189, 190, 194, 195, 203, 206, 220, 221, 226
British physicians visiting Germany, 155
Buchenwald (concentration camp), 189, 203, 211
Büchner, Franz, 8
Bumm, Ernst, 47, 48, 52, 126, 127
Burg, Meno, 22, 23

Canaris, Wilhelm, 137, 206, 207, 209, 211
Carl Schurz Foundation, 171, 178, 179
Cellini, Benvenuto, 53, 59
Christiansen, Friedrich, 88, 90
clinic. *See* Mayo Clinic; Strassmann Women's Clinic (three Berlin addresses); Berlin, Rudolf Virchow medical complex
Club of October 3 (Klub vom 3. Oktober), 205, 207, 212. *See also* Dehler, Thomas; Landahl, Heinrich; Robinsohn-Strassmann group; Stark, Otto; Strassmann, Ernst-Karl-Otto
concentration camps. *See* Auschwitz; Buchenwald; Dachau; Flossenbürg; Sachsenhausen; Theresienstadt
Confessing Church (Bekennende Kirche), 157, 158, 207, 211

Conti, Leonardo, 7
conversions, religious. *See* religion, conversions
Corinth, Lovis, 41, 45, 52, 54, 154
Croton on the Hudson. *See* Hemlock Hague

Dachau (concentration camp), 159
Dahlem. *See* Berlin, Dahlem
Darwin, Charles, 44, 186
"Degenerate Art," 154, 229. *See also* Barlach, Ernst; Corinth, Lovis
Dehler, Thomas, 205, 208, 212
deportations. *See* Auschwitz; Buchenwald; Dachau; Flossenbürg; Jews in Germany, persecution; Sachsenhausen; Theresienstadt
Dibelius, Martin, 101
Dibelius, Otto, 158
Diepholz (town near Bremen/Germany), 125, 167, 179, 181, 182
Dohnanyi, Hans von, 115, 206, 209, 210
Do-X (German airplane), 87–90, 135, 138, 153, 216
Duncan, Clara, 168, 177, 178
Dürselen, Ilse, 122, 134, 162

Earhart, Amelia, 85, 86, 88
Ebert, Friedrich, viii, xiv, 73, 223. *See also* Rathenau, Walter
Eckener, Hugo, 86, 90, 143, 216
Eichmann, Adolf, 198
Elsas, Fritz, 205, 207
Ernst Strassmann Foundation (Ernst-Strassmann-Stiftung), viii–xi, xiv, 10, 204, 223
Esch, Putzi, 192, 193, 197
espionage, 136–138. *See also* Germans in the US
euthanasia, 7, 8, 103, 115
    beginnings, 109–110
    See also Auler, Hans; Conti, Leonardo; Schneider, Carl; Wagner, Gerhard; Zucker, Konrad

Faitini, Camilla, 199
Federal Order of Merit (*Bundesverdienstkreuz*), viii, 196, 220
"Final Solution," 198. *See also* Auschwitz; Buchenwald; Dachau; Flossenbürg; Jews in Germany, persecution; Sachsenhausen; Theresienstadt
Fischer, Heine, 7
Fleischmann, Max, 207
Flossenbürg (concentration camp), 211
Forster, Rudolf, 79, 83, 86, 87, 141, 142
Fraenkel, Gertrud. *See* Strassmann, Gertrud
Fraenkel, Konrad, 199, 220
Fraenkel, Max, 49
Fraenkel, Susanne, 200
Franck, Philip, 36, 52, 121, 145
Franz, Karl, 47, 48
Frederick the Great, King of Prussia, 2, 3, 160

Freiburg im Breisgau (town and university in Baden/Germany), 76, 94, 124, 125, 130, 133, 184, 192, 198, 199, 201
Freund, Wilhelm, 5
Fribourg (Freiburg) im Üchtland (town and university in Switzerland), 93–96, 104–107, 151, 162, 164, 182
Friedländer, J. N., 4
Friedländer, Käte, 130, 172
Friedländer, Luise (Ferber), 130, 172
Friedrich, Crown Prince of Prussia, 28, 30–32
Friedrich Wilhelm IV, King of Prussia, 18, 22, 23, 31
Friedrichsgymnasium. *See* Berlin, Friedrichsgymnasium
Fritz Strassmann Institut (Institute for Forensic Medicine of the Humboldt University Berlin, Institut für Rechtsmedizin der Humboldt Universität Berlin), xi, 5, 60, 63, 220
Fritz Strassmann Medal, 63, 220

Gardens, Helmut, 228, 229
German Association for Legal Medicine (Deutsche Gesellschaft für Rechtsmedizin), 63
German physicians (non-Jewish), during the Nazi era, 6–8, 108–109, 114–116, 124–126, 127, 155. *See also* Brandt, Karl; Conti, Leonardo; euthanasia; Fischer, Heine; Lenz, Fritz; Nazi eugenics; Schneider, Carl; Wagner, Gerhard; Zucker, Konrad
German Society for Gynecology (Deutsche Gynäkologische Gesellschaft), 44
Germans in the US
  "enemy aliens," 182, 187, 216
  espionage in the US, 136–138
  visitors to the US, 141–143
Germany, history of
  assassination attempt (July 20, 1944), 10, 207, 209, 211
  civilian resistance against Hitler, viii–ix, 10, 155, 160, 189, 202–203, 205–207, 209–210, 212, 223
  denazification, 218–219, 225
  development of forensic medicine, 60–62, 194
  military resistance against Hitler, 10, 160, 205, 206, 209, 211–212, 223
  Napoleonic Wars, 14
  after 1945, ix, x, xi, 196, 200–201, 205–206, 212, 214–223, 225, 228–229
  Olympic Games (1936), 117–118
  politics (1919–1932) (Weimar Republic), 6, 51, 73, 90–91, 99–100, 160, 223
  politics (1812–1848) (including Prussian reforms), 4
  politics (1848–1871), 4–5, 24–27
  politics (1871–1914), 26–34, 47–49, 66–67
  politics (1933–1939), 6–8, 108–115, 119–120, 127–131, 136–138, 151–153, 155–156, 161, 163–164, 179–182, 205–207
  politics and events of 1933, 1–2, 110, 136, 205
  Revolution of 1848, 4, 21–24

religious resistance against Hitler, 157–159, 207
World War I, 6, 10, 39, 41, 50–51, 66–73, 131, 190–191, 194
World War II, 105–106, 143–145, 182, 184, 198, 200, 208–212, 217
See also Berlin, Reichstag fire; Bonhoeffer, Dietrich; Confessing Church; Kreisau Circle; Niemöller, Martin; Nuremberg Laws; Robinsohn-Strassmann group; Stauffenberg, Claus Graf Schenk von; World War I; World War II
Giessen (town in Hessen/Germany), 37–39, 44, 46, 47, 118, 137, 152
Ginsberg, Siegmund, 37
Gladow, Dorothea, 120–122
Glogau, Otto, 29
Goebbels, Joseph, 90, 110, 112, 138, 184, 199
Goerdeler, Carl, 160, 205–208, 211
Goethe, Johann Wolfgang von, 7, 14, 35, 42, 53, 59, 76, 77, 80, 95, 96, 156, 159, 162, 168
Gohrbandt, Erwin, 115
Göring, Emmy, 90, 111
Göring, Herrmann, 83, 84, 90, 91, 108, 111, 222
Gradenwitz, Menachem Mendel, 13
Gradenwitz, Otto, 96, 97
Great Service Cross (*Grosses Verdienstkreuz*), 216
Griebl, Ignatz, 137
Groedel, Frances, 126
Groedel, Franz, 5, 125, 126, 178
Groedel, Isidor Mayer, 5, 125
Groh, Wilhelm, 99, 102, 103
Grünfeld, Ernst, 207
Grynspan, Herschel (Grynszpan, Herszel), 180
Guhrauer, Judith. *See* Strassmann, Judith
Gundolf, Friedrich, 97
Gusserow, Adolf, 38, 47
Guttenberg, Baron Karl Ludwig von und zu, 209
Gutzwiller, Carl, 94
Gutzwiller, Emilie (Meyer), 93, 96
Gutzwiller, Ernst, 106
Gutzwiller, Gisela. *See* Strassmann, Gisela
Gutzwiller, Hellmuth (Hellmy), 96, 104, 162, 164, 214, 224
Gutzwiller, Marianne, 96, 162
Gutzwiller, Martin, 96, 104, 162, 164
Gutzwiller, Max, xiii, 10, 38, 39, 51–53, 92–107, 145, 162, 164, 177, 178, 213, 224. *See also* Max Gutzwiller Saal
Gutzwiller, Rosemarie, 224
Gutzwiller, Ruth, 98, 107, 162
Gutzwiller, Ursula, 96, 107, 162

Häfeli, Emil, 116, 121–123, 128, 178
Hague, Robert L., 135, 139–141, 143, 144
Hahn, Otto, 156
Hauptmann, Gerhart, 45, 51, 66, 95, 97, 113, 120, 121, 122, 161, 214

Index

Hauptmann, Marie ("Rautendelein"), 45, 120
Heidelberg (town and university in Germany)
  anti-Semitism at the university, 100–103
  Heidelberg and Holocaust, 103–104
  Heidelberg University (Ruperto Carola), 10, 59
  importance to German academic life and history, xiii, 3, 8, 10, 37, 59, 92–104, 118, 124, 125, 152, 194, 224
  Nazi takeover of, 98–103
  See also Max Gutzwiller Saal
Heinkel, Ernst, 83, 84, 86, 90, 138, 215, 216
  Heinkel airplane company, 135
Hemlock Hague (Croton on the Hudson, Peekskill), 144, 145–148, 150, 182, 214, 216
Herrmann, Karl Friedrich Wilhelm, 137
Heydrich, Reinhard, 198, 209, 211
Hildebrandt, Franz, 158
Himmler, Heinrich, 110, 222
Hindenburg, Paul von, 2, 72, 84, 88–91, 110, 111
Hindenburg airship, 143
Hippauf, Herr, 17, 226
Hirschwald, A., 24
Hirschwald (Hartwell), Herbert, 193, 196
Hirschwald (Hartwell), Hildegard. *See* Strassmann, Hildegard
Hirschwald (Hartwell), Rudolf, 193
Hirschwald (Hartwell), Walter, 193
Hitler, Adolf, 1, 2, 6, 7, 8, 10, 67, 69, 83, 90, 99, 103, 105, 106, 108–110, 115, 118, 126, 143, 149, 151, 154, 155, 157, 159–162, 170, 172, 178, 182, 184, 193, 198, 205–209, 211–212, 215–217, 221, 222, 225
Hitler, Alois, Jr., 161
Hoffmann, Dorothea, 97
Hoffmann, Ernst, 92, 93, 97
Hohenzollern von (leading dynasty in Prussia), 4, 5, 21, 23, 28, 30, 45, 55–56, 78. *See also* Augusta, Empress of Germany; Frederick the Great; Friedrich, Crown Prince of Prussia; Friedrich Wilhelm IV, King of Prussia; Viktoria Luise, Princess of Hohenzollern; Wilhelm I, Emperor of Germany; Wilhelm II, Emperor of Germany; Wilhelm, last Crown Prince of Prussia
Holocaust, x xiv, xv, 103–105, 149, 155, 198–200, 227
  killing centers in occupied Eastern countries (Poland and Soviet Union), 8, 199
  See also Auschwitz; Buchenwald; Dachau; Flossenbürg; Jews in Germany, persecution; Sachsenhausen; Theresienstadt
Houston, Texas, xiii, xv, 9, 147, 163, 168, 176–179, 180–183, 185–188
  Texas Medical Center, xv, 9, 5, 182–184, 186
Hübner, Arnold, 202, 204
Humboldt, Alexander von, 23

Jaray, Sandor, 45, 49, 215
Jasperson, Karsten, 8

Jenny Marx School for Specialized Medical Occupations (Jenny Marx Schule für Medizinalfachberufe), 214
Jewish physicians in Germany (other than Strassmanns)
  contributions to medical science and techniques, 3–5, 9, 24, 37, 44–45, 47–50, 52–54, 59, 60–62, 101, 116, 117, 124, 127, 151, 160–161, 186
  emigration to the US, 176–177
  historical rise in the eighteenth century, 3–4
  practice in Bad Nauheim, 5, 125–126
  practice in Berlin, 4–5
  practice and opposition in the late nineteenth and early twentieth centuries, 47–48
  See also Freund, Wilhelm; Friedländer, N. J.; Groedel, Franz; Groedel, Isidor Mayer; Schoenewald, Sally; Schott, August; Schott, Theodor; Spielberg, Otto; Stern, Moritz
Jews in Germany
  assimilation, x xi, 3–4, 6, 10–11, 39, 62, 74, 207, 219, 226
  conversions. *See* religion, conversions, Judaism to Christianity
  deportation, 69, 103, 180, 189, 198–200, 202
  and German nationality, xi, 50–51, 70, 73, 110, 113–114, 122, 141, 157, 158–160, 162, 163, 190, 214
  Jews in Berlin (1925–1933), 109
  migration and emigration (1933–1939), x, xiii, 6, 8, 9, 10, 35, 67, 103, 109, 117, 161, 162, 177, 193, 198, 205, 207, 218, 220, 224, 226
  migration and emigration (until 1933), ix, x, xi, xiii, xiv, 2, 4, 10, 14, 15, 35, 39–40, 48, 94, 103, 109, 219, 227
  migration and emigration to the US, ix, x, xi, xiii, 6, 9, 11, 35, 48, 57–58, 87–91, 106, 112–114, 120, 126, 128–135, 137, 141, 144, 154, 155, 162, 165–169, 171–174, 176, 193, 194, 197, 207, 213, 217, 221, 225, 229
  persecution, including forced labor (1939–1945), 189, 197–200, 203
  persecution and regimentation (1933–1939), 7–10, 62–63, 108–109, 110, 112–114, 119–120, 122, 126, 127–128, 129, 151, 155, 157, 161, 163–165, 179–181, 192–193, 204
  pre-modern education and income levels in Rawicz (Prussian province of Posen), 15–18
  role in political history, 2–7, 13, 21–34, 46, 61–62, 202–212
  statistical information, 4–6, 8, 13, 17, 38, 47, 69, 99, 103, 109, 155, 176, 200, 227
  See also anti-Semitic laws; Auschwitz; Buchenwald; Dachau; Flossenbürg; Holocaust; *Kristallnacht*; Nuremberg Laws; Progressive Party; Sachsenhausen; Theresienstadt
Johnson, Herman, 183–185
Joseph, Willy, 77, 78, 81

Jung, Martin, 110, 111, 127, 128
Junkers (airplane manufacturer), 81, 84, 87, 135, 138, 139, 143

Kaltenbrunner, Ernst, 211
Kauffmann, Robert, 207, 212
Keiler, Helene. *See* Strassmann, Helene
Keiler, Max, 43
Keiner, Elisabeth. *See* Strassmann, Elisabeth
Keiner, Ernst, 155, 198–201, 225
Keiner Springer, Annemarie, 10, 155, 189, 196, 197–201, 225
Kirchert, Werner, 8
Klemm, Hanns, 90, 91
    Klemm airplane company, 85, 90, 135
Klepper, Friederike Minna, 218
Koblanck, A., 48
Koch, Fritz, 208
Koch, Walter, 125, 184–185
Kochhann, Heinrich, 27
Koenig-Warthausen, Friedrich Wilhelm Freiherr von und zu, 84, 85, 88
Kollwitz, Käthe, 5, 54
Kortner, Fritz, 141, 142
Kreisau Circle (Kreisauer Kreis), 207, 211
Kristallnacht (Night of Broken Glass), 56, 165, 176, 193, 207
    in Bad Nauheim, 180–181
    in Bremen, 181
Kuhlmann, Friedel-Marie, 121
Küper, Willy, 133
Kuhnert, Dr., 114, 115, 116, 120, 123

Landahl, Heinrich, 205
Lange, Bernd-Peter, viii, 223
Lange, Hermann, viii, 223
Lange, Margarethe, viii, 223
Lange-Quassowski, Jutta, xii, xiv, xv, 223
Langerhans, Paul, 4
Lasker, Eduard, 30
Lehmann, Ernst, 143
Lehmann, Henni. *See* Strassmann, Henni
Lehmann, Karl, 33, 194, 195
Lenz, Fritz, 7
Leonhard, Betty, 43
Leszno. *See* Lissa
Levin, Arthur, 37
Levy, Berthold, 39
Levy, Joseph Bender, xiv, 33, 35, 36, 145
Levy, Julius, 39, 51, 197
Levy, Marie, 189, 193, 196, 197, 198
Levy, Martin, 51
Levy, Richard, 189, 193, 197, 198
Levy, Therese, 35, 36
Lewis, Mary, 139, 140
Liebknecht, Karl 61, 73

Liman, Carl, 60
Lissa (town in Poland), 3, 15, 17–20, 33, 226
Löhlein, D. N., 37, 44, 47
Lübke, Heinrich, 196, 216, 220
Ludendorff, Erich, 72, 160
Luxemburg, Rosa, 6, 61, 73

Manville, Valerie Claire (Sunny, Mrs. Thomas Manville), 117, 137, 141, 166, 167
Marr, Wilhelm, 29
Martin, August, 54
Martin, Eduard A., 47
Marwitz, Gertrud, 200
Marwitz, Ilse. *See* Strassmann, Ilse
Marwitz, Marie, 197
Marx, Karl, 49, 214
Masur, Charlotte, 43
Masur, Elisabeth, 43
Masur, Emil, 42–43
Masur, Frieda. *See* Strassmann, Frieda
Masur, Gerhard, 33, 40, 42, 43, 78, 117, 144, 219–220
Masur, Heinrich, 43
Masur, Paula, 43
Max Gutzwiller Saal (Heidelberg University), 224
Mayer, Helene, 141
Mayo, Alice, 170
Mayo, Charles H. (Charlie), 9, 50, 58, 117, 120, 121, 126, 127, 131, 132, 164, 168, 170, 171, 174, 186, 187
Mayo, Charles W. (Chuck), 130, 131, 170, 171, 175, 178
Mayo, Joe, 170–171
Mayo, William J. (Will), 9, 50, 58, 111, 113, 117, 120, 121, 127, 131, 132, 164, 168, 170, 172, 173, 186, 187
Mayo Clinic (Rochester, Minnesota), 9, 58, 117, 126, 131, 132, 168–172, 175, 177, 180
McDonald, Eugene F., 145, 146, 150. *See also* Zenith Radio Corporation
medicine in Germany
    economic aspects, 6–7, 47, 49–50, 54–55, 119, 114–115, 118–119
    forensic/legal medicine, 9, 59–63, 194, 213, 220
    medical innovations and new surgical operations, 44–46, 53–54, 56, 115, 116–117, 124, 127, 160, 215
    medical publications, 24, 44–46, 50–51, 59, 160–161, 194
    university medical studies, nineteenth century, 21, 37, 46–47
    See also Fritz Strassmann Institut; Fritz Strassmann Medal
medicine in the US (with regard to German immigrants)
    economic aspects, 171, 178
    forensic/legal medicine, 195, 195–196, 220
    medical surgeries and innovations, 183, 185–186
    publications, 171
    See also Mayo Clinic; Houston, Texas, Texas Medical Center; United States, immigration policy toward Germans (including physicians)

Index

Meineke, Friedrich, 219
Mendelssohn, Moses, 3
Mendelssohn-Bartholdy, Felix, 42, 120, 153, 160, 179
Mengele, Josef, 8
Meyer, Karl, 96
Meyer, Louis, 19
Meyer, Paul, 49, 51, 217
Meyer, Robert, 161
Meyer, Ulla, 120
Meyerbeer, Giacomo, 32
Milch, Erhard, 84, 86
Mischling. *See* person of mixed heritage
Moellendorff, Erika von, 127
Molower, Schmuhl. *See* Strassmann, Schmuhl
Moltke, Helmuth von, 32, 67, 211
Mommsen Theodor, 29, 92, 97, 160
Mücke, Amalie Frieda, 119, 122
Mueller, Ernst, 144, 148
Mueller, Rosel, 144
Müller, Fritz, 157, 158
Müller, Heinrich, 198
Müller, Johannes, 24

Nagel, Otto, 36
Nazi eugenics, 7
Nazis and "Jewish science" (after 1933), 160–161
New York City, xiii, 1, 9, 33, 57, 58, 67, 74, 84, 85, 87–89, 106, 114, 126, 128, 131, 132, 14, 135–150, 151, 153, 165–169, 173, 176, 177, 179–182, 185, 13–195, 197, 214, 220
Newton, Isaac, 44
Newton, Silas, 144
Niemöller, Martin, 39, 157–159
Nuremberg Laws, 7, 112, 120, 131, 155, 176, 192, 194, 204
Nuremberg trials, 8, 225

Olshausen, Robert, 37, 47
Olympic Games, 87–88, 117–118
Oster, Hans, 206, 209, 211

person of mixed heritage (*Mischling*), 7, 130, 141, 163, 193, 203, 229. *See also* Jews in Germany, persecution; Nuremberg Laws
Pfannschmidt, Karl Gottfried, 5, 52, 162
Pfeiffer, Erich, 137
Posen (Poznan), district in Poland, xi, 9, 10–20, 25, 35, 43, 64, 109, 226
   Jews in Christian schools in, 17
Posner, Käthe, 144
Prestin, Hella. *See* Strassmann, Hella
Prestin, Resi. *See* Strassmann, Resi
Priestley, Klea, 170, 171
Priestley, Jim, 170, 171
Progressive Party (Fortschrittspartei), 4, 24–32, 64. *See also* Bamberger, Ludwig; Lasker, Eduard

Prussian Assembly (Preussischer Landtag), 14, 22, 23, 25–27, 29, 32
Prussian-Danish War, 64–66
Przyjemsky, Count Adam Obracht Pryżna, 13, 226, 227
Puntarenas (town in Chile), 9, 13, 40, 41

Rasche, Thea, 90, 138, 215
Raschkow. *See* Raszkow
Raszkow (Raschkow) (town in Poland), 155, 202, 212
Rathenau, Walther, 6, 61, 204
Rawicz (town in Poland), viii, xiv, 3, 4, 9, 11, 13–17, 19, 20, 33, 35, 39, 42, 64, 155, 189, 202, 212, 213, 214, 219, 225–228
   1848 riots in, 18–19
   Jewish merchants in, 13
   Strassmann family in, 13–20
Rawitsch. *See* Rawicz
Reichstag fire. *See* Berlin, Reichstag fire
Reicke, Georg, 33
Reinhardt, Max, 45, 74–76, 142, 148
Reis, Eva Maria (Korte), xiv, 130, 226, 229
Reis, Hans, xiv, 130, 214, 226, 229
religion, 198
   Catholicism, 13, 17, 18, 93, 94, 95, 100, 148–149, 188, 189, 192, 205, 207, 226, 227, 229
   Christian hostility toward Jews, 26, 29–32, 206
   Christianity, 3, 4, 16, 17, 19, 26, 29, 31, 33, 39, 62, 94, 109, 113, 114, 117, 149, 156–159, 192, 193, 198, 206, 207, 226
   conversions, Judaism to Christianity, 3–5, 31, 38–39, 43, 48, 62, 100, 109, 114, 126, 192, 207
   conversions, Judaism/Protestantism to Catholicism, 93–94, 148–149
   German Christianity, 157–159
   Judaism, xi, xiii, 2, 3, 5, 8, 11, 12, 14, 16, 17, 22, 29–33, 35, 36, 39, 47, 48, 62, 94, 97, 100, 103, 108–110, 112, 118, 126, 149, 158, 182, 189, 193, 204, 207, 213, 226
   Protestantism/Lutheranism, 13, 17, 18, 31, 38, 39, 43, 94, 123, 149, 157–159, 189, 192, 203, 206, 226
   religious resistance against Hitler/Nazi Germany. *See* Germany, history of, resistance against Hitler
   religious views of Paul Ferdinand Strassmann, 39, 114, 123, 152, 154, 156–159
   See also Confessing Church; Niemöller, Martin
Reuter, Ernst, 146, 212, 223
Revolution of 1848
   in Germany/Berlin. *See* Germany, history of, Revolution of 1848
   riots in Rawicz. *See* Rawicz, 1848 riots
Reynolds, Robert R., 138–141
Richter, Eugen, 30
Riefenstahl, Leni, 83, 84
Robinsohn, Hans, 204–207, 212, 223
Robinsohn-Strassmann group (Robinsohn-Strassmann-Gruppe), ix, 10, 155, 205–212, 223

Rochester, Minnesota, 9, 50, 57, 58, 113, 126–127, 130–132, 142, 163, 164, 168–175, 176–179, 181. *See also* Mayo Clinic
Röhricht, Eberhardt, 157
Roosevelt, Eleanor, 5, 125, 146, 147, 150
Roosevelt, Franklin Delano, 5, 125, 126, 138–140, 180
Rosemeyer, Bernd, 123, 141, 142–143
Rosenberg, Anton, 37, 123
Rosenberg, Ernst, 118, 130
Rosenberg, Hedwig. *See* Strassmann, Hedwig
Rosenberg, Julie (Homberger), 37, 123
Rossberg, Fritz Ewald, 137
Rudeloff, Marianne, 122, 123, 229, 230
Rudolf Virchow medical complex. *See* Berlin, Rudolf Virchow medical complex

Sachsenhausen (concentration camp), 159, 181
Sauerbruch, Ferdinand, 8, 115, 116, 118–121, 152, 215
Schiller, Friedrich, 76–80, 95, 123, 157, 196
Schmeling, Max, 141, 143, 178
Schneider, Carl, 8, 103
Schoenewald, Sally, 5, 126
Schönaich-Carolath, Princess Hermine von, 5, 55–56, 120, 163, 221
Schott, August, 5
Schott, Theodor, 5
Schulze-Delitzsch, Herrmann, 25
Schürmann, B., 112, 116, 119, 120, 121, 123, 128, 129
Schutzjuden (protected Jews), 13
Schwarze, Leni, 218
Schwarze, Martha, 182
Schwarze, Otto, 179, 182, 217
Schwarze, Rolf, 182, 217–219, 222–223
scouts of Moses (symbolic grape carriers), 2, 3, 14, 15, 115, 120, 213, 215, 226
Siemens (airplane engine company), 87, 135, 143
Siemens-Helmholtz, Ellen von, 5, 113
Sittenfeld, Julius, 24
Society for Scientific Medicine (Gesellschaft für Wissenschaftliche Medicin), 21
Sonnemann, Emmy. *See* Göring, Emmy
Spielberg, Otto, 5
Stahl Arthur, 126
Stahl, Friedrich Julius, 31, 219
Stark, Oskar, 205
Stauffenberg, Claus Graf Schenk von, 115, 209
assassination attempt on Hitler, 211–212
See also Germany, history of, military resistance against Hitler
Stern, Moritz, 5
Stoeckel, Walter, 120, 127, 160, 161
Stoecker, Adolph, 26, 30–32
Stoecker, Wolfgang, 210
Strassmann, Angelika (also Angelica, born 1930), 1, 126, 133, 134, 159, 172, 174, 187, 215

Strassmann, Antonie (1901–1952), xi–xv, 9, 10, 38, 42, 43, 46, 50, 57, 68, 74–92, 107, 111, 117, 121, 128, 129, 131, 132, 134, 135–150, 151–153, 162–164, 166–168, 171, 172, 178, 179, 182, 183, 188, 195, 213, 214–216
Strassmann, Arnold (1861–1940), xiv, 155, 202–204, 212, 226
Strassmann, Bernhard (1831–1897), 17, 24, 25, 213
Strassmann, Bertha (1824–1906?), 3, 15–17, 19, 20, 64, 213
Strassmann, Beverly Ilse (born 1957), xv, 188, 224
Strassmann, Chune (dates unknown), xiv, 3, 14–15, 155, 202, 212, 213
Strassmann, Diana Louise (born 1955), xiv, xv, 41, 224
Strassmann, Elisabeth (1899–1990, married to Ernst Keiner), 10, 155, 189, 197, 198, 201, 225
Strassmann, Emilie Ottilie (née Backhausen, ?–1920), 202–204, 212
Strassmann, Ephraim (also Eduard, dates unknown), xiv, 155, 202, 212
Strassmann, Erika (1923–1923), 126
Strassmann, Ernst (1868–1923), 9, 36, 37, 39–42, 156
Strassmann, Ernst Karl Otto (1897–1958), viii, ix, xi, xiii, xiv, 10, 155, 189, 200, 202–213, 222–223. *See also* Ernst Strassmann Foundation
Strassmann, Erwin (1895–1972), viii, xiii, 2, 9, 11, 34, 38, 43, 45, 46, 48, 51, 53, 54, 56, 66, 68–73, 75–78, 81, 86, 89, 92–94, 105–108, 110–115, 117, 120, 122, 123, 124–134, 140, 141, 143, 144, 149, 153, 156, 161–164, 166–175, 176–178, 180, 182–188, 216–219
Strassmann, Ferdinand (1835–1931), 5, 20, 21, 32–34, 48, 59, 65, 155, 213, 225
Strassmann, Flora (née Levy, 1840–1910), 35, 193
Strassmann, Franz (born 1958), 222
Strassmann, Fred (also Friedrich Werner, born 1929), xiii, xiv, 10, 56, 57, 189, 192, 193, 195–197, 201, 215, 220–222
Strassmann, Frieda (1869–1945), 33, 40, 42–43, 117, 159, 219
Strassmann, Fritz (1858–1940), xi, xiii, xiv, 5, 6, 9, 29, 35, 36, 41, 46, 56, 59–63, 73, 117, 189, 192–194, 196, 197, 213, 220. *See also* Fritz Strassmann Institut; Fritz Strassmann Medal
Strassmann, Fritz (1902–1980) (nuclear scientist, no relation to Strassmann family), 156
Strassmann, Georg (1890–1972), viii, xiii, 6, 9, 10, 56–57, 61–63, 117, 189–198, 200–202, 220–222
Strassmann, Gertrud (1859–1916, married to Albert Fraenkel), 193
Strassmann, Gisela (1896–1942, married to Max Gutzwiller), xiii, 10, 36, 38, 39, 43, 46, 76, 78, 92–107, 120, 145, 151, 162, 164, 177, 179, 180, 224
Strassmann, Gisela (born 1935), 203
Strassmann, Hedwig (née Rosenberg, 1889–1959), 35, 37–41, 45–47, 49, 51, 55, 57, 58, 66, 67, 74–76, 86,

92–94, 106, 107, 108, 113, 116–120, 122, 123, 130, 132, 133, 139, 141, 143–145, 147–148–150, 151–165, 168, 174, 179, 180, 181, 182, 214, 216, 230
Strassmann, Heiman (1797–1881), xi, 3, 9, 13–20, 35, 155, 202, 213, 226, 242
Strassmann, Heinrich (1834–1905), xiii, 14–20, 21, 22, 24, 25, 33, 35, 36, 38–43, 47, 64–66, 96, 119, 202, 213, 219, 226, 227
Strassmann, Helene (1872–1942, married to Max Keiler), 40, 42–43, 119, 155, 156, 159, 189, 200
Strassmann, Helene (née Stang or Streng, dates unknown, married to Ernst Strassmann), 41, 156
Strassmann, Hella (née Prestin, 1897–1931), 203
Strassmann, Hellmuth (1894–1916), xi, xiii, 11, 35, 38, 39, 41, 43, 45, 46, 51, 66–71, 73, 92, 96, 111, 113, 121, 123, 133, 152, 161, 214, 230
Strassmann, Henrietta (Henni), 33, 154
Strassmann, Hildegard (1902–1990, married to Herbert Hirschwald/ Hartwell), 193, 196
Strassmann, Hildegard (née Tolzmann, 1904–1996), 203, 226
Strassmann, Hugo, 202
Strassmann, Ilse (née Wens, 1895–1993), xi, xiii, 33–34, 78, 110, 111, 120–123, 124–134, 153, 159, 166–175, 179, 182, 184, 185, 187, 217, 218
Strassmann, Ilse (née Marwitz, 1895–1989), 56–57, 117, 193–196, 197, 199–201, 220–222
Strassmann, Joan Elisabeth (born 1953), xv, 224
Strassmann, Judith (née Guhrauer, 1795–1875), 15, 16, 19, 42, 213, 226
Strassmann, Louise (née Cohen, 1835–1889), 25, 31–33
Strassmann, Louise (née Levy, 1844–1915), 35, 39–42
Strassmann, Margarethe (née Rosenthal, 1846–1919), 33
Strassmann, Meta (née Kraft), 200
Strassmann, Monika (born 1945), 203
Strassmann, Paul Ferdinand (also Paul, 1866–1938), xi–xiii, 1, 3, 5, 9, 35–45, 46–59, 62, 66, 67, 71, 74–78, 86, 92–94, 96, 98, 104, 106, 110–123, 128–131, 133, 142, 151–165, 168, 172, 174, 178–180, 182, 186, 189, 194, 202, 214–216, 219, 221, 224, 228, 230
Strassmann, Priska (née Albert, dates unknown), 189–192, 196, 198–201
Strassmann, Reinhard (1900–1971), xiv, 189, 203, 204, 226
Strassmann, Reinhard (born 1942), 203
Strassmann, Reinhold (1893–1944), xiii, 6, 10, 62, 63, 117, 189–201, 202, 220
Strassmann, Renate (also Renata, born 1924), 1, 89, 126, 130, 133, 134, 136, 159, 172, 182, 187, 215
Strassmann, Resi (1910–1981), 203, 204, 208–210, 212, 223
Strassmann, Rose (née Borchardt, ?–1934), 41, 62, 189, 192
Strassmann, Samuel (1826–1879), 17, 21, 24, 25, 33, 35, 52, 60, 202, 213, 226
Strassmann, Schmuhl (Molower, ca. 1760–ca. 1825), 3, 13, 14, 156, 189, 202, 213, 214, 226, 227, 242
Strassmann, W. Paul (also Wolfgang, born 1926), 89, 120, 126, 133, 136, 146–150, 159, 163, 172, 174, 175, 182, 187, 214–216, 224–230
Strassmann, Walter (1870–1937), xiii, 62, 121, 155, 193, 196, 198
Strassmann, Werner (1891–1899), 189
Strassmann, Wolf (dates unknown), 33
Strassmann, Wolfgang (1821–1885), xi, xiii, xiv, 4, 5, 9, 14–17, 21–34, 48, 52, 64, 154, 160, 194, 213, 225, 226
Strassmann, Wolfgang (1930–1941), 203
Strassmann Bistrot, Berlin, 34, 225
Strassmann Haus (Strassmann House), xi, 5, 63, 215
Strassmann Street (Strassmannstrasse), Berlin (between 1938 and 1946: Ermeler Street), 34, 225
Strassmann Women's Clinic (Berlin, Luisenstrasse 45, Strassmann's first small polyclinic), 44, 48, 51, 116, 133, 171, 173, 228
Strassmann Women's Clinic (Berlin, Oranienburger Strasse 57), 44, 48, 50
Strassmann Women's Clinic and Polyclinic (Berlin, Schumannstrasse 17 and 18, and home of the Strassmanns), 3, 5, 9, 36, 45, 48–57, 73, 82, 89, 92, 96, 108–123, 126, 130, 132, 135, 144, 152, 155, 156, 161, 162, 168, 171, 214, 215, 217, 222, 228, 230. *See also* Jenny Marx School for Specialized Medical Occupations; Strassmann House
Streicher, Julius, 110
Stuttgart, 77–78
Sutermeister, Ruth (née Gutzwiller), 214

Texas Medical Center. *See* Houston, Texas, Texas Medical Center
theatre in Germany, early twentieth century, 74, 76–77, 79–81. *See also* Berlin, Deutsches Theater; Hauptmann, Gerhart; Reinhardt, Max
Theresienstadt ghetto, 35, 104, 119, 189, 196, 198, 220
history of, 199–200
Thirty Years' War, 13
Thun, Ferdinand, 171, 178
Tolzmann, Hildegard. *See* Strassmann, Hildegard
Treitschke, Heinrich von, 29
Tübingen (town in Germany), 42, 94, 125, 194, 220

Udet, Ernst, 83–84, 86–87
Ullstein, Leopold, 29
United States
German immigrants to the US (besides Strassmanns), 58, 179, 185–188
immigration policy toward Germans (including physicians), 9, 131–132, 167, 176–178, 182, 216
international politics (1933–1945), 140, 143, 145
as viewed by the Strassmanns and other German emigrants, 2, 57–58, 126–127, 131, 134, 166–169, 174
Unter den Linden. *See* Berlin, Unter den Linden
Unus, Heinrich, 153

Index

Viktoria Luise, Princess of Hohenzollern, 55
Virchow, Rudolf, xiv, 4, 5, 21, 24, 27, 29–32, 48, 59, 160
Virchow Klinik. *See* Berlin, Rudolf Virchow medical complex

Wagner, Gerhard, 7, 109, 120, 155
wars. *See* Germany, history of, World War I; Germany, history of, World War II; Prussian-Danish War; World War I; World War II
Warthausen, Baron von. *See* Koenig-Warthausen Friedrich-Wilhelm Freiherr von und zu
Wegener, Paul, 74–77, 79–81, 148
Weimar Republic, 6, 51, 73, 99, 101, 223. *See also* Germany, history of, politics (1919–1932)
Weissensee, Jewish cemetery. *See* Berlin, Weissensee, Jewish cemetery
Wens, Ferdinand, 125, 179
Wens, Gerhard, 125, 126, 128, 129, 179, 181, 217
Wens, Gertrud, 179
Wens, Ilse. *See* Strassmann, Ilse
Wens, Käthe Luise (née Schwarze), 125, 130, 134, 164, 172, 174, 179, 180–182, 184, 187
Wens, Ulrich, 11
Wilhelm I, German Emperor, 23, 45, 51, 55–56, 66
Wilhelm II, German Emperor, 72, 118, 133, 163, 174, 221
Wilhelm, Crown Prince of Prussia, 78, 79, 140
Wilson, Louis B., 131, 132, 168
Winterstein, Eduard von, 75, 76
World War I, 7, 10, 11, 39, 41, 50–51, 55, 58, 66–73, 83, 92, 97, 124, 131, 138, 139, 145, 148, 171, 183, 189, 190, 193–194, 199. *See also* Germany, history of, World War I
World War II, 9, 10, 36, 69, 105–106, 143–145, 151, 170, 177, 182, 184, 198, 200, 208–212, 216, 217. *See also* Germany, history of, World War II
Wrangel, Friedrich von, 23, 66
Wroclaw (town in Poland). *See* Breslau

Zehlendorf. *See* Berlin, Zehlendorf
Zenith Radio Corporation (Hearing Aid Division), 145–146
Zimmer, Gerhart, 112, 120–123, 151
Zucker, Konrad, 8, 103